TO THE
L.C.C.
TRAMWAYS
AF304751

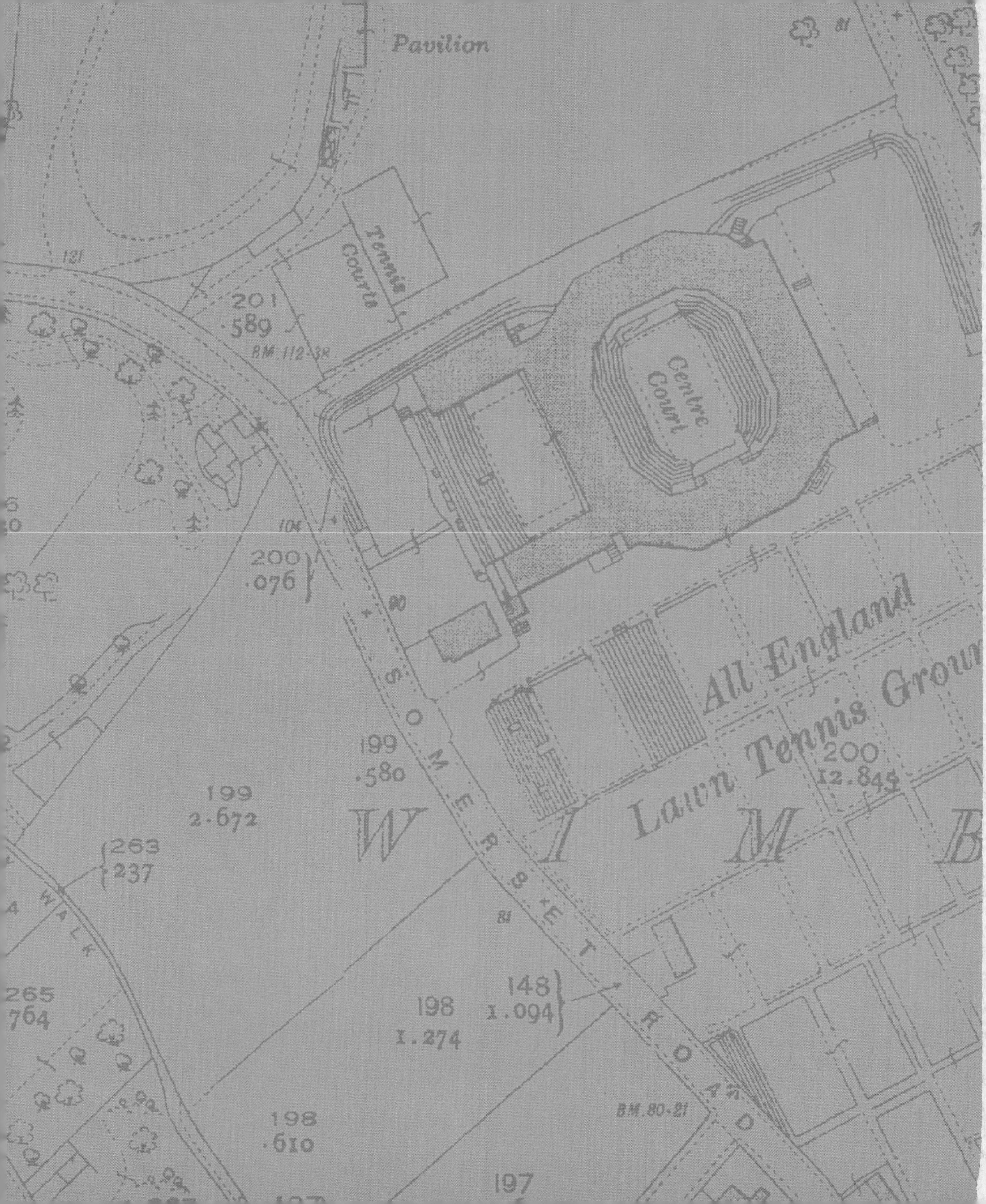

Pavilion
121
201
·589
BM.112·38
Tennis Courts
104
Centre Court
200
·076
81
All England
Lawn Tennis Groun
200
12.845
199
·580
199
2·672
263
237
W
I
M
B
WALK
265
764
81
148
1·094
198
1·274
ROAD
BM.80·21
198
·610
197

WIMBLEDONIA

This book was first published in May 2021 under the title *The People's Wimbledon*.
The stories and anecdotes were collected between the summer of 2016 and March 2020.

Pitch Publishing Ltd
A2 Yeoman Gate
Yeoman Way
Durrington
BN13 3QZ

Email: info@pitchpublishing.co.uk
Web: www.pitchpublishing.co.uk

First published by Pitch Publishing 2026.
Text © 2026 Richard Jones.

1

A CIP catalogue record for this book is available from the British Library.

13-digit ISBN: 9781836804222
Design and typesetting by Olner Pro Sport Media. Visit www.olnerpsm.co.uk
Printed in India by Replika Press

WIMBLEDONIA

THE ULTIMATE BOOK OF
WIMBLEDON TENNIS
COLLECTABLES

RICHARD JONES

with Amisha Savani

CONTENTS

PART ONE   *Memories of Wimbledon*

PART TWO   *Wimbledonia*

PART THREE   *A New Era*

FOREWORD

This is a book for people who love Wimbledon. It will appeal to fans of all ages around the world for whom the experience of Wimbledon, whether through attending The Championships or simply enjoying the extensive coverage on television, has left a lasting sense of affection and enthralment. It will fascinate those who thrill to the exploits of the great players but equally dwell with delight on particular items, objects or moments that recall a happy memory or a sense of fun. Its colourfully illustrated pages exude the passion of author Richard Jones and his lifelong enthusiasm for history, memorabilia and quirky stories from Wimbledon.

This is an eclectic book of history, memories, stories and images. You can open at any page, start reading and let your attention take off in its own direction, the mind fascinated by an unexpected detail or the eye suddenly catching an image which you had forgotten but immediately recall. It captures the love for Wimbledon felt by so many people from across the wide spectrum of the tennis community.

There are reminiscences of first visits to The Championships. I can recall my own, more than fifty years ago, and still visualise the scene in the evening glow over the Centre Court as two players reached a level of intensity that I had never previously experienced. I will never forget the warmth, the light, the sound of racket on ball, the reverential quiet and the deafening applause in that special place.

We at the All England Club are proud of the club's history as a pioneer of the game and as a continuing guardian of its heritage. A familiar sight at the Wimbledon Lawn Tennis Museum and our Library over the past years has been Richard visiting and checking up on facts, exploring new leads, selecting images and reviewing what he delightfully terms Wimbledon's 'ephemera' in the Museum's collections. I admire his passion, his determination and his desire to share his enthusiasm with all Wimbledon fans.

Richard celebrates many leading writers who have enhanced our enjoyment of the game over its history. He rightly asserts that 'printed books remain an important vehicle for communicating this rich heritage'. This book well communicates that heritage and I wish it much success. May all fans enjoy it and feel their spirits lift with warm nostalgia and affection for the magic of Wimbledon.

IAN HEWITT
Chairman
The All England Lawn Tennis & Croquet Club
2019–2023

This is the story of Wimbledon in the words of those who were there. People of different generations and diverse backgrounds, but all with one thing in common: they love Wimbledon. The storytellers are mostly ticket-buying spectators, but amongst them you will find a sprinkling of well-known administrators, broadcasters, coaches, journalists, officials and players. Their stories are illustrated with reproductions of items of Wimbledon memorabilia such as postcards, press cuttings, programmes and tickets – many of which are from the actual day they illustrate – along with some rarely seen items of tennis ephemera from the Wimbledon Lawn Tennis Museum.

The reminiscences were collected in conversation and in writing, from the start of the 2016 Wimbledon Championships through to the spring of 2020. Some are presented in their entirety, extracts from others have been incorporated into the book's narrative. Quite a few fascinating contributions have had to be omitted altogether due to lack of space, but every single submission added important detail to the story of *Wimbledonia*.

The book is in three parts. The first, Memories of Wimbledon, contains descriptions of The Championships from 1877 to the

" *That first visit to Wimbledon changed my life.* **"**

start of the Second World War, followed by eye-witness accounts of visits to Wimbledon during the period from 1946 to 2019. The second part of the book is called Wimbledonia and tells the stories of the most popular types of Wimbledon memorabilia: programmes, postcards, art, books and films. Part Two also contains a chapter about the Wimbledon Lawn Tennis Museum and the Kenneth Ritchie Wimbledon Library, both

of which were instrumental in making this book possible. Part Three brings the Wimbledonia story up to the present day.

Just as great champions such as Suzanne Lenglen, Rod Laver, Martina Navratilova and Roger Federer write their names into history through their on-court achievements, there should also be a permanent record of those very special individuals whose outstanding creative work has done so much to bring Wimbledon to the people over the last century and a half. Such a Roll of Honour would surely include the names of Henry Jones (whose pseudonym was 'Cavendish'), George Hillyard and Francis Burrow, early Wimbledon officials who recorded their recollections of The Championships in print; journalists Arthur Wallis Myers, 'Jackie' Smyth and Lance Tingay; commentators Max Robertson, Dan Maskell and John Barrett; printer Edwin J. Trim; photographers Arthur and Michael Cole; and the remarkable Alan Little, the doyen of Wimbledon's facts and figures and author of over 100 books and other publications about The Championships. Their collective experience spans Wimbledon's entire history, and they are our guides on the journey that guides on this fascinating journey.

When people take a nostalgic look back at their visits to Wimbledon, certain themes recur. These include travelling to Wimbledon, ticket ballots and queuing, impressions of the Club and grounds, favourite players and memorable matches, 'people-watching' and food and drink. One theme, however, is mentioned more than any other. 🎾

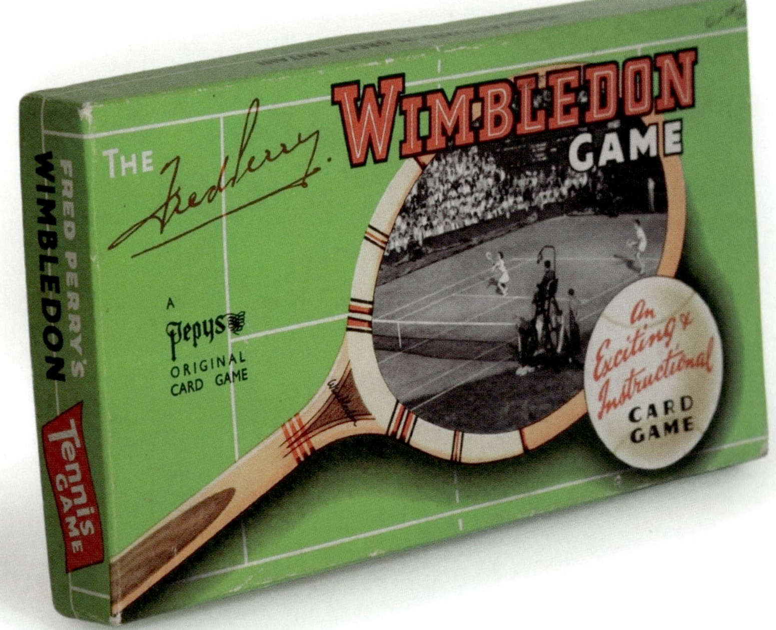

Wimbledon card game, 1960

Wimbledon on the BBC

Watching Wimbledon on BBC Television is one of the highlights of the British summer. The BBC's wall-to-wall, free-to-air coverage has been a fortnight-long advertisement for The Championships for more than half a century, each year prompting thousands of people to make their first visit to The All England Club.

certain. When planning the first live TV broadcast from Wimbledon in 1937 Gerald Cock, the BBC's Controller of Television, expressed real doubts in an internal memo: 'It may, of course, prove after tests that Wimbledon is hopeless from the television point of view.' Fortunately these fears turned out to be groundless, and the TV

> **❝***My earliest memory of Wimbledon tennis was when an elderly neighbour invited myself and a friend round to her house to watch her TV.***❞**

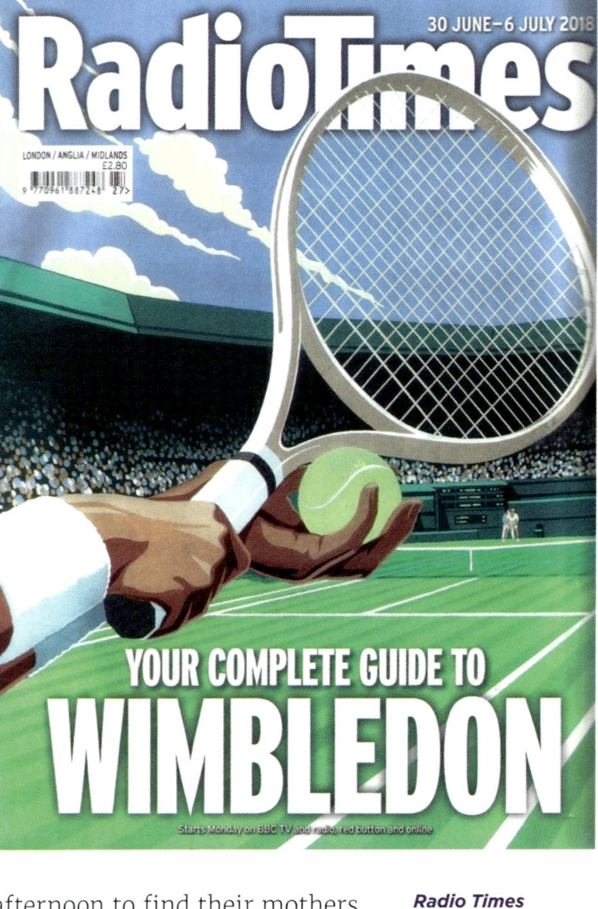

The British Broadcasting Corporation made the first experimental wireless broadcasts from the Centre Court in 1927, and has been bringing Wimbledon tennis to the British public ever since. The televising of Wimbledon began in 1937, when pictures with 'running commentaries' were broadcast for an hour each day, starting at 3pm.

The popularity of radio coverage of The Championships had been predictable, but with television the technical challenges were greater and eventual success much less

broadcasts from the Centre Court were a great success.

It was not until the live broadcast of Her Majesty Queen Elizabeth II's Coronation in 1953, however, that the new medium of television really caught the British public's imagination. From then on, demand for TV sets soared, although it was not until the 1960s that Wimbledon's BBC Television audiences outstripped radio for the first time.

During the summers of the 1950s, before breaking up for the school holidays, many British children arrived home in the

afternoon to find their mothers listening to Wimbledon on the radio or, if they were amongst the fortunate few, watching the matches on TV. Thus was the baby-boomer generation introduced to Lawn Tennis and to Wimbledon, and such was the game's appeal, many were 'hooked'. The irresistible lure of The Championships applied to adults, too.

The BBC's relationship with The All England Club stretches back to 1927, and for the first three decades the Corporation enjoyed a monopoly position as

Radio Times magazine, 30 June - 6 July 2018

1877
Inaugural Wimbledon Championship Meeting, Worple Road

1884
First Wimbledon Ladies' Championship

1877 1878 1879 1880 1881 1882 1883 1884 1885 1886 1887 1888 1889 1890 1891 1892

the UK's sole radio and television broadcaster. The Television Act of 1954 opened the gates to competition, and from 1956 to 1968 the BBC shared the rights to cover Wimbledon with Independent Television (ITV). The launch of BBC2 in 1964 made it difficult for ITV to compete, and the BBC has now been the home of Wimbledon tennis for British audiences for more than 90 years. Britain's first-ever colour television broadcast was made from Wimbledon on Saturday, 1 July 1967 and was a great success, although very few people had colour TV sets at the time.

In such a long relationship, the voices and personalities of the commentators become an important part of the listeners' and viewers' experience. Max Robertson was BBC Radio's lead tennis commentator from 1946 to 1986, and a number of contributors to *Wimbledonia* have marvelled at his extraordinary shot-by-shot descriptions of every point in a match. On BBC TV, Dan Maskell's habit of never using two words when one would do endeared him to the watching millions, and his catchphrase 'Oh I Say!' is recalled with affection by many. From 1961 to 1972

Dan's popular co-commentator was 1947 Wimbledon champion Jack Kramer, and the 'Jack and Dan' partnership is still warmly remembered today.

Dan Maskell's successor as BBC TV's 'Voice of Wimbledon' was former British player and Davis Cup Captain John Barrett. Following in Maskell's footsteps was no easy task, but Barrett did it well, one of the high points of his broadcasting career coming in 1987 when he described Pat Cash's impromptu post-match ascent to the Players' Box. In 2000 John was the Master of Ceremonies for the Millennium Champions' Parade on Wimbledon's Centre Court – a warm, emotional occasion seen by millions of viewers all over the world.

Other popular BBC presenters and commentators at Wimbledon mentioned by our contributors include Peter West, Harry Carpenter, Desmond Lynam, Gerald Williams, Bill Knight, Paul Hutchins, Christine Truman, John Inverdale, Pam Shriver, Barry

Davies and Sue Barker. Davies, who is of course best known as a football commentator, recalls how he found his way into the TV commentary box at Wimbledon: 'I was a presenter of tennis on BBC Television for six or seven years, doing other British tournaments covered by the BBC, but I didn't have a role at Wimbledon. My break into commentating came when the BBC started covering more courts at Wimbledon, and they thus needed more commentators. My first match as a commentator was on the old No.1 Court, and just as the match was about to start a floor manager spilled coffee all over my notes!'

Elsewhere in *Wimbledonia* John Rowlinson, the BBC's former Deputy Controller of TV Sport, describes how he had to deal with a complete washout on his first day on duty as editor of live programmes from Wimbledon. John was later The All England Lawn Tennis Club's Director of Television from 2002 to 2009 and went on to become Head of

1897
Doherty brothers trigger
Wimbledon boom

1902
Slazenger balls first
used at Wimbledon

1908
Olympic Tennis at
Worple Road

1893 1894 1895 1896 1897 1898 1899 1900 1901 1902 1903 1904 1905 1906 1907 1908

Planes, Trains and Automobiles

Broadcast for the London 2012 Olympic Games. As if that were not enough, John also contributed the title for this book!

The overwhelming majority of those who have passed through the gates at Somerset Road and Church Road over the years had their first taste of The Championships through radio or television, and most of those through the services of the BBC. Thanks to its long-running strategic partnership with The All England Lawn Tennis Club, the BBC is still the gateway to Wimbledon. ⊘

People travel to The Championships from all over the world, and from just around the corner, using every conceivable mode of transport. When the tournament began in 1877, the fortunate ones travelled to The All England Club's Worple Road ground by horse-drawn carriage or Hansom Cab.

> **" The shuttle bus from Wimbledon station was an ancient coach that dropped us off in Somerset Road. "**

Journeys to Wimbledon sometimes take on epic proportions. In 1975, for example, Bob Everitt travelled from the Midlands in the back of his tennis club Captain's Ford Escort van. 'We were thrown around the interior of the van whenever the Captain was required to negotiate a roundabout or a sharp turn.' The passengers couldn't see out, apart from the small rear windows, but, as Bob recalls, 'this probably heightened our anticipation of the tennis thrills to come.'

Many of our contributors, including television presenter John Inverdale, first visited

Wimbledon on a coach trip from school, although in John's case, it was a minibus. Nowadays school trips are a lot more difficult to organise, but teacher Simon Etheridge from Bishop's Stortford has found a remarkable way of introducing his students to Wimbledon. He organises an autumn visit to SW19 each year, with coachloads of students visiting various local places of spiritual and sporting interest including, of course, The All England Lawn Tennis and Croquet Club.

However short or long your journey to Wimbledon, the last few yards are always filled with an overwhelming sense of anticipation. These days there is only one public entrance to Wimbledon, but in earlier times there were turnstiles on both sides of the grounds. Special buses from Wimbledon station dropped their passengers off in Somerset Road, and those from Southfields in Church Road. Passengers from Wimbledon describe mounting excitement as the bus moved slowly down Marryat Road before dropping them off by the big tree growing out of the pavement. Shared taxis made that journey too, but in a less memorable way. ⊘

1922
All England Club moves to Church Road

1919
Suzanne Lenglen's
Wimbledon debut

1924
No.1 Court opens

First public ballot for
Wimbledon tickets

1909	1910	1911	1912	1913	1914	1915	1916	1917	1918	1919	1920	1921	1922	1923	1924

Just the Ticket!

The Wimbledon ballot and queue are established traditions which date back to the early years of the 20th century. In the world of sport nothing is more greatly prized than a ticket to Wimbledon, and no sporting ticket has generated more stories and anecdotes.

For every person lucky enough to have a Wimbledon ticket, there are at least ten more who wanted that ticket. Some of the stories in this book reflect the joy and elation of securing a ticket to the world's most prestigious tennis tournament, and the determination of those who are unlucky to 'try, try and try again'.

The demand for Wimbledon tickets has outstripped supply from the days of the Renshaws and the Dohertys at Worple Road, and that was the driving force behind the move to the present ground in 1922. At the time, sceptics thought the new Centre Court with its 13,500 capacity might prove to be a costly white elephant, but they could not have been more wrong.

The first public ticket ballot was held in 1924, and these have continued ever since. At various times it has been possible to apply for single tickets, pairs, or series of tickets covering several days' play. In the very early days it was possible to purchase a season ticket for the entire fortnight. Up to 1979 separate ballots were held for Centre and No.1 Court tickets, and until quite recently applicants could indicate preferred days. In the days before electronic banking, The All England Club returned thousands of uncashed cheques and postal orders to unsuccessful applicants each year.

Success or failure in the Wimbledon ballot is a perennial talking point amongst tennis lovers. Nowadays the traditional public ballot is supplemented by separate ballots for members of the Lawn Tennis Association's British Tennis scheme and for registered tennis players who are members of LTA–affiliated clubs.

In 1932 a reduced ground admission charge was introduced for people arriving after 5pm. This opened Wimbledon up to a far broader audience, and contributors to *Wimbledonia* share happy memories of after-work evenings at The Championships. With play only starting at 2pm, it was sometimes possible to arrive at five o'clock and still see three complete matches.

It is not known when overnight queuing began, but as early as 1927 there were press reports

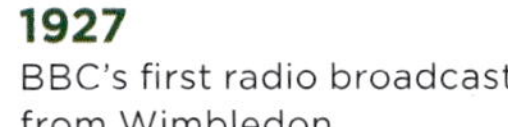

1927
BBC's first radio broadcast from Wimbledon

1937
BBC's first television broadcast from Wimbledon

1926
Jubilee Champions Parade

1934
Fred Perry and Dorothy Round complete British 'double'

1925 1926 1927 1928 1929 1930 1931 1932 1933 1934 1935 1936 1937 1938 1939 1940

of people queuing outside the grounds from 5am. Overnight queuing was certainly a well-established Wimbledon ritual by the 1960s, as some of our contributors testify. In 1965 Elsie Rosam from Dorking arrived at 9.30 on Friday morning to make sure she would get in to see the Ladies' Singles, Ladies' Doubles and Mixed Doubles finals the following day.

Chris Gorringe worked at Wimbledon for over 30 years and served as CEO from 1983 to 2005. During his career he saw a big increase in the demand for daily tickets, necessitating considerable changes to the queuing arrangements. 'It all began with Bjorn Borg and John McEnroe. Between them they generated huge interest, and the Queue became much more high profile.'

The Somerset Road and Church Road queues each had their own distinct characteristics, and were much loved by those who returned to Wimbledon year after year. From 1997 everyone entered the grounds through newly built turnstiles in Church Road. There were still two queues, but the southerly one now stretched straight up the hill towards Wimbledon Village, bringing to an end 75 years of queuing in Somerset Road.

In 2008 the entire 'Queue', as it was now officially labelled, moved off the pavement and onto the grass in Wimbledon Park. 'When the Queue moved into Wimbledon Park we lost something,' Chris Gorringe recalls. 'When the Queue was on the street, the players saw people queuing to see them play.'

The public ballot and the Queue are expensive to manage, but they are important Wimbledon traditions. 'The Honorary Stewards and Service Stewards are key to the success of the Queue. The local Councils have always been very helpful, too,' said Chris. 'The Queue is very democratic. If you stay long enough, you will get in.'

> **"** *People of all ages would queue. Lots of them spent all night on the pavement.* **"**

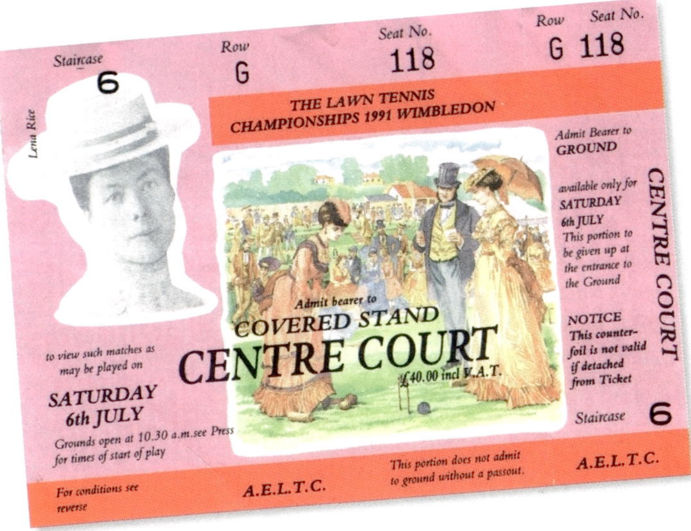

1946
Max Robertson's first commentary from Wimbledon

1949
Dan Maskell's first commentary from Wimbledon

1941 1942 1943 1944 1945 1946 1947 1948 1949 1950 1951 1952 1953 1954 1955 1956

Vantage Points and Landmarks

When 80 of the world's top men boycotted The Championships in 1973 it made absolutely no difference to the enthusiasm of the public to come and watch the tournament. Three hundred thousand people attended the fortnight that year, the second-highest attendance in Wimbledon's history.

The reason for this is simple: the players are important, but it is Wimbledon itself that is the star attraction. People who have been to Wimbledon are drawn back time and time again to feel the magic and to re-enact the joyful rituals of a summer's day at The All England Lawn Tennis Club. Contributors to this book wistfully describe their favourite vantage points, many of which are now long gone, and the resourcefulness required to get to them.

Many first-time visitors find The All England Club's grounds much bigger than they had expected, but are nevertheless struck by the intimacy and warmth of the place. Today, as in the past, ground ticket holders make a beeline for the free seats around the outside courts, although there is now the added attraction of a prime spot on Henman Hill where the big show-court matches are shown live on a giant video screen. In the past the Free Standing Room on Centre and No.1 Courts afforded the same opportunity, as many of our correspondents recall.

Other favoured locations included the narrow internal corridor between Centre Court and the old No.1 Court which gave a close-up ground-level view of play on the latter, albeit with regular interruptions as heads bobbed up and down, and the top-floor corridor at the southern end of the Centre Court which gave a panoramic view of nearly all the outside courts. The back row of the free seating on the west side of the old Court 3 gave a splendid view of Court 2 if you stood up and turned around, and, from 1922 until 1970, a small grass bank on the eastern side of the grounds gave a good view of a line of three adjoining courts, the middle of which had no spectator access whatsoever.

People also fondly remember

The water tower was built to provide an emergency water supply from the lake in Wimbledon Park

such landmarks as the queue lanes, the Change Box, the wooden hut selling 'Photographs of the Players' (later renamed The Bookstall), the Officials Buttery, the water tower, the groundsman's cottage, and the red boxes where departing spectators deposited their tickets for resale in aid of the National Playing Fields Association. Up to the start of the 1980s the Referee's Office at the southern end of the old No.1 Court was a popular spot for watching the stars as they ascended the staircase to the Players' Tea Room above, from where Czeslaw 'Spike' Spychala's voice could be heard over the tannoy as he called players for their matches. ◎

1968
First 'Open' Wimbledon Championships

1961
All-British Ladies'
Singles Final

1967
First BBC TV colour broadcast from Wimbledon
Attendance exceeds 300,000 for the first time
Wimbledon World Professional Championships

1957   1958   1959   1960   1961   1962   1963   1964   1965   1966   1967   1968   1969   1970   1971   1972

At 2pm Precisely

When tennis players come to Wimbledon you know that what you are seeing is their best effort, for it is the tournament that defines their careers. Whatever a player is capable of, you will see it on the lawns of SW19. 'The atmosphere was palpable,' wrote Ruth Hartgill of her first visit in June 1949. 'The scene was like nothing I had ever seen in my short life.'

From 1919 to 1982, play on all courts at Wimbledon started 'at 2pm precisely'. Not a minute earlier, or a minute later. The pace of play was much quicker than it is today and, with 'The Fortnight' falling at the height of the English summer, four matches could usually be completed on each court before dusk. If play finished early on either of the main show courts, an extra fifth match was sometimes added to the programme from matches listed in the Daily Order of Play as being 'On Courts To Be Arranged'.

The 2pm start meant that many spectators only needed to take half a day off work to attend The Championships. Workers typically had only two or three weeks' paid holidays each year, so eking out this leave entitlement was important. In the amateur era many of Wimbledon's competitors also had jobs, so the 2pm start helped them too.

Contributors to the book remember these days with nostalgic affection. With the gates opening at noon there was plenty of time to have a picnic lunch, watch the stars practising or go and 'bag' a seat next to one of the outside courts. The free seats on the old Court 3 were very popular, affording a great view of the matches on that court as well as the external scoreboards of Centre and No.1 Courts. Heaven for a tennis fan was a prime seat on an outside court, a packed lunch and a copy of *The Daily Telegraph*. A transistor radio came in handy too, as Wimbledon often coincided with the Lord's Test.

In 1959 David Orchard from High Wycombe had a different reason for arriving at Wimbledon with plenty of time to spare: 'An early arrival was vital in order to join the queue waiting for the gates to open at noon prior to the headlong dash for standing room on the Centre Court.' He was rewarded by seeing the graceful Brazilian Maria Bueno win the first of her three Wimbledon singles titles.

Nowadays the pace of life has increased, and that world of patient anticipation is long gone. Since 1983 play has been starting earlier on the outside courts. First at 12.30pm; then, from 1992 at noon; from 2012 at 11.30am; and, in 2019, at 11.00am. The gates open earlier, too, but there is now little time for visitors to savour the Wimbledon atmosphere before play starts. Indeed, play has already commenced by the time many people get into the grounds. It's non-stop action from the moment you arrive, which is no bad thing. ⊘

> **❝** *An early arrival was vital in order to join the queue waiting for the gates to open at noon prior to the headlong dash for standing room on the Centre Court.* **❞**

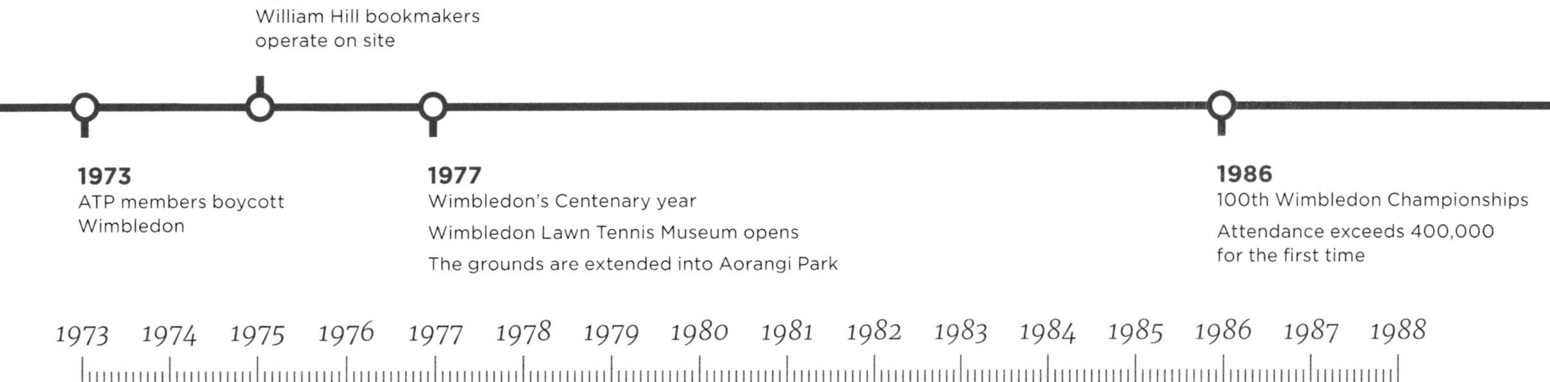

Popular Players & Memorable Matches

Despite his incredible achievements at Wimbledon, Novak Djokovic is often said to feel a lack of love from the Centre Court crowd. By contrast, Carlos Alcaraz's huge popularity stems not just from his sublime, near-magical skills, and his extraordinary achievements – it is also due in large part to the way he goes about the game: courteously, quickly and a smile on his face.

Contributors reveal exactly what triggers love for a player. High in the list of these characteristics are personality, vulnerability, a pleasing style of play and, particularly important nowadays, getting on with the game. Some players lose Brownie points for playing too slowly and too noisily, and by showing a lack of consideration to officials and opponents with their exaggerated rituals and routines.

Little mannerisms live long in the memory, however, and often help endear a player to the public. Good examples are Ken Rosewall's drooping shoulders and look of abject despair when he missed a shot; Rod Laver slapping his thigh for the same reason, and roughing up his leather racket grip on the net cord; Pancho Gonzales flicking sweat from his eyebrows before

> **❝***I always loved watching Ken Rosewall, and every year I would go along thinking 'this year he will win it.'***❞**

serving; and Jimmy Connors scraping the toes of his shoes on the grass. Serena Williams always wears longer sleeves for doubles than for singles.

Many players are fondly remembered in these pages, but ironically it is one of Wimbledon's most diminutive stars who stands head and shoulders above the rest when it comes to the affection in which he is held by the public. Australian Ken Rosewall delighted the crowds for a quarter of a century with his sublime touch play, invariably repulsing challenges from bigger and more powerful opponents. It is a source of sadness for many that he did not win Wimbledon despite four appearances in the final, the first and last of which were 20 years apart.

Men's tennis has been in the ascendancy at Wimbledon in recent years, but this is an exceptional era. For the most part, women's tennis has been at very least equal to the men's, and has often led the way.

Maureen Connolly, Maria Bueno, Christine Truman, Evonne Goolagong, Chris Evert, Martina Navratilova, Steffi Graf, and Venus and Serena Williams are amongst Wimbledon's biggest-ever stars, and all are warmly remembered here.

Amongst the matches that have lived long in the memory is the 1950 men's doubles quarter-final in which Americans Budge Patty and Tony Trabert beat Australian duo Frank Sedgman and Ken McGregor 6-4, 31-29, 7-9, 6-2. Patty went on to beat an exhausted Sedgman in the men's singles final the following day.

Sometimes the most memorable matches are not the most important ones. Octogenarian Keith Stephens from Upminster still remembers the first-round match in 1952 in which Felicisimo Ampon of the Philippines came back from two sets down to beat the 11th-seeded American Ham Richardson 1-6, 5-7, 6-2, 6-3, 6-0. 'Little Ampon was everywhere,' recalls Keith, who is still an active tennis player himself.

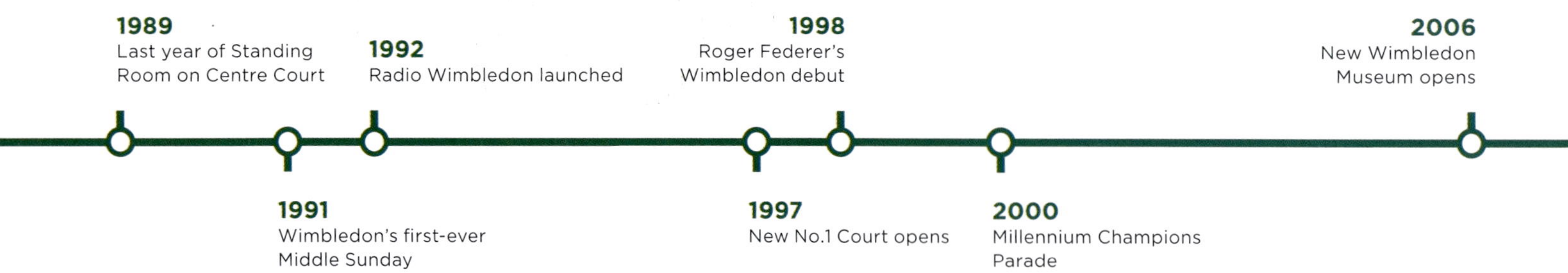

The Look of Love

Roger Taylor's dramatic five-set quarter-final victory over the emerging Swede Bjorn Borg in 1973 is remembered by more than one of our contributors, as is the 1975 Gentlemen's Singles Final in which Arthur Ashe upset the odds to beat fellow-countryman Jimmy Connors. Connors's plaintive cry 'I'm trying, for Chrissake!' stills chimes with many.

Bjorn Borg's classic five-setters against Vitas Gerulaitis in 1977 and John McEnroe in 1980 are remembered here, as are, amongst many others, Jimmy Connors's remarkable fightback against Mikael Pernfors in 1987, the Roger Federer versus Rafael Nadal final in 2008 and the extraordinary John Isner/Nicolas Mahut marathon in 2010. The most dramatic of all, surely, is also the most recent: the 2019 men's final between Novak Djokovic and Roger Federer, the first singles match in Wimbledon's history to be decided by a fifth-set tiebreak.

'People-watching' is very much a part of the Wimbledon scene, as a number of contributors have observed. Ruth Hartgill was barely a teenager when she attended The Championships for the first time in 1949. 'I immediately fell for my first tennis hero, Budge Patty. He seemed so elegant, had a forehand volley to die for and classy dress – cream flannel shorts and a grey sweater.'

When you step inside the Wimbledon grounds you are entering a different world. On the lawns and walkways of SW19, beautiful and famous people rub shoulders with thousands of ordinary tennis lovers. Wimbledon is where glamour is on parade, and aspirations are nurtured.

Up until 1980 crowds of people used to stand outside the old Referee's Office, hoping to catch a glimpse of a star as he or she came down the adjacent flight of

stairs from the Players' Tea Room. If not a tennis star, then perhaps a celebrity of stage or screen. Roger Milne, who first went to Wimbledon in 1973, remembers: 'Another place to see the stars was right in front of the Centre Court building. Crowds were kept behind barriers as the limos dropped off and picked up players. I recall that all the drivers looked like glamour models.'

It is not just players and celebrities who catch the eye at Wimbledon. Spectators make an impression, too, as Susan Morgan Thomas of Tunbridge Wells recalls: 'I went to work in the City that day dressed in my

SUE BARKER

VITAS GERULAITIS

From Bath Buns to Sushi

Sushi, bento, salad. Salmon, steak, stew. Hamburgers, pizza, fish and chips. Wimbledon coronation chicken with toasted almonds, apricots, green beans and Moroccan couscous. Strawberries and cream. Those are just a few of more than 50 menu choices which were available to our contributors Omar Bopal, David Brown, Andrew Fulcher and Mark Kuhn from ten eateries dotted around the grounds of The All England Club during the 2019 Wimbledon Championships.

A century earlier, a simple pot of tea accompanied by a selection of sandwiches and cakes provided ample refreshment for Wimbledon's hungry hordes. It is said that for some time during the Worple Road years food was supplied to the Club by the enterprising landlord of the Swan

best hat, dress and high heels. People always dressed up for Wimbledon in those days.' The year in question was 1959, and back then the Centre Court crowd would have largely been made up of fashionably dressed women and men looking rather formal in jacket, collar and tie. There were practical reasons for this apparent uniformity, particularly for the men. Money was tight, clothes were expensive, and the leisurewear market had not yet taken off.

Behaviour was different, too. The social order was clearly defined, and deference, a legacy of the Victorian class system, was still shown to one's supposed 'elders and betters'. The Centre Court audience paid rapt attention but made little noise, apart from polite applause between points.

Since Open Tennis came to Wimbledon in 1968, spectators' dress styles have gradually become more eclectic and their behaviour less inhibited. The Centre Court is a much noisier place than it once was. However, if you want to mingle with fashion, glamour and celebrity, Wimbledon is still the place to go. ✇

Annabel Croft Great Britain

public house (now The Rushmere) on the Ridgway, halfway between the Club and Wimbledon Common, and early photographs of the Worple Road ground show people taking afternoon tea in quite a formal setting. There are white linen tablecloths and uniformed waitresses, and almost every seat is taken. This tradition was maintained through the inclusion of an expanded Tea Lawn in the new grounds at Church Road, where the City-based firm of Ring and Brymer was engaged to provide the refreshments.

In 1936 J. Lyons and Company took over as Wimbledon's caterers, a role it retained until 1962. This go-ahead company had been founded in 1887 by the Gluckstein family and was named after Joseph Lyons, its first manager. The company was hugely successful and was renowned in particular for its high-quality leaf tea and packaged cakes which were made at its famous Cadby Hall factory in Hammersmith, just a few miles from The All England Club. Lyons' Art Deco-style Corner Houses with their 'Nippy' waitresses were the stylish forerunners of today's fast-food restaurants and coffee shops, and the company's distinctive delivery vans were a familiar sight on Britain's streets.

Amongst 'Joe' Lyons' most popular offerings to the Wimbledon public was the classic 'Bath Bun', a sweet bun with pieces of crushed sugar on top which went down perfectly with a hot cup of tea. This Wimbledon favourite gets its name from the English spa city of Bath where it was first made in the mid-18th century.

J. Lyons and Company was Wimbledon's caterer from 1936 to 1962

For many years a Bath Bun accompanied by a suitable beverage was one of the culinary highlights of a day at The Championships. Peter Gregory of Northwick Park was at Wimbledon on 4 July 1967 and sums things up nicely: 'We had a brief walk round the grounds and I bought the obligatory Bath bun.'

In addition to its traditional English offerings, J. Lyons was also instrumental in bringing the American fast-food culture to Britain. The Wimpy hamburger was successfully trialled in Britain at the 1954 Ideal Home Exhibition, Chelsea Flower Show and the Wimbledon Lawn Tennis Championships, where it was particularly well received by the public.

The Bath Bun was a Wimbledon staple for more than half a century, but the Wimpy hamburger, popular though it was, didn't last as long in the gentrified surroundings of The All England Lawn Tennis Club. 'There was a refreshment area in front of the old No.1 Court,' recalls Peter Gregory, 'and one sign rather amused me; it was advertising the sale of "Wimpy's"' but they clearly suspected that much of Wimbledon's clientele would have no idea what these were, as in brackets underneath was the explanation "A hamburger in a bun with onions". I recall that in one of the following years the Club banned the onions following complaints of the smell!'

In fact, it was not just the onions that were banned, as Norman Cohen of Stanmore recalls: 'I read in one of my tennis magazines that the best meal at The Championships was a "Wimpy" and it was! Alas, due to the smell of the fried onions reaching the Royal Box, this concession disappeared.'

Many contributors have commented on the popular service provided by J. Lyons and Company. From 1963 to 1998 Wimbledon's food and drink was supplied by the Town and County Catering Company, and during this time the 'Oscar' hotdog was introduced. Our contributor Steven Lynch describes an unforgettable moment when, unexpectedly coming face to face with Chris Evert, his starstruck teenage friend offered her a bite of his Oscar! ◎

Souvenirs of Wimbledon

People love to keep souvenirs. They are a simple way of keeping happy memories alive. Tickets, postcards, photographs, programmes, badges, booklets, selfies, autographs and all kinds of objects and ephemera; whether you are a film buff or a theatre-goer, a music lover or a football fan, there's a fair chance you'll have some of these items tucked away.

Many football fans have bought a programme at every match they have ever attended, and some have collections running into thousands amassed over a lifetime of watching the game. 'I have a programme from when I took my son to his first game,' one fan remarked. 'It means more to me than my £20 grand car.'

Scrapbooks, photograph albums and autograph books are amongst many people's most cherished possessions. Others just tuck things away in drawers and look at them once in a blue moon. This particularly applies to Wimbledon Championships tickets and programmes, which for several decades during the mid-20th century were attractively printed in a range of bright colours which changed from day to day during The Fortnight. They were just too nice to throw away, which explains how a number of contributors have been able to put precise dates on their stories even though the events they are recounting happened a long time ago.

The earliest known item of Wimbledon tennis memorabilia is the four-page programme produced for the Gentlemen's Singles Final in 1877, an example of which is to be found at the Wimbledon Lawn Tennis Museum. Simply entitled 'List of Players', this folded sheet contains the 22-man draw plus a 'Plan of the Grounds' showing the 12 grass courts laid out in three rows. This flimsy document was the forerunner of the magazine-style official programmes that would later

Evonne Goolagong Cawley autograph, circa 1980s

become Wimbledon's best-selling and most-collected items of memorabilia.

The programme is interesting for a number of reasons. First, throughout its four printed pages there is no mention of the word 'Wimbledon'. It was just a small folded card, but it cost the princely sum of sixpence, a lot of money in those late-Victorian days. Also, the programme is not for the whole tournament, but just for the final day, suggesting that the tournament organisers

If you went down after work the full programmes were sold out and they only offered you a slimmer stapled set of draw sheets with an order of play.

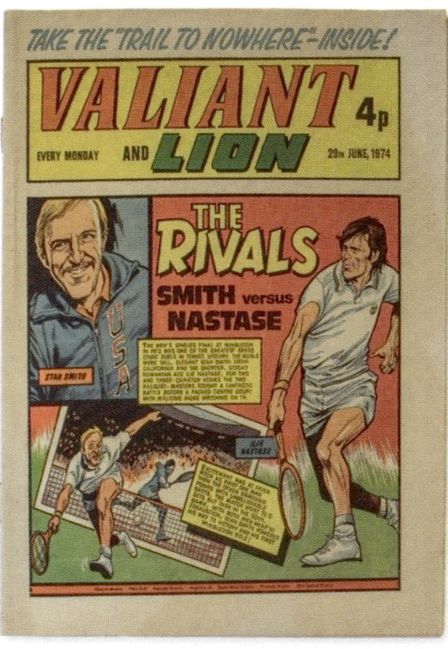

Wimbledon special edition magazines and comics

were looking for ways to cash in on the anticipated bumper finals-day crowd. The names of the winners of each match have been printed in, with only the tournament winner's name not yet known. Little did anyone know that the name later to be entered there would go down in world sporting history.

The earliest admission ticket in the Wimbledon Museum's collection is for the 1919 Championships, but tickets must surely have been issued many years before that, perhaps even as early as 1880 when F.H. Ayres brought two movable stands to the Centre Court. Wimbledon's printed tickets are, in the main, stylish and attractive, and for this reason people tend not to throw them away. The distinctive typefaces and imagery evoke the spirit of the eras in which they were produced. They are also of interest to historians and collectors for the information they contain such as price and conditions of entry.

The first Wimbledon Championships in 1877 were well timed. Technological change was in full swing, and advancements in graphic design, photography and printing over the next few years soon made it possible for attractive designs to be incorporated into practical items such as tickets, programmes and posters. The success and popularity of the tournament became a catalyst for the creative arts, spawning an ever-increasing raft of printed ephemera items which were highly collectable.

Tickets and programmes aside, Wimbledon's first real venture into merchandising came around 1905 when Edwin Trim and

Company, a family printing and stationery business based in the town, began printing postcard-sized black and white photographs of the players and general views of The All England Club's courts. These were sold inside the Worple Road grounds during The Championships, probably by members of the Trim family. This was the beginning of Wimbledon's love affair with postcards, a popular tradition which continues to the present day.

The Trim company continued to sell postcards to the public when The All England Lawn Tennis Club moved to its present home in Church Road in 1922, again from a temporary retail unit. Situated near the Centre Court's South West Hall, this 'pop-up' shop offering 'Photographs of the Players' was upgraded several times before finally being turned into a permanent structure with a concrete base in 1959.

By the early 1970s the small shop selling an expanded range of photographs, magazines and books had become inadequate, with crowds of people jostling to reach the display counter and make their purchases. The opportunity for change came in the Centenary year of 1977 with the opening of the Wimbledon Lawn Tennis Museum, and with it Wimbledon's first year-round shop. A special range of Centenary products was offered for sale including such items as tee shirts, bookmarks, pens and a limited-edition Spode commemorative plate. Postcards were sold from a purpose-built display wall.

In addition, a much larger Museum Shop opened in a permanent wooden building near

Wimbledon Queue giveaways

to the Tea Lawn, between Gates 3 and 4. This was open during The Championships only, its service counter four times as long as the old postcard booth.

After a century of selling just programmes, postcards, books and magazines the product range began to expand rapidly, with new lines of souvenirs and giftware being added each year. These included Museum booklets (from 1977), Wimbledon Official Films (from 1974), Wimbledon Official Annuals (from 1983) and Wimbledon Tournament Posters (from 1986). Other popular

My love for this place remains undiminished.

Wimbledon collectables include badges, mugs, towels and limited–edition prints.

Later on an octagonal wooden postcard hut was added, and the process of commercialisation was further accelerated by the opening of 'The Wimbledon Shop' as part of the new No.1 Court complex in 1997 and a new, much-enlarged year-round retail outlet facing onto Church Road when the new Wimbledon Lawn Tennis Museum opened in 2006.

In the early years of the 21st century Mark McCormack's International Management Group (IMG) took over the running of Wimbledon's retail operations. IMG expanded the range enormously, concentrating on branded apparel and giftware. Recent years have seen Wimbledon managing its own retail operations once again, and in 2017 a new range of branded clothing, footwear, equipment and gifts was launched as 'The Wimbledon Collection'. Traditional fan-friendly products such as postcards, books and magazines are less prominent in this new retail environment, but they are still there – just!

Today visitors to The Championships can make their purchases from three main Wimbledon shops and seven satellite outlets around the grounds, plus one in Wimbledon Park serving the Queue. Shopping is now an integral part of the Wimbledon visitor experience, and in 2019 more than 450,000 items were sold to the public during the 13 days of The Championships. All this retail activity stems from the same basic impulse that made postcards so popular more than a century ago: the desire to take home a souvenir of Wimbledon, and keep happy memories alive.

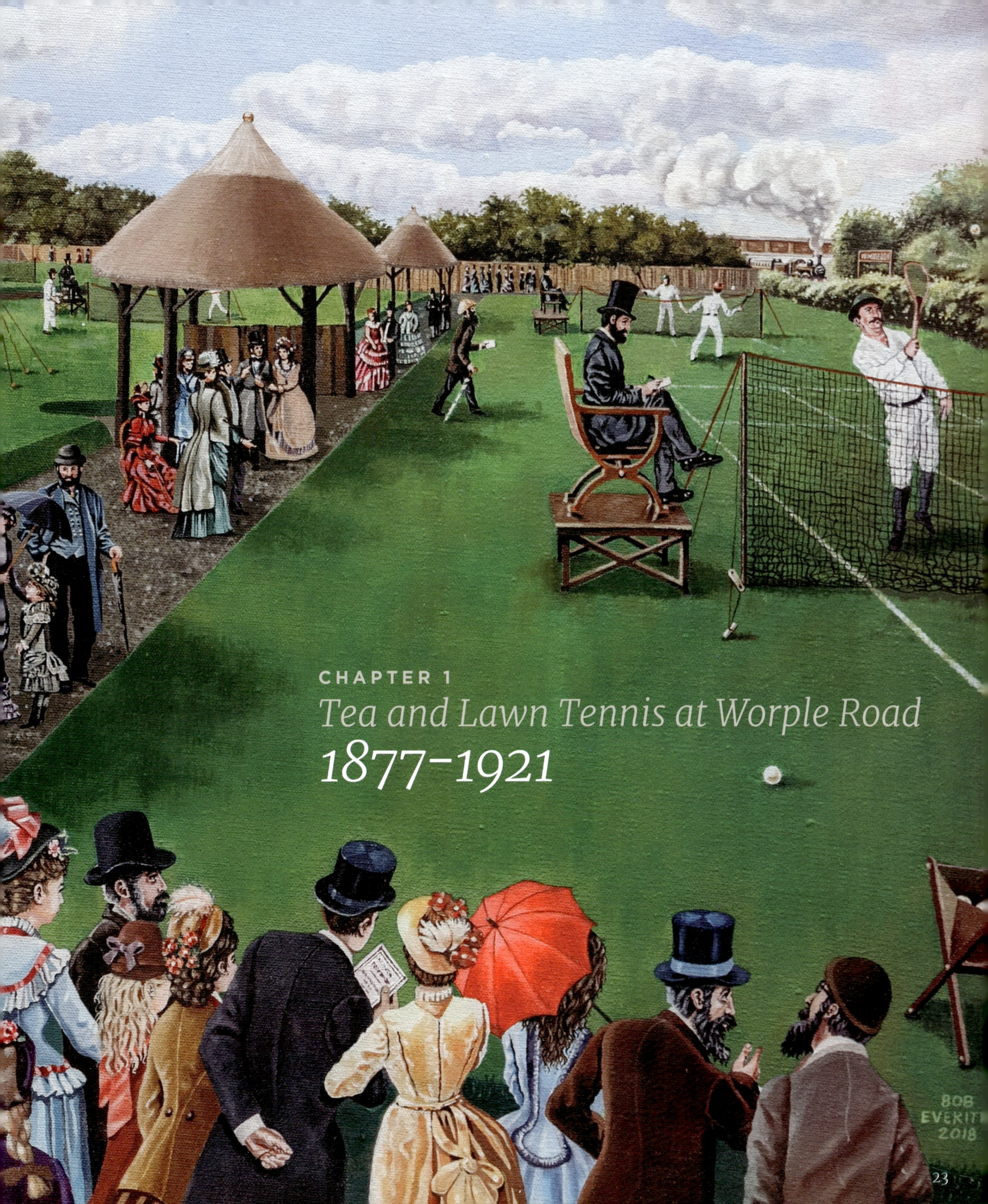

Tea and Lawn Tennis at Worple Road

1877–1921

It is the classic scene from the early days of lawn tennis: a gentle game of mixed doubles on a grass court surrounded by summer trees in bloom. The gentlemen are wearing long flannel trousers, shirts with long sleeves rolled up to the elbows and cricket caps. The ladies are resplendent in voluminous, ankle-length dresses topped with white aprons, and elaborate hats, more suited to a stroll along the promenade at a fashionable seaside resort than participation in a competitive physical sport. A cluster of spectators is watching the play with detached interest, whilst partaking of afternoon tea.

This was Lawn Tennis in the very early days, a garden-party pastime for the privileged few, and this relaxed atmosphere was much in evidence during the early Championships staged at the All England Croquet and Lawn Tennis Club's first home at Worple Road, halfway between Wimbledon and the neighbouring railway suburb of Raynes Park. Photographs of the Worple Road grounds during the early tournaments show ever-increasing space being devoted to the provision of afternoon tea to the gentle folk who made up the majority of Wimbledon's spectators in those days. In mid-19th-century England, affluent Victorians who had made their money during the Industrial Revolution were looking for new leisure pastimes that could be enjoyed by both men and women. The reason for this was simple: there was a shortage of eligible young men for the daughters of well-to-do parents to marry. Strict codes of etiquette and behaviour made it difficult for young ladies to mix socially with potential partners, so sports and games which brought the sexes together were much in demand.

Women had long been involved in sports, but in Victorian times a new impression of the ideal woman emerged: feminine and refined, but also somewhat dependent and fragile – in short, an attractive young lady who needed looking after by a handsome man of means and substance. The flushed cheeks and perspiration associated with athletic exercise remained acceptable for men, but were seen as highly undesirable for women. Women's participation in sport actually declined during the 19th century. Women's cricket, for example, had begun as early as 1745, but Victorian attitudes resulted in it having all but died out by the 1830s. Sport was seen as the province of men, providing them with the opportunity to demonstrate their masculinity.

Throughout its history tennis has always benefitted from

Original Sphairistike box, 1874

Walter Wingfield, inventor of Lawn Tennis

technological advances, and two key 19th-century developments were instrumental in the launching of the game. In 1839, an American named Charles Goodyear (after whom Goodyear tyres were later named) had discovered the process of vulcanisation which made rubber resilient and led – amongst other more important things – to the manufacture of the world's first bouncy rubber balls. Around the same time, Scot Alexander Shanks and Englishman Thomas Green were manufacturing the first lawn mowers, enabling Victorian country house gardeners to create immaculate, close-cut lawns.

The first popular lawn game was croquet, in which heavy balls are knocked through metal hoops with a long-handled wooden mallet. Croquet was all the rage during the 1860s, fulfilling the Victorian need for a civilised garden game for both sexes. But after a while the croquet craze subsided, and the arrival in 1874 of a new garden game called 'Sphairistike' – named after the Greek word for a ball game – was perfectly timed.

Sphairistike, or Lawn Tennis, as it soon became popularly known, was the brainchild of Major Walter Wingfield, a retired army officer with a good deal of entrepreneurial flair. His game was supplied in boxed sets containing rackets, balls, nets and poles, a book of rules, and pegs with which to mark out a 'portable court'. This latter element enabled Wingfield to make a successful application for a patent in February 1874.

Lawn tennis was a modern outdoor adaptation of the indoor game of 'Royal' or 'Real' tennis which had been played across Europe for hundreds of years. The most historically important real tennis player was King Henry VIII of England (1485–1547), who had a court built at Hampton Court Palace in the early 16th century.

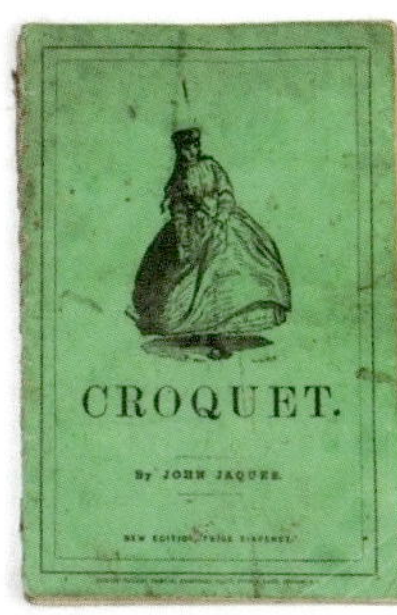
John Jaques's Laws of Croquet, 1867

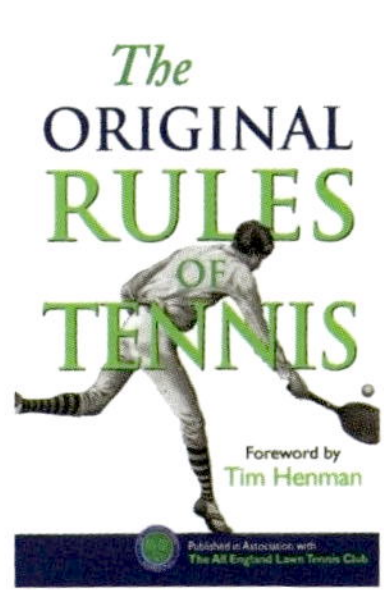

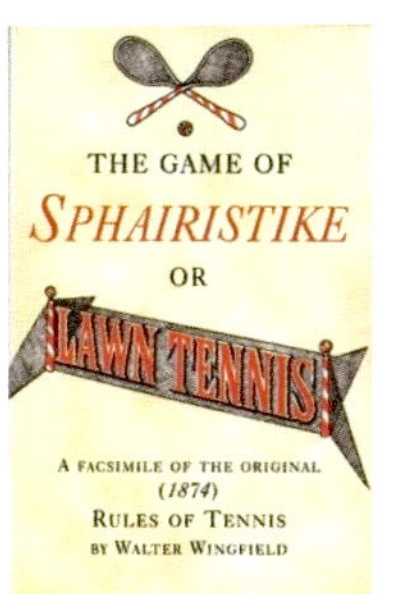

History records that Henry played real tennis in a velvet jacket, a fine shirt, long stockings and shoes with felt soles. Long before that, the game had been played by monks and wealthy aristocrats in various European countries including Italy, Spain and France. Remarkably, real tennis is still played at Hampton Court today.

Following the award of his patent, Wingfield launched his new game commercially in the spring of 1874. His boxed sets were advertised in *The Field* – 'The Sporting Gentlemen's Newspaper' – and despite a high price of five guineas the game was an immediate success. Lawn tennis was soon being played in the gardens of the wealthy up and down the British Isles. *The Field* also had many subscribers in America, and the game travelled there within weeks of its UK launch. In a few short years it was being enjoyed by thousands of people throughout the world. ◉

The first Wimbledon Championships were hastily arranged and commenced on Monday, 9 July 1877, with 22 gentlemen paying an entry fee of one guinea (one pound and one shilling in 1877, but equating to more than £100 today)

In 1875 the All England Croquet Club in Wimbledon responded to an increasing clamour from its members by setting aside one of the croquet lawns on its four-acre site for use as a lawn tennis court. The Club had been founded in July 1868 at a meeting chaired by J.H. Walsh, editor of *The Field*, at the newspaper's London office, and had moved into the ground in Worple Lane, just off Worple Road, a year later.

The Victorians were not only sports lovers, they were also great organisers, and it was inevitable that tournaments would be set up for the more competitively minded players of the new game of lawn tennis. The All England Club had regularly held croquet tournaments, so the first Lawn Tennis Championship was, therefore, a logical development.

The Club had added four more tennis courts at its Worple Road grounds in 1876, and changed its name to the All England Croquet and Lawn Tennis Club in April 1877. However, by the early summer of that year the Club's finances were far from healthy, and it was decided to stage an open lawn tennis tournament in order to raise funds.

'The Lawn Tennis Championship Match at Wimbledon', circa 1888 by Arthur Hopkins

The first Wimbledon Championships were hastily arranged and commenced on Monday, 9 July 1877, with 22 gentlemen paying an entry fee of one guinea (one pound and one shilling in 1877, but equating to more than £100 today). The first prize worth twelve guineas was won by 27-year-old Spencer Gore, a local all-round sportsman whose main love was cricket. Gore also won a silver trophy worth twenty-five guineas which had been donated by the proprietors of *The Field*. The tournament was played over 11 days, including a two-

The only scheduled day of play for that inaugural Championship was the first. After that, play would take place on such subsequent days as were necessary to complete the tournament. The fact that there was just one Championship event – the Gentlemen's Singles – and that there were only 22 entrants, meant that a total of just 20 matches were played during the tournament, 19 on the first four days and the rain-delayed final a week later.

Although the plan of the grounds suggests that 12 courts were available, only a few would have been needed for tournament matches, the remainder being given over to practice and social play. It is quite likely that the early lawn tennis players were so keen that after playing their relatively short matches in the tournament they might have played on just for fun.

The first Wimbledon final was further delayed by three days of heavy rain, eventually taking place on the afternoon of Thursday, 19 July 1877. Word of mouth amongst elite London society coupled with a report in *The Field* resulted in a large crowd of 200 spectators paying one shilling (just under £6 today) each for admission. A small temporary grandstand was erected for the occasion, but there is no evidence to suggest that Wimbledon's authorities had ever previously considered that the public would come in large numbers to watch what had essentially been, up to that point, a humble garden game.

day break for the Eton versus Harrow cricket match at Lord's, one of the major sporting and social occasions of the English summer season which had in the past attracted crowds of around 20,000 spectators.

The pause in proceedings at Wimbledon was in all probability not to avoid competition with the cricket match, but rather because many at The All England Club wanted to go to Lord's to see it. Spencer Gore himself was an Old Harrovian, and also a keen cricketer, remarking after his Wimbledon victory that he much preferred cricket to lawn tennis.

Richard Sears, 1886

Centre Court, Worple Road, 1903

For its inaugural Lawn Tennis Championship in 1877 The All England Club's organising committee comprising Julian Marshall, Charles Heathcote and Henry Jones – the latter better known to readers of *The Field* as 'Cavendish' – had wisely made a number of changes to the game Major Wingfield had launched three years earlier. The original hourglass-shaped court was replaced with a rectangular one, and the first-to-15 points method of scoring was superseded by the 15, 30, 40, deuce, advantage system still used today. The key change, however, took place during the period from 1878 to 1882 when the height of the net at the posts was gradually reduced from five feet to three feet six inches, thus signalling the beginning of the end of the 'pat-ball' game played in country house gardens and ushering in a new era of attacking tennis with greater spectator appeal.

Reports in *The Field* and other periodicals quickly spread word of the success of the first Wimbledon Championships, stimulating the growth of tournament tennis in Great Britain and beyond. Lawn tennis tournaments had been held in the US as early as 1876 but the first official US Championships were not staged until 1881, when Richard Sears defeated William Glyn of Great Britain 6-0, 6-3, 6-2 in the final at Newport, Rhode Island. Sears would go on to win the title for seven straight years before losing to fellow-countryman Henry Slocum in 1888. On the other side of the Atlantic, the arrival of two Leamington-born twin brothers signalled the start of Wimbledon's first golden era.

Right from the start attendances at Wimbledon had been steadily rising. In the *Wimbledon Compendium* Alan Little records that the final, then known as the Challenge Round, in which the previous year's champion defended his title against the newly crowned winner of the 'All-Comers' Final', was watched by 700 people in 1878, 1,100 in 1879, and 1,300 in 1880. Now, with the net reduced in height, the popular Renshaw twins, William and Ernest, spearheaded a new era of exciting attacking play, and big crowds came to Wimbledon to see them. One or both of the brothers reached the Wimbledon singles final for ten consecutive years from 1881 to 1890, and during five of those years they teamed up to win the men's doubles title as well. 'Willie', as he was affectionately known, was the more charismatic and

Worple Lane (now Nursery Road)

successful of the two, winning six consecutive singles titles from 1881 to 1886 and a seventh in 1889. Ernest won his sole singles title in 1888, but reached the Challenge Round on three other occasions, narrowly losing out each time to his brother.

William and Ernest Renshaw, along with Richard Sears, were the first lawn tennis stars, and their celebrity reached far beyond aficionados of the sport, attracting bigger and bigger crowds to Wimbledon during the 1880s. In his book *Forty Years of First Class Lawn Tennis*, All England Club Secretary George Hillyard described the effect the Renshaws had on the Wimbledon public: 'Who that witnessed lawn tennis of the eighties doesn't remember the Renshaw rush? When, whatever match was in progress, and however exciting it might be, the moment the famous twins appeared on the scene, the whole gallery arose as one man, and there was a perfect stampede of spectators and chairs to whatever court they were going to play on.'

A posed studio photograph from this period shows the Renshaws dressed in their tennis clothing which derived much in its style and functionality from cricket attire: long flannel trousers; white shirts with sleeves rolled to the elbow; necktie; and military belt. This is how the fashionable sportsman was dressed in late-Victorian times, and this was the first of many fashion trends to emanate from the manicured lawns of SW19. ◯

Ladies' tennis tournaments were staged in various locations during the late 1870s and early 1880s, but it was not until 1884 that women made their debut at Wimbledon. Thirteen entrants competed for a silver cup worth twenty guineas, and 19-year-old Maud Watson, a rector's daughter from Coventry, beat her elder sister Lillian 6-8, 6-3, 6-3 in the final to become Wimbledon's first-ever Ladies' Singles champion. That same year three American players, Richard Sears, Arthur Rives and Dr James Dwight of Boston – who later became affectionately known as 'the father of American lawn tennis' – were the first overseas entrants to play in The Championships. Also in 1884, the first Gentlemen's Doubles Championship was played at Wimbledon. Tennis was coming

powered flight took place, and the Paris Metro and the New York Subway opened. Not only could people travel more freely, they also became healthier and lived longer as new vaccines were developed to combat ailments and illnesses which had previously been untreatable. People's preoccupations were local, but within a decade or two world affairs would be on everyone's minds.

The game of lawn tennis evolved equally quickly. The early players had been well-to-do socialites seeking amusement and exercise. What they could not have anticipated was the rapid growth of Walter Wingfield's garden game as a competitive spectator sport, although even the very first Wimbledon final in 1877 had been watched by 200 paying spectators, with hindsight a clear indication of things to come. Three years later, F.H. Ayres & Company provided two temporary grandstands, and Courts 7 and 8 were merged to create what became known as the Centre Court. By the mid-1880s permanent stands had been erected on three sides of the court, along with a sectioned-off area for the press. The name Centre Court – so synonymous with tennis today – was a logical one, for at Wimbledon's first home in Worple Road the main court was indeed surrounded on all sides by the other 'outside' courts.

Despite the rapid advancement of lawn tennis as a serious competitive sport, the players at Wimbledon still placed a high value on the sporting ethic of the true amateur. A great example of this came during the All-Comers' Final of 1889. Trailing by two sets to one and match point down, William Renshaw slipped and dropped his racket as he approached the net to volley. His opponent Harry Barlow had an easy shot to win the tournament, but instead chose to tap the ball gently back, giving Renshaw time to scramble to his feet and pick up his racket. Renshaw recovered to win the point, the set, the match and, eventually, the Championship.

By the 1890s tennis clubs had been established all over the world, but top-level competition was still only for the privileged classes with leisure time to play in tournaments, particularly where long-distance travel was involved. Within countries and continents the train took the strain, but the pioneering few who crossed the Atlantic did so in style in luxury ocean-going liners. At the other end of the social spectrum, members of the working classes were quite willing to spend a shilling (or its equivalent in cents or centimes) to read illustrated weekly news magazines which focused on the social activities of high society. Tennis was very much a part of that glamorous lifestyle.

of age as an international sport for all.

In the 1880s the world was entering an extraordinary period of technological and social change. Within a few short years, the petrol-fuelled car was invented, the first

At Athens in 1896, lawn tennis was one of the original nine sports included in the first Olympic Games of the modern era, with Ireland's John Boland earning the distinction of becoming the first Olympic tennis champion. At the Paris Games four years later Charlotte Cooper, a three-times Wimbledon singles champion, won the inaugural Ladies' Singles tournament to become Britain's first-ever female Olympic champion.

Wimbledon endured a dip in popularity in the mid-1890s after the Renshaws retired from tournament play, but within a few years fortunes were revived by the arrival of another pair of brothers, Reggie and Laurie Doherty, born just a few hundred yards from The All England Club in Hartfield Road, Wimbledon.

The Dohertys were handsome, sportsmanlike and supremely talented. Earlier champions had played other racket sports before turning to lawn tennis, and – with one or two exceptions – would never have had the inclination to travel abroad to compete. Reggie and Laurie Doherty, however, had styles of play that owed nothing to other sports. They were lawn tennis players through and through, and their achievements testified to their prowess and skill. Reggie won Wimbledon for four straight years from 1897 to 1900, and his brother Laurie then went one better, triumphing in five consecutive years from 1902 to 1906. They won the Wimbledon doubles together eight times in nine years. Laurie also won the US Singles Championship in 1903,

No. 33.   MISS SUTTON

May Sutton (USA), Wimbledon's first champion from overseas

and, with Reggie, the US Doubles Championship in 1902 and 1903.

Both the Doherty brothers died young – Reggie in 1910 at just 38, and Laurie in 1919 at 43 after serving in the Royal Naval Reserve during World War I. They had brought record crowds to Wimbledon, and their passing was much lamented by tennis lovers both in Britain and America. The All England Club's Doherty Gates stand as a permanent memorial to their greatness.

Since the Dohertys, Great Britain has only produced three male Wimbledon singles champions: Arthur Gore (1901, 1908, 1909), Fred Perry (1934–1936) and Andy Murray (2013, 2016).

In the Wednesday, April 24 1901 issue of *Lawn Tennis and Croquet* magazine, a 'Wimbledon Correspondent' reported that 'Great changes have been worked at Wimbledon in the winter. The pavilion, which dates from 1868, and very early croquet, has been almost completely rebuilt. A large and handsome room has been constructed on the second storey for the ladies, and the gentlemen's dressing room is also new, and a great improvement on the old one,' adding 'Two thousand two hundred turfs were laid down in the winter. The pavilion at Wimbledon was the first croquet pavilion ever erected. We are glad to see it made up to date.'

In 1905 Wimbledon had its first overseas champion when Plymouth-born May Sutton, whose family had emigrated to California when she was a young girl, beat Britain's reigning title-holder Dorothea Douglass in the Challenge Round. In the years prior to the American's victory, Britain's Maud Watson, Blanche Bingley (later Mrs Hillyard), Charlotte 'Lottie' Dod, Charlotte Cooper (later Mrs Sterry) and Dorothea Douglass (later Mrs Lambert Chambers) were all multiple champions, between them winning all but two of the Ladies' Singles Championships between 1884 and 1904. Entries during these years were very low, sometimes in single figures, and it was not until the arrival of Suzanne Lenglen after the First World War that women's tennis really began to flourish at Wimbledon.

Also in 1905, 27-year-old Norman Brookes travelled to

England from his home in Melbourne to compete in the Wimbledon Championships. He came very close to lifting the title, winning the All-Comers' Singles before losing to reigning champion Laurie Doherty in the Challenge Round. Two years later, he returned and was crowned Wimbledon's first overseas Gentlemen's Singles champion.

Sutton and Brookes's victories opened the floodgates of overseas success. Handsome New Zealander Anthony Wilding was a sporting idol in the eyes of the British public, winning the Wimbledon singles title in four consecutive years from 1910 to 1913 before losing his title to Davis Cup team-mate Brookes in 1914. A year later Wilding was killed in France whilst serving with the Royal Marines.

Wilding was a dashing hero straight out of a boy's adventure story. He thought nothing of driving across Europe on his motorcycle to play in a tennis tournament and then driving straight back to play in another one. His book *On The Court and Off* was published in 1912 and immediately had to be reprinted, such was the demand. In 1916 Arthur Wallis Myers's *Captain Anthony Wilding* became the first biography of a lawn tennis player to be published in Britain.

Wilding's successes were based on intensive practice and physical training, as George Hillyard observed: 'I always thought his was the type of genius which is defined by Carlyle as "the capacity for taking infinite pains," rather than what is commonly, and to

Reggie and Laurie Doherty, amongst Britain's finest-ever champions

my mind rightly, understood to be the meaning of that word.'

Victorian codes of behaviour had deemed it unsporting to train and practise for games, but Wilding's success confounded those notions and from then on nearly all top players embraced his serious approach to the game.

Anthony Wilding (New Zealand), champion 1910–1913

Early in the 20th century, lawn tennis took on a truly international identity and there was a flood of overseas entries to Wimbledon.

The Davis Cup was inaugurated in 1900 as an annual team match between the United States and the British Isles, and quickly broadened into an international competition involving many nations. In 1901 the public flocked to Wimbledon to see the much talked-about American players Dwight Davis and Holcombe Ward. These exponents of the 'American Twist' serve had bamboozled the British team during the inaugural Davis Cup match in Boston the previous year, and there was great speculation on how effective it would be in English conditions, with truer courts and harder balls.

Impressions of the Championships

by 'Our Lady Commissioner'

Writing in the July 3, 1901 issue of *Lawn Tennis and Croquet* magazine, Our Lady Commissioner gave a delightful description of the joys and frustrations of a day at Wimbledon:

I don't think Wimbledon is a very nice place to get to, do you? I was told to take the electric railway at the City to Waterloo, and then go by South-Western. You walk for miles down a sloping passage, in which the wind is so strong that it nearly blows your hat off, and then you get into what looks like a barge, and find yourself at Waterloo, where there are other passages, and a lot of steps. When you get to the top somebody tells you that you take your ticket on the other side – the main line, I think it is – and then they say, 'No, you go to the south station.' So you go back, and find that you have got to walk the whole length of a long platform before you get to the booking-office. But you get to Wimbledon Station at last. I thought that the ground was sure to be near the station. So I walked until I was tired, and still there was no ground. But I found it at last – with such an entry! All among horses' heads and legs, and no pavement. I wonder what it would be like on a wet day!

One ought to be rewarded by something specially good when one at last got inside, and I was. There were hundreds of people there, and it was quite like the finals at Beckenham, although it was early in the week. I naturally thought that people who went to see the Championships would all understand the game very well indeed, and I was immensely astonished to find how many of them didn't understand it at all –

men, as well as women. I am sure some of them went away with all sorts of wrong impressions.

I was watching the first match in which the Americans played, and behind me were two gentlemen who met by accident. One of them said to the other, 'Hallo, you here!' 'Yes, came to see the Americans.' 'So did I, which are they?' 'Well,' said the second one, 'the big chap there' (pointing to Mr. Hillyard) is Davis, and the stout little chap (this was Dr. Eaves) is Ward.' 'Ah,' replied the other, 'We don't make men like Davis in this country – what a splendid fellow he is, and I like the look of the little chap, too; he's so jolly brown – quite American.' I don't know why they thought Americans ought to look brown. They never discovered their mistake, and soon went away, saying that they 'didn't see any twist on the service, after all. It was all moonshine.'

But you do hear funny things at Wimbledon. While I was looking at a Ladies' Doubles in which Mrs. Hillyard was playing with Mrs. Sterry, a lady asked me (pointing to Mrs. Hillyard), 'Would you mind telling me the name of that young lady? She doesn't play at all badly.' I said, 'No, she didn't,' for it was Mrs. Hillyard. 'Oh,' replied my questioner, but I mean the one in the short dress.' 'Yes,' I replied, 'that is Mrs. Hillyard.' 'Surely you must be making a mistake.

'I understood that Mrs. Hillyard has won the Championship for years and years.' I replied that except for a year or two she had won it for a long time, and would very likely win it again. She thanked me, and I heard her say to herself as she went away, 'Well, I declare. Why doesn't she look as old as Elizabeth!'

The Tea Lawn, Worple Road

On Thursday I was looking at the match in which Capt. Young and Mr. Hawes, poor dears, were trying to understand the American service. Mr. Davis had just made a tremendous drive, which frightened me very much, for the ball went quite close to me at a fearful rate, when a very young gentleman said to another one aloud in a whisper, 'By George! old chap, wouldn't he make a stunning headmaster!' The other one replied 'I don't know; I fancy the other chap has more sting in him.' They both laughed, and an old gentleman who heard it smiled pleasantly at them. I haven't any idea what they meant, but it must have been rather clever, or they wouldn't all have smiled, would they? So I put it down here.

I was told that, whatever I did, on Thursday I was to see Mr. Agger play Mr. Smith, because, my informant said, it was always 'awf'lly good sport' to see Agger running backwards and forwards on the base-line for all the world as if he was wound up and could not help himself. So I went. I arrived at the centre court, just as Mr. Agger was doing one of these backward and forward runs. He returned the ball from close to one of the side-lines and then bolted as hard as he possibly could to the other side, and kept on going backwards and forwards for ever so long. All this time Mr. Smith was standing almost still, and it seemed positive cruelty on his part to make Mr. Agger exert himself so much on a hot day. I heard someone say, 'It's always like that. Poor chap! he gets nearly killed after a match with Smith.' I felt ever so sorry for him, but he didn't seem to mind in the least, and before long I noticed that Mr. Smith was doing much more than a fair share of the work, and when he was running backwards and forwards himself he did not seem to be getting so much fun out of the game as Mr. Agger, I thought. Indeed I began to be very sorry for him in turn, for Mr. Agger kept on placing the ball out of his reach, and Mr. Smith made double faults and couldn't get his big drives as fast as usual, and it was all up with him.

French superstar
Suzanne Lenglen
made her
Wimbledon
debut in 1919

In early June 1914, a 15-year-old girl won her first major title, the World Hard Court Championship at St. Cloud, Paris. This precocious French teenager was immediately invited to come to Wimbledon to play in The Championships, but her father, who was her coach and mentor, decided it was too soon.

Unknown to them both, Suzanne Lenglen would have to wait five long years for her Wimbledon debut, for during the 1914 Championships Archduke Franz Ferdinand, heir to the throne of Austria-Hungary, was assassinated in Sarajevo. This triggered a chain of events that would quickly lead to the outbreak of World War I. For the next four years, the progress of lawn tennis, and Wimbledon, was halted.

In the early years of the 20th century the spirit of the 'gentleman amateur' lived on. Herbert Roper Barrett, a future captain of the British Davis Cup team, competed in the 1901 Championships under the comical pseudonym of 'D'Agger', reaching the semi-finals of the Gentlemen's All-Comers' Singles, where he lost to eventual champion Arthur Gore. The 'Mr Smith' referred to by 'Our Lady Commissioner' in *Lawn Tennis and Croquet* magazine was hard-hitting S.H. Smith of Gloucestershire, one of the finest players never to become Wimbledon champion.

In 1905 Australian Norman Brookes and New Zealander Anthony Wilding played together in the Davis Cup representing Australasia, and that combined team went on to win the trophy six times before the two nations began entering separately in 1923. The Davis Cup was a powerful driving force in raising standards and developing the sport worldwide, and by 1913 the desire for international cooperation was such that the International Lawn Tennis Federation (ILTF – now known as the ITF) was formed. It had been the brainchild of Duane Williams of Philadelphia, who would sadly never see his grand vision realised, for he was one of the hundreds who died when the ocean liner RMS *Titanic* struck an iceberg and sank on its maiden voyage in 1912. His son Dick swam to safety from the stricken vessel, and went on to become a two-times US singles champion.

When the Wimbledon Championships resumed after World War I there was huge demand from players and the sporting public. The draw for the Gentlemen's Singles was increased to 128, and a ballot was introduced to determine which lucky applicants would get tickets. Both these features have remained in place ever since. Arthur Wallis Myers later observed: 'The reason for the game's remarkable revival was clear. The athletic energies of youth, suppressed for five years, sought a natural outlet and found it in a pastime so cosmopolitan as lawn tennis.'

Norman Brookes sportingly returned to Wimbledon to defend the title he had won in 1914, but at 41 was past his prime and was decisively beaten in the Challenge Round by powerful fellow-Australian Gerald Patterson, 17 years his junior.

After spending the war years honing her tennis skills against men in the safe haven of the French Riviera, Suzanne Lenglen made her long-awaited first appearance on the lawns of SW19. Her arrival brought huge crowds flocking to The Championships, and her style and charisma changed the game of tennis forever.

Wimbledon had never seen anyone like Suzanne. She dressed, played and behaved quite differently from all the other female players of the day. Whilst her fellow competitors wore long-sleeved, ankle-length dresses with extensive corsetry and undergarments leaving only their hands and faces visible, Suzanne wore lightweight, knee-length dresses with short sleeves. Her balletic, all-action style of play often gave the watching galleries glimpses of bare flesh,

In early June 1914, a 15-year-old girl won her first major title, the World Hard Court Championship at St. Cloud, Paris. Suzanne Lenglen was a precocious French teenager who had to wait until the First World War was over to make her Wimbledon debut.

something most Edwardian men and women had never seen in public before. And Suzanne smiled when she played. And she laughed. And she groaned at her very rare bad shots. There was a unique joyfulness in her play, and she loved to perform just as much as the gallery loved to watch her.

The extraordinary Suzanne Lenglen was a 'must-see' star for London's elite social circles in the summer of 1919. At fashionable dinner parties and in West End theatre lobbies everybody was talking about her, and if by some chance you had not seen her play you were, quite simply, behind the times. Chauffeur-driven automobiles were parked in long lines along the narrow Worple Road each day during The Championships whilst their owners jostled for position inside The All England Lawn Tennis Club's tiny grounds in the hope of seeing Suzanne play. Others made their way on foot from Wimbledon station, half a mile away, and with each passing day the crowds grew bigger.

'The interest in her play and personality was phenomenal,' wrote George Hillyard. 'It didn't matter who she was pitted against, a rabbit or a good player, it was all one to the crowd! They nearly broke down some of the stands in their efforts to get a glimpse of her!'

Suzanne Rachel Floré Lenglen was born in the Passy district of Paris on 24 May 1899. When she was five the family moved north to Marest-sur-Matz, near Compiegne, and began spending winters in the warmer climate of the French Riviera. Their winter home was very close to the Nice Lawn Tennis Club and that was where Suzanne began playing the game seriously at the age of 11. Her talent and her father Charles's intelligent coaching soon saw her playing with adults and winning local competitions. In 1914, just after her 15th birthday, she became the World Hard Court champion.

During the war years Suzanne practised her tennis hour after hour on the courts of the Nice Lawn Tennis Club under the constant supervision of her father. It was reputed that he would put small coins on the court as targets, and Suzanne had to hit them. Many top tennis players visited the Riviera during the war years and Suzanne had the benefit of playing with them. By the time tournament tennis resumed early in 1919, she was quite simply unbeatable.

In the early months of 1919 Suzanne entered 15 singles and doubles tournaments in France and won them all. When she travelled across to England in June, she was the favourite to win the Wimbledon title despite

SUZANNE LENGLEN
The first global superstar
of lawn tennis

the fact that she had never played on grass before. Such was Charles Lenglen's confidence in his daughter he did not enter her into any of the pre-Wimbledon tournaments, opting instead for grass-court practice at Queen's Club in West Kensington. His strategy was ultimately proved correct, but only just.

Suzanne opened her Wimbledon campaign on Tuesday, 24 June against Mrs Annis Cobb. Surprisingly the match was not played on the Centre Court, which had a capacity of 3,500, but on one of the outer courts where a small stand had recently been erected. Suzanne's fame had preceded her, and hundreds of people left their Centre Court seats to try to see her in action out on Court No.4. Suzanne was wearing a floppy hat – her famous bandeau would not appear for the first time until a year later – and, in the words of tennis historian Alan Little in his book *Suzanne Lenglen: Tennis Idol of the Twenties*, 'a flimsy, white, calf-length short-sleeved tennis frock'. She leapt about the court before a disbelieving crowd, dispatching her British opponent 6–0, 6–1. Despite the one-sided scoreline Mrs Cobb had done well, for over the years that followed many of Suzanne's opponents were unable to win even a single game.

Suzanne Lenglen played 13 matches at the 1919 Wimbledon Championships: seven in Singles, three in Ladies' Doubles and three in Mixed Doubles, losing in the quarter-finals of the latter in partnership with Frenchman William Laurentz. She was on court nearly every day, and even in those pre-radio days news of her exploits spread across London like wildfire. Everyone who saw her was enchanted – men by her beguiling looks, women by her fashion sense and independence of spirit.

As Suzanne advanced towards the trophy matches in the Ladies' Singles and doubles events, the crowds coming to watch her grew even bigger. To challenge for the singles title, Suzanne first had to win the All-Comers' event, the winner of which earned the right to play against the reigning Wimbledon champion. This she did, winning five matches very easily and only facing a serious challenge from her doubles partner Elizabeth Ryan, whom she beat 6–4, 7–5. Having won the All-Comers' Singles, Suzanne now faced the reigning pre-war champion, 40-year-old Dorothea Lambert Chambers, who had been sitting out waiting for her challenger to emerge.

Dorothea had won her seventh Wimbledon title in 1914, a record, but five years on was not expected to win against a talented and athletic challenger who was less than half her age. The match was more than just challenger against champion, and youth against age; it was tradition against modernity, with Suzanne Lenglen exuberantly representing the bright new generation.

On the eve of the match, Dorothea received a not-wholly-encouraging good luck letter from her friend, six-times Wimbledon champion Blanche Hillyard:

Thorpe Satchville
Melton Mowbray

July 2

My Dear Dollie,

Just one line to wish you the best of luck against the Lenglen. Go all you can & never give up, stick to her till the last ace. I am afraid you can't do it but die hard, your reputation will help you a lot even against a paragon as she is. Thank God she didn't live in my day!!

I shall be with you in spirit & I shall Evil Eye her if I can. I wish I knew which day you play for certain, Remember I have the Evil Eye that has been proved many times.

My Rheumatism is too damnable for words. How on earth Satterthwaite has got to the final I don't know. One of the worst styles of players & I always feel I could have given her 1/2 30 in my best days. Well my dear again good luck & I do hope you won't have the "curse." I wish she may have it if she does have it at all?

Yours affectionately,
Blanche Hillyard

PS I hope Bob won't watch you. He brings you bad luck I am sure.

The Centre Court at Worple Road showing the Royal Box and the pony roller

> *"The interest in her play and personality was phenomenal. It didn't matter who she was pitted against, a rabbit or a good player, it was all one to the crowd! They nearly broke down some of the stands in their efforts to get a glimpse of her!"*

George Hillyard on Suzanne Lenglen

'Bob', of course, was Dorothea's husband Robert Lambert Chambers, and when the match got underway, the defending champion surprised everyone. Despite Suzanne moving quickly to a 4-1 lead, the veteran British player showed true grit and determination, plus considerable tactical nous, only losing the set 8-10 after herself holding two set points. The next two sets were see-saw battles, with Dorothea taking the second 6-4 and holding two match points at 6-5 in the third. Suzanne saved the first of these with a shot off the frame of her racquet, and that was as close as her opponent would get to her eighth Wimbledon singles title. She netted a drop shot on her second match point, and a relieved and exhausted Suzanne went on to close out a remarkable 10-8, 4-6, 9-7 victory after just over two hours' play.

Three days later Suzanne partnered Elizabeth Ryan to a narrow victory against Dorothea and Ethel Larcombe for her second Wimbledon title. The Suzanne Lenglen story had begun. ◓

Over the years, the Wimbledon Committee had done all it could to meet the needs of ever-increasing numbers of players and spectators within the tight physical constraints of the Worple Road grounds. Even before the war there had been rumblings about a possible move to a new, bigger ground; Suzanne Lenglen's arrival in 1919 made such a move inevitable and urgent. Over the years permanent stands had been built around the Centre Court, which now seated 3,200 spectators, but it was estimated that nearly 8,000 were present when Suzanne played Dorothea in the 1919 Challenge Round.

In 1920 Suzanne Lenglen returned to Wimbledon to defend her singles and doubles titles. She was joined by the other superstar of world tennis, America's 'Big' Bill Tilden, who was making his Wimbledon debut. Suzanne not only retained her singles title, beating Dorothea Lambert Chambers once again in the Challenge Round, she was also successful in the Ladies' and Mixed Doubles, making her the first player, male or female, to win three Wimbledon titles in a single year.

In the year since her first Wimbledon victory Suzanne had become a worldwide celebrity, and a fashion trendsetter. In his biography of Suzanne, Alan Little described her new look: 'the public saw a smarter and more sophisticated Suzanne, dressed in clothes designed by Jean Patou, the Paris couturier, and sporting the new "bobbed" hair style. On court she wore a loose, one-piece frock. Her dresses were always uncreased as she never sat, once dressed for tennis. The soft hat was replaced by what became known as the "Lenglen bandeau", several yards of georgette, varying in colour from heliotrope to lemon, swathed around the hair. Later, Suzanne chose multi-coloured silk chiffon for the bandeau, which was usually held in place by a diamond arrow. With every match she changed the colour of the bandeau and matching cardigan. She scarcely ever wore jewellery.'

Bill Tilden, like Suzanne, was an eye-catching extrovert and a big crowd-puller, and his rivalry with fellow-American 'Little' Bill Johnston further fanned the flames of Wimbledon's popularity. After Tilden's 1920 victory, and with the prospect of many more to follow, The All England Club purchased a large plot of land in Wimbledon Park and began making plans to build a grand new tennis complex there.

The last year at the old ground was a poignant one, as All England Club President Herbert Wilberforce reflected in *Forty Years of First Class Lawn Tennis*: 'Those who, like myself, have known the old ground for over forty years feel a tinge of regret at leaving a place round which so many recollections of their youth hang clustered; there was a homeliness and a friendliness about the earlier gatherings which one cannot expect to find in the more magnificent surroundings created by Stanley Peach.'

Wimbledon's move to larger grounds did not come a moment

William T. Tilden II, affectionately known as 'Big Bill'

too soon. In 1921, Worple Road's biggest-ever crowd watched the All-Comers' Singles semi-final in which Manuel Alonso, a Spaniard with, according to Wallis Myers, 'court movements as rapid as Renshaw's and a most engaging style', beat Japan's Zenzo Shimizu 3–6, 7–5, 3–6, 6–4, 8–6. Lenglen and Tilden successfully defended their singles titles, and fittingly it was Suzanne who hit the very last shot on the old Centre Court at Worple Road in the final of the Ladies' Doubles, a smash which, according to Wallis Myers, 'nearly knocked Mrs Peacock over'. ◯

CHAPTER 2
Wimbledon, Everyone?
1922–1939

The 1920s and 30s was a period of artistic creativity, political uncertainty and economic strife. Mass-circulation newspapers and magazines, cinema newsreels and radio broadcasts kept people fully up to date, not only with important world affairs but also with the activities of the rich and famous. The media told of the outrageous social excesses of the 'Bright Young Things', wealthy young people from privileged backgrounds whose reckless hedonism was a direct reaction to the horrors of the First World War. Celebrity culture was alive and well, and globe trotting tennis stars were very much a part of it.

When the new Centre Court opened in 1922, the young generation of the Jazz Age saluted a soaring totem of sporting modernity. As has been the case throughout its history, Wimbledon astounded the public with the breadth of its vision and the height of its achievement. The new stadium made lawn tennis a world leader, and the decade that followed saw the opening of the sport's other great arenas: White City, Sydney (1922), Forest Hills, New York (1923), Roland Garros, Paris (1928) and Kooyong, Melbourne (1932). ◓

The 1922 Wimbledon Championship meeting was the wettest on record up to that point. Day after day it rained, and on several days during the first week virtually no play was possible on the uncovered outside courts. It was a great achievement by referee Francis Burrow and the Wimbledon Committee to get the tournament finished, but the Gentlemen's Singles Final was not played until the third Monday and the three doubles finals two days after that.

The Championships had originally been scheduled to commence at 2.45pm on Monday, 26 June 1922, but it was raining heavily when play was due to start. Fortunately the weather eased and at 3.30pm King George sounded a gong to signal the formal opening of The All England Lawn Tennis and Croquet Club's new ground, which the official programme described as being at 'Wimbledon Park'. After deliberately hitting his service return into the net on the opening point, Britain's Leslie Godfree rushed forward and pocketed the very first ball hit on the new Centre Court. This memento stayed on the family's mantelpiece for over half a century, until it eventually fell apart.

Suzanne Lenglen, now aged 23, returned to win her fourth consecutive Ladies' Singles title, but to the disappointment of many, Bill Tilden, the champion in 1920 and 1921, did not come across from America to complete his hat-trick. Had he done so, Tilden would have had to play through all the rounds, for after consultation with the players the previous year the Challenge Round system had been abolished. The Gentlemen's Singles title was won by Australia's Gerald Patterson, the 1919 champion. Despite the absence of the leading American men, Wimbledon was now firmly the hunting ground of overseas stars, and the British press was already beginning to lament the lack of home success, a theme that would be prevalent in the coverage of Wimbledon during all but a few of the next 100 years.

Despite the awful weather, the inaugural Championships at the new Wimbledon were a success, and the great risk of building a Centre Court that could hold 10,000 more people than the one it replaced proved fully justified. As Wallis Myers observed, 'The entry was a record; Royalty came down often; thousands of would-be onlookers were turned away. The first New Wimbledon, if wet, was welcomed.'

The project had been brilliantly planned and executed by George Hillyard, the Secretary of The All England Club. He had micro-managed every aspect, from supporting the day-to-day work of architect Stanley Peach through to the choice of yew trees planted to eventually provide a dark backdrop to each of the 12 outside courts. These would eventually grow to a height of five feet, providing a perfect background. All but 100 of the Centre Court's 9,989

Wimbledon 1926. The front cover of the Official Programme for the Jubilee Championships showed players from the 1870s and 1920s dressed in contemporary tennis attire as their handshakes bridged the generations.

Monday, 26 June 1922. The gong is in position as King George V formally opens the new Centre Court

seats had an uninterrupted view of the entire playing area, and the remainder were designated 'restricted view'. Peach's design ensured that shadows could not encroach onto the Centre Court until after 7pm.

Only a few aspects of the original plan were not implemented. It was deemed too risky to bring the original turf from Worple Road, in case the new ground was not ready in time. Turf was brought in from Cumberland instead. Three planned courts and a pavilion on the west side of the new ground were not ready in time, and after the success of the 1922 Championships the space allocated to these was given over to two new show courts instead. The original No.2 Court opened in 1923, and the No.1 Court a year later. A distinctive feature of the new ground was the Water Tower on the eastern perimeter, intended to be used in emergencies to pump water from the lake in Wimbledon Park.

In the period from 1922 to 1979, although three times the size of the original Worple Road site, the Wimbledon grounds were much smaller than they are today, with the northern end of the Centre Court marking the boundary of The All England Club's estate. During this period, all the outside courts were to the south of the Centre Court and the old No.1 Court. Many visitors who made their Wimbledon debut prior to 1980 still have a tendency to think of these bench-lined courts, with their often jam-packed walkways, as the 'real Wimbledon'. 🎾

Church Road in the 1920s. Spectators and automobiles mingle on the Promenade.

During the 41 years in which The Championships were staged at Worple Road, the nature of the tournament and the demographic of the spectators changed considerably. The early Championships had a small number of entries and there were relatively few matches for the public to watch. The combined number of entries for all Wimbledon Championship events – singles and doubles – rose and fell from year to year at first, but the overall trend was a marked increase as the number of Championship events grew. For the first seven years, there was just one event, the Gentlemen's Singles. In 1884 Ladies' Singles and Gentlemen's Doubles were included in the programme, and in 1913 Ladies' Doubles and Mixed Doubles were added. Entries rose from 22 in 1877 to 53 in 1884, 67 in 1900, 165 in 1910 and, in the last year at Worple Road, 327.

With so many more matches being played, there was scope

for many other talented players to become familiar faces at Wimbledon. These included the popular Allen brothers, Charles and Roy; Toupie Lowther, Kenneth Powell, who fell in World War I; Aurea Edgington, Theodore Mavrogordato, and Evelyn Colyer. These and many other colourful personalities

each had their own coterie of supporters, and were capable of attracting a good-sized crowd when they took to the court.

The number of spectators increased too, but this growth was constrained by the lack of space at the Worple Road ground. In the *Wimbledon Compendium*, Alan Little noted that the scene at the ground was 'very congested when 6,000 people were present'. When the figure reached 7,500 the ground was said to be 'packed to suffocation'.

Arthur Wallis Myers was present in 1906, the last year in which the Doherty brothers competed seriously at Wimbledon, and observed that 'the galleries were overflowing'. Of the 1914 Championships, the last before the outbreak of war, he commented: 'For two or three years, ever since Wimbledon had developed into an affair of nations and even of continents, the capacity of the original ground to hold the multitude of sightseers had been strained. The stands girdling the centre court had been enlarged to the limit of available space; if a spectacular match was staged on a side court the crush was intolerable.'

Of the environs of the Worple Road ground, he wrote: 'The approaches to the gates and the accommodation for motor cars were totally inadequate. Peaceful residents in Wimbledon backwaters complained that their view was obstructed and their privacy disturbed by queues of waiting cars; the police, however sympathetic, felt that the traffic problem was beyond them; the cry for more room was becoming insistent. Long before the new ground at Wimbledon Park was purchased and made

For two or three years, ever since Wimbledon had developed into an affair of nations and even of continents, the capacity of the original ground to hold the multitude of sightseers had been strained.

ready, the management realised that the popularity of the game had outwitted them; their pride was their embarrassment; they realised that sentiment must give way to common sense, that the picnic days of Wimbledon, loved by the old habitué, were numbered. The crush of 1913 had been an ominous portent; that of 1914 cast the die; and if the war had not intervened it is almost certain the New Wimbledon would have risen much earlier.'

The 'old habitué' Wallis Myers referred to included the last of the upper-class garden-party set who had been joined at Wimbledon in recent years by thousands of upwardly mobile working folk who were enjoying better pay, working conditions and annual holiday entitlements. For them, Wimbledon was an expensive day out, but now firmly within reach.

When The Championships moved to Church Road in 1922, the capacity of the Wimbledon grounds was instantly trebled, and with blanket reporting in the print media augmented by radio coverage from 1927 and television a decade later, attendances continued to grow steadily. It had been estimated that a maximum of 70,000 may have attended The Championships in the last years at Worple Road; by 1932 the aggregate attendance for 12 days at Church Road had reached 219,000. 🎾

A great stadium, like a great theatre, needs star performers, and during the 1920s the new Centre Court was graced by some of the biggest personalities in the history of lawn tennis. Suzanne Lenglen remained peerless until she turned professional in 1926, and the two Bills, Tilden and Johnston, were joined at the top of the men's game by fellow-American Frank Hunter, and France's Jean Borotra, Henri Cochet, Rene Lacoste and doubles specialist Jacques Brugnon, the latter quartet becoming popularly known as the 'Four Musketeers', after the characters in Alexandre Dumas's 19th-century adventure novel *The Three Musketeers*.

Jean Borotra (left) was one of France's popular 'Four Musketeers' who were favourites with the Centre Court crowd during the 1920s. Champion in 1924 and 1926, 'The Bounding Basque' competed at Wimbledon for over 50 years

Clockwise from top left: Rene Lacoste, Jacques 'Toto' Brugnon, Henri Cochet and Jean Borotra

1922

A Visit to Wimbledon

Jessica Bousfield, HUNTINGTON, NEW YORK

Confectionery box, 1920s

In July 1922 Jessica Bousfield of Huntington, New York crossed the ocean to visit relatives in Britain. Whilst here, she had the good fortune to see the great Suzanne Lenglen in action on Wimbledon's Centre Court. This account is from Jessica's letter dated July 9, 1922 to her family back in New York:

Saturday morning we went for mail, and I made inquiries about going to Bath and about where Esther lives. Then we considered the tennis matches at Wimbledon. Grabbed a hasty lunch, and took an Underground to Southfields where we drove to the Wimbledon Club. There was a line (or queue, as the British say) stretching for some distance, but we knew Molla Bjursted Mallory was to meet Suzanne Lenglen, and it would be too good to miss, so we stood in line over an hour, and at last got in but there were no seats left, and we could just see over people's shoulders. First there was men's doubles between French and Belgian representatives. Then men's singles, Australians I think, Anderson & Patterson. In the middle of their match about four, it started to rain and they covered the court with a mackintosh, and the crowd waited in the rain for two solid hours. We wouldn't have left for anything. And that British crowd was a sporting crowd. I mean they were friendly and jolly and in good spirits in spite of the rain.

Just before the rain began there was a commotion and everyone rose and looked in the direction of the Royal box, and in came the King and Queen. They looked just like their pictures, so that I had to pinch myself to be convinced that I was really there.

At six, the rain stopped, and (we had stood the whole time to keep our places) the game continued. Then at six-thirty, we were afraid they wouldn't get to the ladies singles, so we started to go home. Then thought better of it – got some food, and returned to find Suzanne & Molla hard at it. The French girl won so easily. Mrs. Mallory didn't seem to have her heart in the game. She didn't put up a very good fight, and it was very disappointing. Another set was played – splendid mixed doubles – Lycett and Miss Ryan – Campbell & Mrs. Peacock – a very snappy match.

It was after eight when we left, and so we stopped for a bite on the way home. . . .

Loads of love to you all,
Jessica

P.S. Let [Jessica's brother Lester's nickname], tell me what our papers said about Mlle. Lenglen and Mrs. Mallory.

The match between Suzanne Lenglen and Molla Mallory at Wimbledon in 1922 was a significant one, for only nine months earlier the American player had beaten Suzanne in the US National Championships at Forest Hills in a controversial match which saw the Frenchwoman retire due to illness after losing the first set. It was the only singles defeat of Suzanne's adult career, and afterwards she was lambasted as a 'quitter' in the American press. Molla Mallory was a fine player, but Suzanne's 26-minute win over her at Wimbledon in 1922 provided the perfect riposte to her American critics.

Suzanne Lenglen's British Tour Party, 1927. From left to right: Karel Kozeluh, Evelyn Dewhurst, Suzanne Lenglen, Charles Cochran (Promoter), Vivien Glasspool, Dora Koring and Howard Kinsey

In 1922 Suzanne arrived at the new Wimbledon a three-times singles champion, and she extended this winning sequence to five titles before illness forced her to retire from the 1924 Championships after a strenuous three-set quarter-final victory over her friend and doubles partner Elizabeth Ryan. Britain's Kitty McKane benefitted from a walkover to reach her first Wimbledon final, where she beat the 18-year-old US champion Helen Wills, who was making her Wimbledon debut.

Suzanne won her sixth title in 1925 and looked set to make it seven the following year until an extraordinary sequence of events led to her withdrawing from The Championships and subsequently signing a contract to turn professional.

Nineteen twenty-six began well for Suzanne when she beat Helen Wills in their long-awaited first encounter in the final of the Carlton Club tournament at Cannes on the French Riviera. The 20-year-old Californian had just won her third consecutive US singles title, and many pundits believed that she would be the player to at last end Suzanne's 12-year unbeaten run. There was a huge clamour for tickets for the match, and even the erection of a large temporary stand – doubling the usual seating capacity to 3,000 – could not satisfy the demand. Suzanne won the match in straight sets, 6–3, 8–6, but young Helen had done enough to show that she was the rightful heir to the Frenchwoman's crown.

Later that year, Suzanne won the French singles title for a sixth time, but the Parisian crowd was denied a possible return match between Suzanne and Helen when the American was laid low with acute appendicitis. In Helen Wills's absence, Suzanne was the overwhelming favourite to win her seventh Wimbledon singles title, but fate decreed otherwise. Suzanne won her opening match against Mary Browne but then found herself at the centre of a controversy when the Queen arrived at Wimbledon expecting to see her play, only for the Frenchwoman to be absent due to a breakdown in communications with Francis Burrow, the referee. Despite an attempt at mediation by her fellow-countryman Jean Borotra, the rift could not be healed, and to the shock of her thousands of fans Suzanne retired from the tournament, citing an arm injury. She turned professional a few weeks later, and never played at Wimbledon again.

Suzanne Lenglen lost just one completed singles match in her entire senior career, to Mlle Broquedis in the final of the 1914 French Championships. It was a close three-set match, and Suzanne was just 15 years old. For the next 12 years, until she turned professional in 1926, Suzanne went undefeated in singles play, save for a retirement against Molla Mallory at Forest Hills in 1921. She was never beaten in singles at Wimbledon, and between 1919 and 1925 won a total of 15 Wimbledon titles, including six in singles. She also won 19 French Championships titles, again including six in singles, and two Olympic gold medals. As Alan Little observed: 'Suzanne's opponents measured their success in singles by the number of points they won. If they played extremely well they would count the number of games. Three were able to claim a set, but only one a match.'

Suzanne had elevated lawn tennis from the sports pages to front-page headline news. She swept aside old Victorian values of dress and decorum, playing with a graceful, athletic style in daring outfits that revealed more female flesh than had ever been seen in public before. She was charismatic, enigmatic and a fashion icon; the first global superstar in women's sports. 'She gave to tennis an importance never previously attached to any sport,' wrote tennis couturier Teddy Tinling in his autobiography.

Suzanne appeared in successful professional tours of North America in 1926 and Britain in 1927, and visited Wimbledon several times as a spectator in the 1930s accompanied by her friend Lady Sophie Wavertree, the London socialite. Suzanne's love for tennis never diminished, and in 1936 she opened a tennis school at Auteuil, not far from Roland Garros. In 1938 she was appointed director of the French National Tennis School, but a few weeks later she contracted pernicious anaemia, an illness from which she never recovered. Suzanne Lenglen died in Paris on 4 July 1938, aged just 39. ◓

Slazenger catalogue, 1922. Slazengers have been Wimbledon's official suppliers of tennis balls, court furniture and surrounds since 1902

In men's tennis, the 1920s saw a fascinating battle for supremacy between Frenchmen Jean Borotra, Rene Lacoste and Henri Cochet, and America's Big Bill Tilden. Tilden was a larger-than-life character who has to be considered in any discussion about the greatest players of all time. He won his first Wimbledon singles title in 1920 at the age of 27, and his third and last ten years later, making him Wimbledon's second-oldest singles champion. Tilden, a great student of the game and a brilliant technician, was no stranger to controversy. As a champion in the amateur era he was constantly at odds with officialdom over his off-court earnings from writing and journalism, and in later life he served a jail term for a sexual offence. Tilden continued to play high-level competitive tennis up to his death in 1953 at the age of 60.

The Frenchmen of the 1920s were very popular with the Wimbledon crowds. Following American Bill Johnston's victory in 1923, they monopolised the Gentlemen's Singles, winning a brace of titles each between 1924 and 1929. Jean Borotra, the first-ever Frenchman to become Wimbledon Gentlemen's Singles champion, was a business man who sometimes flew from Paris in the morning for an afternoon match at Wimbledon. He played the game with energetic zeal, and had an infectious sense of humour which the Centre Court crowd loved. Borotra won at Wimbledon in 1924 and 1926, and reached three other finals during the 1920s. He carried on playing in The Championships until 1964, 42 years after his debut.

Rene Lacoste succeeded Jean Borotra as champion in 1925 and won again in 1928. Nicknamed 'the Crocodile', he was an astute tactician and had a series of epic battles with Bill Tilden during a short career punctuated by ill health. He retired at just 25, going on to be the co-founder of the Lacoste clothing brand with the distinctive crocodile logo.

Henri Cochet, like Borotra and Lacoste, made his Wimbledon debut in the first Championships at the new ground in 1922. He was an exquisite touch player who loved to half-volley, and won the title in 1927 and 1929. To complete the French quartet, doubles expert Jacques 'Toto' Brugnon won the Wimbledon men's doubles title four times, twice with Cochet in the 1920s and twice with Borotra in the 1930s. He was also a mainstay of the French team which won the Davis Cup in six successive years from 1927 to 1932. 🎾

A ceremony was held on the Centre Court during the 1926 Championships to mark Wimbledon's 50th anniversary. Most of the former winners present to receive commemorative gold medals were British, accompanied by recently crowned champions from Australia, France and the USA, the emerging powers in world tennis. At the highest level lawn tennis was now a truly international game, and during the remainder of the 20th century home successes at Wimbledon were to prove increasingly rare.

As the 1920s drew to a close, tennis, like other major sports, remained high profile as people sought distraction from the world's growing economic and political uncertainties. The first radio broadcasts from Wimbledon in 1927 added to the already considerable public interest in The Championships, and it seemed that whatever problems might beset the outside world, tennis in general and Wimbledon in particular were destined to go from strength to strength.

In just the same way that Suzanne Lenglen had dominated Wimbledon in the early 1920s, America's Helen Wills was head and shoulders above her rivals in the latter years of the decade and throughout the 1930s. Sandwiched in between, Britain's Kathleen McKane/Godfree was the Wimbledon champion in 1924 and 1926. But, fine competitor that she was, Kitty was only keeping the throne warm, for it was clear to all that Helen was Suzanne's natural successor. 🎾

Helen Wills Moody, eight-times Wimbledon champion between 1927 and 1938

In the women's game, the 1930s was the decade of the USA's two Helens, Wills and Jacobs. Helen Wills was a tennis machine with powerful, accurate groundstrokes who was aptly nicknamed 'Miss Poker Face'. She first came to Wimbledon in 1924, profiting from Suzanne Lenglen's absence through illness to reach the final where she lost in three sets to Great Britain's Kitty McKane, in what proved to be the only defeat of her career at The Championships. Always playing in her trademark white sunshade – which countless fashion-conscious women around the world copied – Helen Wills (later Mrs Wills-Moody) would go on to win eight singles titles at Wimbledon and 19 Grand Slam singles titles in all. Her nearest rival was fellow-Californian Helen Jacobs, who was always her closest challenger without ever threatening her supremacy. Jacobs lost to Wills in no fewer than six major singles finals, but nevertheless ended her career with five Grand Slam titles, all but one of which were won when Helen Wills did not compete.

Helen Wills's career record was remarkable. Between 1922 and 1938, she played 24 Grand Slam singles tournaments, reaching 22 finals and winning 19 titles. Between 1927 and 1933 she won every singles tournament she entered, and recorded 161 consecutive match victories, all but one of which were in straight sets. Helen's accomplishments were not restricted to the tennis court, for she was also a successful artist and writer.

Two other women players made worthy contributions to top-flight tennis during the 1930s. Great Britain's Dorothy Round was a Sunday School teacher from Worcestershire who refused to compete on the Sabbath, but this was not such an impediment to a tennis career then as it would be today. She won two Wimbledon singles titles, in 1934 and 1937, and the first of those victories was the most recent occasion on which a British woman and man were crowned Wimbledon champions in the same year. In the final Championships before World War II, America's Alice Marble won playing an attacking serve-and-volley game never seen before by a woman at Wimbledon and which would influence generations of female champions to come. Her total of four Grand Slam titles would almost certainly have been higher but for the outbreak of war. 🎾

The opening day of The Championships, 1928. The Order of Play board shows first-round matches in progress, including Australia's Gerald Patterson, the champion in 1919 and 1922, against Britain's Leighton Crawford

In comparison with the earlier photograph on pages 46 and 47, the yew trees between the courts have thickened considerably and motor vehicles no longer use the Promenade (apart from one delivery van!). As recently as the 1970s a local council dustcart used to make its noisy way along the Promenade every evening during play

The 1930s was a golden decade for men's tennis, too, with leading European stars Fred Perry, Bunny Austin and Gottfried von Cramm striving to overcome a host of top-class American players including the veteran Bill Tilden, Wilmer Allison, Sidney Wood, Frank Shields, Ellsworth Vines, Don Budge and Bobby Riggs. Add to that list Australia's Jack Crawford, and you have a compelling cast of characters that would grace a Hollywood epic, and – courtesy of Perry and Vines – Hollywood was exactly where tennis was headed.

In 1931, there was a surprise Wimbledon winner when Sidney Wood was presented with the trophy after injured fellow-American Frank Shields defaulted. This was the first, and is currently the only, singles final walkover in Wimbledon history. The 1933 final was a five-set thriller in which Australia's Jack Crawford beat defending champion Ellsworth Vines of the USA in what many who saw it considered the greatest match of all time. Vines turned professional shortly afterwards, and would later switch to professional golf.

Final Programme with full results, 1934. This bound official programme was given to Fred Perry to commemorate the first of his three Wimbledon Gentlemen's Singles victories.

Frederick John Perry was born in Stockport, Cheshire on 18 May 1909, the son of working-class parents, whose father later became a Labour MP. Perry was a born winner, despite, as he put it, coming from 'the wrong side of the tracks'. His first sport was table tennis, where he became world champion at 19. Then he switched to lawn tennis, winning eight Grand Slam singles titles between 1933 and 1936. Perry's single-mindedness was seen by many as arrogance, and at first he was not universally liked by the tennis public. That all changed when he won Wimbledon three years in a row from 1934 to 1936, and led Great Britain to four straight Davis Cup triumphs. Perry was a national hero, turning professional in 1936 and embarking on a tour of North America the following year in a head-to-head contest against Ellsworth Vines.

Perry had a singular personality, as those who knew him testified. 'Instead of "Good Shot" Fred would say "Very Clever",' recalled 1947 Wimbledon champion and pro tour promoter Jack Kramer. Bobby Wilson, who was part of the British Davis Cup squad coached by Perry in the 1950s, said: 'Fred was so confident. He would only talk about his victories, never his losses.'

Perry was a handsome man with a superb physique, and in America he had Hollywood starlets falling at his feet. He married one – Helen Vinson – in 1935, and in 1937 he and Vines invested some of the profits from their tour by buying the Beverly Hills Tennis Club. The link between tennis and Hollywood was thus firmly cemented, and Perry later went on to exploit his fame still further by founding the eponymous sportswear brand with the famous laurel leaf motif. ◍

Worthington's ale advertisement, circa 1930s

By the start of the 1930s the Australian, French and US Championships stood alongside Wimbledon as the four most coveted titles in world tennis. In 1933 Australia's Jack Crawford became the first player – male or female – to win the first three of these titles in the same year. Having done so, he was urged by the Australian Lawn Tennis Association to try for the clean sweep by travelling to New York to compete in the US Championships at Forest Hills. Physically and mentally exhausted, Crawford lost in the final after leading Great Britain's Fred Perry by two sets to one. He had fallen just one set short of his goal. In the build-up to the US final an American journalist had likened the feat of winning tennis' four major tournaments in the same calendar year as akin to scoring a 'grand slam' at bridge, a most rare occurrence indeed. The term stuck, and from then on the press referred to the Grand Slam as the ultimate achievement in tennis, and it became the holy grail for the game's top players.

The first player who deliberately set out to achieve the Grand Slam – albeit without making his intention public – was jazz-loving American Don Budge. The year was 1938, and he began his campaign already holding the Wimbledon and US titles from the previous year, along with a Davis Cup winner's medal. His strategy for 1938 was to concentrate solely on the four major tournaments, and to conserve energy whenever possible. As a result he suffered a number of surprising losses at lesser events during the year, but when the big tournaments came round he was ready. He secured the Australian and French titles without undue difficulty, and won at Wimbledon for the second year running without the loss of a set. In the US final, Budge was pitted against his friend and Davis Cup team-mate Gene Mako. The 23-year-old Budge came out on top in four sets, and the game's first Grand Slam had at last been achieved.

The Second World War was about to interrupt top-flight tennis for six long years, but not before another extraordinary young American player had made an indelible mark on the game's history. Bobby Riggs from Los Angeles came to Wimbledon for the first and only time in June 1939 – just weeks before the outbreak of war – and won all three titles: singles, men's doubles and mixed doubles. No other player has ever achieved this feat on his or her Wimbledon debut, but sadly the war deprived Riggs of the opportunity to defend these titles. By the time of the next Wimbledon Championships in 1946, Riggs had turned professional and was ineligible to compete. Throughout his life, Riggs had a reputation as a gambler, and he claimed to have won $100,000 by betting on himself to win all three titles at Wimbledon in 1939. His nickname 'The Hustler' was well merited. ✇

Right: In 1926 the Duke of York played in the Gentlemen's Doubles at Wimbledon. He later became King George VI.

Far right: Popular British player Betty Nuthall was US National Singles Champion in 1930

The increased draw sizes at Wimbledon during the 1920s and 30s led to many more players becoming popular crowd favourites. These included British players such as Eileen Bennett, Nigel Sharpe – first-round victor over Henri Cochet in 1931 – and 'Bounding' Betty Nuthall; along with regular overseas visitors including Silvia Henrotin, of France; Gottfried Von Cramm, of Germany; and, most remarkably, Chile's Anita Lizana.

The diminutive senorita from Santiago was just 19 when she first played at Wimbledon in 1935, and her infectious smile made her an instant favourite with the British public. She was a fine player too, and by the time of her third visit in 1937 she was seeded third and one of the favourites to lift the title. Anita lost in the quarter-finals but fulfilled her potential by becoming US National Champion at Forest Hills a few weeks later. At the end of the year Arthur Wallis Myers placed her No.1 in his unofficial world-ranking list, and another observer hailed her as the 'second Suzanne Lenglen'. Whilst in Britain, Anita met Ronald Ellis, a leading Scottish player, whom she married a few days after the 1938 Wimbledon Championships. Mrs Ellis played at Wimbledon again after the war, but was not a serious contender.

In 1937 three 'firsts' were recorded at Wimbledon. On Sunday, 9 May a Service was held on the Centre Court to celebrate the Coronation of King George VI, who had ascended to the throne the previous year when his brother Edward VIII abdicated to marry Mrs Wallis Simpson. During The Championships a few weeks later, the BBC made its first live television broadcasts from the Centre Court. Two cameras were used; one in a fixed position at the end opposite the Royal Box and another with a telephoto lens at the south-east corner giving close-up shots of

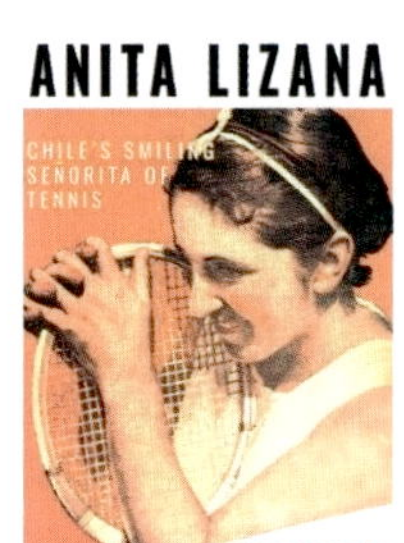

The biography of Anita Lizana, by her daughter Ruth Weston

the players. The vision signals were transmitted by wireless to London's Alexandra Palace from where they were relayed directly to the few thousand viewers able to receive them at that time.

In the same year, players withdrawing from The Championships at the last minute were replaced from amongst those who had been beaten in the final round of the qualifying competition. The tradition of 'Lucky Losers' was born.

'Flicker' books enabled readers to see moving images of top players in action

As the 1930s drew to a close, professional tennis began to pose a serious threat to Wimbledon and the world's other major amateur tournaments. Increased international competition made it increasingly difficult for top players to compete on a part-time basis. Since the amateur code ruled out direct payment, players increasingly relied on expenses payments from tournaments and national associations, a system open to widespread abuse. Some expenses payments were vastly inflated in order to attract top players, an 'under-the-counter' system which became known as 'shamateurism'.

A far greater threat, however, was the impending global conflict which would result in a six-year hiatus for Wimbledon and most of the tennis world. 🎾

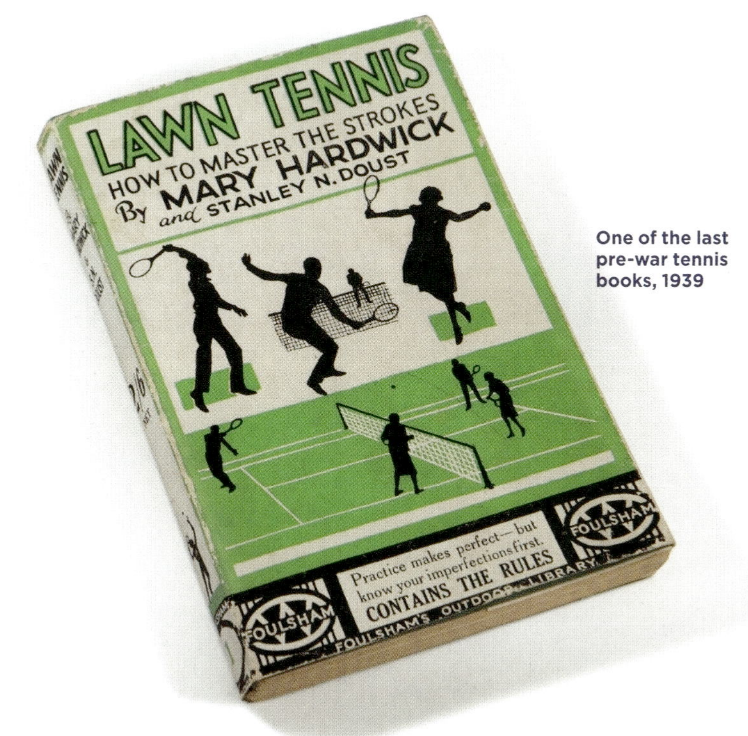

One of the last pre-war tennis books, 1939

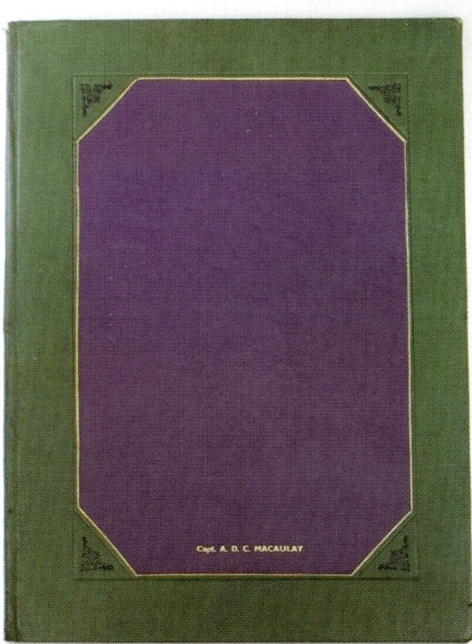

Wimbledon Championships, 1937. During the 1930s special leather-bound Final Programmes with full results were presented to champions and tournament officials. This one was given to Duncan Macaulay, the Assistant Referee

F.R. Burrow, Championships' Referee, 1919–1936

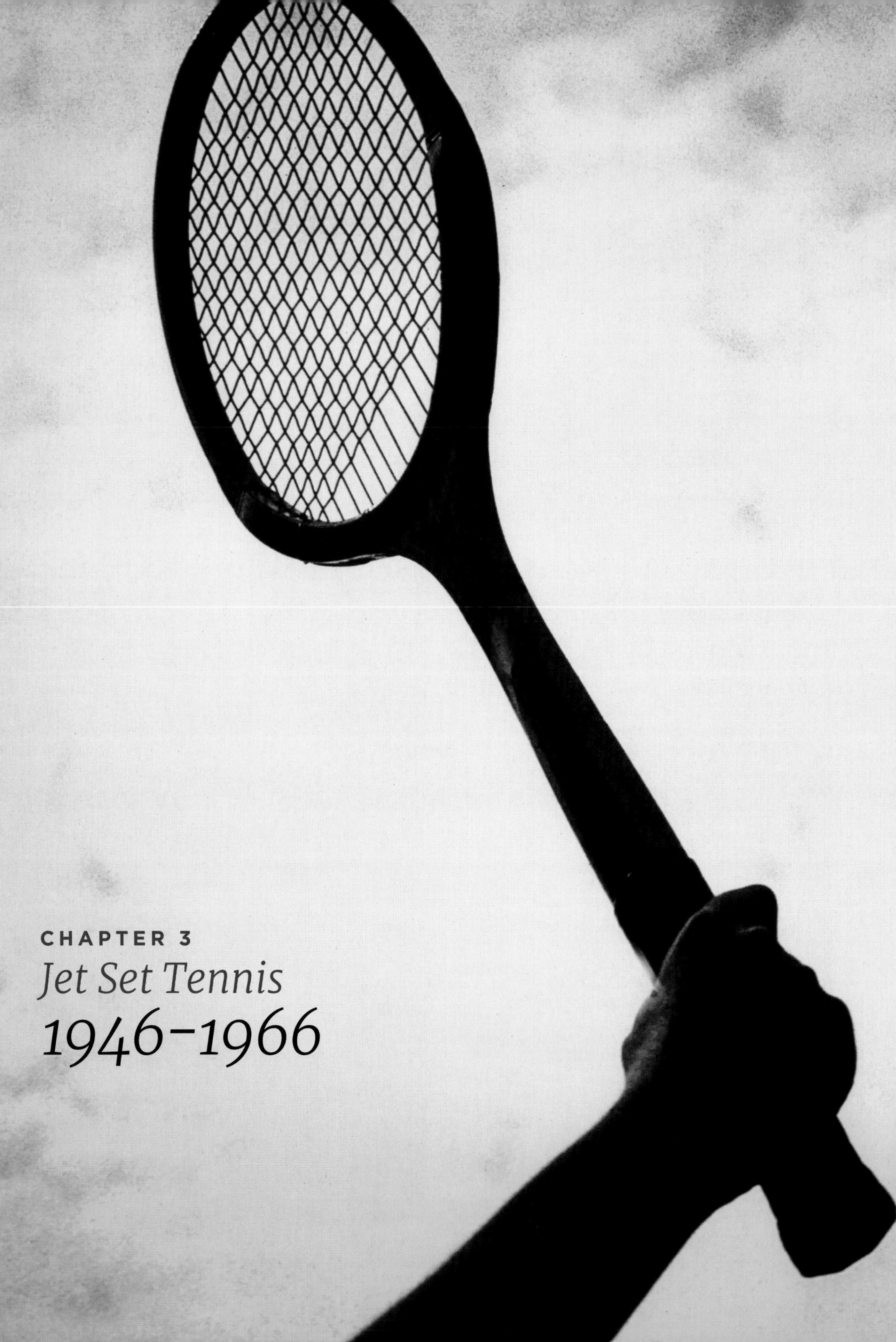

CHAPTER 3
Jet Set Tennis
1946–1966

'Cowboy' busker,
Church Road, 1946

The first few Wimbledon Championships after World War II are still remembered with nostalgic affection by many tennis lovers, and today we are fortunate to be able to enjoy their first-hand accounts of those years. After six years of hardship and privation, the British people were in the mood to live life to the full, and sport was quick to restart with record crowds attending football and cricket matches, race meetings and, of course, Wimbledon.

Alan Little, who three decades later was to become Wimbledon's Honorary Librarian, recalled the very first Championships after the war:

'I listened to the 1946 Men's Singles Final between Yvon Petra and Geoff Brown on the radio, and decided to go next day, the final day of the fortnight when the Ladies' Singles was held.

'I took the special bus from Wimbledon Station to the All England Lawn Tennis Club, arriving in Somerset Road at around 9.30am. There was a busker there dressed as a cowboy, complete with spurs and hat. He was coining it in!

'I got in right at the back of the west side Centre Court free standing area, away from the hot sun. When play was about to start a kindly lady asked if I could see. When I said "not much", she called out to everyone in front to let a small boy through and I ended up at the front!

'I couldn't believe how hard Pauline Betz and Louise Brough hit the ball. I'd never seen anything like it before, but when

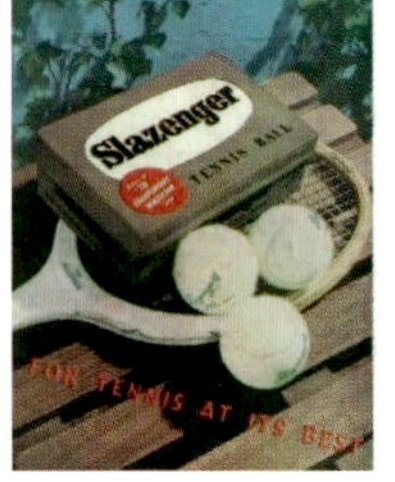

the Men's Doubles finalists came out, they hit the ball even harder! I was "hooked" on the game for life. All four finals were over by 6pm.'

When tennis resumed in 1946 the world had changed in many ways from pre-war days. The British class system was still in place, but ordinary folk were now much more worldly wise and had greater aspirations for themselves and their children. Over the next decade intercontinental travel would increasingly be by air rather than sea, dramatically reducing journey times, and more families would acquire television sets and other modern conveniences, or 'mod cons' as the advertisers called them. In the short term, however, life was still tough. Despite the elation of victory, the immediate post-

On the night of Friday, 11 October 1940 a 500-pound bomb fell on the Centre Court, causing damage which was not fully repaired until 1949

war years saw a further period of austerity in Britain, with the food rationing introduced during the war continuing for another eight years.

During the war, The All England Club had been looked after by Norah Cleather, a long-serving member of the Club's administrative staff who had been appointed Acting Secretary when Dudley Larcombe retired due to ill health in 1939. Her reward for keeping the Club going for six years was to be immediately replaced as Secretary by Duncan Macaulay, whose unstinting efforts led to the resumption of The Championships in June 1946, only nine months after hostilities ended. This was a major organisational achievement, for the Centre Court, like many other buildings in the Wimbledon area and countless more across London, had suffered bomb damage during the Blitz of 1940. Tennis balls were in short supply, and only limited catering could be offered to spectators. But somehow, under Macaulay's stewardship, the 1946 Championships went ahead.

The nation's spirits were lifted a few weeks before the 1953 Championships when street parties all over the country marked the Coronation of Her Majesty Queen Elizabeth II. A year later, on Sunday, 4 July 1954, rationing finally ended, just a day after Maureen Connolly had overcome Louise Brough to win her third consecutive Wimbledon title. ◌

MY EXPERIENCE WHILST ON DUTY AT THE WIMBLEDON LAWN TENNIS CLUB DURING WORLD WAR 11.

The All England Tennis Club can be a lonely and eerie place at night for two young firewomen.

It was our duty to report any incidents in the immediate area. The air raid warning had gone, but it was very quiet, so I laid myself down on the camp bed which was in the watchroom by the Somerset Road gate.

Suddenly we heard the familiar engine of a flying bomb. It was getting nearer and nearer, and I prayed that it would not stop.

The noise got louder and we knew it was going over our heads. To our our horror it cut out, and I remember thinking this is the one with my name on it.

I heard a loud swish like a mighty wind, and it missed us by only a few yards to drop on the famous Wimbledon courts.

I had covered my head with a blanket and could hear bits of plaster coming down from the ceiling and things dropping off the walls. Luckily neither of us were hurt, only covered in dust. It was not long before the fire appliances arrived from Wimbledon Fire Station and everything was under control.

Everytime I watch the Tennis Championships, I think of that night. I did not realize at the time that I was stationed at such a famous place. — Kathleen Clayden.

Kathleen Clayden from Wandsworth was just 17 when she joined the Auxiliary Fire Service in 1938

During the 1930s American men had won six of the ten singles titles on offer at Wimbledon, while the country's women had done even better, winning seven singles titles during that decade. After the war that golden generation was succeeded by an even more successful one, with all the singles titles bar one between 1946 and 1951 being won by American players.

Tournament tennis had continued uninterrupted in America during the war years, and the US had not had to endure the food rationing suffered by many of the other leading lawn tennis nations. As a result, American players were fitter, stronger and competitively sharp, giving them a distinct advantage – not that they needed one, for they were a fine group of players. How ironic then that the first post-war Wimbledon Championships should be won by a French clay-court specialist, 30-year-old Yvon Petra, one of the few leading players who had played at Wimbledon before the war. Petra's victory was just a blip, however, for Americans won both men's and ladies' singles – and most of the world's other major singles titles – in each of the next five years.

Yvon Petra's successor as Wimbledon champion was a man who would ultimately become one of the most influential figures in tennis history. John Albert 'Jack' Kramer was born on 1 August 1921 in Las Vegas, and had it not been for the war he may well have become the world's top amateur player in the early 1940s. As it was he had to wait until 1947, winning the Wimbledon and US singles following wartime service in the

US Coastguard. Kramer perfected the art of percentage tennis – attacking his opponents' weaknesses whilst minimising his own unforced errors – and always played in a trademark white tee shirt.

Kramer turned professional immediately after winning the 1947 US Championship, and on his first pro tour he decisively beat reigning professional world champion Bobby Riggs by 69 matches to 20. The following year, he beat rookie pro Pancho Gonzales 96-27. In 1952 he took over as promoter of the tour whilst still an active player himself. His shrewdness, business acumen and organisational skill brought the professional game to its greatest-ever heights during the 1950s and early 60s, with huge crowds watching the stars such as Ken Rosewall, Pancho Gonzales, Lew Hoad and Rod Laver at world-famous venues such as New York's Madison Square Garden and London's Empire Pool Wembley. This success added to the pressure that eventually led to the establishment of Open

Tennis in 1968. In the 1960s, Kramer became a household name in Britain as a result of his broadcasts from Wimbledon alongside Dan Maskell, the popular pair becoming known simply as 'Jack and Dan'. ◎

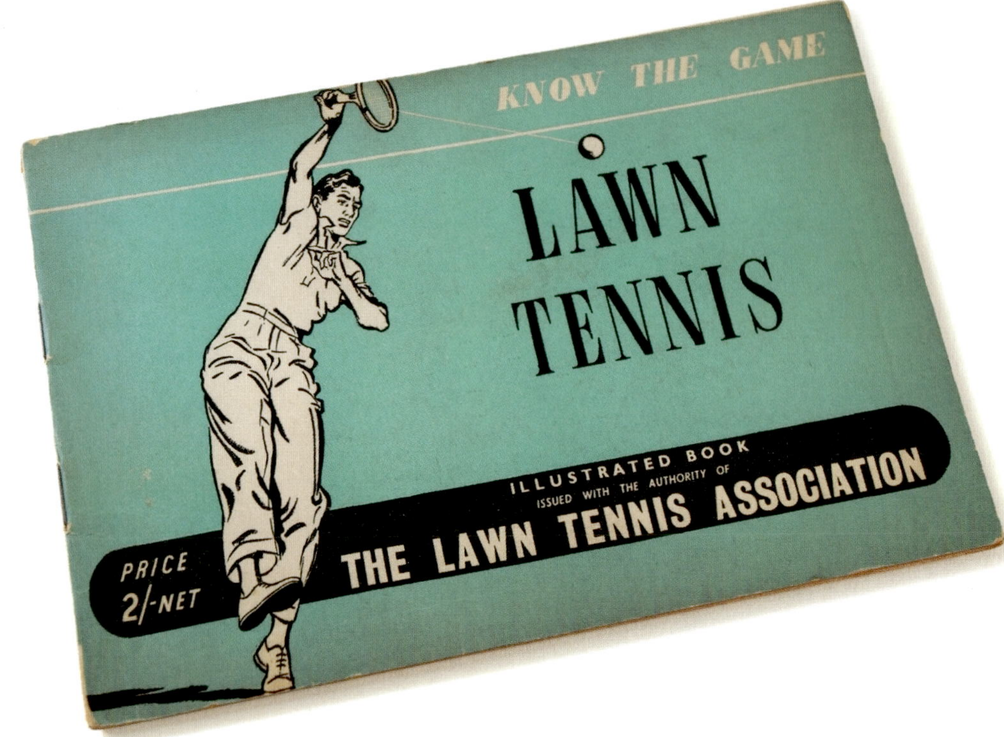

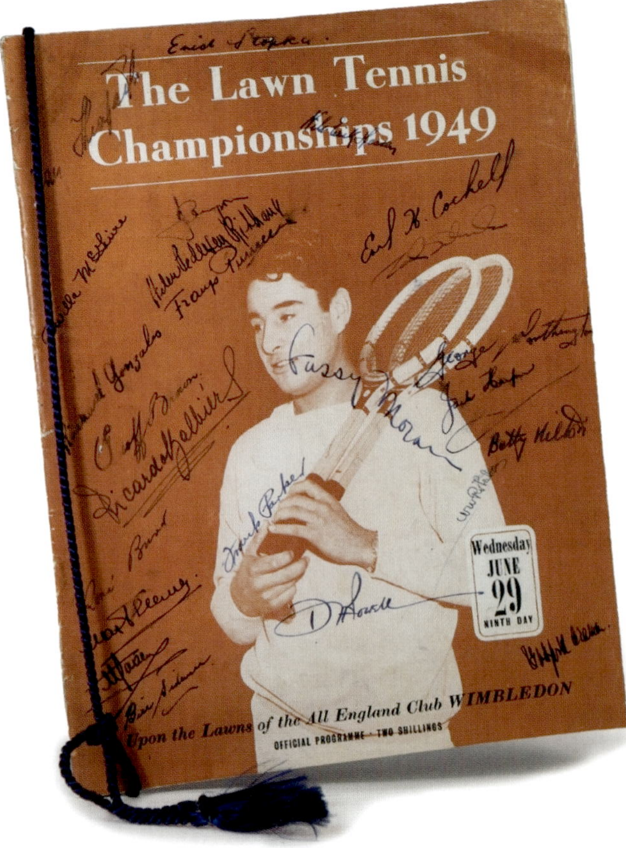

Wimbledon Official Programme with ribbon bookmark, 1949, signed by various top players for Enid Stopka who worked in the Wimbledon Secetary's Office for more than 30 years

In the years immediately after World War II the USA completely dominated both amateur and professional tennis. This resource-rich nation had a production line of champions: Jack Kramer, Bob Falkenberg, Ted Schroeder, Budge Patty, Gardnar Mulloy, Dick Savitt, Vic Seixas and Tony Trabert swept up major singles titles, whilst in the women's game Pauline Betz, Margaret Osborne, Louise Brough, Doris Hart, Maureen Connolly and Shirley Fry more than matched the achievements of their male counterparts. Ironically, though, it was their fellow-countrywoman 'Gorgeous' Gussy Moran's appearance on the Centre Court in 1949 wearing panties with white lace trim that did most to boost the public's interest in tennis. These had been designed at Miss Moran's request by British couturier Ted Tinling, whose use of coloured trim a year earlier had led to the introduction of Wimbledon's 'all white' clothing rule.

Many of America's champions came from Southern California, where there was an abundance of high-quality cement courts and a favourable year-round climate. Add in the collegiate coaching system and the excellent organising skills of Perry T. Jones, Secretary and later Manager of the Southern California Tennis Association, and you have the perfect recipe for tennis success.

The nation that was to challenge the United States for world tennis supremacy during the 1950s and on into the 1960s also enjoyed many of these favourable conditions. In Australia tennis was mainly played on grass courts, but it too enjoyed good year-round weather for outdoor sports, and there was a seemingly never-ending queue of youngsters taking up cricket and tennis in the hope of emulating national sporting heroes like Don Bradman, Norman Brookes and Jack Crawford. Indeed it was Brookes the administrator who played a large part in creating the conditions for Australian post-war tennis prosperity.

In 1950, former player Harry Hopman was appointed Captain-Manager of the Australian Davis Cup team. This role involved not only the Davis Cup but also travelling with the group of players selected each year by the Australian Lawn Tennis Association to represent the nation at the major tournaments such as the French Championships, Wimbledon and the US Championships at Forest Hills. Hopman was a strict disciplinarian who believed in the importance of the players being in peak physical condition. Right from the start, his methods were successful and as a result he enjoyed unquestioning loyalty from all the top Australian players. The Davis Cup was won in America in 1950, and the two nations met in the Challenge Round during every year in the 1950s, with the Australians winning the trophy in all but two of those years.

Hopman's stars in the early years of the 1950s were John Bromwich, Ken MacGregor and Frank Sedgman, and later they were succeeded by Mal Anderson, Neale Fraser and Ashley Cooper. But in 1952 two young players emerged who were to become Australian sporting legends.

Lewis Alan 'Lew' Hoad was born on 23 November 1934 in the Sydney suburb of Glebe. Kenneth Robert Rosewall had been born across the city just three weeks earlier on 2 November 1934. By 1953 they were well known in Australia as junior

A Champion's Persistence

Angela Mortimer, WIMBLEDON

O**ne day I saw an item in our local paper which said that a well-known coach, Mr Arthur Roberts, was offering free tennis coaching to promising players under 12 who lived in the Torquay area. I was 15 and I lived in Plymouth, but I was determined to give it a try.**

I made the long bus journey, but when Mr Roberts saw me he said: 'You are too old, and you live too far away.' He took pity on me, though, adding: 'As you've come so far you might as well have a hit against the practice wall.' With that he went off to coach the other children.

I hit against the wall for hours, and when Mr Roberts returned he was very surprised to find me still hitting. 'If you are that determined, you deserve a chance,' he said, 'but you still live too far away.' Later we moved to Kingskerswell, just outside Torquay, and I went straight back to the Palace Hotel to see Mr Roberts and claim my free coaching!

tennis players with prodigious talent, and it was no surprise when Harry Hopman selected 'The Boys', as they were affectionately known, for the Davis Cup squad that year. Australia once again reached the Challenge Round, and yet again USA were the opponents. The tie was played at the Kooyong Club in Melbourne and attracted a then world-record crowd of 17,500 spectators for each of the three days' play. 'The Boys' fully justified Hopman's faith in them, with Rosewall heroically overcoming Vic Seixas 6–2, 2–6, 6–3, 6–4 in the deciding fifth rubber to lift the trophy for Australia. It was the greatest Davis Cup Final ever, and cemented the positions of Australia and the USA at the top of world tennis. ◐

During the 1950s the world was changing rapidly. Jet airliners made travel fast and easy, but the Cold War and the rise of Communism and the Soviet Bloc created new political barriers between sporting nations. Standards rose as top players were able to travel rapidly around the world to compete. Sportsmen were full-time professionals, although in the tennis world it would take the authorities until 1968 to publicly acknowledge this. In the meantime, amateurs and professionals were kept apart, with only the former allowed to compete at Wimbledon.

In 1957 Althea Gibson from South Carolina became Wimbledon champion just a few weeks before her 30th birthday. She was the first black player, male or female, to win a major tennis title anywhere in the world. 'The Black Bombshell', as she was dubbed in the press, won Wimbledon again in 1958, and the door was now well and truly open for people of all backgrounds to succeed at a sport which had at one time been the exclusive preserve of the white privileged classes.

American women won the Ladies' Singles title at Wimbledon for 15 consecutive years between 1938 and 1958 until this period of dominance was halted by one of the most popular players ever to grace the Centre Court, Brazil's Maria Bueno. Maria was the darling of Wimbledon for a decade, her graceful game and Latin beauty accompanied by an easy-going manner that was in stark contrast to the business-like approach of the American and Australian women who were her main rivals. Chief amongst those were Billie Jean Moffitt and Margaret Smith, who under their married names of King and Court would go on to win more titles than Maria, but could never match her popularity.

Britain mounted a spirited challenge at Wimbledon in the post-war years. During the late 1940s and early 50s Tony Mottram was a fine player and a great student of the game, and he was well supported by the less gifted but wholehearted Geoff Paish. In the 1950s and early 60s they were followed by a string of talented young players including Billy Knight, Bobby Wilson, Mike Davies, Roger Becker and Mike Sangster, all of whom gave great pleasure to the Wimbledon crowds and were capable of beating the world's leading players on their day.

It was in the women's game, however, that the home nation achieved the greatest success. Angela Buxton reached the Wimbledon Final in 1956, and won the Ladies' Doubles title in the same year in partnership with Althea Gibson. Teenagers Ann Haydon and Christine Truman were very promising, too, but it was 29-year-old

Angela Mortimer who became Britain's first female champion for nearly a quarter of a century when she beat Truman in an all-British final in 1961, Wimbledon's 75th Championship meeting.

Christine was the darling of the Centre Court, and in the final won the first set before suffering a fall. Her subsequent defeat was almost as newsworthy as her opponent's triumph. Plymouth-born Angela was the second Wimbledon champion from that city, following in the footsteps of May Sutton, winner in 1905 and 1907. She had learned her tennis under the tutelage of renowned coach Arthur Roberts at the Palace Hotel in Torquay, and during an illustrious career she also won the French and Australian singles championships. Angela later married John Barrett, a leading British player, Davis Cup captain, writer and broadcaster. ⊘

In 1959 and 1960 a diminutive freckle-faced youngster from the Queensland outback town of Rockhampton finished runner-up in the men's singles at Wimbledon. Little did the watching world know that Rod Laver would go on to raise tennis to a new level and usher in an exciting new era in the game's illustrious history.

The 1960s saw a creative explosion in art, design, fashion, literature, music and technology. The baby-boomers born in the immediate post-war years were teenagers now, and they unhesitatingly tossed aside the drab austerity of the 1940s and 50s. The sky was no longer the limit, as Soviet cosmonaut Yuri Gagarin proved when he became the first man in space in April 1961. A dreary monochrome world was transformed into vivid colour, and in tennis a revolution began that would change the sport forever.

A few weeks after Gagarin's historic flight, another rocket was in the news. Australia's Rod Laver – playfully nicknamed the 'Rockhampton Rocket' by his fellow-Aussie players, because of his lack of speed – claimed his first Wimbledon singles title. Laver had first played at Wimbledon as a 16-year-old in 1956, losing in the first round of the men's singles but reaching the final of the junior boys' event. He had served his Wimbledon apprenticeship by finishing as runner-up in the men's singles in both 1959 and 1960, but Laver's 1961 victory was the springboard for an amazing year in 1962, in which he not only repeated his Wimbledon success but also added the singles championships of Australia, France and the USA to become only the second man in history – after Don Budge in 1938 – to clinch the coveted Grand Slam.

Laver's dominance, along with that of Billie Jean King and Margaret Court in the women's game, came at a time when total attendances during Wimbledon fortnight were regularly exceeding 275,000, and the tournament was also being broadcast live on BBC Television. Tennis players were household names, but they were not being paid, not officially at least. Something had to change.

A proposal to introduce 'Open' tennis, in which amateurs and professionals could compete together at major tournaments such as Wimbledon, was put before the International Lawn Tennis Federation in 1960, but narrowly failed to achieve the required two-thirds majority.

Needing to secure his financial future, Grand Slam-winner Rod Laver accepted Jack Kramer's offer to turn professional, and as a result missed five consecutive Wimbledon Championships between 1963 and 1967.

Despite the annual defection of champions to the professional ranks, Wimbledon continued to prosper. The rivalry between Margaret Court (née Smith), Billie Jean King (née Moffitt) and Maria Bueno captivated the public, and in Australia's Roy Emerson the men's game had a dashing new hero. After American Chuck McKinley interrupted Australia's period of success in 1963, Emerson won the Wimbledon title in the following two years, each time beating his fellow-countryman Fred Stolle in the final. He was on course for a hat-trick when, in a 1966 quarter-final against Owen Davidson, yet another Australian, he crashed into the umpire's chair whilst chasing a wide ball. Emerson played on, but Davidson went through to the semi-finals where he was beaten by eventual champion Manuel Santana, of Spain. ⊘

1949

Memories of Wimbledon

Ruth Hartgill, REIGATE

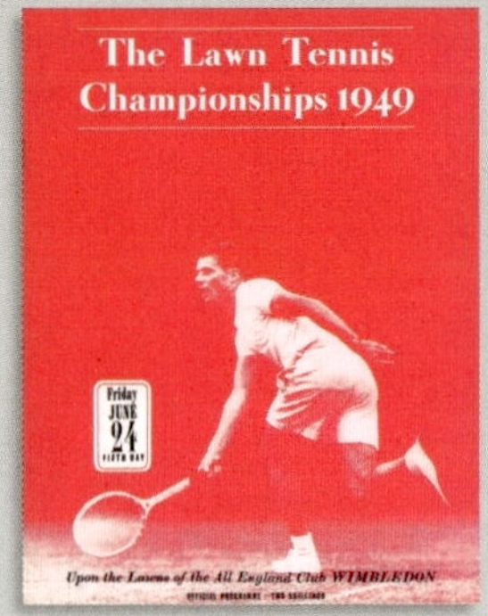

My first visit to the Championships at Wimbledon was on Day 6 1949. I had no great expectations, it was just exciting to be spending a rare day out with my father who had only recently been 'demobbed' and returned to his studies and to renew his interest for his daughters. It was the only visit that I can remember not approaching the Club along Marryat Road where for many years there was a remarkable Monkey Puzzle Tree in one of the gardens. As many visitors remark, excitement gathers as the crowds pour down Church Road on foot. We chose to turn into Somerset Road.

The atmosphere to me was palpable and the scene was like nothing I had ever seen in my short life; in those days almost all the spectators dressed up for the occasion and their behaviour was very civilised compared to nowadays. The first building to my left was the head groundsman's immaculate cottage and grounds. Gradual rebuilding over the years makes it impossible for me to decide exactly where the refreshment area was, but it was the next significant place on the left. The caterers were J Lyons & Co and on that first visit my treat was a buttered Bath Bun washed down with an amazing orange drink called Quosh which bore no resemblance to the only orange squash available outside the grounds. Some food was still rationed at this time. Next on the same side where one of the information booths is now situated came the postcard outlet mainly stocked with black and white photos of the more popular players. Looming over all was the ivy-covered Centre Court building about which so many people have written extravagantly and I found it just magical (and still do!).

We only had ground tickets, but we easily found seats for Court 3 where we were very close to the players. An impressionable, barely teenaged, very immature girl, I immediately fell for my first tennis hero, Budge Patty. He seemed so elegant, had a forehand volley to die for and classy dress – cream flannel shorts and a grey sweater. The players did not wear track suits, carried maybe two or three rackets, wooden framed, and their own towels, not an 'overnight rucksack' or even a tennis bag in sight. Since there were no chairs for them to sit on, the only place for them to put their belongings was under the umpire's chair with the Robinson's Barley Water. Nadal would have found management of his three bottles tricky, not to say impossible! The ball boys, all from Dr Barnardo's, wore grey shirts and long trousers with a red belt. The balls were white and were changed at the end of each set.

The officials did not wear uniform and the majority were male. In the absence of today's clever electronic equipment the score was recorded on a large sheet of paper printed in green to record every detail of play. I have used these sheets many times, not at Wimbledon of course, and during the infamous,

> **"***We had no television at the time, but I listened to Max Robertson's excellent commentaries when they were broadcast and I was free.***"**

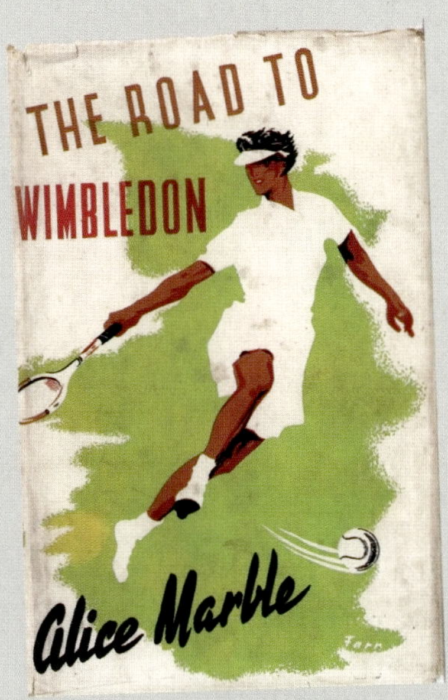

super-long match I recalled how we reversed the strokes for each point when games were so long that the page ran out of space and I wondered what strategy the umpire of that day would have used for the match between Isner and Mahut!! There was no time rule between points, and because there was no opportunity for delay when changing ends and none of this nonsense of selecting balls, re-arranging clothing, bouncing each ball many times before the toss, etc., more matches could be scheduled on each court.

My father cannot have been aware what a can of worms he was opening that day. I became a tennis anorak devouring all I could read about the game and regurgitating it to anyone who would listen. Our local library had exactly three books on the subject: *Wimbledon Story*, *Road to Wimbledon* and *Tennis is my Racket*, all of which I knew from cover to cover, but my father took *The Daily Telegraph* and I read every report, written in those days by John Olliff.

We had no television at the time, but I listened to Max Robertson's excellent commentaries when they were broadcast and I was free.

Seventy years after her Wimbledon 'debut', Ruth Hartgill still looks forward to her annual visits to The Championships

Sadly the men's final was played on Friday when I was trapped in the classroom. All the four other finals were played on Saturday on the Centre Court, so lady players could be involved in three finals on one day. Any of these would have been worth equal pay if financial reward had been available.

The weather was splendid for the whole fortnight.

1950

Electric Excitement

Nick Darby, EAST GRINSTEAD

I first visited The Championships in 1950, and I've been at least once every year since. In the days before covered courts it was disappointing that my first day consisted of watching nothing more exciting than the covers getting wetter and wetter but I was lucky enough to be allowed another day off school to go again. I do remember though the electric excitement generated by the atmosphere, the crowds, the famous names, the buildings and stands of the Centre and No.1 Courts and our proximity to the players. It is just the same today.

I have vivid memories of standing in the queue and of the way players' names were displayed on court before electronics took over. I also remember clearly the excitement of seeing Jaroslav Drobny playing which was such a thrill because he often practised at our club in East Grinstead. Many years later I still look forward with bated breath to my day at Wimbledon and to staying until the last stroke is played.

1952

My First Visit to Wimbledon

Ann Roberts, INGATESTONE

My first visit to Wimbledon was in 1952. I interrupted my A level studies to accompany my parents who went regularly, usually three times during the first week. They seemed to have no difficulty queuing for tickets to either Centre or Court 1.

On this occasion we only managed to get tickets for Court 1, which, although impressive, was quite noisy as the crowds paraded behind our seats. I remember seeing the Australian Frank Sedgman and also a young Swede, Lennart Bergelin, who had sore feet as I recall he was only wearing plimsolls.

Later in the afternoon my parents suggested we try to get onto Centre Court. We managed to find our way into the standing area and I can still vividly remember being awestruck by the ambience, magnificent yet intimate. I forget who was playing that day but I remember it was the first year Hoad and Rosewall appeared, two exciting 18-year-olds from Australia, the same age as me.

Nowadays it is difficult to believe that four best of five set matches were scheduled even though play did not start until 2pm. There were no tiebreaks or sitting down at change of ends in those days!

Over the succeeding years I have visited Wimbledon on many occasions, sometimes having been lucky to secure tickets in the public ballot or through my tennis club but that first visit will stay long in the memory.

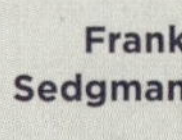

Frank Sedgman

Top-seeded Frank Sedgman was head and shoulders above his rivals at Wimbledon in 1952. He dropped only two sets, and in seven matches won 136 games and lost only 57. The match Ann Roberts saw was on the first Friday, when he despatched fellow-Australian Don Candy 6-2, 6-1, 6-0 on No.1 Court. Ann was very fortunate to see Frank Sedgman in his last year as an amateur at Wimbledon. After winning the tournament he turned professional and did not play in The Championships again until 1971. Don Candy was one of the characters of the tennis tour in the 1950s, and there are several humorous anecdotes about him in the classic book *A Handful of Summers* by Gordon Forbes.

Ann's mention of Lennart Bergelin probably relates to a subsequent visit in 1953, 1954 or 1955, as the Swede did not play at Wimbledon in 1952. Bergelin later became famous as Bjorn Borg's coach in the 1970s.

1952

Memories of Wimbledon

Bobby Wilson, WELWYN

My mother took me to Wimbledon in 1946 to see the first post-war men's singles final in which Yvon Petra of France beat America's Geoff Brown. I don't remember anything about the match, but I do recall annoying my mother with my repeated requests for ice cream. I've always preferred playing the game to watching.

Encouraged by my mother I joined Finchley Manor Lawn Tennis Club in 1946. It was a medium-sized club, and the champion had played at Wimbledon a couple of times. At 14 I could beat all but one of the male players at the club. At 16 I was club champion. Whenever I showed signs of getting too big for my boots my parents quickly brought me down to earth. They wouldn't let me get conceited.

I was selected for coaching with Dan Maskell at Wimbledon. He was a very nice man, an old-style gentleman. He never raised his voice, and was always very encouraging. My progress was very swift. In 1951 I was British Junior champion, and in 1952 I won the Junior event at Wimbledon.

I was only 16 when I made my Wimbledon debut in 1952. I managed to win my first-round match against Jean Moreau of Belgium in straight sets, but I then found myself facing Jaroslav Drobny, the number two seed and one of the favourites for the title. He stepped up to serve the first point of the match and hit an ace straight down the middle. He then did the same thing twice more, but at 40-love his first serve was a fault. The prospect of a second serve made me think 'here's my chance', but when the ball came over I caught it on the frame and it flew right out of the court. Drobny had a very effective serve, a good forehand and good volleys, but his backhand was relatively weak. I managed to hold serve three times in the third set, which was a comfort.

In my early years the Wimbledon courtesy cars would not come out as far as Hendon, where I lived, so I arranged for one to pick me up at Golders Green station. It never turned up, and I had to dash to Wimbledon by tube.

I was never scared of playing on the Centre Court. My first match there was in doubles, in partnership with Billy Knight in 1953. My first singles match on the Centre Court was against Budge Patty in 1955. I had won the French Junior Championship twice, and while in Paris I had practised with Patty. He gave me a few pointers which proved most helpful, and I modelled my game on his. It was like playing against myself.

In 1977 I partnered Jackie Fayter in the Wimbledon Mixed Doubles and we came up against John McEnroe who was playing with Mary Carillo. When Jackie and I won the first set, McEnroe shouted out 'I give up!' I walked to the net with my hand outstretched, and the umpire said to me 'What are you doing?' I said 'The match is over, he has given up,' but the umpire told us to play on. Eventually we lost 7-5 in the third set, but I always felt that if the umpire had taken him at his word then that might have put an early end to his outbursts.

During my career I played against or practised with 22 male Wimbledon champions, including five pre-war winners. I partnered several female champions, too, including Maureen Connolly at Surbiton. She was head and shoulders above anybody else.

Today I love watching Roger Federer because of the way he moves and volleys. That's why I like Federer, because of the way he comes in. Rafael Nadal is superb, too. Novak Djokovic bores me to tears.

1952

Fast Car to Wimbledon

Billy Knight, EAST HADDON

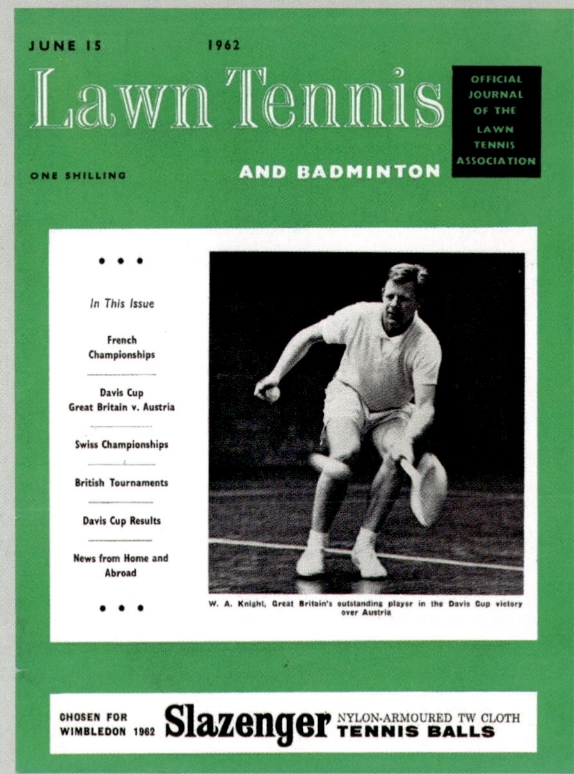

I was four or five when the war started. I can't remember any tennis being played during the War. All the men were away, and times were hard. There were no tennis balls. I first played tennis at the age of 11, after the war. My parents were both club players, and I used to go along with them.

I played mostly with my mother, because my Dad was working. In those days, parents spent a lot of time at the tennis club. I played a lot with my sister Jean, too. I had the opportunity to play tennis every day of my life. The courts were just ten minutes walk from our home, three minutes' by bike. The club had shale courts, so we could play in winter. Ernie Blincow taught me the game, and I became the best player in the club.

The LTA organised for Emlyn Jones, Dan Maskell and Fred Perry to travel around the country looking for promising young tennis talent. Emlyn was the organiser, Fred hit with all the kids and Dan did a running commentary. They took a portable wood court around with them, eventually selecting around 120 kids from parks and clubs all over the country. The lucky boys and girls were all invited to Wimbledon where, at the age of 12 or 13, we all played competitive sets, which was great. The big group was finally whittled down to just 20 or 30, and the chosen few included Mike Davies, Bobby Wilson, Roger Becker, Tony Pickard, Alan Mills and myself.

When I was around 13 or 14 we went to Devon on holiday and I played in the tournaments in Budleigh Salterton and Torquay. On one occasion we went past a club where matches were going on and I asked my Dad if we could go and watch. He said it was too expensive, but pointed to a gap at the bottom of the fence and I squeezed in through there. When I was inside a gentleman told me to 'clear off.' It was Henry Billington, Tim Henman's grandfather.

I was British Junior champion in 1952 and 1953. In 1952 I beat Bobby Wilson in a very close final. In 1952 I'd played in a lot of tournaments and decided to enter the Northern qualifying tournament for Wimbledon. At that time Bill Threlfall was the Navy champion, and he decided to enter the Northern qualifying event rather than the Southern one, thinking it might be easier. Surrey and Middlesex were hotbeds of tennis, and that made the Southern qualifying event much harder to come through. I beat Threlfall in the final qualifying round.

I'd made it to Wimbledon, but there was a problem. In the first round I was scheduled to play the second match on Court 2 against Jaroslav Drobny, but I had two GCE exams at school in the morning. I did the exams, then a friend of my father rushed me to Wimbledon in a fast car. You could never do that nowadays, with so much more traffic on the road.

I never really did very well on the grass at Wimbledon. Clay was my favourite surface. I played in the French, German and Italian Championships, all on clay. My biggest win was at the German Championships in Hamburg. My favourite British tournament was the British Hard Court Championships at Bournemouth. I won the title there in 1958 and was runner-up in the next two years.

I played against Borotra and Cochet. Cochet was a lovely, quiet man, who used no gamesmanship. I played Cochet at Harrogate when I was 16. Borotra was a real character. He was in his fifties then, but was still able to beat Geoff Paish in the final of the British Indoor Championships at Queen's.

Lew Hoad was stupendous. He was so powerful, It was like playing against a steamroller. Lew suffered with his back from very early on, from his early twenties. Ken Rosewall hit the ball just a couple of inches over the net. He never missed.

1952

Wimbledon

Keith Stephens, UPMINSTER

am 85 and I have strong memories of my first visit to Wimbledon in 1952. The match that stands out was the one in which little F. Ampon beat Ham Richardson 1-6, 5-7, 6-2, 6-3, 6-0.

The American player was one of the top seeds, but little Ampon was everywhere, coming back from two sets down to completely overwhelm him in the end.

Felicisimo Ampon of the Philippines played at Wimbledon from 1948 to 1953. Ham Richardson was the 11th seed in 1952. Sixty-seven years after his first visit to SW19 Keith Stephens remains an avid tennis player and Wimbledon watcher

1954

Memories of Wimbledon Tennis Championships in Days Gone Past

Frances Funnell, WIMBLEDON PARK

used to come down from Highgate to Wimbledon in my teens to watch the tennis and those were the days when one could see the 'planets' of the tennis world on the outside courts, not just on Centre, One or Two.

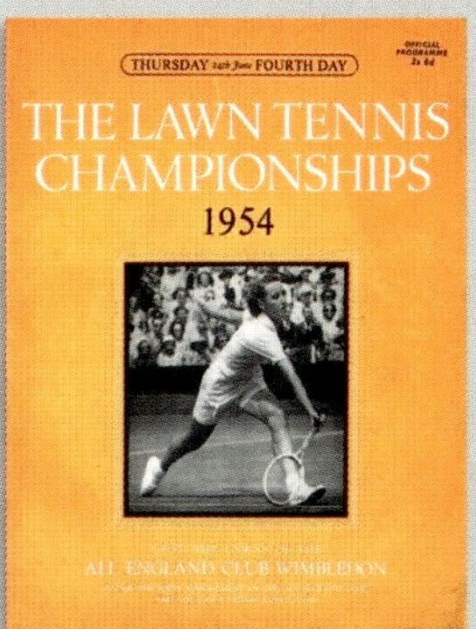

In those days I stood and the first memory to tell is of the final between Jaroslav Drobny and Ken Rosewall. Being around Rosewall's age and loving his tennis I was rooting for him. My neighbour, rather older, was rooting for Drobny who I think was then 35 – in his thirties anyway – an unimaginable age to be still at the top of his game in those days! – and not expected to win. After a very exciting match the unthinkable happened and Drobny

The second memory is of standing on the Centre Court watching a match between Arthur Ashe and Jimmy Connors. Again, a great match full of struggle on both sides. At one point Jimmy was definitely getting the worst of it from Ashe and someone in the crowd yelled 'Come on, Jimmy!' At which point the frustrated Connors turned to the crowd and yelled back 'I'm trying for Christ's sake!' Appreciative roars of laughter from the crowd.

I've been coming to Wimbledon since the 1950s queuing most of the time because I rarely get tickets and I shall continue to go until

> **"***Don't worry. Rosewall will win this Championship one day.***"**

won to great acclaim. I was very downcast and I remember my neighbour saying to me, 'Don't worry. Rosewall will win this Championship one day.' And I replied to him, 'I do hope so, but sadly it doesn't always follow.' And sadly, it didn't. For my money one of the greatest players in the game never to have won Wimbledon.

I'm unable to do so because the frailties of Anno Domini will have taken over! It has always been one of the highlights of my year.

1956

My First Visit to Wimbledon

Paul Eisenegger, BARNET

I t was 1956. The year of the Suez crisis. The year Grace Kelly married Prince Rainier of Monaco but more memorably the year of my first visit to Wimbledon.

I was 16 and Dave Walker, who captained the school Second VI, 18 and the period June/July was exam time. O levels for me and A levels for David. We'd had a very enjoyable partnership over the previous weeks with the team winning five out of seven fixtures and had become good friends.

We were both very keen on our tennis but in those days our knowledge of Wimbledon was limited to the newspapers, irregular coverage on the small black and white TV screens of the time and probably most importantly to my imagination. The voice of Max Robertson commentating on the wireless. Although I played club tennis I had never experienced a grass court, it was either *En Tout Cas* red shale or asphalt all weather then; moreover, the idea of a visit to The Championships was entering the realms of fantasy.

Finals Day that year was Saturday, 7 July when all the matches were played except the men's singles which always took place on the Friday. A few days before the finals I was offered two No.1 Court tickets which had been allocated to my club which nobody wanted presumably choosing to watch on TV. The plan was to arrive at about 10am and join the ticket holders' queue and hope that when the gates opened at noon a dash to the unreserved standing on Centre Court could be achieved. If this failed there would still be junior and plate finals to watch on No.1. I then set about tempting David away from a day of revision and finally convinced him that a day of relaxation would refresh his brain for his final exam on the Monday.

Louise Brough

<blockquote>You could count the footsteps of the serve volleyers by the bare patches from baseline to net.</blockquote>

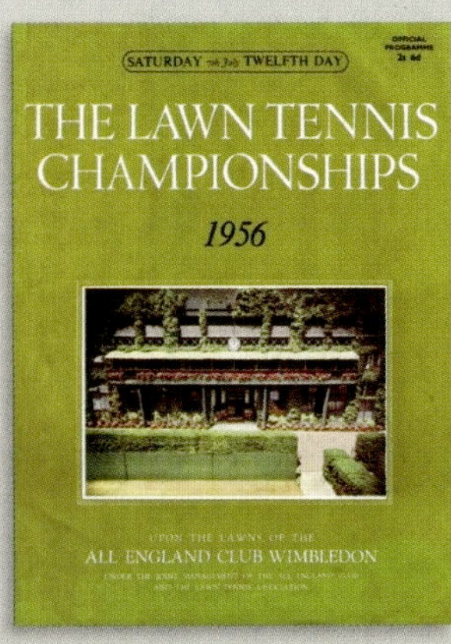

We both lived in Finchley so took the Underground to Southfields. Even on the train we felt the excitement as it gradually filled with fans who spilled out of the station mostly to the line of buses to take them to the ground. We walked down Church Road (I've never yet used the bus) and took in all the pop-up stalls in the front gardens selling drinks, snacks, souvenirs, fake programmes et cetera and of course the ticket touts asking 'Any spare tickets?' in a low voice. It was all a complete revelation.

On arrival we found the ground entry queue to be hundreds of yards long with many having been there overnight but the ticket holders' queue was quite short which filled us with hope. The next two hours passed quite quickly enjoying the buskers and the good humour of a British queue all 'talking tennis'.

Saturday, 7th July, 1956.—Intended Order of Play, at 2 p.m. precisely.

CENTRE COURT.	No. 1 COURT.
1. Miss A. Buxton (G.B.) v. Miss S. Fry (U.S.A.) *Final of Ladies' Singles*	1. Mrs. T. D. Long v. Miss I. Buding *Final of All England Ladies' Plate*
2. L. A. Hoad and K. R. Rosewall v. N. Pietrangeli and O. Sirola *Final of Gentlemen's Doubles*	2. G. Mulloy v. H. W. Stewart *Final of All England Plate*
3. Miss F. Muller and Miss D. G. Seeney v. Miss A. Buxton and Miss A. Gibson *Final of Ladies' Doubles*	3. R. Holmberg (U.S.A.) v. R. Laver (A.) *Final of Boys' Singles*
4. V. Seixas and Miss S. Fry v. G. Mulloy and Miss A. Gibson *Final of Mixed Doubles*	4. Miss A. S. Haydon (G.B.) v. Miss I. Buding (G.) *Final of Girls' Singles*

NOTE.

The Committee, while adhering as closely as possible to the order of play given, are unable to guarantee that it will be maintained in its entirety.

The Ladies' Singles Final that year was between the hot favourite Shirley Fry (USA) and Britain's Angela Buxton.

On the stroke of noon the gates opened and after a sprint to the Centre Court we managed to get a good spot in the standing area, mission accomplished.

Well, we were actually there and just let the experience wash over us. The colour, the buzz of the crowd, the sense of intimacy of the court, the Royal Box and, of course, *the anticipation.* I seem to remember that a military band entertained us from courtside, but I do definitely recall being surprised by the brown areas of the worn court; you could count the footsteps of the serve volleyers by the bare patches from baseline to net.

The Ladies' Singles Final that year was between the hot favourite Shirley Fry (USA) and Britain's Angela Buxton. The American although only seeded at five had beaten both Althea Gibson and Louise Brough in her quarter and semi-final matches. Angela Buxton, seeded six, had come through the weaker half of the draw beating the unseeded Pat Ward in the semi-final but getting a walkover against the No.2 seed Beverley Fleitz in the quarters who had discovered she was pregnant and withdrawn on medical advice.

As expected Angela Buxton was overwhelmed 6-3, 6-1 but we were entranced by the whole experience admiring the quality of play, the expertise of the ball boys, watching out for doubtful line calls and joining in the audience reaction. I don't remember who made the presentations but I guess it was Marina Duchess of Kent who was the president of the club. One slightly odd thing that always stuck in my mind was the fabulous golden tan of all the players that was enhanced by the spotless white tennis gear – to me they looked like sporting gods.

I must now admit to a very strange trick of the memory. After the Ladies' Singles all three doubles finals were played and neither David nor I could remember any of the players we'd seen after that first match. Bearing in mind these included Hoad, Rosewall, Pietrangeli, Sirola, Seixas, Mulloy and repeat appearances of Shirley Fry and Angela Buxton who won the Ladies' Doubles with Althea Gibson I can only imagine that the initial experience was so strong that the rest of the day's tennis faded from the memory. However, I'm quite sure we arrived home very tired but very happy. As a footnote, had we taken our seats on No.1 Court we would have seen youngsters called Laver and Ann Haydon competing in the juniors finals. Also, David need not have worried about his

Max Robertson was the BBC Radio's Voice of Wimbledon from 1946 to 1986

lost day of revision – he went on to study at Oxford.

Subsequently David and I lost touch for about 30 years but met up again at a school reunion when his first words to me were 'Do you remember our day at Wimbledon?' We now meet regularly and no Grand Slam is complete without one long phone call analysing the progress of the tournament. Over time we have both visited The Championships many times watching great players and nail-biting matches, exploring the outside courts and marvelling at the changes but the thrill of that first visit 61 years ago has never left us.

Paul Eisenegger's account will resonate with many who visited Wimbledon during the post-war years of the 1940s and 50s. It was a golden era, with American women and Australian men the dominant forces in world tennis, and increased media attention bringing ever-increasing crowds to The Championships

1957

Dreaming of Wimbledon

Christine Truman, ALDEBURGH

At the age of ten I was dreaming of playing at Wimbledon and in the Wightman Cup. I ate, slept and dreamt tennis. I wanted to be like Lottie Dod, who won Wimbledon at 15, but I wasn't allowed to enter until I reached 16. In 1957 I made my Wimbledon debut and, unseeded, reached the semi-finals. I lost to Althea Gibson who went on to become champion, but instead of being pleased to have reached the semi-finals, I was disappointed, because I was not going to win Wimbledon as a girl like Lottie had done. At 16 I was tall and blonde, and there was a huge media reaction.

Probably one of the best matches I played on the Centre Court in my whole career was in 1961 when Margaret Court – Margaret Smith as she was then – was the No.1 seed and the best new thing; she was from Australia, a superb athlete, she was winning everything, and she was expected to win Wimbledon. We played on Centre Court, it was the quarter-final, and she won the first set, I won the second and it went level on serving right up until she led 6-5 and had two match points. She put two very easy volleys out and I came back to win the third set 9-7. And that was, as you can imagine, a British girl winning on the Centre Court in a quarter-final against the No.1 seed, one of my best moments. That was possibly my biggest match at Wimbledon.

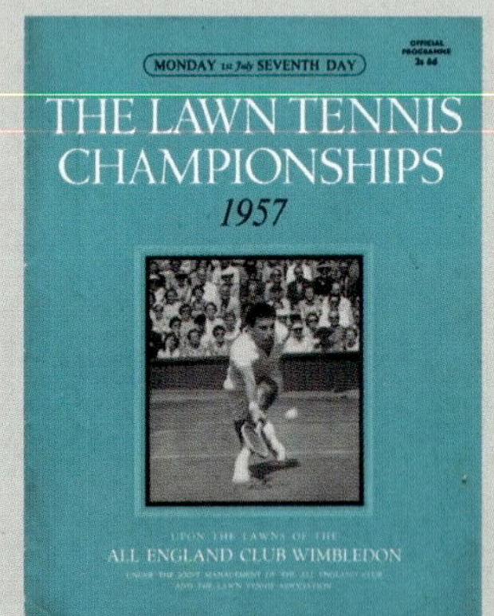

In the next round I played the South African girl Renee Schuurman, who was the No.2 to Sandra Reynolds, who I always beat during my career. Renee was more of a doubles player, and it was a bit of a weakened draw that year as Maria Bueno had pulled out through injury, as had Darlene Hard, so playing Renee was a bit of a light relief and I won 6-4, 6-4 in the semi-final, and now I was in the final.

It was an all-British final. Angela Mortimer – as she was then – beat Sandra Reynolds in the semi-final, and so here we were, the first all-British final probably for a 100 years or so I think! I was 20, Angela was 29 I believe, so time wasn't on her side. I led 6-4, 4-3 and 40-30 and there was a little bit of a drizzle and I slipped and fell and lost my concentration really, and she being experienced took advantage of that and came back to win the next six games and lead 3-0 in the third set. I hardly won a point. You didn't have medical time-outs then or any time-outs at all, no toilet breaks or sitting down at change of ends. I came back but I never got ahead again. I lost 7-5 in the third set which, you know, for a final was a very close and good match. I was very disappointed, as were friends and family, but my parents had taught me not to make a fuss, and they were pleased that that was what I had done. Afterwards I received a telegram from Winston and Clementine Churchill. That was my heyday, really.

1958

My First Visit to Wimbledon

Geoffrey Gammon, SURBITON

My enthusiasm for lawn tennis was sparked by my family's acquisition of our first small, black and white television in June 1957, which enabled me to watch a live broadcast of matches from Wimbledon that year. First I watched the men's singles final, in which the iconic Lew Hoad, at his magnificent best, beat Ashley Cooper 6-2, 6-1, 6-2 in 57 minutes. Next day, top seeds Hoad and Neale Fraser lost the men's doubles final to unseeded veterans Gardnar Mulloy (43) and Budge Patty (33). Together, the two matches made me an instant tennis fan.

Lew Hoad

Neale Fraser

Next summer, after my first year exams at University College, London, a fellow student and friend suggested a visit to The Championships on the second Monday. The first week of the 1958 event had been severely disrupted by rain, which meant that some third, as well as fourth-round matches had not been completed. This was serious, because the men's final was then played on the second Friday, with some players having to play best of five sets on successive days.

On arrival, we bought ground passes for five shillings and headed for the standing room on the two main show courts. The main event on Centre Court was British hope Bobby Wilson taking on star Italian player Nicola Pietrangeli, whom he beat in straight sets. My friend headed to the standing area there. The old Centre and No.1 courts were then adjacent, and I opted for the latter. There, 1957 Roland Garros champion Sven Davidson

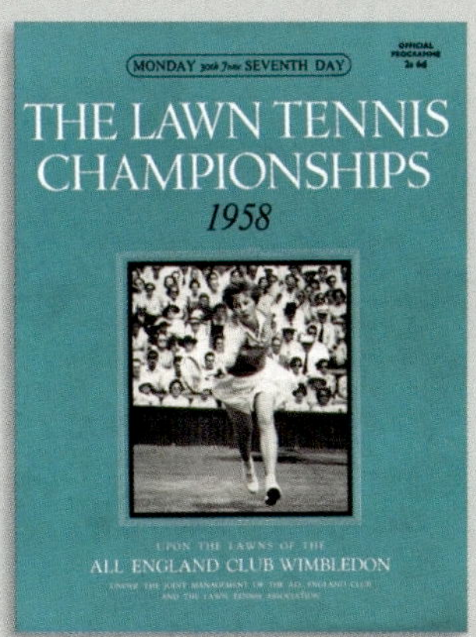

(the best Swede prior to Borg) was playing Patty, who had so impressed me the previous year. So I stood while they competed for three hours in a fiercely contested 54-game five setter, which was won by the younger, fitter man, Davidson. There were, of course, no timed changeovers or chairs for the players to rest their weary limbs; that had to wait until 1974.

Needing to stretch my legs and release the built tension of this fine contest, I strolled round the outside courts. I watched two of the matches for a few minutes. One pitted Angela Mortimer against Christiane Mercelis in a third-round match. I had no inkling that Angela would reach the final, losing to Althea Gibson, or become champion herself three years later. In the other, I had the unexpected pleasure of seeing 36-year-old

Jaroslav Drobny beating a 19-year-old opponent for the loss of six games; both players were left-handed. The latter was a scrawny youth who hit the ball hard but was unable to cope with the veteran's variety and guile. His name was Rod Laver, whom I only saw again live when he played and beat Ken Rosewall when the pros competed at Wembley in 1964.

For the record, the event was completed on time, although the men's semis on Wednesday were split between the two show courts. With Hoad now a professional, Cooper duly won the singles final over Fraser, but they lost the doubles final to Davidson and Ulf Schmidt. I had greatly enjoyed my first visit to this great and unique tournament, and it is always a pleasure to return there.

1959

My First Visit to Wimbledon

David Orchard, HIGH WYCOMBE

My first visit to Wimbledon was in 1959. I was a 14-year-old tennis enthusiast who had been captivated two years earlier by the BBC broadcast of the Wimbledon Championships that had been viewed on our family's newly acquired black and white television set. I obtained my first ticket through my school as from their small allocation I was able to acquire a ground pass ticket for the final Saturday. This act left me in bad odour for a short while, as I had to drop out of a school match in order to attend but I considered that a small price to pay.

The whole day was filled with excitement, starting with the journey into and across London to arrive at the famous Southfields station and join the procession towards The All England Club for the first time, with the iconic ivy-covered walls of the Centre Court appearing in view as we neared the Club. An early arrival was vital in order to join the queue waiting for the gates to open at noon prior to the headlong dash for standing room on the Centre Court. Being young, small and fairly athletic was an advantage as access to the hallowed area was readily gained and the generosity of the fellow spectators ensured that I was manoeuvred to the front in order to have a good view. There ensued a two-hour wait until the start of play, so there was ample opportunity to take in the atmosphere whilst consuming a packed lunch and listening to the excited chatter of the fellow spectators, most of whom were clearly experienced and knowledgeable. There was keen anticipation as with only the men's singles final having been played the day before there were four finals to look forward to with some players featuring in more than one, as at that time most players played in all three events.

At 2 o'clock the excitement level rose as the Ladies' Singles finalists Maria Bueno and Darlene Hard entered the court preceded by the dressing room attendant carrying

Darlene Hard

the rackets, as was the then custom. Miss Hard was the higher seed and more experienced player coming into the match but this proved to be the first occasion that a Wimbledon crowd was treated to the athletic skills and grace of Maria Bueno in a singles final. The match was very much in contrast to what is seen today as both players frequently attacked from the net and with no sit-downs at the change of ends it was over in less than an hour, with Bueno winning an all-action match in straight sets. Following the presentation of the trophies on court by the Duchess of Kent the venue was made ready for the all-Australian men's doubles final between top seeds Neale Fraser with Roy Emerson and singles runner-up Rod Laver with Bob Mark. This was a closely fought match that demonstrated a high level of serve-volley technique without becoming very exciting. The top seeds prevailed in a

Christine Truman

lengthy four setter with the abiding memory of a first view of Laver and Emerson who would go on to become two of the game's greats.

Following the customary presentation of the doubles trophies in the Royal Box, it was the turn of the Ladies' Doubles finalists to take the court and there was British interest with Christine Truman partnering Beverley Fleitz of the USA against all-American duo Darlene Hard and Jeanne Arth. Home hopes were high as the first set went to the former pair but the more experienced team came

through comfortably in the next two sets. Miss Hard then joined three finalists from earlier as she partnered Rod Laver to a two-set victory over Neale Fraser and Maria Bueno in the mixed doubles.

Following the last presentation of trophies the spectators trudged wearily from the Centre Court. After a long and exciting afternoon I was a very tired young man as I joined the crowds retracing their earlier footsteps as they made their way home, my head still buzzing with the images of the day. A lifelong love affair had begun.

Wimbledon's custom of playing four of the five finals on the very last day, which in those days was a Saturday, commenced in 1933 and continued until 1968. From 1969, the second year of Open Tennis, the Gentlemen's and Ladies' finals were switched round, with the Ladies' showpiece match being played on Friday afternoon and the men's a day later. Since the introduction of scheduled play on the second Sunday in 1982, the Ladies' Final has reverted to its original Saturday slot with the Gentlemen's Final bringing the curtain down on The Championships on Sunday afternoon.

Roy Emerson

Beverley Fleitz

1959

Seven Decades of Wimbledon

Susan Morgan Thomas, TUNBRIDGE WELLS

Jaroslav Drobny

Susan's first experience of watching top-class tennis came in 1946 when, as a ten-year-old, she attended the Welsh Championships which were staged at her local Newport club. The tournament took place the week after Wimbledon each year and attracted some of the world's leading stars, including Jaroslav Drobny and Lew Hoad. Susan visited the tournament as a spectator every year from 1946 to 1958. 'Sport was very important in the town; rugby in the winter and tennis in the summer,' Susan recalls.

Fast forward a dozen years to the autumn of 1958 and after leaving Nottingham University Susan took a job in London working for Shell International, thus paving the way for a love affair with Wimbledon which continues to the present day.

Of her very first visit to Wimbledon in 1959, Susan remembers: 'I went to work in the City that day dressed in my best hat, dress and high heels. People always dressed up for Wimbledon in those days.' Her colleagues asked why she was dressed up. 'I'm going to Wimbledon after work this evening,' she replied, adding 'My ticket was 1'6d.'

Leaving her office in the City, Susan would travel out to Wimbledon and watch the evening's play, often from the free standing room on the Centre Court. 'In those days the standing room was mainly occupied by schoolgirls,' Susan recalled.

'Wimbledon was a bit of a mystery to many people. Not many people knew how to go about getting tickets. I often went in the evening, and on Saturdays when I did not have to work.'

Susan recalled some of her favourite players from seven decades of Wimbledon: 'I was there on the Saturday when Virginia Wade won in 1977. It was a very popular victory, and it is the reason my email address ends in 77.

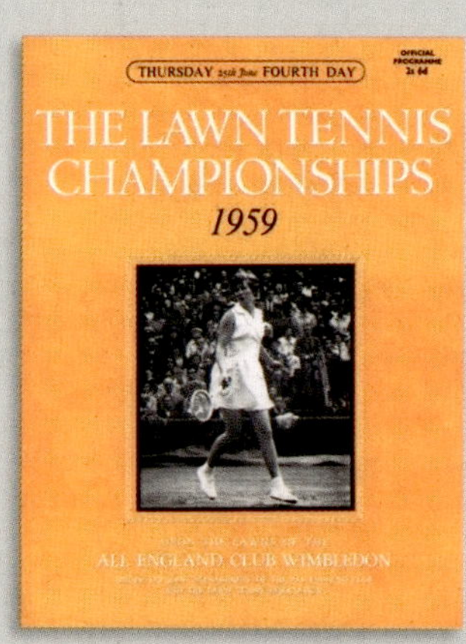

'I always loved watching Ken Rosewall, and every year I would go along thinking "this year he will win it." But he never did. Interminable baseline rallies bore me,' Susan remarked. 'I like Roger Federer so much because he gets away from the baseline.'

Other favourites over the years include Billie Jean King (in her earlier years, before she became 'political'), Stan Smith, Martina Hingis, Lindsay Davenport and Martina Navratilova. Susan tells a great story about the latter. 'Years ago there was no tunnel for the players, and you used to see the

Ken Rosewall

❝*In those days the standing room was mainly occupied by schoolgirls.***❞**

stars walking around the grounds. One day I was on my way to Wimbledon with my friend and we saw Martina Navratilova coming in our direction on her bicycle. To our delight she stopped and talked to us. It made my day!'

During Susan's time there have been many changes at Wimbledon, but the magical atmosphere has remained. 'I used to like the old No.1 Court,' she recalled. 'My friend Janet and I play a game of "spot the changes" when we go to Wimbledon.'

Of tennis itself, Susan remarked, 'It's become a bit of a science now,' but it was clear from listening to her that her love of the game, and particularly the grass courts of SW19, remains undimmed. 'Tennis is my passion,' Susan said, as if that were ever in doubt!

Susan Morgan Thomas hails originally from Newport in Monmouthshire but now lives in Tunbridge Wells. She first went to Wimbledon in 1959, and still goes to the tournament today.

1960

> **❝**I used to like the old No.1 Court. My friend Janet and I play a game of 'spot the changes' when we go to Wimbledon. **❞**

Early Days at Wimbledon

Edward Tidy, WIMBLEDON PARK

I remember:

Maria Bueno who added colour to black and white TV

Rod Laver who danced around the court like a ballet dancer

Chuck McKinley who blamed the cameras every time he lost a point

1965

My First Visit to Wimbledon

Jeremy Hudson, RAYNES PARK

My first visit to the Tennis was in 1965, when I was aged 12. For a few years before this I had avidly followed the tennis on television, and Fred Stolle (twice a defeated men's singles finalist) and Maria Bueno (Champion in 1964) were my favourite players.

My family lived in Raynes Park, and I attended a local grammar school. My father taught at another local school, and through the school regularly obtained complimentary tickets ('whites' as they were called), which were ground passes which could be used on any day of The Championships. On this occasion, in 1965, my father took my younger brother and me to the tennis one very warm and sunny afternoon during the first week.

In those days Centre Court and Number One Court both had large standing areas. There were two standing areas on Centre Court, one on either side of the court and quite close to the front, each accommodating a couple of thousand tennis fans. Anyone with admission to the ground was entitled to stand on Centre Court, and that is where the three of us went. I remember we saw a second-round Ladies' Singles match between the great Australian player Margaret Smith (as she then was) and an Austrian girl. Research of the record books confirm that the latter would have been Miss L.M. Leyrer, and that she lost 6-0, 6-1 to the eventual Champion.

Of that occasion I remember sitting on a concrete barrier, to get a better view. What struck me most was seeing the tennis in 'colour' for the first time! After watching on a black and white TV, it was marvellous to be able to see bronzed tennis players in action clad all in white, set against the all green surrounds of Centre Court, the lush grass, the gleaming varnish on the net posts and wooden tennis rackets, the uniforms of the service personnel guarding the entrances, and all the colours of the crowd. Watching the tennis side-on for the first time made one appreciate the sheer speed of the ball and the force of the serves and groundstrokes. Margaret Smith looked every inch a superstar.

After the match we left Centre Court to find an ice cream. As we strolled along the main concourse we noticed poor Miss Leyrer gazing out of an open changing-room window, no doubt reflecting ruefully on the hammering she had just experienced!

This was my first attendance at a major sporting occasion, and the first time I had seen a major celebrity (sporting or otherwise) in the flesh. It was also the first time I had been in such a large audience (in those days Centre Court held over 13,000), and experienced the roar of the crowd responding to a moment of brilliance on the court. It was a day I have never forgotten.

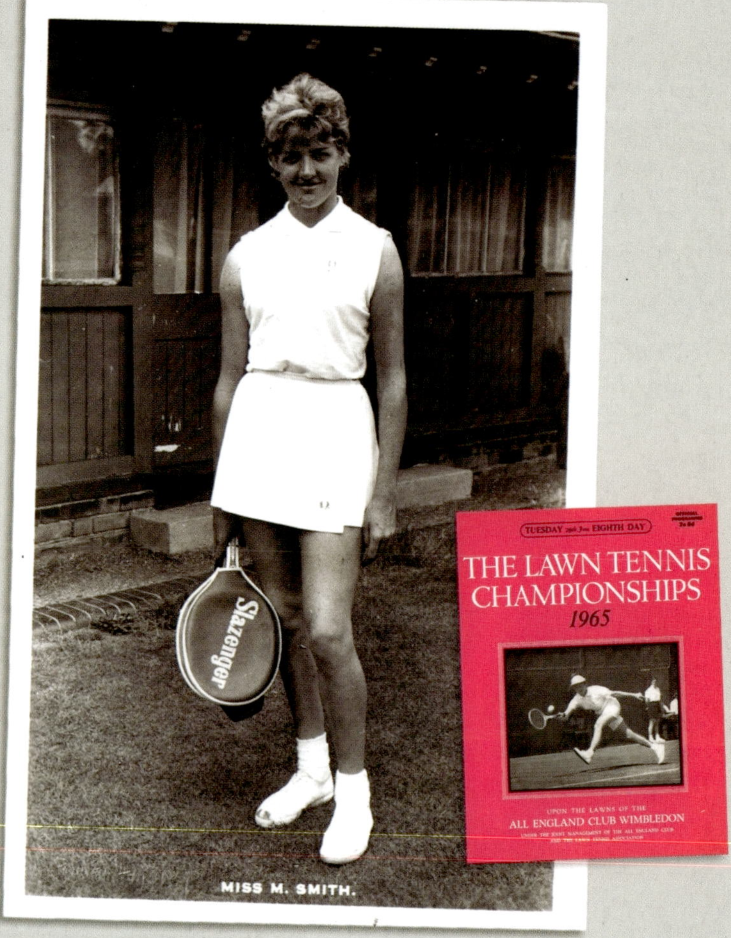

Margaret Smith

> **"***After watching on a black and white TV, it was marvellous to be able to see bronzed tennis players in action clad all in white, set against the all green surrounds of Centre Court.***"**

1965

My Wimbledon Debut

Julie Heldman, SANTA MONICA

was playing a Dutch player whom I'd never heard of, so I assumed that I was the favourite. Although we were scheduled for the second match we didn't get on court until 8pm. I'd been practising at Queen's Club because I didn't know then that it was possible to practise at Wimbledon. I asked 'where do we practise?' and they just said 'Queen's'.

Anyway the court at Wimbledon was much faster than any other grass court I'd ever experienced, and after losing the first set 6-2 I realised I had to do something pretty quick or I was out. So I began getting down really low, with my butt nearly touching the ground, and I won the last two sets 6-0, 6-0. Apart from the match I remember the crappy food, and being frozen!

It was cold and oppressive. There were three locker rooms, and I was in the third (lowest) level of the three. At the time, I knew Wimbledon was supposedly hallowed ground, but it didn't seem so special to me. I was staying at an inexpensive hotel near the Brompton Road, and Wimbledon sent a car to take me to The All England Club. That was special.

For several years, I played mixed doubles with Torben Ulrich, who taught me a great deal, including how to rush the net in tandem and when to duck when he hit a smash. I was also amazed by his twinkle-in-the-eye irreverence towards Wimbledon's officials. One match,

we won the toss, and we elected to serve first. Torben handed me the balls, so I served, but I made a terrible hash of it. Two games later, he handed me the balls again, saying 'You can do better this time.' I was shocked, and so was the umpire, who said something like 'Mr Ulrich that is not proper. It's your turn to serve.'

Julie Heldman

Torben Ulrich

Julie Heldman and Torben Ulrich were two of the great characters of world tennis in the 1960s and 70s. Julie was one of the nine women who signed symbolic $1 contracts with her mother Gladys, the pioneering publisher of *World Tennis* magazine, to turn professional in 1970, thus turning their backs on the tennis establishment and paving the way for the eventual formation of the WTA Tour. One of the best wins of Julie's career came at Queen's Club in the 1973 London Grass Court Championships, when she beat rising superstar Chris Evert. Julie's autobiography, *Driven – A Daughter's Odyssey*, was published in 2018.

Torben Ulrich was a mystical figure – a jazz musician who was sometimes found meditating on an empty outside court at Wimbledon. He had already been playing at Wimbledon for 20 years when he first teamed up with Julie in the Wimbledon Mixed Doubles in 1968. They continued their partnership until the Dane's last Wimbledon appearance in 1972, at the age of 43.

1965

My First Visit to Wimbledon

Bernard Fullerton, BRINGSTY

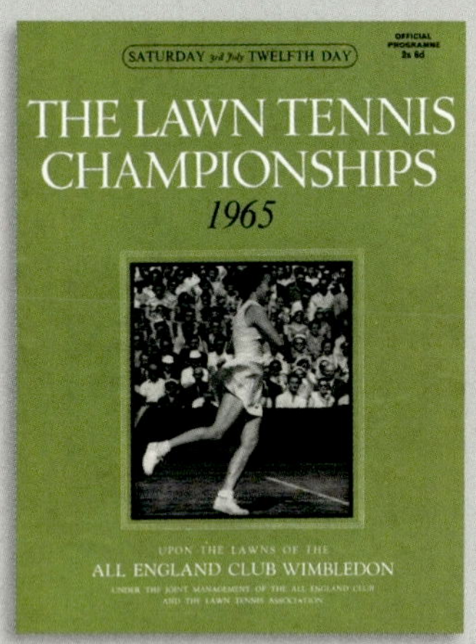

On reflection, more than half a century later, I can't help feeling that I should have been at school. It was a Tuesday in June, surely the school holidays hadn't commenced?

My school friend, Tim, and I decided that we would travel to The All England Club to watch tennis at the famous tournament. It was on the second Tuesday of The Championships, ladies quarter-finals day. Previously I had only watched Wimbledon on the television, black and white only in those days.

The queue to get in was long but moved reasonably fast, no security checks needed then. I saw the order of play: Christine Truman was due to play the American number four seed Nancy Richey, the first match on Centre Court. The unseeded Truman had beaten Carole Graebner, the number six seed, earlier in the tournament. I remember watching the match on TV. The BBC ceased transmission of this match before it had finished, with Truman leading. No Internet then, I frantically rang the AELTC to learn the result but got no reply. I had to wait until a radio sports bulletin, much later in the day, to learn of Christine's victory. The ATP/WTA app is just so brilliant.

For those without Centre Court tickets limited standing room was available. I was 15 and fast, I didn't need to use my elbows! The two-hour wait before play started passed and the players entered the court to loud applause. Those who had been sitting in the standing area stood up. Fast I may have been, tall I wasn't. Peering between the shoulders of those in front of me, my view was restricted. That did not stop my enjoyment though. I confess I was loud, my hero

direction as her racket was going in the opposite way, but winning the point. The Centre Court was enraptured; it was a very close match which could have gone either way. The final point was greeted with the loudest cheer of the day, and probably of the week, a 6-4, 1-6, 7-5 victory to Truman.

Tim, who hadn't wanted to stand to watch a tennis match, had gone off in a different direction after we'd entered the grounds. However, we met up later and, as we passed one of the Centre Court exit gangways, a very nice woman gave us her tickets as she was leaving for the day. So we spent the rest of our visit seated

> **" *I confess I was loud, my hero was cheered whenever she won a point. Christine Truman was Britain's favourite tennis player, as she was mine.* "**

was cheered whenever she won a point. Christine Truman was Britain's favourite tennis player, as she was mine.

Richey was an accomplished player, in my opinion never getting the appreciation she deserved. She had the ability to beat Christine with her consistent, solid ground strokes. But on this day Christine's volleying, if sometimes a touch erratic, proved decisive. I'm sure I remember Christine going in one

on the magical Centre Court. What a wonderful day I had.

The following day Tim phoned me. His mother had been reading the *Daily Express*, and the Truman/Richey match was the main feature on the back page. She noticed that there was a picture of the crowd, and who was centre of the group of spectators in the photograph, yes that noisy teenager!

Christine Truman (left) and Nancy Richey after their quarter-final match in 1965. Christine squeezed home 6-4, 1-6, 7-5.

1965

My First Attempt at Getting into a Final Saturday

Elsie Rosam, DORKING

I arrived at the Marryat Road entrance of the Wimbledon Tennis Championships on Friday at 9.30am complete with sleeping bag and a carrier full of goodies to keep me going. I wanted to queue to see the three finals on the Saturday. There was only a handful already queuing and we soon became friendly and chatted excitedly about what had been happening over the fortnight. In those days the men's final and men's doubles final were played on the Friday and as the crowd grew, transistor radios were keeping us informed as Roy Emerson beat Fred Stolle. There was lots of noise and cheering.

We were so near the front of the queue that our little gang knew that we would definitely be getting onto Centre Court on Saturday. As play finished, some of the players came over for a chat on their way home and that gave us a ripple of excitement and we enthused about that for some time. The weather had been dry and warm all day but it certainly cooled off as it grew dark. Most of us were tucked into our sleeping bags quite early. Rows of long sausages with heads popping out. There was a gentle buzz and rustling up and down the now rapidly growing crowd which snaked up to Church Road and beyond. I don't think we got much sleep but it didn't matter. There was a toilet opposite near where we were and this was in constant use during the night.

At 6am an official gave us a queue ticket number and told us to disappear until 12 noon. I went home to Surbiton. I later found myself rushing back to get into my queue space. I remember, as 1 o'clock approached we all concertinaed closer together so we could be 'on our marks'!

As the gate opened we clattered through to the turnstile and paid as quickly as possible, and ran to get our space on the Centre Court. In those days there was quite a large space for 'standing room only' and this filled up very quickly. I was right in the middle, leaning on the barrier that separated me from the seats in front. I can remember taking a

MISS J.A.M.TEGART

Judy Tegart

> **❝** *I can remember taking a deep breath and thinking 'Wow, I've made it'.* **❞**

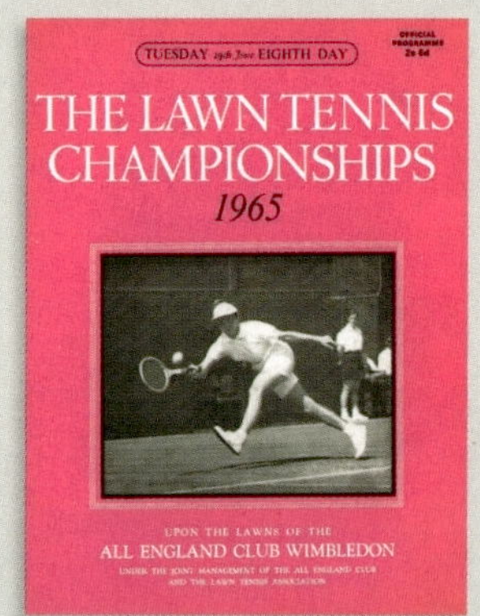

MISS. N. RICHEY.

Nancy Richey

Tony Roche

deep breath and thinking 'Wow, I've made it'. The standing barrier meant that I was head and shoulders above everyone and the court was so close it was awesome.

Ladies' Final was between Margaret Smith and (my favourite) Maria Bueno. Smith overpowered Bueno to win the huge Championship plate but it could have gone either way. Ladies' Doubles followed. Bueno and Richey beat Durr and Lieffrig and the day finished with a delightful, but serious Mixed Doubles Final between Tony Roche who partnered Judy Tegart, and the winning duo, Ken Fletcher and Margaret Smith. The Mixed Doubles was very fast and exciting. Lots of good serves and volleying that looked quite dangerous if you were punished at the net.

It was an incredible day and I went home exhausted. I did find out subsequently that I could have got a good seated ticket near the front because an amount of tickets were kept especially to be sold on the day. With this experience I was

out queuing again in 1966, 1967, 1968 and 1970 (and sitting down). I missed Mrs Jones beating Mrs King in 1969, but I've got lots of great memories!

Ken Fletcher

The three or four precious hours of free time between the early morning issuing of queue tickets and the re-assembly of the queue just prior to the opening of the gates enabled people to freshen up and enjoy their afternoon's tennis.

CHAPTER 4
A Happening in SW19
1967–1984

I n the mid-1960s The Beatles were leading their
millions of fans on a psychedelic trip away
from society's rigid old structures towards a
new egalitarian world of peace, love and self-
expression. Youth culture prevailed, and clothes
and hairstyles gave outward expression to this
inner liberation. The boutiques of Kensington,
Carnaby Street and Chelsea's King's Road were
prime Saturday destinations, and would have been
weekend-long ones had the law not prevented
shops opening on Sundays.

Whatever the current fashion
might be, Wimbledon's players
and spectators are always at its
leading edge. This was never
more true than in the late 1960s,
when pop musicians, film stars
and fashion models were the
trendsetters, and tennis stars
and Wimbledon's spectators were
quick to follow. Having been
clean-cut and clean-shaven at the
start of the decade, male tennis
stars ended it with long hair and
sideburns. Sixties supermodel
Twiggy set the style for women in
tennis, and as the men's hair got
longer, the women's got shorter,
except for the few like Virginia
Wade who kept their beautiful
long tresses. Tennis skirts and
dresses were shorter, too – once
again mimicking high-street
fashion where the mini-skirt was
de rigueur. ◯

World No.1
Ilie Nastase was
twice a runner-up
at Wimbledon

By the start of the 1960s, the
majority of British homes had
television sets. Housewives and
schoolchildren could watch
Centre Court and No.1 Court
matches live, albeit on small
screens in black and white, and
dads also got to catch an hour or
two of action from Wimbledon
when they got home from work.
Wimbledon was on the BBC
where there were no adverts, so
the cameras just stayed on the
players all the time, even as they
changed ends. With this intense
scrutiny, the players' looks and
mannerisms became well known
to the watching audience, which
numbered millions of people.

With Wimbledon enjoying
ever-increasing TV coverage,
more and more people came to
The All England Club to watch
the world's best amateur players
in action. This new breed of
spectators were not all tennis
aficionados; indeed many were

oblivious to the existence of the
professional game. To them,
Roy Emerson, Fred Stolle, John
Newcombe, Tony Roche, Tom
Okker, Dennis Ralston, Manuel
Santana, Bobby Wilson, Mike
Sangster and Roger Taylor were,
quite simply, the best players in
the world. In 1967, during 'The
Summer of Love', a Wimbledon
Championships stripped of
such luminaries as Laver, Hoad,
Rosewall and Gonzales, all of
whom were plying their trade
on the pro circuit, still attracted
a record aggregate attendance
of 301,896.

1967 was also the year of the
BBC's first colour broadcasts
from Wimbledon. The sun
shone brightly every day, and
the grounds were packed.
Behind the scenes, however, all
was not well. ◯

Ever since 1926, when Suzanne Lenglen turned professional, Wimbledon had been suffering defections of its star players to the pro ranks. Fred Perry in 1936, Don Budge in 1938, and Bobby Riggs in 1939 were just a trickle compared to the post–World War II flood which saw virtually every male Wimbledon champion during the 1940s, 50s and early 60s turn professional. Australia's Roy Emerson, Wimbledon champion in 1964 and 1965, was the notable exception, although it was rumoured that he received just as much in so-called 'expenses' as professional stars did from their lucrative contracts. A number of attempts were made to unify the sport through the creation of 'Open' tennis, where amateur and professional players could compete together in the same tournaments, but all came to nothing. In 1967, Wimbledon and the British Lawn Tennis Association took unilateral action which changed the game forever.

Rod Laver was the world's No.1 male player from 1963 to 1967 but, having accepted Jack Kramer's offer to turn professional after his 1962 Grand Slam success, spent those years playing his tennis on portable canvas courts laid down in ice rinks, concert halls and hockey stadiums which were a far cry from the historic homes of tennis such as Roland Garros, Forest Hills and Wimbledon. All that changed, however, when The All England Club Chairman Herman David announced that Wimbledon would stage a professional tournament on the Centre Court in August 1967, and that the 1968 Wimbledon Championships

EVONNE CAWLEY

Evonne Goolagong, (later Mrs Cawley) brought sunshine and smiles to the Centre Court

would be open to both amateur and professional players.

At the Lawn Tennis Association's Annual General Meeting on 14 December 1967, the LTA's Councillor for Kent, Derek Penman, gave an impassioned speech in which he said that the main reason behind the drive for Open Tennis was 'not to stage open tournaments, but to remove Shamateurism and hypocrisy from the game'. His plea won unanimous support, and over the following three months Penman, LTA Chairman Derek Hardwick and The All England Club Chairman Herman David travelled the world explaining Britain's decision to the other leading tennis nations. Within a year, they all followed Britain's example and made their tournaments open to amateur and professional players.

The first 'Open' tournament was played at Bournemouth in the spring of 1968, and Mark Cox of Great Britain made history as the first amateur to beat a professional in an ILTF-sanctioned event when he downed veteran American Pancho Gonzales. The tournament was won by Australia's Ken Rosewall, Laver's closest rival in the professional ranks who also won the 1968 French Open – the first-ever Open Grand Slam event. Ninety sixty-seven French champion Roy Emerson – the last Roland Garros winner of the amateur era – did well to reach the quarter-finals before losing to 40-year-old Gonzales, thus illustrating the considerable superiority of the professionals. This was underlined when Rod Laver won his third Wimbledon title a few weeks later, six years after his second back in 1962.

In August 1967 Rod Laver won Wimbledon's first-ever professional tournament, beating Ken Rosewall in the final on the Centre Court.

ADRIANO PANATTA

Talented and handsome, Italy's Adriano Panatta was popular with Wimbledon crowds in the 1970s

During the 1970s corporate America saw the vast financial opportunities of Open Tennis, and aspiring agents and promoters including Lamar Hunt, Dave Dixon, Donald Dell and Mark McCormack were instrumental in signing groups of players and redefining the tennis landscape. Disputes were inevitable as self-interests clashed, and players and fans were usually the victims.

Wimbledon was boycotted by many of the top men in 1972, denying Australia's John Newcombe the opportunity to win his fourth singles title in six years, and he was absent again in 1973 as most of the top 100 voted to strike in support of Nikki Pilic, a Yugoslav Davis Cup player who was in dispute with his country's tennis federation. Jack Kramer, in his role as Executive Director of the newly formed Association of Tennis Professionals (ATP), represented the unhappy players in their dispute, and as a result his much-loved commentary-box partnership with Britain's Dan Maskell came to an end when Kramer was fired by the BBC.

During the 1973 Championships 17-year-old Bjorn Borg was repeatedly mobbed by adoring teenage girls. When he was beaten in five tough sets by Britain's Roger Taylor in the quarter-finals on the Centre Court, the Swede was surrounded by photographers and female admirers whilst gallant winner Taylor was almost completely ignored. America's Jimmy Connors, also a quarter-finalist, was arrogant, brash and sometimes foul-mouthed, and was goaded into further excesses by his friend and doubles partner Ilie Nastase, whose nickname 'Nasty' was well justified.

The game had a new generation of young stars including Borg, Connors, Nastase, Vitas Gerulaitis, Chris Evert and Evonne Goolagong, and a new generation of fans who were younger and louder than the respectful audiences of the pre-Open era. These new fans idolised the tennis players like pop stars, and the players responded, shedding the etiquette and inhibitions of earlier times. The second-largest aggregate attendance in Wimbledon's history proved that, to the British public at least, the tournament was bigger than the players.

Jimmy Connors won his first Wimbledon title in 1974, crushing all his opponents including 39-year-old Ken Rosewall in the final, but was surprisingly beaten in the 1975 final by 31-year-old fellow-countryman Arthur Ashe, whose clever mix of touch and power completely disrupted Connors's punishing groundstroke game.

In 1976, players, officials and spectators had to endure the unremitting heat of London's drought year. Wimbledon's parched yellowy-brown courts were lightning quick, and photographs show all the fans to be brown-skinned with the English summer only just starting. The Wimbledon Long Bar struggled to cope with the never-ending demand for ice-cold drinks, a sweaty mass of potential customers pressing forward genially in the hope of eventually being served. Rumania's Ilie Nastase was long overdue a Wimbledon singles title, and his untroubled progress through to the final made his coronation as champion seem a formality. Swedish superstar Bjorn Borg had other ideas, however, and in the final his more substantial game triumphed over the artistic but by comparison lightweight Nastase.

The 20-year-old Bjorn Borg who won the first of five consecutive Wimbledon singles titles in 1976 was a very different person to the hard-hitting blond teenager who had wowed the girls at Wimbledon just three years earlier. Gone were the purple-trimmed Slazenger shirt and Adidas Robert Haillet shoes, replaced by the iconic Fila candy-stripe shirt with blue collar and red trim, and Diadora shoes. Borg's flowing locks were now held in place by a Fila headband, making him look more like an eastern guru than a tennis player. His game was different, too. He still hit the ball very hard, but the flashy part of his game had gone, replaced by the more patient, tactical approach which would win him five Wimbledon and six Roland Garros titles between 1976 and 1981. ✇

1982

The 1969 Wimbledon Championships saw an epic first-round encounter in which 41-year-old Pancho Gonzales staged a remarkable comeback against Charlie Pasarell, winning an extraordinary 112-game match 22–24, 1–6, 16–14, 6–3, 11–9. Rod Laver won his fourth Wimbledon title and Britain's popular Ann Haydon Jones her first, beating World No.1 Margaret Court in the semi-finals and No.2 Billie Jean King in the final. Ann also won the Mixed Doubles in partnership with Fred Stolle. The following year she became one of the few Wimbledon singles champions not to defend her crown, having already retired to start a family with her husband Pip.

The momentous decade that had begun with two rockets ended in similar fashion. In July 1969 Apollo 11 astronaut Neil Armstrong became the first man to set foot on the moon, and a few weeks later 'Rocket' Rod Laver sealed his second Grand Slam, this time casting aside all doubts about the merit of his earlier achievement by beating all comers, both amateur and professional. The changes in tennis stemming from Wimbledon's unilateral decision to go open were far from over, however, and during the next few years there would be disputes, lawsuits, player strikes and boycotts as the new order was gradually and painfully pieced together. ✇

In celebration of Wimbledon's Centenary in 1977 the Wimbledon Lawn Tennis Museum and the adjacent Kenneth Ritchie Library were opened. Both were located on the first floor of the newly expanded Centre Court building, in the north-east corner. Following the arrival of an outspoken 18-year-old New Yorker on the scene that year, the popularity of tennis soon scaled new heights as the behaviour of some of the top players plumbed new depths. Born in Wiesbaden, Germany, where his father was serving in the US Air Force, John Patrick McEnroe blew away the last vestiges of the amateur days when sportsmanship and camaraderie were considered more important than titles and prize money.

During the late 1970s through to the mid-1980s more people than ever before attended tournaments, watched tennis on TV and, most importantly, began to play the game themselves. Sales of rackets, balls and equipment reached an all-time high, and modern indoor facilities were built in many parts of the developed world. This explosion in popularity was fuelled in no small measure by the great Wimbledon rivalries between Bjorn Borg and John McEnroe, and Chris Evert and Martina Navratilova.

The Centenary Wimbledon Championships in 1977 had a British singles champion who received her trophy from Queen Elizabeth II. Virginia Wade won the title at her 16th attempt, just nine days short of her 32nd birthday. Her success followed those of her fellow-countrywomen Angela Mortimer (1961) and Ann Jones (1969), but it was to signal the start of a long barren spell for British players at Wimbledon. Sweden's Bjorn Borg won the men's title for the second consecutive year, but the real story of the tournament was the emergence of a new young star in the tennis firmament.

Wimbledon Centenary Plate, 1977. One thousand nine hundred and seventy-seven numbered plates were made by Royal Doulton

Eighteen-year-old John McEnroe was about to take up a place at Stanford University and had come to Wimbledon to play in the junior boys' event. As is often the custom with promising juniors, he was also entered for the men's singles qualifying tournament. McEnroe duly qualified and found himself involved in two Championship events on his Wimbledon debut, as he was also entered for the Mixed Doubles in partnership with fellow-American teenager Mary Carillo, with whom he had unexpectedly won the French Open Mixed Doubles title a few weeks earlier. Such was McEnroe's precocious talent that he reached the semi-finals in singles, losing in four close sets to Jimmy Connors, and the quarters in the Mixed, winning three matches before bowing out, these successes forcing him to scratch from the junior event. The nine singles matches that McEnroe played in qualifying and then reaching the last four in the main draw created a Wimbledon record that may never be beaten.

Following his breakthrough at Wimbledon 1977, McEnroe completed his tennis education quickly. By 1979 he had won his first Grand Slam singles title at the US Open and was ranked No.2 in the world behind Bjorn Borg. But McEnroe was a flawed genius, and his increasingly frequent

Dodging Des

was in the Somerset Road queue one evening in the mid-1970s when I saw the BBC's Desmond Lynam approaching, microphone in hand. The friends I was with were inside watching the tennis, and I'd been left to hold the fort. I liked Des, but I had no desire to share the secrets of queuing for Wimbledon with him or his radio audience, so when he was about to turn his attention to me I slipped off to the toilet, only resuming my place in the queue when he had passed by.'

The rivalry between John McEnroe and Bjorn Borg was celebrated in wax at Madame Tussauds, London

Love him or loathe him, no one could deny that John McEnroe had brought a new youthful following to tennis. He would eventually go on to win three Wimbledon singles titles and five men's doubles titles, four of these in partnership with his boyhood friend Peter Fleming. Overall he won 17 Grand Slam titles in singles and doubles during his career. McEnroe was front-page as well as back-page news, and the same was true of Czech-born Martina Navratilova who dominated women's tennis for a decade from the late 1970s. Martina was talented but not in great physical shape when she made her Wimbledon debut as a 16-year-old in 1973, but she emigrated to the US and transformed her body and her game, eventually winning 18 Grand Slam singles titles between 1978 and 1990. Her rivalry with fellow-American Chris Evert was legendary, and they faced each other no fewer than nine times at Wimbledon, with Martina winning seven of those matches which included five finals. Martina was open and honest about her sexuality at a time when very few sportspeople came out, and the tabloid press loved to turn her relationship problems into front-page news.

The more tennis was in the news, the more advertisers and sponsors were attracted to the sport. Borg retired suddenly in 1981 at just 25 years of age, leaving McEnroe as undisputed leader of the men's game. After winning Wimbledon three times in four years, the American took a two-year sabbatical in 1985 and two German teenagers immediately stepped up to continue the march of youth at Wimbledon. ◎

and vitriolic outbursts against umpires and linesmen threatened to overshadow his achievements. His behaviour at Wimbledon 1979 was that of a spoilt child; he repeatedly argued about line calls, confronted umpires and called for the tournament referee to come on court. All this was disrespectful and distracting to his opponents, and many ordinary tennis lovers were pleased to see him beaten in the fourth round by fellow-American Tim Gullikson. McEnroe was booed onto the Centre Court for the 1980 final against Borg, but left a gallant loser after an epic five-set match which saw the Swede clinch his fifth and last Wimbledon title.

When McEnroe had his first public spat with authority at Wimbledon in 1978, he instantly became an anti-establishment figure who made Wimbledon interesting for a whole new audience. Umpires who had previously seemed dignified and respected now appeared hapless, frozen in the headlights of McEnroe's tirades.

1967

A Centre Court Memory

Ian Hewitt, LONDON

My first year visiting The Championships was 1967. As a junior tennis player, I had entered the famous grounds as a nervous teenager a few years earlier, playing for my school in the Clark Cup and then, even more nervously, playing at 'Junior Wimbledon' (as then called) held for Britain's Under 18s. But that was all on The All England Club's red shale courts, with barely a spectator around.

In 1967, however, I was at The Championships in the capacity as a scoreboard operator! Lucky enough to be at Oxford University – much to the surprise of my parents – I was in the University tennis team and several of us were invited, as per the custom then, to join the team operating the electric scoreboards on Centre Court and nearby No.1 Court. A tough job – and we were even required by the supervisors to work 'one hour on' and 'two hours off' such was the concentration involved in manually turning the right switch immediately after (not before) the umpire had announced the score! We worked with a fantastic courtside view, from what is now the TV commentary box, and we could watch the play afterwards.

1967 – it was a momentous year for Wimbledon, but it is strange how the memory works. I do not recall now that it was the first year of colour TV transmission. Indeed, I do not recall Britain's Roger Taylor beating South African Cliff Drysdale in that first televised match or his great run in reaching the semi-final. It would be the last year of 'amateur' tennis before the 'professionals' were permitted to play.

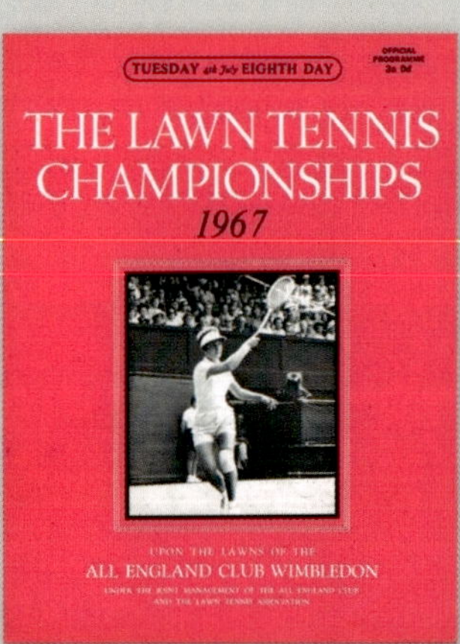

Matches and Wimbledon years pass by. Yet, indelibly in my memory is a match late on the first Saturday with the evening light casting a golden glow over the Centre Court. I was in the then standing area at the side of the court. I recall vividly the scene as a last-16 match took place between American Charlie Pasarell (who, in an earlier round, had defeated the previous year's winner, Manuel Santana) and Brazilian Thomas Koch. A close and captivating match entered a phase with both players 'in the zone' and barely missing a shot. Five sets with strong serves, every return seeming to be made, lobs and magnificent

Charlie Pasarell

passing shots – with the Brazilian clinching the match 6-4 in the final set.

Spellbinding. In the gently fading light, and in this magical arena, both players were seeing the ball 'like a football'. This for me was tennis and competition at its finest. I was fortunate to be there. It became a lasting memory.

Ian Hewitt is a former county tennis player and a respected researcher of sports history. His books include *Sporting Justice – 101 Sporting Encounters with the Law*, *Immortals of British Sport – A Celebration of Britain's Sporting History Through Sculpture* and the award-winning *Centre Court – The Jewel in Wimbledon's Crown*, the latter co-edited with John Barrett. Ian succeeded Philip Brook as Chairman of The All England Lawn Tennis and Croquet Club in December 2019.

Thomas Koch

1967

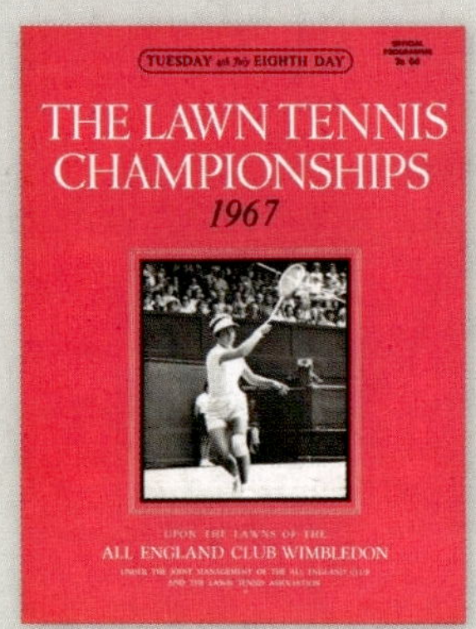

My First Visit to Wimbledon

Peter Gregory, NORTHWICK PARK

In the summer of 1967 I completed my GCE O levels and although, if you were staying on at school for the 6th Form, you were still meant to report in daily, in practice this was not enforced. As a result two school mates and I decided to pay a visit to Wimbledon. None of us had ever been there before as the tournament always clashed with school time and exams and TV viewing had to be confined to the evenings and the first and second Saturdays. The day we selected was Tuesday, 4 July which was ladies' quarter-finals day. That year turned out to be the last all amateur tournament and the first to be covered by colour TV on BBC 2, although the TV audience must have been quite small as at that time very few people had colour TV sets.

We met up at Northwick Park underground station and travelled to Southfields Station. On the way we speculated that we would probably have no chance of seeing any tennis on the Centre Court but that we should see some good quality doubles on the outside courts.

Upon arrival at Southfields we boarded one of the special buses to the AELTC grounds. We arrived at the grounds at about 1.30pm and entered them. I purchased a programme that I was surprised cost as much as 2s 6d (12.5p) as I was used to only paying 1s (5p) at Wembley Stadium when attending football matches there. More in hope than anticipation we followed the signs to the Centre Court standing area and were amazed that within ten minutes we were actually standing in the enclosure on the Centre Court just as the players were coming out for the first match.

My first impression on entering the Centre Court was how small the playing area was and the energy of the ball boys who continually scampered across the court to retrieve the loose ball after each point. One of the ball boys had very red hair and apparently, so a newspaper article revealed a couple of days later, was showing up well on the colour TV broadcasts. First on the Centre Court was the title holder Billie Jean King and Britain's number two Virginia Wade. As the match started the applause was very polite and subdued being just slightly louder when Wade won a point. The only comment I recall hearing shouted was a 'Well played Miss Wade' from a gentleman in the stands who sounded like a retired Colonel. Virginia put up a good show in the first set but the result was never in doubt as King triumphed 7-5, 6-2. Little did I dream that some ten years later I would be standing on the same court watching Virginia win the title.

Looking around the court during the interval between the first two matches I recall that much of the audience in the stands was quite well dressed and amongst the visitors in the Royal Box was Roy Jenkins (then Home Secretary

> **❝** *One of the ball boys had very red hair and was showing up well on the colour TV broadcasts.* **❞**

and soon-to-be Chancellor of the Exchequer) and TV entertainer Bernard Braden.

Next match on was between two unseeded players, the 18-year-old American, Rosie Casals, and Australia's Judy Tegart. Rosie was very much the 'new kid on the block' and had caused a sensation in the previous round on the middle Saturday when she knocked out the number two seed Maria Bueno. She was only 5' 2" in height and was a bundle of energy on court with a great array of shots and, from her performance that day, was to remain a firm favourite of mine for the rest of her career. She beat Tegart that day 7-5, 6-4 in a close match and most spectators thought that we were witnessing a future Wimbledon champion that day, her height drawing comparison with 'Little Mo'. Alas that was not to be, although she did win a number of grand slam doubles titles mostly in partnership with Billie Jean King.

Following the conclusion of this match many of the spectators in the Centre Court standing area left and we were able to actually sit down and rest our by now aching legs and witness the next match which was the continuation of a lengthy men's doubles between Leschly and Ulrich of Denmark and Krishnan and Mukerjea of India. In those days many of the sets in the men's doubles were very lengthy and this was no exception with the Indian pairing winning in five sets, two of which went to 11-9. I recall Jan Leschly sporting long hair and a headband which was most unusual for the male competitors at that time.

Next on Court was a men's doubles quarter-final between a young British pair, Peter Curtis and Graham Stilwell, versus Australia's John Newcombe and Tony Roche, the number one seeds. The standing area started to fill up again as the 'evening crowd' started to arrive and we had to stand again. In those days it was common for spectators to come straight from work and head towards the Centre Court. Newcombe and Roche won the first set and we thought 'this is going to be over in straight sets, let's rest our aching legs and watch

Tony Roche won five Wimbledon doubles titles in partnership with John Newcombe between 1965 and 1974

some tennis on the outside courts' where we could sit.

We had a brief walk round the grounds and I bought the obligatory Bath bun. There was a refreshment area in front of the old No.1 Court and one sign rather amused me, it was advertising the sale of 'Wimpys' but they clearly suspected that much of Wimbledon's clientele would have no idea what these were, as in brackets underneath was the explanation 'A hamburger in a bun with onions'. I recall that in one

of the following years the AELTC banned the onions following complaints of the smell!

Having secured some seats on one of the outside courts we heard increasing roars from the Centre Court as the British pair were making a comeback taking the next two sets. We decided to return to that court but on arrival found massive queues since everyone was now sensing a possible upset. How we regretted that decision to leave the court, as we could now not get back and eventually, after we had left the grounds, the British pair triumphed 8-6 in the final set.

As indicated above we were feeling really tired and at about 7pm decided to leave the grounds and go home. It was a thoroughly enjoyable day and for me became a journey I would continue to make annually up to the present time, having not missed a Wimbledon since. It is a great shame that there is no longer a standing area on the Centre Court as it gave many youngsters the chance to take in the unique atmosphere that used to exist on the Court. I find the present arena, although much improved in many ways, sterile in comparison to those days.

On the way home I read the programme and noticed an advert stating that the 'Wimbledon World Professional Lawn Tennis Championship' was to be held on the Centre Court in August; little did we realise that the professionals would also be attending the following year's Wimbledon to play in the main championship.

Peter Gregory's account of his first day at Wimbledon captures many recurring themes of the 1950s, 60s and 70s, including 'bunking off' school, happy hours in the Free Standing area and the consumption of the 'obligatory' Bath Bun.

1968

Lew Hoad – My Hero

Tim Andrews, BRIGHTON

I**t is 1961. I am standing on a chair stretching up to get my clockwork train set down from the top of my mother's wardrobe. I am taller than the last time I was here and so this time I notice an old newspaper up there amongst the bright red boxes containing the trains, carriages, etc. I bring it down, blow the dust off it and see that it is dated 5th July 1957. I begin to read the report of a man called Lew Hoad who had beaten Ashley Cooper in 55 minutes in the men's singles final at Wimbledon. I am fascinated. Hoad looks incredibly dashing in the photograph which accompanies the report, with his blond hair and superb figure. I loved History at school and this, combined with a growing enthusiasm for sport, draws me into the rapturous description of Hoad's demolition of his fellow countryman that day.**

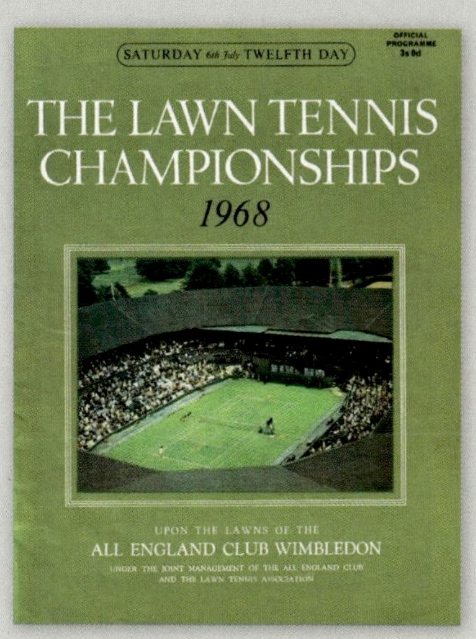

I had never been to Wimbledon or indeed any other major sporting event. My father had died when I was two, leaving my mother with five children under the age of eight to bring up on a widow's pension. She had neither the time or the money to take me to these events and so I grew up not really connecting what I saw on the TV with the possibility that I could go to the real thing. I was an avid Spurs supporter but never thought I could go to an actual match until one Saturday in 1966, a friend of my mother's took me to White Hart Lane.

My sister Sally was responsible for a similar breakthrough as far as tennis was concerned. In 1968, she went on a school outing to Wimbledon and came back full of it. I recall her telling me excitedly that Ann Jones had walked past her. Suddenly, it occurred to me that I could do the same. Sally and I bunked off school and made our way to SW19.

We arrived at the entrance in Somerset Road and I was utterly enthralled by the majesty of the buildings painted dark green, clad in the purple green of the ivy and the lush green of the grass courts – it was in colour! We wandered around the outside courts and watched players whose names I had read in newspaper reports and heard mentioned on TV but now they were real people within touching distance – Drysdale, Tiriac, Roche, Laver, Jones, Wade, Buchholz, Okker, Curtis, Stilwell, Cliff and Nancy Richey, Fletcher, Emerson and Newcombe. I was hooked.

My sister and I somehow managed to wangle our way out of school for a second time in the following week and wandered around the outside courts but then I saw that on the Centre Court, Lew Hoad was playing in the men's doubles partnered by Owen Davidson. We made our way to the Free Standing behind the Umpire's chair and there he was, not quite as athletic as he had appeared in the photographs on the back page of the *Daily Express* of 5th July 1957 nor quite as dominant in his play. Every so often he would curse over a misplaced volley or the failure to reach a drop shot expertly chipped over the net by Santana or Fletcher, his opponents that day. The sun appeared from behind a cloud and

> **"***We arrived at the entrance in Somerset Road and I was utterly enthralled by the majesty of the buildings painted dark green, clad in the purple green of the ivy and the lush green of the grass courts – it was in colour!***"**

threw a glow onto the crisp white of the players' shirts and shorts whilst, at the same time, casting a shadow over one corner of the court. I stood there and allowed my eyes to drift around the court from the Royal Box along the criss-cross patterns in the concrete above the standing area to the scoreboard and then back to the increasingly irascible figure of Hoad who trudged off at the end, with his partner, Owen Davidson, beaten in straight sets and looking bowed and bitter at his failure to reach the heights to which he had ascended

Owen Davidson

Lew Hoad in action during the Wimbledon Championships, London, July 1968

a decade earlier. What he did not know was that there was a 17-year-old boy watching his hero from the stands who was sufficiently captivated by what he had just seen to ensure that he would return every year thereafter for the next 48 years.

In particular, I have wonderful memories of the personalities of the players, their strengths and their weaknesses. The beautiful backhand topspin drive of Laver and the smack of admonishment on his thigh after a rare error, the curving serve of McEnroe always on a short fuse, the thudding volleys of Roche and his sharp words to Connors at the net which immediately halted any further play-acting on the latter's part, the unerring accuracy of Rosewall's passing shots and his drooping shoulders during his demolition in the 1974 final, the athleticism of Sampras and his collegiate good manners, Connors scraping his toes on the grass, Gonzales lifting his sweat-soaked shirt off his shoulder, Margaret Court, tall and feminine wiping the palm of her hand on her skirt, Billie Jean bullying and competitive, Evert serene and unhurried, Navratilova the champion, the dainty Evonne Goolagong and Ann Jones, British, buxom and at last a winner, and now a frequent presence in the Royal Box.

It is also about friendships made in the queue and fostered. Harry, Richard, Bob, Joan, Irene, Karl, Gill, Christine, Neal, John, Jeannie and Penny and love, laughter and silliness. All this is Wimbledon.

Ninety sixty-eight – the year I first saw Lew Hoad play, the year I fell in love with Wimbledon.

1968

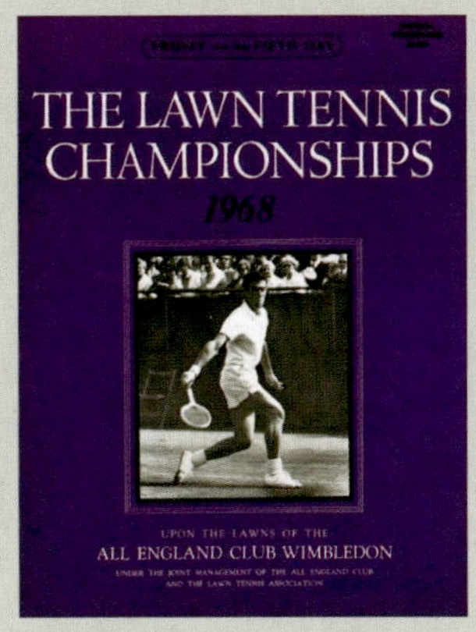

Superman's New Weapon

Colin Triplow, NEW ASH GREEN

It seemed too good an opportunity to miss. A school trip giving an afternoon out of school watching tennis, a game I had just started playing, at Wimbledon. Wherever that was. Whilst I didn't know exactly where Wimbledon was, I did know that, in tennis terms, it was right at the top – the most important tournament in the world – so this trip was a big deal.

Imagine my disappointment, therefore, when I learnt that the date of the school trip, 29 June 1968, was a Saturday rather than a weekday, so no time out of class. Never mind, I was just beginning to get into tennis, and this would be an opportunity to see the best players in the world in action, up close and personal, and in colour rather than on our black and white TV. We'd have seats on Court No.2, which, I was told, was one of the best courts there.

Up until February that year my main sport had been athletics. I'd done pretty well at it too, winning the Under-14s' high jump at the London Schools Championships the previous year. Then, on 29 February 1968, disaster struck. Warming up for a cross-country run I broke my leg – badly. I had Osgood-Schlatter Disease, apparently. In fact, I had the most

extreme case the doctors who treated me had ever seen. An almost non-stop train of student doctors came trooping in to see me during my stay in hospital. I became a bit of a novelty, but at least I didn't get too bored.

When I came out of plaster it was time for physiotherapy. The physiotherapist asked me if I played squash. I'd never seen a squash court, let alone played the game. Badminton? No, didn't even own a racket. Tennis? Well, yes, sort of. I'd played a little bit with a few mates down the park. 'Okay,' said the physio, 'play a lot more.' An hour of tennis was equivalent to a six-mile run in terms of therapeutic benefit because of the changes in direction and flexing of the knee, he said. So, tennis became my new sport. I dragged anyone I could out onto court. School friends, my sister, even a guy who lived in the same

street who I'd seen down the park playing with his kids. The more I played, the more I enjoyed it.

Ninety sixty-eight was the big one in tennis. It was the first year of Open Tennis, with professionals returning to compete against amateurs in the world's biggest tournaments. The French Championships at Roland Garros in May had been the first 'open' Grand Slam tournament, but some of the top players, amateurs and professionals, had skipped the event. No one was skipping Wimbledon, they were all going to be there. This was crunch time – reputations were on the line in the first full-on showdown between the amateurs and pros.

As it was the first open Wimbledon there was a lot of talk about it and great coverage on the TV. Although I can't say I was avidly following the event, I had a pretty good idea of what was going on. One thing I wasn't aware of, however, was that because of the amount of rain there'd been in the first week the start of play on the Saturday we were going had been brought forward to 1pm instead of 2pm. The coach taking us had been booked on the assumption of a 2pm start, and it wasn't until we were on our way that I learnt of the earlier start, and that we'd probably miss a chunk of play because of it.

We didn't actually get into the ground until after 2pm, and by the time we'd been marched past the mightily impressive frontage of Centre Court (which I immediately

> **❝** *There seemed to be something different about Graebner's rackets lying on the grass. Maybe it was the white headcovers with red trim, but I couldn't really put my finger on it. Then he removed the headcover from the racket he was going to play with, and it was like the Sword being drawn from the Stone.* **❞**

Mark Cox in play against Thomaz Koch of Brazil on No. 1 Court at Wimbledon, during the Davis Cup inter-zone semi-final, 31 July 1969

wanted to see), to Court No.2 and briefed on how to behave – don't shout out, don't clap double faults, applaud politely, and, most importantly, don't disgrace the school – and then told when and where to meet up, we'd missed the first match completely. The second match between Mark Cox and Daniel Contet of France was already underway. What immediately struck me was how green and white things were – green courts, green court covers (thankfully not in use), green umpire's chair, green scoreboards, green sight screens at the back of the court – contrasting with bright white lines on the court, white tennis balls, and the pure whiteness of the players' clothes and shoes. Cox's shirt had a tiny bit of coloured trim around the collar and sleeves, Contet's was pure white.

Having heard a lot of 'Quiet please' from the umpires on TV I was surprised how noisy things were on Court 2, and amazed to see that there was a public walkway from the concourse outside Court 1 through to the outside courts running along each side of the Court. There was a constant stream of people wandering up and down these paths, stopping to watch a bit of play, then continuing on their way, all the time talking, and generally making a bit of a racket (pardon the pun).

Cox versus Contet was an eye-opener. I didn't realise just how hard the guys hit the ball, and Cox's swinging left-hand serve and heavily sliced backhand that seemed to lay down on the grass were very impressive. Contet had a two-handed backhand – very unusual in those days, a short, compact, awkward-looking shot. Every now and then we'd hear a loud cheer from behind us, and we were told that it was the noise from Centre Court after a particularly good rally or shot. The more I heard cheering the more I wanted to be in there, and by the time Cox had finished off Contet in straight sets I'd made the decision to try and get onto Centre Court. Centre Court was what I'd seen on TV, and whilst I had nothing against Court 2, I wanted to see for myself what all the fuss was about.

With my friend Pete in tow, I left Court 2 and made my way to Centre Court in the hope of perhaps catching a glimpse of play. Just as we arrived, there was thunderous applause, the umpire called 'Game, set and match to Ralston', and hundreds of people started piling out of the court. Some well-dressed young men near us were asking those leaving if they'd finished with their tickets, so I did the same. Most gave me a stern look with a 'Well, of all the nerve!' expression, whilst others looked at me with an expression of total bemusement, as if I was speaking in a foreign language. However, one rather elderly moustachioed gentleman in a very smart white-trimmed blue blazer stopped, turned to his wife and asked if she'd seen enough for the day, then with just a hint of a smile, handed me their tickets and said, 'Enjoy the rest of play.'

What a result! Laughing, then shouting thank you loudly, we dashed off to find our seats, only to find we were going completely the wrong way and we had to ask a steward for directions. When we eventually found our seats I was totally blown away. No public walkways here, but an arena purpose-built to showcase tennis. Still very green and white though. We were directly behind the umpire, and three or four rows in front of the old free standing area. Looking around we certainly had a better view than a number of people, some of whom were sitting behind the substantial metal pillars which, at that time, held up the Centre Court roof. Everyone was extremely well dressed. Collar and tie was the order of the day for the men, and smart Sunday best dresses for the ladies.

A murmur in the crowd was followed by polite applause as the players for the next match walked on from the end of the court to our right. A tanned man with a slightly toothy grin, and a much taller man with a crew cut and horned-rim glasses who bore a striking resemblance to Clark Kent before he turned into Superman, made their way to the umpire's chair. Both carried three or four rackets under their arms. I glanced at the scoreboard to see who they were. Nameplates with 'M Santana' and 'C E Graebner' had been slotted into place. Not really being sure who was who I turned to the gentleman

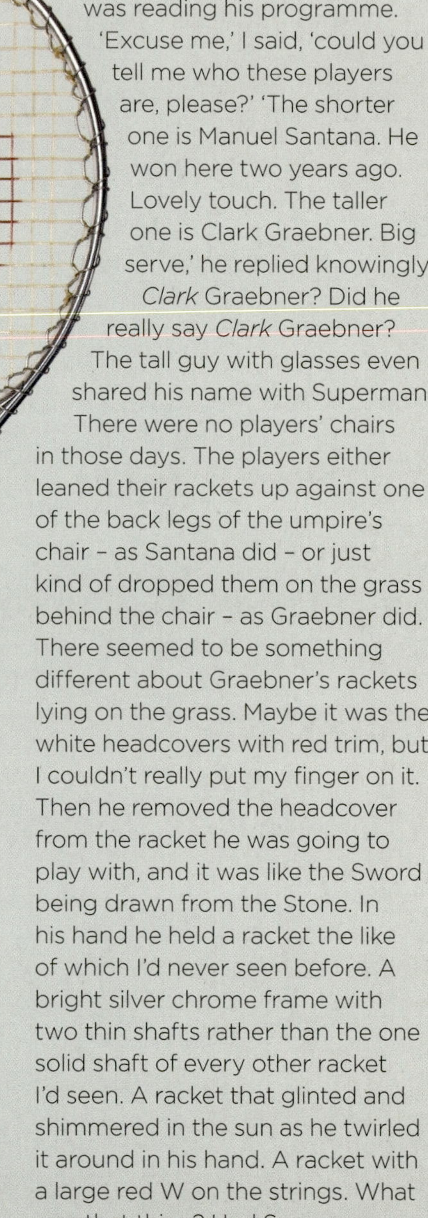

The Wilson T2000 steel racket, first manufactured in 1967 and based on a design by Rene Lacoste

seated on my left-hand side who was reading his programme. 'Excuse me,' I said, 'could you tell me who these players are, please?' 'The shorter one is Manuel Santana. He won here two years ago. Lovely touch. The taller one is Clark Graebner. Big serve,' he replied knowingly.

Clark Graebner? Did he really say *Clark* Graebner? The tall guy with glasses even shared his name with Superman!

There were no players' chairs in those days. The players either leaned their rackets up against one of the back legs of the umpire's chair – as Santana did – or just kind of dropped them on the grass behind the chair – as Graebner did. There seemed to be something different about Graebner's rackets lying on the grass. Maybe it was the white headcovers with red trim, but I couldn't really put my finger on it. Then he removed the headcover from the racket he was going to play with, and it was like the Sword being drawn from the Stone. In his hand he held a racket the like of which I'd never seen before. A bright silver chrome frame with two thin shafts rather than the one solid shaft of every other racket I'd seen. A racket that glinted and shimmered in the sun as he twirled it around in his hand. A racket with a large red W on the strings. What was that thing? Had Superman brought a new weapon down with him from Planet Krypton? I took a look at Santana's racket. A bland, plain lump of wood in comparison. How could he hope to compete with that?

As the players warmed up I was mesmerised by Graebner's racket, by the way the frame sparkled as light reflected off it, by the sound it made as it whistled through the air, and the solid thud as he hit the ball. From the headcovers of his other rackets I saw that it was made by Wilson, hence the W on the strings, and I could see there was something else written at the throat of the cover. I *had* to find out what it said, and clambered over the seats in front of me and down to the front. I could see 'T2000' clearly. So that must be what it's called, I reasoned – the Wilson T2000.

As play got underway the difference in the two competitors' playing styles was marked. Santana did, indeed, have lovely touch, whilst Graebner seemed to be armed with a cannon. When Santana served there was a sound like a champagne cork popping. When Graebner served it sounded like gunfire. Mark Cox had been impressive, but this was a serve of ballistic proportions, and he seemed to be serving aces at will. How could Santana even see the ball coming? He was making no impression on Graebner's service games, but was managing to hang on to his own to stay on level terms. When the score reached 5-5 the guy on my left said, 'Santana will get a bead on that serve soon, and when he does the American won't have anything to fall back on.' Maybe he was right; after all, Santana was a previous champion, but from where I was sitting it looked like he was struggling just to stay in the game – and he didn't have that shiny steel 21st-century-looking racket his opponent had.

Every time Santana seemed to be making inroads in a Graebner service game, Graebner would wield the wand of steel and bang down an ace. It was obviously all down to that racket.

Games were much quicker in those days. Serve and volley was the dominant style of play, and whilst Santana was more than happy at the baseline he still came to the net whenever he could. The change of ends was a shorter affair too. No chairs to sit on, just a quick towel down, a swift slurp of water or squash, and back onto court. The only delays in the action came when the ball boys dashed to a large rectangular box at the side of the court to bring out a new set of balls. My colleague on my left informed me that the box was actually a refrigerator that kept the balls at the optimum temperature for tennis. They certainly took their tennis seriously at Wimbledon!

A couple sitting a few rows in front of me were clearly great Santana fans. They cheered heartily (or at least, as heartily as spectators did at that time), whenever their man played a particularly good point, and groaned audibly when Graebner served an ace or crunched a massive forehand for a winner. When Santana dropped serve at 7-7 and Graebner powered through another service game to take the set 9-7 they began to get restless.

They became more and more agitated as Graebner, buoyed by his one set lead and looking more relaxed, began to motor away from Santana in the second set. What really seemed to be winding them up, however, was what Graebner did at the end of his service games. Back then a double-handed

Manuel Santana

backhand was a rarity, and most players held two balls in their hand when serving, and played the point out holding the second ball if it wasn't needed. Graebner, however, put the second ball in the pocket of his shorts. At the end of the game, regardless of where he was on the court, he would take the spare ball out of his pocket and let it fall to the ground for the ball boys to come and pick up. This was all too much for the Santana fans, who called his behaviour 'disgraceful', 'ungentlemanly', and 'uncouth' amongst other things. It may have been any, or all, of these, but it didn't stop him breezing through the second set 6-2, as he began to batter Santana's much weaker delivery with a forehand almost as

intimidating as his serve. Anything in the air – forget it. The shiny silver blade in his hand whooshed down like an executioner's axe and ended the point dismissively.

I couldn't believe the power of Graebner's game. He ripped through the third set 6-1 as a dispirited Santana, smiling bravely but shaking his head as ball after ball flew past him, faded away. The guy on my left and the couple in front had departed before the end, perhaps not wanting to see a former champion go out in this way. I couldn't see how anyone could possibly beat Graebner, and felt sure I'd just seen that year's men's singles winner.

My friend Pete pointed out that time was now getting a bit short, and, although there was a doubles match scheduled for Centre, I decided to have a wander around the grounds before heading to our meeting point. So far my experience of Wimbledon had

been limited to the march from the gates to Court No.2, and then the short walk from No.2 to Centre. I wanted to see what else there was. What made Wimbledon *Wimbledon*, if you like.

TV coverage only showed matches on Centre and Court No.1, so I had the idea that every court at Wimbledon was surrounded by large grandstands full of people. So it was a bit of a surprise to find that seating around most of the outside courts mainly consisted of just a few park benches, whose occupiers jealously guarded their territory, and that the vast majority of spectators stood behind a low green canvas barrier that ran the length of each side of the court. There were occasional polite shouts of 'Can you move back a bit, please? You're blocking my view' from people on the park benches, as those standing leaned a little too far over the barrier in search of a better view. These courts seemed

a world away from the majesty and prestige of Centre Court. There were also three courts joined together side by side, with the canvas barrier along the side of the two outer courts of the three. These reminded me a bit of my local park courts, and seemed even more removed from the grandeur I'd been experiencing less than half an hour ago. Was this really the same tournament?

There were doubles matches going on all over the place on these outside courts, and I moved from court to court, catching a bit of the action from each match as I went. The teamwork and interaction between partners was fascinating to watch, and the whole game was so different from the doubles me and my mates played down the park you'd have thought we were playing to a different set of rules. The umpires on these outside courts didn't have microphones to amplify their voices so they had to shout the score out after each point – which some did louder than others – and there wasn't a full complement of linesmen on all the courts, so the umpire called the unmanned lines as well.

A match on one of the courts in the distance caught my eye, or rather, the racket being used by one of the players on that court caught my eye. With the sun beginning to lower in the sky, I could see light being reflected off what looked like the same racket Clark Graebner had been using. I made a beeline for that court, and, sure enough, there was another T2000 in action. This one was being used by a girl whose name I've long since forgotten, but she and her partner were winning their match quite comfortably. I

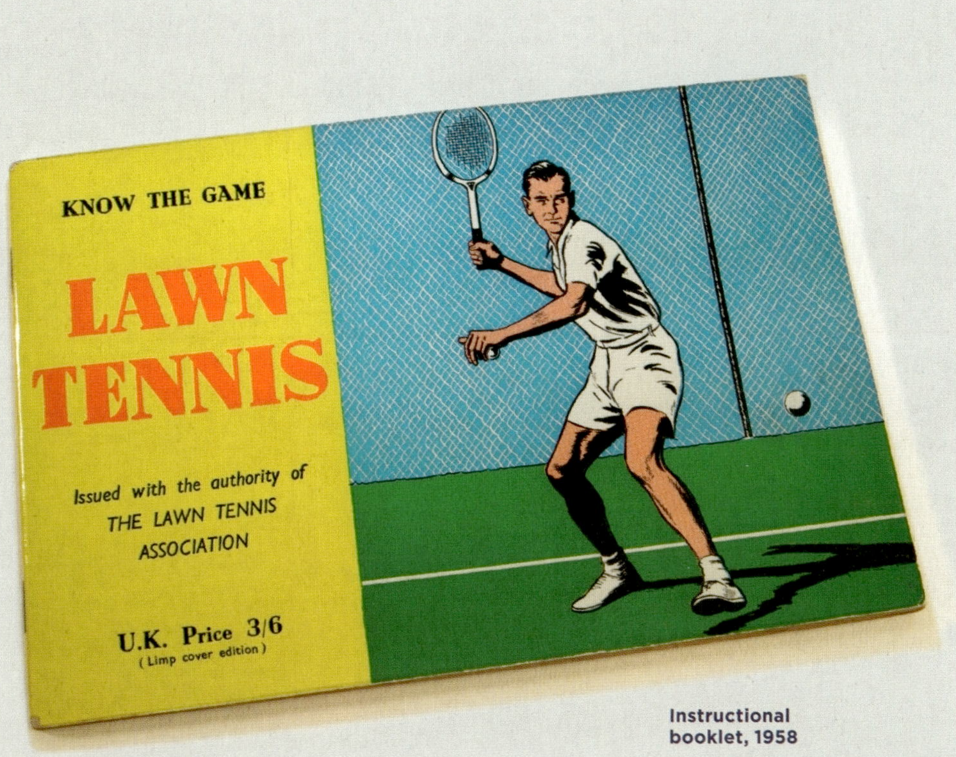

Instructional booklet, 1958

put it down to the racket. Get one of those in your hand and you became invincible.

By now time was getting very tight, so it was time to make my way back to the designated meeting point. I didn't want to go. This game had got me well and truly hooked. I found everything about it – the power of the men, the grace of the ladies, the almost gladiatorial one-on-one of the singles, the camaraderie of the doubles – alluring and appealing. It was something I wanted to be part of. And Wimbledon itself was clearly the place to aspire to. No imposters here, just the best in the world.

I was the last to arrive at the meeting point, and it was pointed out to me by the master in charge that I was two minutes late! Oh well, at least I hadn't disgraced the school, unless asking those leaving Centre Court if they had finished with their tickets fell under the 'disgracing' banner, in which case the disgrace had been worth it anyway.

On the journey back there was lots of excited talk about who had done what, and who had seen who. Pete and I were the only ones who'd gatecrashed Centre Court, but a couple of the other lads had managed to get onto Court No.1, and seen one of the top three seeds in the Men's Singles, Andres Gimeno of Spain, go out to a 'long-haired hippy with a headband', as one of them described him, called Ray Moore. They said that Moore had played with a shiny metal racket with a red W on the strings that whistled through the air as he swung it. Did anyone with one of those rackets ever lose?

I settled back to reflect on what had been a wonderful day and to plan my assault on Wimbledon and the sport that I could feel was about to become an obsession. Two things were immediately abundantly clear. Firstly, I wanted to get back to Wimbledon as soon as I possibly could. The second, more important, thing was that the way to world domination in tennis was clearly by using a Wilson T2000. There was just one question – how could I get hold of one???

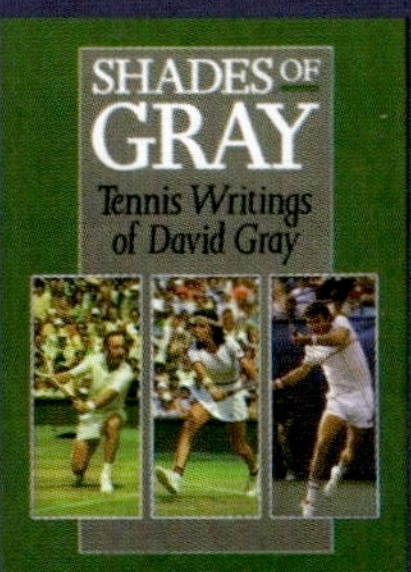

1968

Wimbledon '68

Ray Moore, PALM DESERT, CALIFORNIA

South Africa's Ray Moore was an unexpected star of the first Open Wimbledon in 1968, knocking out third-seeded Andres Gimeno of Spain en route to the quarter-finals.

Gimeno was one of the top players returning to Wimbledon after a period of self-imposed exile in the pro ranks, but it was not Moore's victory but his appearance that caught the attention of the media. His frizzy but well-groomed blond hair was way beyond shoulder length, and was held in place by the kind of headband that a decade later would become Bjorn Borg's trademark. Moore's victory over Gimeno came on Wimbledon's middle Saturday, and the Sunday morning papers quickly dubbed him 'the hippie tennis player'. Moore wasn't a hippie, of course, but why let the facts get in the way of a good headline?

'It was a great time, the start of Open Tennis,' Ray recalls. 'I had been an amateur, and he was a pro, so we'd never met before. You just go on court and adapt. He had a chip backhand, and I liked playing against players like that. I didn't like the guys who hit out on their backhand, but Gimeno's style suited me.'

Moore smiles when reminded that his win got him top billing on BBC television news: 'We played for two reasons, firstly to win and also for recognition. That victory changed my career.' He followed up his defeat of Gimeno with a fourth-round win against America's Tom Edlefsen. That put him through to a quarter-final against another American, big-serving Clark Graebner. 'I was intimidated against Graebner,' he remembers. 'We didn't have coaches and advisors like today's players, if I had maybe I'd have done a little better.'

When he retired from the tour, Ray Moore went into partnership with Puerto Rican friend and fellow former player Charlie Pasarell.

Together they began working to develop tennis in the Coachella Valley, the desert region a couple of hours' drive from LA that was the playground of Hollywood's rich and famous. They turned round the struggling La Quinta tournament to the point where a new, larger venue was required, and as a result the Indian Wells Tennis Garden was opened in 2000.

Ray Moore in action at Wimbledon, 1971

1968

My First Wimbledon

Peter Woodman, HATCH END

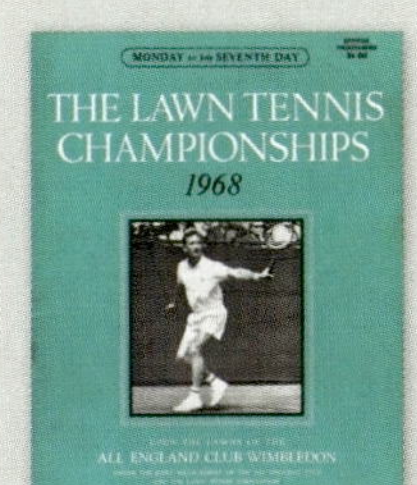

t was 1968 and it was the first Open Wimbledon. I was nearly 18 years old and at a boarding school in Sussex. There was great excitement as a bunch of us were being taken to Wimbledon. It was the first week and we had Number One Court tickets.

To my horror, we awoke that morning to pouring rain. To show how bad it was, not a ball was bowled in any of eight County Championship cricket matches that day.

We set off for SW19 more in hope than in expectation. We arrived to a gloomy sight – the rain still falling and the covers on. But by mid-afternoon it brightened. The covers came off, out came the players and we were away.

On No.1 Court I saw Pancho Gonzales against Alex Metreveli. Pancho was past his best then, but still won in four. There were few crowds then and you could just walk into Centre Court and stand. So after the Pancho match I strolled in to see Rod Laver take on Marty Riessen. I was amazed at how small the Centre Court was. TV made it look enormous. Rod was far too good for Riessen (the Australian would go on to be champion that year and in 1969) and after I stayed on to watch Bob Hewitt beat Lew Hoad.

It was great just dipping in to matches on the outside courts, too. I've been to Wimbledon most years since that far-off June day, but there's nothing like the first time.

In the 1960s the BBC broadcasts from Wimbledon involved just a small number of fixed camera positions behind the baselines on Centre and No.1 Courts. There was no coverage of the outside courts, and many first-time visitors to The Championships were surprised by the speed of the ball, the intimate atmosphere of the Centre Court and the number of matches being played simultaneously on the outside courts during the day.

1969

Memories of Playing at Wimbledon

Marian Boundy, FINCHLEY

first competed at Wimbledon in 1953 when I was 17, when I was studying to go to university, and emigrated to Canada the year after I graduated. I returned to England in 1964 but for a few years played little or no tennis.

At the ripe old age of 33 I decided I would love to compete at Wimbledon again, had half a crown's worth of coaching from Frank Wilde at The All England Club, and was accepted for Qualifying, where I beat Dorothy Head Knode in the first round and managed to win the next two rounds. I had just joined a company in May and had assured my boss that I would not want to take lots of days off work to play tennis, but ended up having to ask for four days. Tennis had gone professional the year before, and I was rewarded with £50 for my participation in the first round.

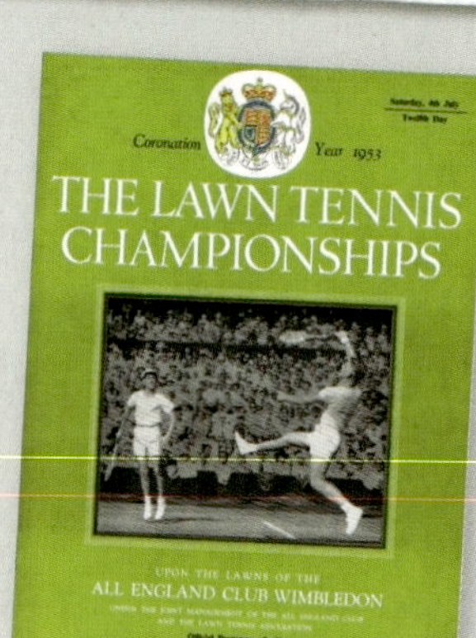

1953 I lost my first match in the Ladies' Singles but the experience of playing in The Championships was quite overwhelming in other ways too. British competitors were given free tea, and a free lunch if their match was scheduled first in the afternoon.

I still remember the anchovy and egg bridge rolls provided at tea-time. Above all I had the chance to see the greatest tennis players in the world battling against each other. Maureen Connolly was magnificently accurate with her groundstrokes, but it was the match between Jaroslav Drobny and Budge Patty that has remained vivid in my memory. It was almost dark when it ended and hardly anyone could tear themselves away from their seat on Centre Court. The then Duchess of Kent gave the players a personal memento of the match.

1954 On Court 6 I lost in two sets to the Swiss No.1, Ruth Kaufmann. There had been no chance to practise on grass beforehand, and I found the Wimbledon grass unbelievably fast.

My partner in the mixed doubles, Peter Moys, and I won a round and were then put on Court One (the old one, of course) where we won the next round and were

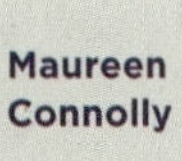

Maureen Connolly

Marian Boundy is now known by her married name of Marian Werner.

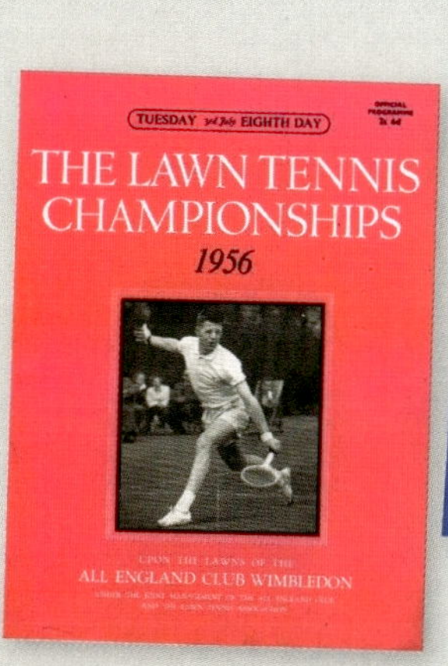

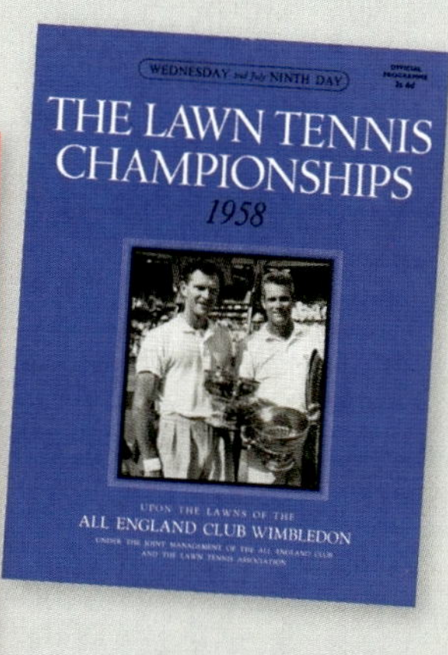

1969

The Queue

If you queued for Wimbledon in 1969, you had the choice of lining up in Church Road or Somerset Road. Both queues had the same number of tickets each day, usually around 250 for the Centre Court and 500 for No.1 Court.

scheduled to play there again that afternoon. I remember that I had miscalculated the time the intervening match would take and that Lorna Cornell helped me to dress hurriedly as the packed crowd were beginning to handclap. The reason for the full attendance was that our opponents in the last 16 were Mrs. Margaret du Pont and Ken Rosewall. I managed to ace her with a second serve as she had never seen me play before and did not know that my second serve was a shaky dolly-drop and she could not reach it. At one point I passed Rosewall down the line. Such small incidents remain in the mind of lesser players. I still remember that year's final between Drobny and Ken Rosewall, tense to the last shot. Most of the crowd wanted Drobny to win, not because they did not like Rosewall, but because he was much younger and would have other chances. Would we have been less enthusiastic, had we known that Rosewall would never win the title?

1955 I win my first round, then lose to the Belgian No.1, after being 6-0, 5-2 up. Friends who were watching went away at that point, and were amazed to see in the next day's paper that I had actually lost.

In the Members' seats Danny Kaye comes and sits beside me. I exclaim 'hard cheese' at one point, to which he says, 'Don't you mean tough cheddar?' That was another wonderful feature of Wimbledon, meeting celebrities one had only ever seen in films or the theatre.

1956 I am very short of match practice, during my university years at Bristol, and am petrified on the second day when the Referee, Col. Legg, insists on putting my match against the Spanish Maria-Josefa de Riba on Centre Court.

Our name boards had been put up when the Colonel changed his mind because the light on the court had become too bad. By that time I had gone to a jelly and lost in two sets on Court 5. But I have never been so grateful for the shadows that spread across the Centre Court! I did not play in 1957, the year I graduated.

1958 I won a round in the ladies' doubles with Pat Wheeler (Roberts) and a round of the mixed doubles with Geoff Ward. That September, I emigrated to Canada.

1969 I return – as a professional!

At 7am one of Wimbledon's Honorary Stewards came along the pavement issuing queue tickets, entitling the holders to go away for three hours or so to freshen up. For those who lived within reasonable travelling distance, this was enough time to take the bus or train home, have breakfast and a bath, and then get back to the queue by 10.30am. The queue then moved in three stages. First, at 11am, they opened the outer gate so that the people at the front could go inside to the first window where court tokens were issued and money could be changed. The token entitled the holder to purchase a ticket at the second window, which was at the end of a covered queue lane about a hundred yards further on. Payment was in cash only, and you had to have exactly the right amount of money at the ticket window.

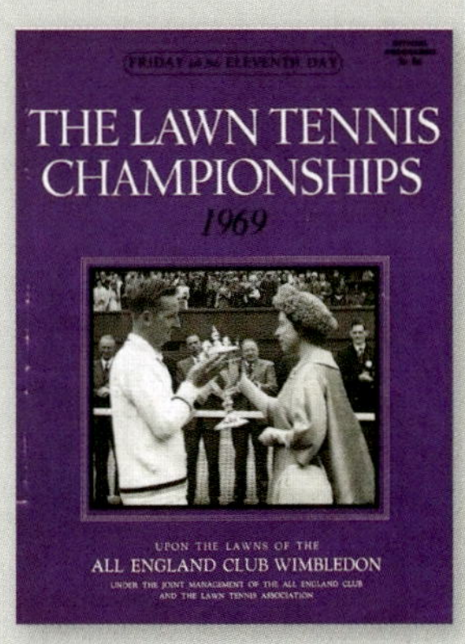

1969

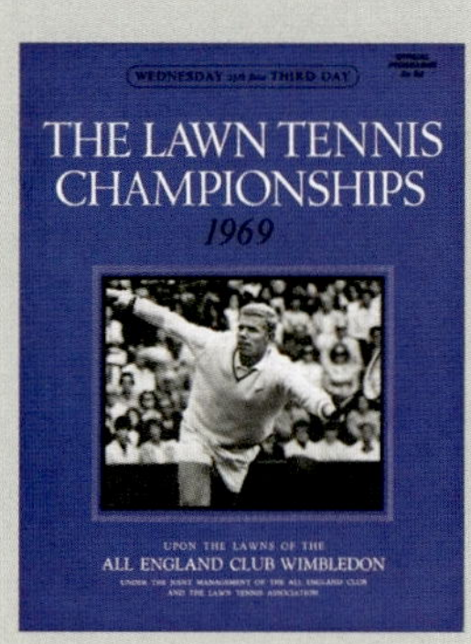

My Love for this Place

Geoff Masters, QUEENSLAND

As a child, some of my earliest tennis memories were of listening on the radio to various Davis Cup Challenge Round finals involving some of the greats of our sport, especially of course our Australian players.

After those initial interests, I started following these players' progress throughout the year, especially when Wimbledon time came around. Listening to the like of Rod Laver playing and winning at Wimbledon way back in 1962, when I was 12 years old, was especially pleasing given he was a Queenslander like me!

As my own junior successes evolved in Australia, by the time I was 16 I had decided that I too would like to pursue tennis as a career, so in 1969, aged 18, I set off to try my luck.

After initial stints playing events in small English tournaments such as Sutton and Guildford, where I had some success, I was hopeful of maybe getting accepted into Wimbledon. Not to be however, and instead was banished to the qualifying tournament at Roehampton, where I lost in the last round. I did however make it into the mixed doubles main draw, and remember coming into the grounds for the first time, and feeling almost overawed. I have a fabulous memory of watching Pancho Gonzales play Charlie Pasarell to a standstill on Centre Court though, and desperately hoped to be able to get onto Centre Court myself one day. I also had the great fortune of watching many of Rod Laver's matches, and escapes, while winning the third leg of what was to be his second Grand Slam.

By 1973 I was a regular main draw player, and one of my greatest disappointments was to make arrangements to have my dad come to London to watch me play at Wimbledon, only to have all of us in the ATP boycott the tournament, so he never did see me play there!!

By 1975 I was a capable singles player on the world stage, but better in the doubles format. In singles I had defeated 1973 winner Jan Kodes on Court 3, and another year lost to Bjorn Borg in the last 16 while Bjorn was on his five-year undefeated reign.

My first venture onto Centre Court came in 1976, when my partner Ross Case and I were making a name for ourselves, and played the previous year's doubles winners Vitas Gerulaitis and Sandy Mayer in the quarter-finals. We had a win, and subsequently played Stan Smith and Bob Lutz on Centre Court, as well as the final against Raul Ramirez and Brian Gottfried, which we lost in five sets.

We came back in 1977 to take the title over fellow Aussies Phil Dent and John Alexander, again on the hallowed Centre Court.

I have been fortunate to return to Wimbledon so many times since my retirement from full-time tennis in 1980. Initially as an invitee in the over 35s Invitational Doubles, then as an invitee in the over 45s Invitational Doubles. These days I return as a commentator for Channel 7 Australia, and never tire of this mystical place. Like so many before, my love for this place remains undiminished.

Australia's Geoff Masters in action at Wimbledon in the 1970s

The 1950s, 60s and 70s were a golden era for Australian men's doubles teams at Wimbledon, but none was more popular than Queenslanders Ross Case and Geoff Masters. Their silky skills and seamless teamwork led them to victories over many seemingly more powerful opponents and made them great favourites with the Centre Court crowd.

1970

In the Summertime

John Inverdale, KINGSTON UPON THAMES

How much of the following is fact and how much fiction is lost in the mists of time. How to remember so long ago?

It was 1970. If you're that kind of person, you remember it by music. 'In the Summertime' by Mungo Jerry. Everywhere.

The minibus definitely left from my school in Hampshire early in the morning, and we probably/surely had a packed lunch. Almost certainly egg sandwiches. Every time I see an egg sandwich I think of school. And an orange. Satsumas hadn't been invented then. Somehow you had to peel the orange without splattering juice all over your uniform. Impossible.

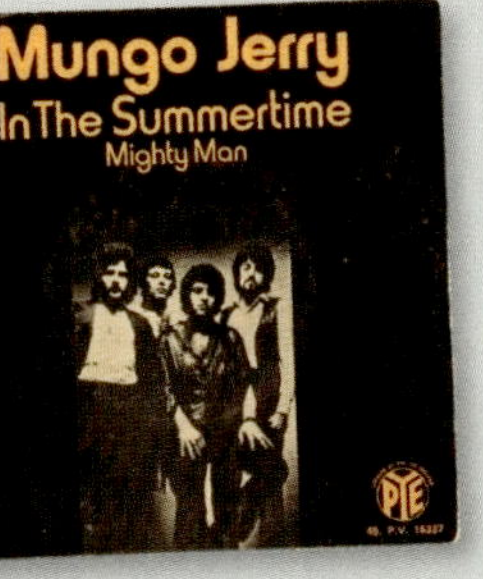

Car Park 4 where all the buses park these days didn't exist then. Where did we park? What did we see? Who did we see? Now that's the easy bit. We saw Helen Gourlay, an Australian tennis player. And I remember that because I had an autograph book and she signed her name on the same page as Colin Cowdrey, for reasons that I can't recall but she did. And after that wandered around the outside courts, had an ice cream or two, irritated our teacher no end by disappearing off in twos and threes, and I surely went off in pursuit of a sighting of John Newcombe and Ilie Nastase – my two heroes of the time.

It's hard to know though. Did anyone get lost? Did the bus go back with less children on board than arrived? Presumably our teacher counted us out and counted us all back again. I've got a feeling his name was Mr Egan but it might not have been.

No phones. No iPods. No radios. If you wanted music for the journey home, you stored it in your head.

Ch.ch.ch..ch.ch .ah...

In the summertime, when the weather is hot ....

> **"**No phones. No iPods. No radios. If you wanted music for the journey home, you stored it in your head. Ch.ch.ch..ch.ch .ah... In the summertime, when the weather is hot ...**"**

Known for his infectious enthusiasm and occasional on-air mishaps, John Inverdale presented BBC Radio's popular Wimbledon coverage during the 1990s, bringing the best out of an around-the-grounds commentary team that included Christine Truman, Fred Perry, Gerald Williams, Tony Adamson and others. He went on to present BBC2 Television's highlights show *Today At Wimbledon* for 15 years, and currently works as a commentator for BBC Television whilst also presenting ITV's much-admired coverage of the French Open.

1970

The Most Beautiful Place in the World

Norman Cohen, STANMORE

1970 My first Wimbledon. I was overwhelmed by the sheer size and beauty of the place.

I attended on middle Saturday and was shocked to hear of Rod Laver's defeat by Roger Taylor. Although fiercely patriotic, as a Laver worshipper, I was distraught at his loss. An abiding memory was of an evening newspaper seller shouting out 'Taylor beats Laver!' to advertise his wares.

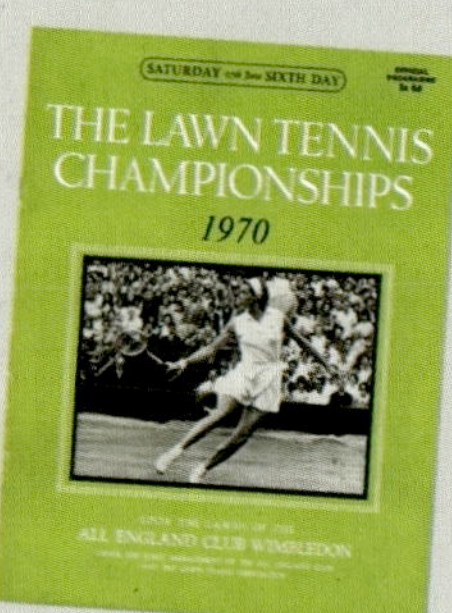

1971 It was the middle Saturday and John Newcombe was practising on the outside courts.

Newk, as ever the showman, picked up a 'singles stick' and pretended to throw it as a javelin at the 'Rocket' – one way to remove your deadly rival from the draw!

1972 The first time I saw Roscoe Tanner who had an amazing serve both for power and that 'kicking mule' on the second delivery from an incredibly quick action.

Later, standing (happy days!) on Centre Court watching and revelling in the shot making of Ilie Nastase v Tom Gorman – sheer joy – oh, those topspin lobs. There was a very exciting, fresh atmosphere at Wimbledon that year, probably due to the absence of the WCT players. I read in one of my tennis magazines that the best meal at The Championships was a 'Wimpy' and it was! Alas, due to the smell of the fried onions reaching the Royal Box, this concession disappeared.

1973 Boycott Wimbledon! A desperate year for The Championships. I watched John Feaver play eventual finalist Alex Metreveli on Centre Court.

At first Metreveli struggled against Feaver's 'Cannonball' serve but class prevailed. The other abiding memories of that day – the No.1 seed and newly crowned French Champion, the (cracked) genius, Ilie Nastase, lost to Sandy Mayer on Court 2 – a disaster for this already denuded tournament. I didn't see this match but because so little noise was coming from the spectators I knew the fans' favourite, Nastase, was losing. Later I headed for a far outside court to watch a nostalgia filled, all British ex-Davis Cup players doubles between Peter Curtis/ Roger Taylor v Alan Mills/Bobby Wilson – a 'blast' from the amateur days. Even later I saw a match that ended around 10pm, the latest I ever watched a game finish (pre-roof), on Court No.2, under cloudless skies – a true midsummer's night – featuring the earlier defeated Nastase playing with Connors entertaining a rapt crowd and beating Mike Machette and (the then unknown) Raul Ramirez, 8-6 in the fifth.

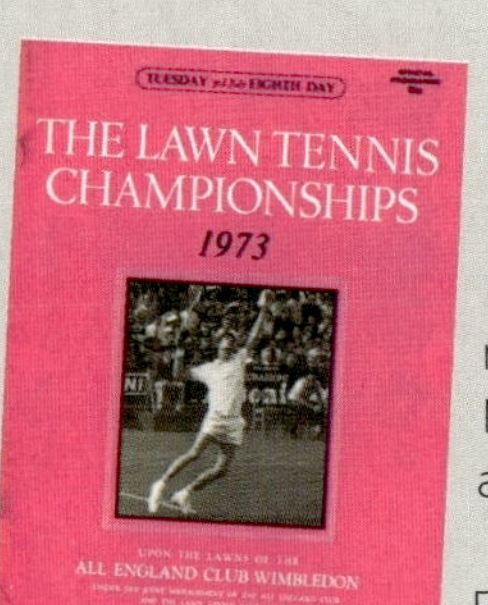

1974 Wet, Wet, Wet – no, not the pop group – the deluge at SW19. The last 16 moved back to the second Monday and the place was absolutely packed.

I was watching Adriano Panatta on the old Court No.6, a natural amphitheatre, a wonderful court for spectators. A load of schoolgirls were making a very loud noise causing Panatta annoyance and he reacted by very gently lobbing a ball into the noise where it softly hit one of the girls on the forehead and she had no idea what had happened. The great Kenny Rosewall – I was elated that this veteran beat Newcombe and Stan Smith on his way to the final, at nearly 40, but devastated when he lost to Jimmy Connors. On middle Saturday standing on Centre watching Newcombe/ Tony Roche v Ray Keldie/ Rayno Seegers – as usual in those days special atmosphere watching men's doubles, the worst thing wrong with present tennis, the doubles now just a devalued side-show. Right behind me in the front row seats was the late, great Richard Attenborough who gave me a big smile when I quickly mentioned his football club, Chelsea.

In 2011 Norman Cohen completed 25 years' service as an umpire at Wimbledon.

1975 Kenny Rosewall's last Wimbledon in the men's singles – watched him play Roche on Centre – the end of an era.

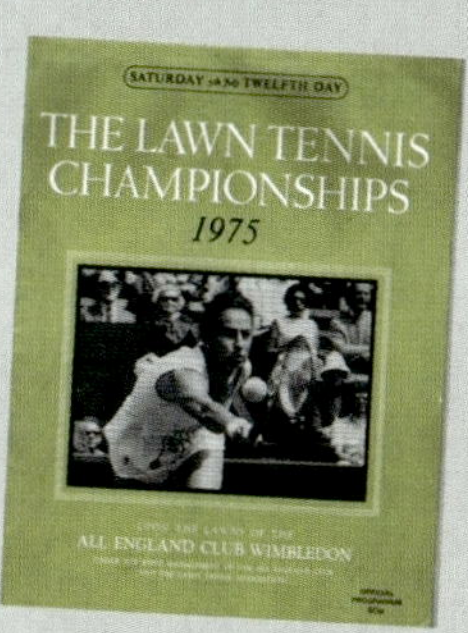

1976 The year of THE summer – drought, day after day of record temperatures, invasions of ladybirds and at Wimbledon, brown courts!

As usual I was there on the middle Saturday which just happened to be the hottest day of the year. The first aid building was jam-packed with people overcome by the heat. I watched Stan Smith play Teimuraz Kakulia on an outside court. During the match Stan hit a terrific winner and I let out a 'stage whisper' of 'Great shot, Stan!' Stan, as always the gent, looked over at me and gave me a great big smile in acknowledgement.

1977 No unusual memories just the warm glow of reflecting on one of the great Wimbledons.

Wonderful matches every day, NO Rain, with the bonus of a classic men's semi-final, Borg v Gerulaitis, and final and, of course, Virginia finally succeeding.

1978 After the Lord Mayor's show – cold, cold, cold.

I'm going to stop there, as I could go on forever. Every time I hear that word 'WIMBLEDON' even if it has nothing to do with tennis, my ears prick up and my heart sings. Wimbledon is, for me, the most beautiful place in the world.

1970

Wightman Cup at Wimbledon

John Nicholson, MOTSPUR PARK

MRS. J. R SUSMAN.

The second week of the 1961 Championships coincided with the start of our school summer holidays, and there was the possibility of an all British Ladies' Singles Final. That's when my interest in tennis began. Angela Mortimer and Christine Truman both defeated South African players in their semi-finals to contest the final.

After watching Ann Jones win the Ladies' Singles Championship in 1969 I was determined that next year I would attend The Championships. I was lucky in the Wimbledon ballot and obtained Centre Court tickets for both the first day and the final day. I also purchased No.1 Court tickets for six days of the meeting.

My first visit to The All England Lawn Tennis and Croquet Club did not, however, take place on the first day of the 1970 Championships but ten days earlier on Friday, 12 June on the occasion of the Wightman Cup played on the old No.1 Court between the ladies of Great Britain and the United States of America.

The cost of a ticket for the West Open Stand was 17/6 (equivalent to 87.5p) and our seats were in Row B, the second front row, near the umpire's chair affording an excellent view of the proceedings and close proximity to the players. The team for Great Britain was Ann Jones, Virginia Wade, Joyce Williams, Winnie Shaw, Nell Truman and Angela Barrett (non-playing captain) and for the United States of America Billie Jean King, Nancy Richey, Julie Heldman, Mary Ann Curtis, Peaches Bartkowicz and Doris Hart (non-playing captain).

At the close of play on day one Great Britain led by two rubbers to one. In the opening match Billie Jean King defeated Virginia Wade 8-6, 6-4 in a closely contested encounter. Ann Jones was a convincing winner against Nancy Richey 6-2, 6-3. Ann Jones and Joyce Williams beat Mary Ann Curtis and Julie Heldman 6-3, 6-2 in the first doubles match.

We returned to the same seats on Saturday, 13 June with the air of optimism that Great Britain would regain the Cup which had last been won in 1968. The first match on court was between the third-ranked players with Julie Heldman defeating Joyce Williams 6-3, 6-2. Virginia Wade had an easy win 6-3, 6-2 against Nancy Richey. Great Britain was leading by three rubbers to two with hopes high that Ann Jones would repeat her Wimbledon triumph of the previous year and secure victory for Great Britain. Unfortunately, Billie Jean King was too good in every department of the game and won 6-4, 6-2. Winnie Shaw and Virginia Wade faced Peaches Bartkowicz and Billie Jean King in the deciding rubber and although they led 2-0 in the final set the American pair won 7-5, 3-6, 6-2 resulting in the United States of America retaining the Cup by four rubbers to three.

It was a disappointing end to an eventful and exciting two days but it had been a wonderful opportunity to savour the atmosphere at The All England Lawn Tennis and Croquet Club.

MISS J.M. HELDMAN.

MISS D. R. HARD.

MRS. W. DU PONT.

MISS. N. RICHEY.

It was some consolation that in a matter of days I would be experiencing The Championships for the first time.

It was a thrill to be on Centre Court to see Rod Laver begin the defence of his title. Our seats were in Row S, then the second back row, which enabled us at appropriate intervals to lean out and watch play on the adjacent No.1 Court.

Two thousand and nineteen marked the 50th consecutive year that I have attended The Championships during which time I have seen many exciting matches both on the show courts and the outside courts. I have been fortunate to have had tickets for every men's final in the 1970s. Other highlights include being on Centre Court to witness Virginia Wade's triumph in 1977 and more recently Roger Federer, my favourite player of all time, winning the title in 2004 and 2007.

Looking back, I enjoyed a feast of tennis in 1970. In addition to the Wightman Cup and The Championships I attended the Davis Cup in Edinburgh between Great Britain and Austria, the pre-Wimbledon tournaments at Surbiton and the Queen's Club, the Dewar Cup events in Edinburgh and at the Royal Albert Hall, and the Benson & Hedges tournament at the Empire Pool, Wembley. Sadly, for many years the tournament circuit in this country has been curtailed and there are now fewer opportunities to see the top players in action.

John Nicholson's memoir provides a reminder that over the years it is not just The Championships that have brought world-class tennis to The All England Club. The Wightman Cup was played at Wimbledon 24 times between 1924 and 1972, and between 1904 and 1921 seven of Great Britain's home Davis Cup ties were played at the Worple Road ground. Since the move to Church Road in 1922, 18 of Great Britain's Davis Cup ties have been played at Wimbledon: five on the Centre Court, ten on the old No.1 Court and three on the new No.1 Court. In the pre-World War II years Wimbledon also hosted a number of Davis Cup ties involving two foreign nations, including the epic Inter-Zone Final between Germany and the USA on the Centre Court in 1937.

MISS B. J. MOFFITT.

1971

Wimbledon

Robert and Joan Graham, BURY

Graham Stilwell

My memories from almost 41 years ago come without the aid of a diary! Having said that I do have the aid of a few very precious slides to jog the old brain cells.

The 1971 Wimbledon Championships were very important to me. From an early age, about ten years, I loved to watch Wimbledon on television; way back in the days of monochrome. Part of the fortnight always coincided with our local mill holidays. We never travelled anywhere to stay for any length of time, just day trips on steam trains to Blackpool, Southport, etc., so arrangements could be made around the best matches.

Fast forward ten years. I was married in 1970. In 1971 my husband suggested 'Why don't we go down to Wimbledon this year?' I didn't need asking twice! We managed to book a B&B in the town and travelled down in a recently purchased secondhand Austin A30 van (nicknamed 'Peanut'). We only paid £80 for it but luckily it got us there (and back!).

Our fellow guests were all tennis fans of course. Three of these were ladies; two middle aged and one in her nineties. All members of tennis clubs and all with tickets. The older lady having one for each day. We alas, had none, therefore a spot of queuing was required. But that was for Monday. Another guest was one of the linesmen. Quite a character he was too.

Our Sunday was spent wandering around town. This is where I caught my first glimpse of a tennis player in the flesh! It was Graham Stilwell. Albeit a back view but I would have known him anywhere. During the 60s and 70s I could have recognised most players just by their socks and footwear. I also saw the hallowed ivy-clad walls for the first time through the gates on Church Road. It was a hive of activity beyond in preparation for the following day. A day which would see me attending the tournament I'd loved for so long.

An early morning start was required for Monday. Between 5 and 6 o'clock our host recommended. She also suggested we queue on Somerset Road; Church Road being the more well known and therefore the most popular. Unfortunately it wasn't early enough. There was quite a long queue but, attaching ourselves to the back of it, we awaited our queue tickets. A great system whereby you were given a small ticket with the number of your place in the queue which meant you could go away and freshen up, have a bite to eat, and then return shortly before the gates opened. Although we had only queued for about four hours we decided that something warm and comfortable was a necessity, so queue tickets obtained, we paid a visit to Ely's department store and purchased two lovely thick sleeping bags to keep us warm for the rest of the week's queuing.

Because we were a long way down the queue on the Monday all the tickets for Centre Court had been snapped up long before we got to the front. Court 1 was the next best. Ah, the old No.1 Court.

Tuesday saw us on Court 1 again. We really had to get ourselves sorted out if we were to get seats on Centre!

I don't have tickets for the Wednesday so I'm not sure what happened there. Maybe we were saving up for the finals!

But we did have Centre Court tickets for the Thursday. East Open Stand, Entrance G, Row A, seats 19 and 20. This is the very front row, next to the court and facing

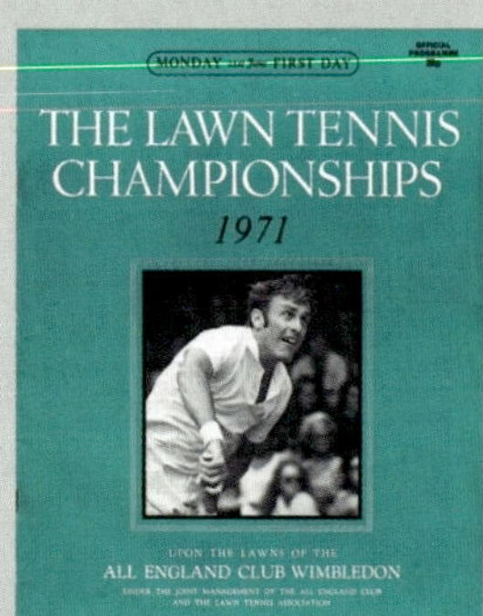

the umpire. Not great for seeing the lines but you are so close to the players. That's the thing about Centre Court, it's really quite small. It looks much larger on the telly. They cost the grand sum of £1.75 each. The equivalent in 2016 was about £126. Wow!

Now Friday was ladies' final day. Alas we didn't have tickets for this, only a complimentary ground ticket given to us by our linesman friend. I think we must have shared this and taken turns to queue for the men's final the following day. Ah, wonderful times when you could queue for the whole of the second week. This, alas, is no longer the case. People of all ages would queue. Lots of them spent all night on the pavement. One particular gentleman wore a suit and trilby hat and made himself comfortable on a deck chair.

Another couple of tickets we managed to get hold of were for the Umpire's restaurant; courtesy of our fellow B&B guest of course. In those days I think it was situated under No.1 Court. What a treat we thought. It being a warm day we each chose a salad. That was a mistake. You wouldn't believe the number of greenfly on our plates! We got into conversation with two lovely ladies who cleared the tables and they told us that the lettuce was never washed!

The match that brings back the fondest memories was the men's doubles semi-final between Rod Laver and Roy Emerson and John Alexander and Phil Dent. I was so thrilled to be watching two of the greatest ever Aussies in action on Centre Court. But as to which day it was, no, I don't remember. It is possible it was late in the day and we managed to get a couple of

tickets through someone kindly handing theirs in for re-sale. I couldn't believe our luck. Laver and Emerson came through and went on to defeat Ashe and Ralston in the final. Unfortunately we didn't manage to see that.

We saw two of the ladies' quarter-finals. Kerry Melville v Judy Dalton and Billie Jean King v Francoise Durr. Our seats were up in the gods on Court 1. A great view of the whole court but a pair of binoculars would have been handy! The height of Francoise Durr's ball toss was quite something. Judy Dalton claimed victory over Kerry and Billie Jean was the winner over Francoise.

The men's semis threw up an all-American clash and an all-Australian clash. The Americans were Stan Smith and Tom Gorman. Victory going to Smith the tall, blond quiet American in straight sets. The all Australian tussle was between John Newcombe and Ken Rosewall. Ken was 36 by now and almost at the end of his career. I was very much rooting for Ken because you knew this was his last chance to add the Wimbledon crown to his long list of tournament wins. But it wasn't to be. Newcombe was merciless winning 6-1, 6-1, 6-3. It was a privilege to watch 'Muscles' at work. We hadn't managed to see Ken in his quarter-final match against Cliff Richey but we had joined about 200 others on the concourse, in front of the external Centre Court scoreboard. Yes, we stood and applauded a scoreboard! You could tell who had won the point from the volume of the applause drifting over from the court. Always a few decibels higher when Ken won the point. Such was his popularity.

Evonne Goolagong

The Ladies' Doubles Final pitted Australia against the US. The pairing of Margaret Court with Evonne Goolagong must have been relatively new I think. They were up against the three-time previous winners in Billie Jean King and Rosie Casals. The Americans emerged as winners, 6-3, 6-2.

We were lucky enough to get tickets for the men's final. Newcombe v Smith. A thrilling five setter with Newcombe emerging victorious. I was so pleased it lived up to its promise. I couldn't have asked for a closer men's final for my first visit. I remember Newcombe leaping over the net.

Our umpire friend was the net cord judge. He was so very proud, just as I was to have had such a wonderful, if exhausting time, at my first ever Wimbledon.

Robert and Joan Graham repeated their long journey from Lancashire to SW19 several times in the years following their first visit. Bob ingeniously took measurements of the Somerset Road pavement and constructed a portable shelter, one side of which could be attached to Peanut and the other to the perimeter wall of The All England Club!

1972

Deep and Meaningful

Steven Lynch, STAINES

My first visit to Wimbledon was actually in 1962, when I was only five. I remember the special bus from the mainline station to the grounds, and also that I spotted a Rolls-Royce somewhere inside – but not much of the actual play. That's a shame, because I apparently witnessed a Wimbledon first – the crowd booing the chair umpire.

'Unprecedented Wimbledon Scenes', shouted one newspaper headline. My mother was almost as shocked. We were on Court Two, watching what I now know was a fourth-round match between Britain's Roger Taylor and Ken Fletcher, the lively Australian. Fletcher took it in five sets, winning with what both players thought was a big service fault. Fletcher sportingly asked for the point to be replayed, but the umpire refused, 'leaving Fletcher embarrassed and Taylor enraged', according to John Oakley in the *Evening News*. The crowd – or at least those of them who were over five – shouted their disapproval, which hadn't happened at Wimbledon before.

My first trip under my own steam came, I think, in 1972. A friend and I went after school, and took advantage of the cheap recycled tickets that went on sale at 5pm. Helped by earlier rain, which had encouraged most people to go home, there were lots of Centre Court seats

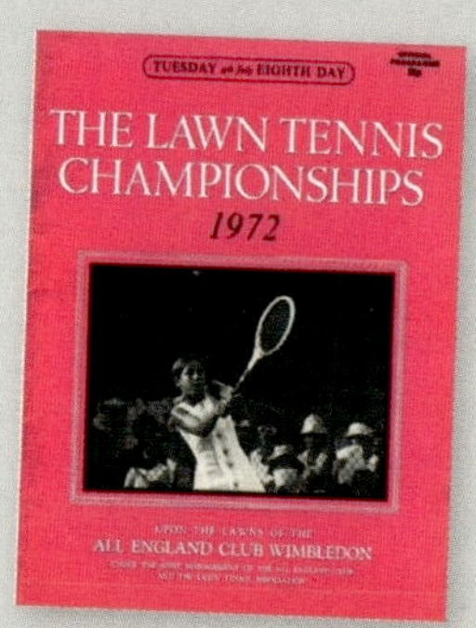

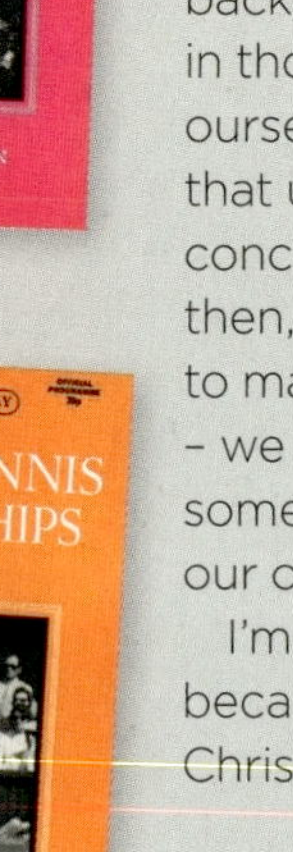

available, and I remember watching the long-haired pair of Ilie Nastase and Ion Tiriac in a doubles match, as play continued to about 9 o'clock. While it was raining we had explored the dusty corridors at the back (not many fussy security men in those days), at one point finding ourselves in the scoreboards that used to overlook the main concourse. They weren't electronic then, and there were piles of letters to make up the participants' names – we were sorely tempted, but somehow resisted the urge to put our own names up there.

I'm pretty sure it was 1972 because that was the first year Chris Evert played at Wimbledon.

Chris Evert in action, 1972

For red-blooded 15-year-olds she was very interesting indeed. Most of the other top women players looked like our mums, but here was someone almost our own age. That she was very pretty and wore remarkably short dresses had not entirely escaped our attention either. The bus journey from the station this time revolved around the killer chat-up lines we would suavely summon to captivate and fascinate in the admittedly unlikely event of being confronted by Chrissie. Back then the Wimbledon catering was less varied than now: about the only hot food available was a giant hot dog known, for reasons lost in the mists of time, as an Oscar. During a rain-break my friend and I grabbed a couple of these and huddled up against the wall of the Centre Court to keep dry. A couple of munches in, a small door opened nearby … and out stepped Miss Evert. Possibly distracted by an overdose of mustard, I dried up – but my friend, to his credit, did manage to mumble 'Would you like a bite of my Oscar?' Oddly, she declined – although she did have the grace to say 'No thank you', which we later agreed technically counted as a deep and meaningful conversation with a famous starlet. Even more oddly, when I finally met her about 30 years later, Chris couldn't remember the incident at all. Strange, that.

Stephen Lynch is the International Editor of *Wisden Cricketers' Almanack*.

1972

My First Wimbledon

Patricia Arthur, PRENTON

I visited my first Wimbledon on Friday 30th June 1972. I travelled by train with my mother from Liverpool and we returned the same day. I don't recall any queues to enter and we must have paid for a ground pass on the day.

There are two matches I can recall watching on outside courts. One was Virginia Wade having an easy win over the Swedish player Ingrid Bentzer. The second was the unseeded American Patti Hogan beating the seeded Kerry Melville. The significance of this match was that in the days of a ninety-six player draw and eight seeds, this was the only win by an unseeded player over a women's seed.

I also recall my mother following the scoreboard on the Centre Court in a close match involving Chris Evert in her first Wimbledon and Mary Ann Eisel. The one player who I can recall seeing wandering around the grounds was the late Karen Krantzcke who is now remembered by the annual Karen Krantzcke Sportsmanship Award.

In the days when play started at 2pm on all courts some people used to travel very long distances by train in order to enjoy a day at The Championships. Night trains took them safely home.

Patricia Arthur's scoreboard-watching mum was indulging in an age-old Wimbledon pastime. When an important match on Centre or No.1 Court reached an exciting climax there would be thousands of pairs of eyes looking up at the ivy-clad wall outside, waiting for the score to tick over.

1972

My First Visit to Wimbledon

Jane Wiltshire, CAMBERLEY

My first visit to Wimbledon was on a school trip in June 1972 when I was 16 years old. We had just finished our O levels and this was a special treat.

We were on Court No.1 in the high stand on the umpire's chair side and were so excited because the third match scheduled was Ilie Nastase.

The first match was Pancho Gonzales v Jurgen Fassbender which seemed to go on for an age followed by Lew Hoad v Ismail El Shafei, which I remember went to four sets. Then, of course, play on the show courts started at 2pm. The teacher said we had to leave at 6pm.

To our disappointment and dismay these two matches lasted over four hours so we never got to see Ilie Nastase play.

Still, we could say we had actually been to Wimbledon!

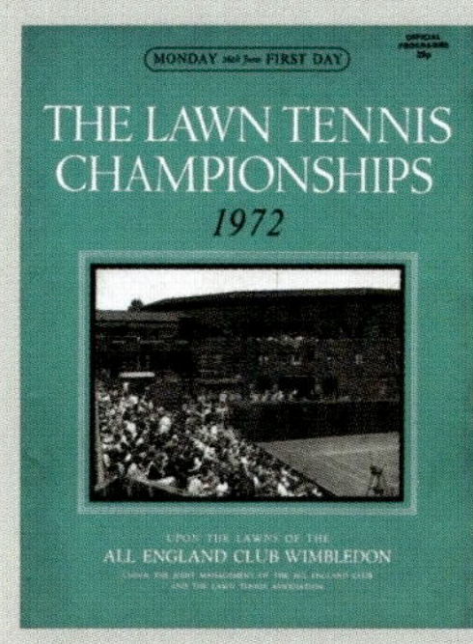

1973

To Somerset Road, by Coach

Roger Milne, PULBOROUGH

I was an armchair tennis fan from the dawn of Open Tennis in 1968 but 1973 was the year I saw my first live tennis at Wimbledon (on Saturday June 30th). This was a notable year for the wrong reasons – the fledgling ATP had called for a boycott by its members over the suspension of Niki Pilic for refusing to play a Davis Cup tie. As a consequence of this there were 50 lucky losers in the men's draw and fans had to find some new heroes to follow (though Ilie Nastase and Roger Taylor defied their Union). As well as my first year 1973 also saw The Championship debuts of Bjorn Borg and Martina Navratilova (Sue Barker too!).

I took the short journey to Wimbledon mainline station and then followed the signs for the shuttle bus to The All England Club. This was not a red double-decker bus as currently used but a rather ancient coach that made its way up the hill through Wimbledon Village and down Marryat Road. My first view of The All England Lawn Tennis Club was thus of a row of people queuing by the concrete slab wall in Somerset Road. That queue snaked around the ground, then across Church Road and up the hill to St. Mary's Church (unknown to me there was then another, even longer queue tailing the other way towards Wimbledon Park. The two queues are now merged).

Back then you would still see a fair number of school parties joining the queue (all in smart uniforms). Play didn't start on any court until 2pm (precisely) and the grounds rarely reached capacity so school parties were able to just turn up during school hours to attend. Now you would have to join the queue before 8am on most days in the first week to be sure of gaining admission. So the schools got left out – good news for the rest of the queuers but maybe not for inspiring children to take up the game.

After a long, slow shuffle I eventually made my way to the entrance gate. I recall that first year there were only three turnstiles though soon after they built a

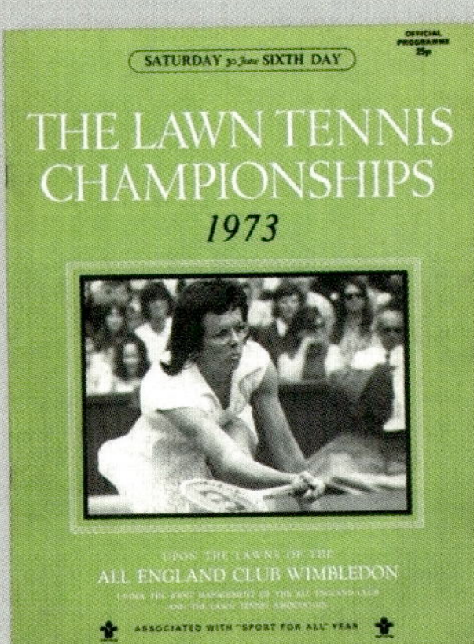

Despite the absence of many top male stars, over three hundred thousand people attended the 1973 Championships

new block with eight turnstiles and some railings to split the head of the queue into three sections (Show court, Court 2, ground admission). The 'sheep pen' as the stewards called it.

Through the turnstiles I found myself right under the stand of the old Number 1 Court and soon found a raised concourse that led between Centre and Number 1 courts. In those days you could stand on that concourse behind the East Stand seating and watch the tennis on Court 1 with your ground admission ticket. Later they put frosted glass along there to avoid congestion but you could still spectate from there in 1981 when I was present to hear John McEnroe's now famous phrase 'You cannot be serious'.

Seeing live tennis on Court 1 that first year was a magic moment. Standing to the side of the court it all looked so much bigger than on television and although it was day 6 of The Championships when I attended the grass still looked so lush. And the atmosphere was electric – tennis on TV would never fully satisfy again.

Television at that time didn't give you an overview of the AELTC ground and all those outside courts that Harry Carpenter, in his BBC bunker, would mention when giving us results but from which we would never have more than a glimpse of players on court. In 1973 Centre and Number 1 Court were on the northern edge of the grounds –

Nikki Pilic

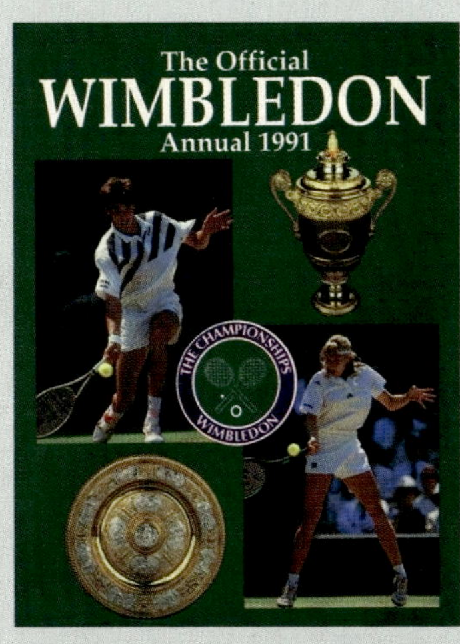

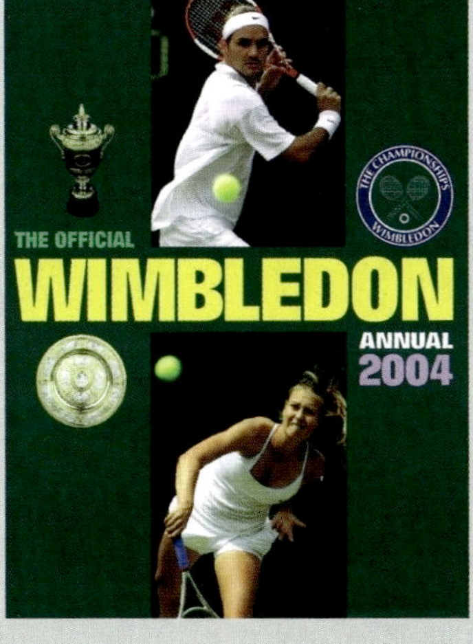

Roger Milne is a keen collector of Wimbledon Official Annuals

Aorangi Park was a rugby ground. Thus all the outside courts were spread out in three rows on the south side. The old Number 2 Court was just across the main concourse from Number 1 (where Court 3 is now), with its banks of seating and standing room for those with a head for heights.

But it was to Court 3 that I made my way to watch a match with one of those new stars in the boycott year. The hype was already in full swing for the young Swede Bjorn Borg and the aisles were packed for his match with the little known Hungarian Szabolcs Baranyi. I stayed there until he went two sets up then moved on, thinking he would soon wrap it up (of course it went to five sets before Borg won). This was a round of 16 clash, all of which were played on the first Saturday rather than the second Monday as now. With no Sunday play the men's final was on a Saturday and the women's on a Friday so week two started with the women's quarter-finals. A lot of matches to get through in week one (though half the women had first-round byes as the main draw was just 96 players).

My favourite court in those early years was Court 6, which was tucked away behind Court 2. That court, and the adjacent Court 7, had had three rows of bench seating added down one side so there was

usually plenty of room to rest your legs whilst watching a match.

My least favourite court was Court 11 on the opposite side (Church Road) to Court 6.

Nowadays the Baseline Restaurant is erected on that site but back then it was a championship match court with spectator viewing down only one side – the side opposite the umpire was just a hedge. Fortunately it did not remain in use for long.

There was unreserved standing room on all courts, including Centre, though you had to queue for it. That remained until disasters at football grounds led to new regulations and all-seater stadiums. A shame as there was never any crowd trouble at Wimbledon.

One trick I soon learned was to climb the stairs to the gangways on the upper level of Centre Court. On the South side you could look out over the outside courts. The area in the middle (above the Royal

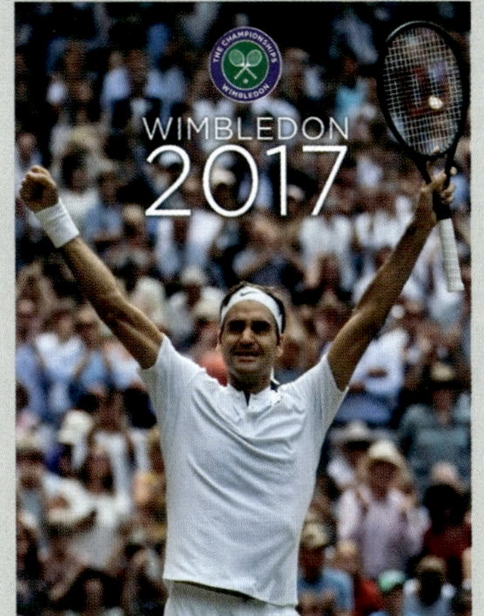

Box guests balcony) was glazed with frosted glass but to either side of that, on the diagonals, you could view multiple courts from above.

The biggest star I saw that day was not at the time playing a match. To the south of the outside courts were some red shale courts (an area now used for VIP marquees). On one of those courts I saw Margaret Court hitting practice serve after practice serve. She beat Britain's Glynis Coles that day though failed to win the title (which would have given her a second calendar year grand slam as she later added the US title to her Australian and French titles).

Another place to see the stars was right in front of the Centre Court building. Crowds were kept behind barriers as the limos dropped off and picked up players. I recall that all the drivers looked like glamour models.

The official programme in those days was a slim, stapled affair with black and white photos costing 25p. If you went down after work the full programmes were sold out and they only offered you an even slimmer stapled set of draw sheets with an order of play.

I've been back to Wimbledon every year since then. There have been many changes, most for the good but I'm still nostalgic for various absent courts and stands around the grounds as well as for the players of that era who I grew up watching.

1973

Tall, Dark and Handsome

Jane Portnell, INGLETON

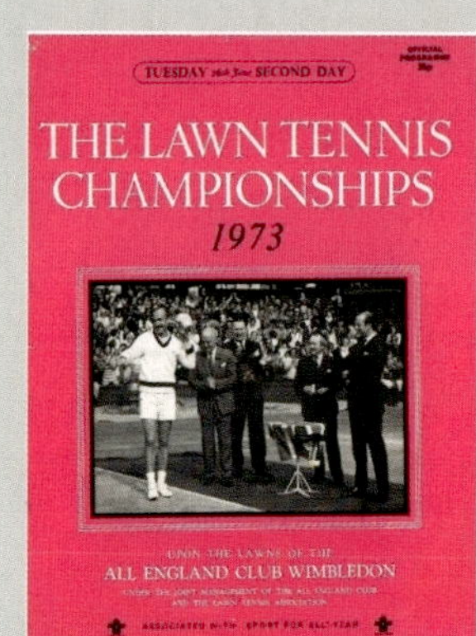

Roger Taylor was my hero! Despite all my friends falling madly in love with Bjorn Borg, it was the tall, dark and handsome Roger Taylor who was my idol.

Living only an hour and a half away from Wimbledon I was lucky enough to be able to go several times throughout my teens on school trips. In those days, free of safeguarding, health and safety policies and risk assessments, we were generally let off the bus and left to our own devices until our return to the bus later in the day. So I found myself at 13 with my friends learning how to jump the Wimbledon queue! Upstanding citizens joined the end of the queue and waited until it wound its way around the grounds to the entrance, but we were teenage convent school girls let out for the day, so we found a better way! We joined the end of the queue which was usually about 15 feet wide and took up a position on the road side of the queue. We would stand and make idle childish conversation and as we did so, every so often we would take a couple of steps forward and shuffle around a little. Others around us would be talking and not really taking notice of our slow progress along the edge of the queue. By this means we made excellent headway along the outside of the queue and if we timed it right we arrived near to the entrance just about the time that the gates opened! With everyone so frantic to get through and run to the Centre Court no-one ever noticed our surreptitious queue jumping!

So it was on the day Roger Taylor played Bjorn Borg in the quarter-finals in 1973, the year of the Wimbledon boycott. The gates opened and we were there ready. We got through and ran as fast as we could to Centre Court and the standing area. We were in! Now we had to wait a couple of hours for play to start. That particular day was very, very hot and the standing area was very cramped and by the time the match started I felt very lightheaded, but I had waited this long and it was Roger Taylor, I wasn't going to miss this for anything. But after half an hour, I had to get out of the furnace that was Centre Court and seek the refuge of the First Aid ladies who poured cold water over my wrists and generally made me feel a lot better. But I was devastated; I knew I would never get a place back on the Centre Court. So once recovered, I and my stoic friend wandered around the outer courts watching tennis and autograph-hunting. We kept an eye on the score of the Borg/Taylor match on the scoreboard outside the Centre Court building and as the game progressed quite a crowd gathered to look up at the scoreboard and follow the game, until the area below the scoreboard was almost as crowded as our little standing area on Centre Court had been. No Henman Hill and big screen to watch in those days. And as we watched the scoreboard, people around started to cheer when the score came up if Taylor had won a point. The more the long five-set match progressed, the greater the cheers became. We could hear the cheers on Centre Court, then we'd wait for the score and then give out a cheer as big as the Centre Court crowd. At the time it was incredibly exciting and probably my first experience of crowd power! Everyone cheered when Roger Taylor won, even the Borg fans.

Returning home in the evening I watched the day's Wimbledon highlights on TV and when covering this match the commentator said that if we could hear a delayed cheer after the Centre Court crowd cheers, it was because there was a big crowd outside cheering as the scoreboard changed, and they panned to the crowd I had been standing in only hours before. It was my first appearance on television but I never saw myself!

This story ends just a few years ago when I was lucky enough to be at a post-Davis Cup party in Glasgow and I was introduced to my former idol Roger Taylor. He is now tall, grey and handsome! I told him about being in the crowd outside Centre Court for his match in 1973. He asked me if I still played tennis and I explained that an arthritic knee prevented me from playing at the time. We then spent ten minutes discussing the various merits and advantages of knee replacements!! So maybe it is thanks to Roger Taylor that I now have a new knee and am playing sport again!

Roger Taylor of Great Britain, seeded third, lost in the men's singles semi-finals to Jan Kodes, the eventual winner, 3 July 1973

1973

Majestic Wimbledon

John Lloyd, PALM BEACH, FLORIDA

Wimbledon was majestic. I was in awe of it. I never really played well in singles at Wimbledon, although I did have some success in doubles.

One memorable match was the Davis Cup tie against Italy in 1976 on the old No.1 Court. My brother David and I were two sets down to Adriano Panatta and Paolo Bertolucci. I thought we were done for, but my brother was very bullish. He had a great presence on court. We turned the match round, winning one set 18-16. If I'd had his mind I'd have been a lot better tennis player. If he'd had my backhand, he'd have been a lot better tennis player!

1974

The Maestro Fights Back

Will Parker, FLEET

I first went to Wimbledon in 1974 on the second Monday, always the best day to go on the outside courts. Late in the evening, I was able to get onto Centre Court to see the great Ken Rosewall, who was something of a hero of mine, taking on the big-hitting American left-hander Roscoe Tanner.

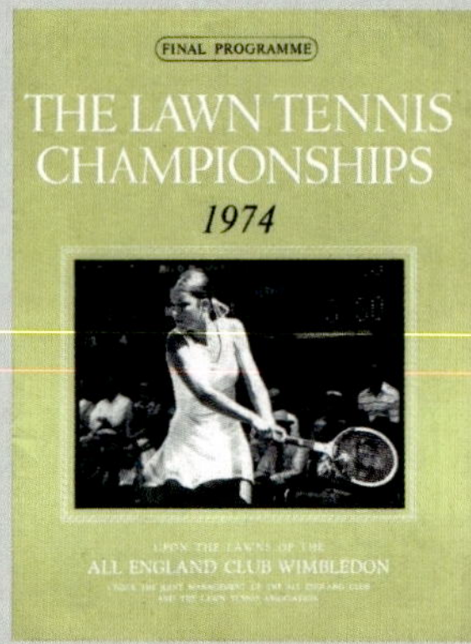

For a set and a half, Rosewall was totally overpowered by Tanner and it looked for all the world that Tanner would win comfortably in three sets, putting the old maestro to the sword. But gradually Rosewall adjusted to Tanner's pace and got into the match and, as he did so, the level of support for him from the crowd rose. Rosewall edged a compelling second set and gradually began to take Tanner's game apart, eventually winning a fantastic match to the crowd's delight by 2-6, 9-7, 6-3, 7-5.

Ken Rosewall

1975

Meeting Arthur Ashe

Sarah Bridgland, HIGH WYCOMBE

My first visit to Wimbledon was a short visit in 1972 and I have to admit that I was by no means a tennis fan at that time. I had played a little at school and watched even less on television. It was at the end of exams and a day out from school, so it was not until I entered the grounds that I felt any of the excitement and awe that the first view of Wimbledon now gives as I walk from Southfields Station.

I saw with my small group of friends some play on the outside courts before it was our turn to see some of a match between Chris Evert and Valerie Ziegenfuss on one of the show courts. I am sure this is when I realised what a wonderful game tennis is and what a magical place Wimbledon is to be a spectator. My parents encouraged my new-found passion and my father joined the tennis club where he worked so that he could enter the ballot for allocated Wimbledon tickets given to the club.

My most special and memorable early visit to Wimbledon was in 1975 when we had tickets for the fourth-round matches. I was thrilled when I read the Order of Play in the paper that I was going to see my favourite player – Arthur Ashe. I remember having a discussion about where my loyalties should be as the match was between Arthur Ashe and the British player, Graham Stilwell. My mother packed us a large picnic and flasks of coffee.

We entered the grounds at Wimbledon soon after the gates opened so that we had time to look around before play started on the show courts. We went to the trading area where there was a stall that sold books and postcards. I purchased a copy of Arthur Ashe's book *Portrait in Motion* that had been published in 1975 and was a diary Arthur wrote between Wimbledon 1973 – Wimbledon 1974.

In those days it was easier to move between the courts and we walked around the outside courts and saw a number of the players practising including Arthur Ashe. My father suggested that I could ask Arthur to sign my book as he came off the court. Arthur wrote in my book 'Arthur Ashe – Thank You'. As he gave me the book back Arthur thanked me and said that he hoped I would enjoy it. I replied that I hoped he would win Wimbledon and he said that he would try his best. We saw amongst other matches Arthur Ashe beat Graham Stilwell in four sets and the book still brings back happy memories of early visits to Wimbledon and of course the thrilling final when Arthur Ashe beat Jimmy Connors to become champion.

Arthur Ashe

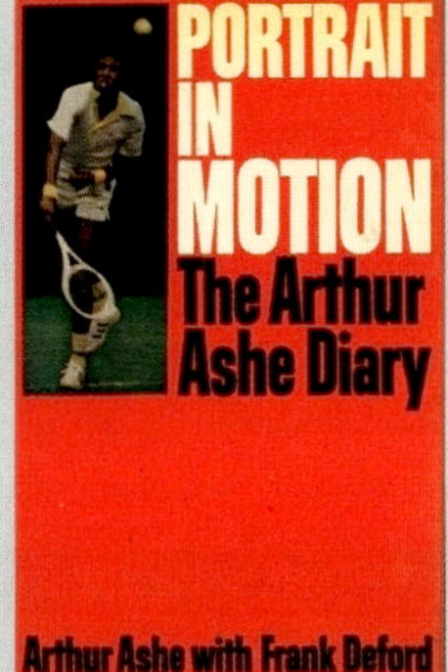

Arthur Ashe's *Portrait in Motion* with its intriguing title and bright-red jacket shone like a beacon from the display wall of the Wimbledon Bookstall. It was an object of desire.

Valerie Ziegenfuss was an American player of the 1960s and 70s. Each year the BBC Television commentators took great delight in mentioning her birthday party, which always fell during Wimbledon fortnight.

❝ What a magical place Wimbledon is! ❞

1975

Early Memories of Wimbledon

Bob Everitt, BILSTON

My very first trip to Wimbledon was in 1975 as a passenger in the back of a two-door Ford Escort Mk. 2 van. I was 19 years old and one of four Club members (two others were juniors) offered a lift to Wimbledon by the Club Captain and his wife on the middle Saturday, fourth-round day.

We were promised ground entry tickets. I have distinct memories of a very uncomfortable ride perched upon one of the two wheel arches, poorly cushioned with blankets and large pieces of upholstery sponge, while we were thrown around the interior of the van whenever the Captain was required to negotiate a roundabout or a sharp turn. With only views from the windows of the rear doors of where we had travelled from rather than where we were going, this probably heightened our anticipation of the tennis thrills yet to come. The older club member and I used our ground tickets to leave the tournament to have a look around. I recall stepping over multiple BBC TV cables next to one of their outside broadcast vans. Eventually, we came across a large wooden Clubhouse, another but far less salubrious tennis club. (Later identified as Wimbledon Tennis Club.) Suitably refreshed, from the club window we could see the outside of Centre Court in the distance, while at the side of the lounge bar stood a television from which we could also watch the action inside Centre Court.

Club members always seemed to travel down to the Club on the middle Saturday, applications had been made for ground and stand tickets for that particular day and the Staffs County Association were suitably obliging. I also have a strong memory of identifying Guillermo Vilas on one of the outside courts. During the warm-up with his opponent, possibly Sandy Mayer, he continually sprayed wild returns off the frame into the spectators, just as if he had never played on grass before. Also little Billie Jean King's startlingly, perfectly round, coiffered, permed hair and scarred swollen knees were, for some reason, very memorable. There was a buzz around the ground when it was discovered that Graham Stilwell had won the second set from Arthur Ashe, the number 6 seed, on the old Number One Court. By the time I got there, standing

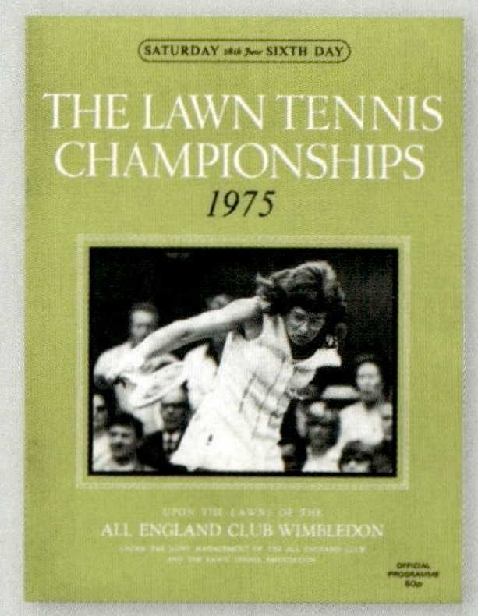

spectators were about eight deep in the gangway between the Centre and Number 1, but by standing on tip-toe I occasionally glimpsed either Ashe or Stilwell fly past through a fleeting gap in the crowd.

On a further trip In 1976 I was fascinated/spellbound by Nastase magically wielding his racket whilst defeating New Zealand's Onny Parun on Centre Court. Three rows from the back of the huge stand with the players hundreds of yards away, the incessant talking and general noise from the spectators during the rallies was unbelievable, more like a marketplace than a studious sporting arena. I could hardly hear the umpire calling the score over the little speakers placed high up in the roof. I felt like to shouting 'Shut up you lot! Don't you know there's a match on this court?'

In 1977, seated at the back of one of the outside court's small stands, I sat watching Virginia Wade play Borg's girlfriend Mariana Simionescu. Wade's struggle in the first set, which she won 9-7, was particularly nail-biting viewing. On the same level of wooden seating to me, about four seats away, two gentlemen journalists were studiously tapping away on typewriters, somewhat precariously balanced on their laps.

> **❝There was a buzz around the ground when it was discovered that Graham Stilwell had won the second set from Arthur Ashe.❞**

1976

Memories of Wimbledon

Chris Bowers, RINGMER

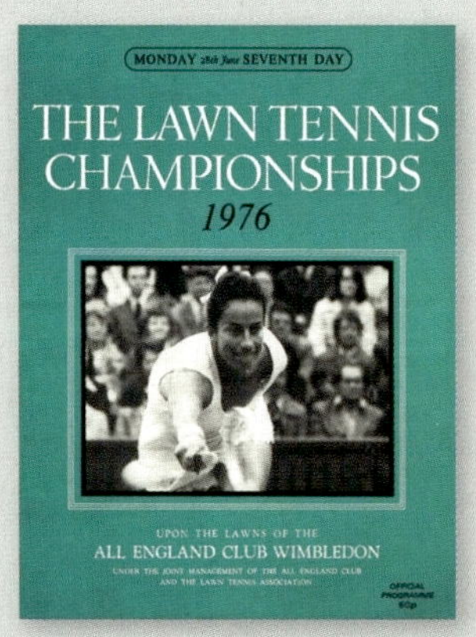

As a kid growing up in the north-west of England, Wimbledon was one of those annual festivals that became part of our year. It belonged to Christmas, New Year, my birthday, the FA Cup Final, our summer holiday and Bonfire Night, to the point where it was a cause of genuine sadness when the fortnight ended.

My first recollections were of Roger Taylor's run to the semi-finals in 1970. I remember my father had the radio on as he did the gardening on a sunny Saturday afternoon, and I caught the strains of Taylor beating Rod Laver, the commentator (Maurice Edelston I presume) getting more and more animated as the plucky Brit closed in on Rod Laver's first defeat at Wimbledon since 1960. I came home from school on the Thursday afternoon to be gutted by the news that Ken Rosewall had ended Taylor's run in the semis.

I think the *Radio Times* played a massive part in cementing Wimbledon in my consciousness, because one year – it must have been 1971 or 72 – it devoted its pre-Wimbledon cover to small action shots of about 24 leading players. They were the same size as the football cards I collected and swapped in those days, and I learned all the names pretty much off by heart. Unwittingly, *Radio Times* had given me a direct passage into the tennis world, from which I've never really escaped.

In 1975 my father's job was moved from Liverpool to London, so our family relocated to Kingston upon Thames. It didn't register that we were just a few miles from Wimbledon until my mother said one Sunday night in June 1976: 'If you get home from school quickly tomorrow, we'll go to Wimbledon for the cheap entry at 5pm.' I think it was £1 admission and 60p after 5pm, so my first-ever time at Wimbledon was the second Monday of 1976 as the sun set on what was then women's quarter-finals day. It wasn't until play was fizzling out in mid-evening that I got to poke my nose into Centre Court for the last few games of a dusk doubles. What struck me most was how small it seemed. Everything was as it looked on telly, but so much closer. It made me wonder whether Wembley was equally intimate (it wasn't, as I found out years later).

The following day I had no school for reasons I can't remember, so I got on my bike and cycled to Wimbledon. I confess to my eternal shame that I queue-jumped. It was mid-afternoon and I wasn't sure what court to head for, when I walked down one of those staircases from the old Court 1 to the areas where ground pass holders queued for free standing room on Centre. At the bottom of the stairs I stopped, looked around me trying to orientate myself, and just stayed put. When the queue began moving, I got onto Centre Court for my first-ever singles match – it was Ilie Nastase crushing Raul Ramirez.

I still feel guilty about the queue-jumping, but if anyone had told me that day that I'd end up commentating on Centre Court, including on Wimbledon finals, I'd have taken it like a shot.

The only problem is that, with the French Open, the grass court warm-up events and Wimbledon occupying a busy seven-week space in the calendar, I have long since stopped seeing the end of Wimbledon as a cause for sadness – these days it's a cause for immense relief and a promise of sleep. But I never lose the memory of those sad Sunday nights when it would be another long 50 weeks before the great tennis festival came round again.

> **"***Radio Times* **played a massive part in cementing Wimbledon in my consciousness. "**

Chris Bowers is a well-known tennis writer and broadcaster. He has written several books on the game, including a best-selling biography of Roger Federer.

1977

The Helen Wills Saga

Onny Parun, WELLINGTON

Helen Wills, 1930s

I n June 1977 I was offered and bought a limited edition copy of Lance Tingay's book *100 Years of Wimbledon*. He had been asked to write it by the AELTC to celebrate its Centenary year. It was leather-bound in green and gold and had 14cwt gilt edges. I had collected signatures since I was a kid and, as I played that Centenary year, decided to get as many ex-Wimbledon Singles Champions as possible to sign this new acquisition of mine.

The book was made perfectly for my task – in the front were two blank pages and the same in the back. I decided to fill the front with the men's signatures and at the back the women.

I obtained many ex-men's Champions as they assembled in Men's Locker Room A (my locker room for that year) before going to the Centre Court for a special presentation.

In 1984 at the 100th meeting of the women, through many various contacts I got most of the ex-Ladies Champions to sign my book.

As well as their signatures on these blank pages I asked each one, on the suggestion of Fred Perry (Men's Champion 1934, 35, 36), to sign again in a middle section of the book where there were draws, with scores, of each year from the quarter-finals on. I asked each ex-Champion to sign the year that they had won and multi winners to sign each year they had won.

As I was nearing completion of the signatures I noticed one glaring omission who had not signed and was still alive – Helen Wills from Berkeley, California who won Wimbledon eight times (3x as Helen Wills and 5x as Helen Wills Moody) in the 1920s and 30s. She had not travelled from her home in Carmel, California for the Centenary in 1977 nor in 1984 for the 100th meeting of the Women's Championships.

I then asked a fellow pro, Jim McManus, also from Berkeley to help me. He suggested Raymond ('Bud') Chandler who had won the Wimbledon Plate event (for losers in the first round of the main singles event) way back in 1929. But, more importantly, he was a childhood friend and practice partner when Helen Wills played at the Berkeley Tennis Club. He personally looked after the financial affairs of an ageing Helen Wills Roark (she married a second time) now retired and living in Carmel, California.

I wrote Bud a letter to see if he would ask Helen Wills to sign my book. He replied that it was unlikely as she had the same phobia as Greta Garbo (they were both born in 1905) – no signatures for anyone or anything! Bud had explained to her all the ex-Champions who had signed but she was unmoved and would not sign.

In 1987 I flew from New Zealand to London via Los Angeles after playing an Oldie Goldie tennis event in Auckland. I had decided to have one last stab at this elusive signature. After going through customs I rented a car and drove north to Carmel. I arrived at 10am and went to the Police Department asking for directions to Helen's house with the address I had obtained from the AELTC – they refused citing privacy concerns for their residents. Clint Eastwood was, at that time, their Mayor.

So I called Bud Chandler in San Francisco and told him my plight – he said he would call Helen and call me back in one hour. He called back and said no answer but he was sure she was at home so he would try again and call me back in another hour. This hourly ritual went on till 4pm – Bud said she finally answered her phone but she had a cold and wouldn't sign today, although she appreciated that I had come such a long way to her hometown. Bud suggested I send the book to him and he would show it to her on his next visit in ten days – with reservations I agreed and sent it from the post office in Carmel hoping it wouldn't get lost and drove back to Los

Helen Wills at Pebble Beach, near her home in Carmel

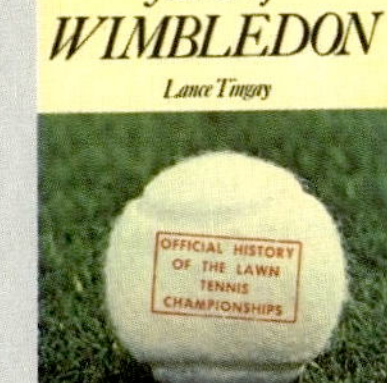

Angeles for my flight back to London.

I called Bud two weeks later and asked if he had any luck – he said, on seeing the book with all the signatures, she declared it the best tennis book she had ever seen and signed willingly. I told Bud I would fly out to San Francisco and pick up the book in person at his law firm's office.

On seeing my book again I checked out her signatures and low and behold – in the middle of the book she signed 3x as Helen Wills and 5x as H.W. Moody with an additional signature of Helen Wills Roark on the blank pages at the back of the book with all the other Ladies' Champions.

Helen Wills dominated her chosen sport as a colossus in an age now long forgotten. Her record speaks for itself – she played in 24 Grand Slam Singles events, was in the finals 23 times and won 19 of them. She won eight Wimbledon singles titles, seven US Nationals and four French Championships. Starting in 1927 in all tournaments she entered she never lost a set to anyone for almost seven years – it is known as 'The Streak'.

The last signature I got for my book was Helen Jacobs. She was known as 'The Other Helen' because she lost four Wimbledon finals to Helen Wills but finally won in 1936 when Wills was side-lined by injury.

In 1989 I had written a letter to Helen Jacobs from London but she replied she would not sign. Still in 1989 I flew to New York and got the last man Sidney Wood who won in 1931 to sign my book. I asked him if he knew Helen Jacobs – he did and even though he hadn't spoken to her for 40 years he called her on the number I gave him.

'Hi Helen, it's Sidney here and there is a Kiwi in my office who needs your signature for his special tennis book.'

'I am sorry but I told him by letter I wouldn't sign'

'Helen, we have all signed it including Helen Wills.'

'OK tell him to come tomorrow.'

The next day I drove through the snow to her house near Philadelphia, knocked on the door and was greeted by a friendly but wary Helen Jacobs. She signed my book, after inspecting it, on the year that she won and right next to

Helen Wills on the blank pages at the back.

She then invited me to lunch and spoke all about her many battles with Helen Wills especially the 1935 Wimbledon final where she lost to Wills after having a match point in the final set! In the late afternoon I left her and drove back to New York to catch my return flight to London. My task was finally over!

I still remember how I got every signature all those years ago – some were easy, some hard, some very hard.

Finally, I salute all those Champions who signed my book but most of all Helen Wills not only because she was a great Champion but because she was the only signer I never met!

New Zealand's Onny Parun was a fine grass-court player who played at Wimbledon from 1967 to 1980, reaching the quarter-finals in 1971 and 1972. He was also a quarter-finalist at the French and US Opens, and won the French Open doubles title in 1974 in partnership with Dick Crealy of Australia. Onny was a keen competitor who always entered the Wimbledon Plate event in years when his main draw progress came to an early end.

Onny Parun, Beckenham 1976

1977

My Love Affair with Wimbledon

John Evans, ROWLEY REGIS

My first visit to Wimbledon was Wednesday 22nd June 1977. It was Jubilee year and I was 15. We were offered places on a coach from a local tennis club. The lady in front of us had a Centre Court ticket, I was very envious, little did I realise that our options would be a little more restricted as I ogled at the order of play from our daily paper. We seemed to arrive very late, play was due to start at 2pm but I don't remember having to queue very much.

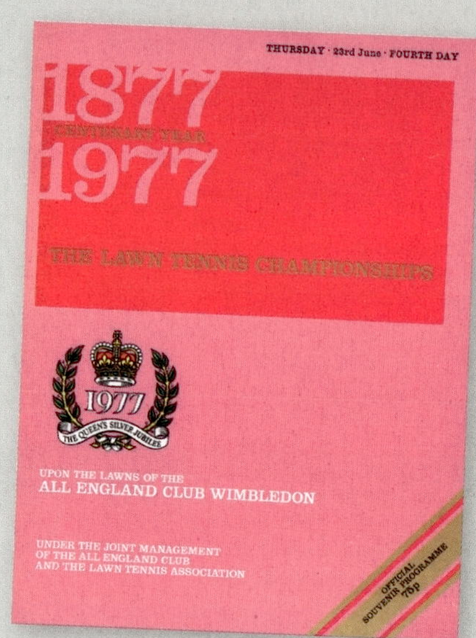

We entered via Somerset Road at the side of Court 2, which seemed to be very crowded as John Lloyd was playing fresh after his shock win over number four seed Roscoe Tanner of America. We walked down the old gangway between Centre and Court 1 and Mark Cox was the first player I ever saw play live. I could not contain my excitement, a real tennis player! It looked so different from TV. He was playing Australia's John Alexander and the match was very close. As the view was not that good we wandered on. At this point I had to persuade my Mom to buy a programme, which she was reluctant to do as it was rather expensive at 75p. Happily she succumbed but at least we now had a map of the grounds. We headed towards Court 6 as I was mad about Sue Barker at the time. I remember battling through crowds only to arrive when she had won, which was great news.

Eventually, we settled on Court 5 as there were some spare seats. I kept looking at this slender, short women's player … I know her I thought! Then the penny dropped, it was Martina Navratilova. She looked quite anxious and appeared terrified the match was going to get out of hand against a Miss Lofdahl-Bentzer of Sweden. She won easily in the end 6-0, 6-3. We then watched a match between Australia's Phil Dent and the older of the Indian Amritraj brothers, Anand. I remember very little about this match but it went to five sets with the Australian prevailing. The high point was Phil Dent exiting the court by us. He politely asked my mom to let him through and she was starstruck that a tennis player had spoken to her!

After a picnic on a piece of grass outside the south side of the Centre Court, we headed for Court 14 where another one of my heroes, Bjorn Borg, the defending champion was playing. Again we could not get through the crowds and word was spreading that he had lost the first two sets to former Australian Open champion Mark Edmondson. I was very worried as we wandered back towards Court 2 where we managed to get into the standing enclosure to watch another one of our favourites Ilie Nastase. I was delighted but then shocked to see him trailing two sets to one to Andrew Pattison of Rhodesia. He then proceeded to lose his serve and at 3-4 down in the fourth set he delayed the match by climbing under the green fence at the back of the court. In spite of frequent requests from the umpire he refused to play on, much to the crowd's amusement. When he did finally agree to play on Pattison had lost all his momentum and we left the match at two sets all as we had to go home. I really felt for Pattison.

On our way out I saw Guillermo Vilas of Argentina, the Australian and French champion, who seemed in control of his match. At this point I got rather upset because I did not want to go home and my Mom had to get very firm with me. It had been an amazing day out on the outside courts. We got home in time to watch the highlights from Wimbledon. Bjorn Borg had come back from two sets down to win and Nastase also won in five. However, the seeds had been sown that day for my love affair with Wimbledon. I have been back every year since!

1978

My First Wimbledon

Richard Hess, PALOS VERDES

grew up in Los Angeles, California with a twin brother, older sister and parents who played and watched tennis. I learned to play as an eight-year old and, at that time, saw players such as Pancho Gonzales, Jack Kramer and many others in the late 1940s. As a ten-year old I asked my father, 'What is the most important tournament?' His answer: 'Wimbledon.' From that day on as our family watches the world's best players come to play the Pacific Southwest tournament in Los Angeles each September, it becomes a dream of mine to some day visit Wimbledon.

That opportunity finally comes in 1978 when I travel with my wife, Jackie, and 14-year-old daughter, Helen, to fulfill this lifelong wish. It is my first visit to a major. In later years I visit all the majors (Wimbledon, US Open, French Open, Australian Open) multiple times; Wimbledon 2018 is my 93rd visit to a major.

Helen and I come for the full fortnight and Jackie joins us for the final three days of tennis and further travel after the tournament. Other reasons for the trip include experiencing the culture, history, people and tourist sites of the UK. Another mission is to trace family history; my mother's father spent his early schooling at Harrow and lived in the Holland Park area of London in the 1880s. I manage to trace one line of my ancestry back to 1215 in Scotland. Speaking of history, before traveling, I memorize the English monarchs and dates of their reigns from 1066 to present day; this holds me in good stead as I enjoy the deeper roots of British and Roman history not available to me in California.

We arrive on Saturday, 24 June 1978, two days before the tennis begins and make our way from Gatwick to Gloucester Road by train and tube to lodging in the Kensington area. So many new experiences all pile up, including jet lag, left-side driving, the Underground, speech and manner of the people and much, much more. On Sunday, we walk to Speaker's Corner and enjoy lively discussions there. Upon return to our lodging about noon, I note that, owing to rain delays, the final day of the Rawlings International at Queen's Club is playing just two tube stops away. We forgo naps to get a tennis appetizer the day before Wimbledon begins. The Centre Court ticket is only £3. Tony Roche defeats John McEnroe in a closely contested final, 8-6, 9-7 (tiebreaks in England are not played until the score is 8-8). Then we watch Bob Hewitt/ Frew McMillan beat Ray Moore/Bernie Mitton 6-8, 9-7, 15-13

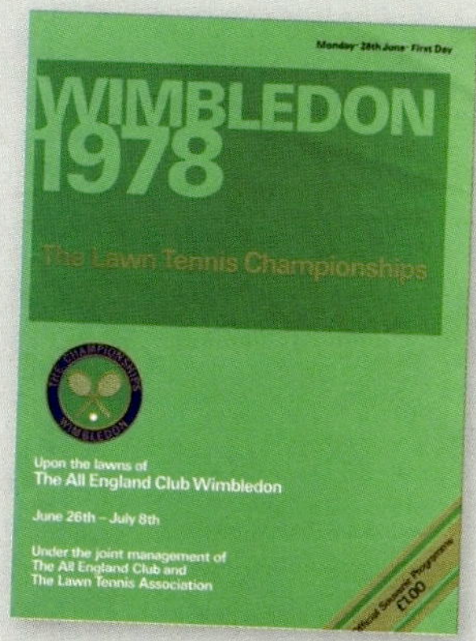

in the doubles semi-final after staving off five match points. Following suitable rest, they play the final as well with Hewitt/McMillan winning 6-2, 7-5 over Raul Ramirez/Freddie McNair after saving three set points in the second set. This is a great introduction to grass-court tennis, though as a child I did attend a grass-court tournament with my parents in the Los Angeles area.

Monday, 26 June is our first day at Wimbledon and there is so much new to take in. We arrive 'early' at 9.30am and the queue is only about two thirds of the way down Church Road toward Bathgate Road. Gates open at 12 noon and play on all courts starts at 2pm. There is time to kill in the queue and we use it to converse with other fans. I had read that the British are reluctant to initiate conversation but are good conversationalists if you initiate. This proves to be true and over the next two weeks I have delightful discussions about language differences, cultural differences, politics, history and the like. What I like the most about the British is their ability to express themselves and their sense of humor. I become a lifelong Anglophile.

> **"***The grounds are spectacular. The Tea Lawn is actually a lawn.***"**

We pay £1.30 for our grounds admission, declining to pay £4.80 for section M (currently section 113) seats on Centre Court. Getting a Centre Court seat is unnecessary because standing room is available to us on all courts. We buy a program for £1.00 and plan our day. Left Luggage is located inside the grounds and the price is 5p per item. We make a standing agreement that if we are separated at the end of the day, we will meet each other at Court 12.

The grounds are spectacular. The Tea Lawn is actually a lawn. Court 2 has a large stand with standing room at the front on the side; Court 1 is even bigger, with standing room in a hallway behind the first ten rows opposite the umpire. There are no courts north of Centre Court and courts 2-14 are south of Centre Court. We watch Ion Tiriac, Ilie Nastase, Guillermo Vilas and Vitas Gerulaitis warm up for an hour before play starts. The tennis balls are white Slazengers. We then move to standing on Court 1 to see Jimmy Connors knock off Jeff Simpson 7-5, 9-8, 6-1. Bjorn Borg is having trouble with hard-serving American Victor Amaya on Centre and we get to standing room to see Borg recover from 8-9, 6-1, 1-6, 1-3 to prevail in the final two sets 6-3, 6-3. Good drama there. We also see Tiriac beaten by James Frawley on Court 12 and Gerulaitis beat Heinz Gunthardt on Court 6. At the end of the day we're back on Centre to see Brian Gottfried leading John Lloyd

Bjorn Borg

two sets to one before rain halts play about 7.30pm. Helen and I are so enthusiastic about the tennis that we decide to remain on the grounds for each of the 12 days of tennis as long as anything is playing.

Our second day, Tuesday, is Ladies' Day and we arrive at the queue about 10.40am, putting us only a few hundred back. Upon entry, about 12.30pm, we head to Court 14 where Tracy Austin will play Diane Desfor in their first-round match. We get front row seats and await arrival of the players. At 14, Tracy is big news as a future star and dresses in a cute pinafore outfit. Helen and Tracy attend the same middle school in Palos Verdes, California, so we want to be sure to see her play. I have seen her at the Los Angeles Tennis Club several times since she was a seven-year-old. Shortly before 2pm, Tracy comes trotting to the court followed by an army of photographers. She briefly looks up, surprised to see Helen, and asks 'What are you doing here?' Tracy wins in three sets and every stroke she hits is accompanied by dozens of camera clicks as the photographers have a field day. Following that, we go to the side of Court 7 to see John McEnroe get upset by Erik van Dillen in five sets. McEnroe had made the semis as a qualifier in 1977 and rates to be a future star. He is full of fire at 19 and, at one time, uses the term 'asshole'. A British gent next to me tells me that's not a term recognized by the British. How times have changed. We see John Newcombe win in four on Court 4 over Dale Collings, and Bob Hewitt beats George Hardie in

five on Court 10 after losing the first two sets (Hardie weeps at the finish). On Court 14 we see Brian Teacher beat Bob Lutz in four and Steve Docherty beat Arthur Ashe in five. Darkness halts play at 9pm.

Wednesday is another full day and we arrive late in the queue, which is around the corner into Bathgate Road about 11.30am. No problem getting in, however, and we start in standing area of Court 2 to see Vilas beat John Feaver in four sets. While waiting we chat with some schoolgirls, about 12 years old, who are part of a convent, which has sent about 350 students to Wimbledon that day. Helen is aghast at their uniforms and is glad she never had to wear such clothing. We next go to Court 1 standing to see Frew McMillan beat Buster Mottram in three and Nastase beat Gianni Ocleppo in three. We also watch John Alexander beating Victor Pecci 12-10 in the fifth on Court 5. Next, it's off to Court 13 to watch Marty Riessen beat Van Winitsky in four and to Court 14 for Phil Dent finishing off Vijay Amritraj 7-5 in the fifth. Good drama today before darkness descends. Other winners on the day are Gerulaitis, Austin, Chrissie Evert and Roscoe Tanner. The setting and tennis is just magical for us.

We get an early start on Thursday, arriving at the queue about 8.30am. It's nearly to the corner and we find a spot on the wall to sit. It starts to rain about 11.15 and is still raining as we get to standing room on Court 1 to see Borg play. We watch it rain the whole day and give up at 5.45pm. No refund policy for rain, even for show court seats. Welcome to Wimbledon 1978!

Friday offers better weather and we join the queue at 11am. Even though it stretches up the hill on Bathgate, we get in the grounds by 12.30pm and are in plenty of time to watch Bob Hewitt beat Colin Dowdeswell in four sets on Court 7 and Billy Martin taking out Van Dillen 7-5 in the fifth on Court 4, followed by Betty Stove beating Stacy Margolin (McEnroe's girlfriend at this time). We also see a bit of Terry Moor beating Ray Ruffels in three on Court 8. Late in the day we immensely enjoy Peter Fleming/McEnroe beating Charlie Fancutt/Paul McNamee in three sets and decide we'll watch as many Fleming/McEnroe matches as we can. Darkness brings play to an end about 9.15pm after another full day.

Saturday play starts at 12 noon to try to make up schedule, so we are at the queue by 9.15am and get in easily. We see Connors beat Tom Gorman in four sets on Court 2 and then John Alexander beating Bob Hewitt in one 8-6 set on Court 12. After the first set Hewitt has a shoulder problem and retires. Sue Barker beats Pam Shriver 2-6, 8-6, 7-5 in a squeaker on Centre and Billie Jean King prevails 4-6, 6-3, 6-3 on Court 12 over Renata Tomanova. Regina Marsikova beats Kathy May 4-6, 6-2, 13-11 in another close contest. Kathy's son, Taylor Fritz, is now on the circuit. Ashe/Yannick Noah win a thrilling match 14-12 in the fifth over Bernie Mitton/Andrew Pattison on Centre. Before the start of tennis, we had watched Ashe drill Noah on his overheads. Fleming/McEnroe are two sets to one up on the third seeds, Bob Lutz/Stan Smith, when darkness halts play. They continue to deliver good fun. Lutz/Smith had already completed a prior round match earlier in the day and are happy to get home for some rest.

Middle Sunday is our day of rest. We do the British Museum for several hours and enjoy remarkable exhibits. Egyptian and medieval presentations are especially captivating. We have a delicious Indian dinner and I discover the delightful combination of lime pickle with lamb curry. The meal has a price of £6 for the two of us. In future visits to Wimbledon I always look forward to enjoying Indian food.

Monday boasts a smorgasbord of tennis starting at noon so we arrive early in the queue and go to Court 1 standing room for Austin losing to Martina Navratilova and Connors over Alexander in three. A brief bit of Nastase over Tanner in four on Centre and Borg in three over Geoff Masters on Court 4 before heading to Court 14 for our match of the day. It is the final two sets of Fleming/McEnroe beating Lutz/Smith 8-9, 13-11 after saving eight match points along the way. This Fleming/McEnroe team might just have some success in the future. Rain ends the day at 8.30pm.

We start Tuesday in standing room on Court 1 and get a front position to see Virginia Wade beat Mima Jausovec 6-0, 6-4 in the quarters and then Connors beat Raul Ramirez in three in their quarter-final. Also, on Court 1 is Tom Okker beating Nastase in four erratic sets. We next go to Court 14 to see Collings/K.W. Hancock beat Tim and Tom Gullikson in four tough sets followed by Alexander/Dent playing Gene Mayer/Hank Pfister. Rain comes at 7pm and ends play for the day.

Wednesday is our lucky day as we are given grounds passes while waiting in the queue. We watch Fleming/McEnroe beat Tito Alvarez/Victor Pecci 6-2, 6-2, 6-4 and later, also on Court 3, see them prevail over McNair/Ramirez 9-7, 8-6, 9-8 in a tight and dramatic quarter-final. They are now in the semis. Helen gets given a ticket for Centre and she kindly lets me use it to see Evert beat Wade 8-6, 6-2 and Martina beat Evonne Goolagong Cawley 2-6, 6-4, 6-4 to set up a final between the top two seeds in the ladies' draw. Later, we see a spectacular doubles quarter with Hewitt/McMillan beating Newcombe/Tony Roche 7-5, 9-8 (11), 6-4. We then watch McEnroe/Stacey Margolin beat Chris Kachel/Ilana Kloss 8-9, 7-5, 9-7 in an exciting contest. We end the day watching a Plate match when darkness intervenes. A word about the Plate matches. It is a consolation tournament for first and second-round losers in the singles. In some years third-round losers and doubles-only entrants were allowed to compete. It is discontinued in the 1980s.

Thursday is special because my wife, Jackie, arrives in the morning and the three of us enjoy tennis from standing room. While waiting in standing room for tennis to begin, an amusing event occurs. The Debenture Seats are directly behind the back of the standing area with the feet of the debenture fans a yard or so above the heads of the

Virginia Wade

standing fans. Shortly before play begins a stiff old gent in the first row of Debenture Seats must negotiate his way to his seat by stepping over various gear on the floor in front of other fans. He starts complaining and sputtering away at the nuisance when a nearby man in the standing area yells out 'Oh Dee-aah'. This is met with much laughter from the fans, both debenture and standing. The gent meekly sits in his seat. My thoughts are that this is perhaps evidence of class tension in the UK expressed through humor. As mentioned before, I find the British to be well ahead of Americans in politeness, articulateness and sense of humor. I love mixing with them.

First up is a ladies' doubles quarter-final where Jausovec/ Virginia Ruzici beat Glynis Coles/Linda Mottram in an agonizingly long and sloppy three-set match. Jackie is fighting jet lag and briefly dozes in standing room. We are packed in so tightly that she remains standing asleep, leaning on fellow fans to keep from falling. Finally, Connors comes on to beat Gerulaitis 9-7, 6-2, 6-1 in the first men's semi. Next up is Borg taking out Okker routinely. At 5-3 in the first set there is some rain delay. Jackie takes a break and someone gives her a pair of Centre seats (Entrance B, row D, seats 40-41) for the remainder, and we see Borg prevail 6-4, 6-4, 6-4. Connors and Borg have looked like two freight trains plowing through the field to meet in the final and now that promise is realized. We go to an outside court to see a plate match with Dennis Ralston getting to 7-7 in the third before darkness halts play.

Friday is the ladies' final between Evert and Navratilova. Helen and I arrive at 10.30am to a very short queue and watch Jeff Turpin from Texas beat Glenn Michibata of Canada in the junior boys' quarters before we go to standing room on Centre. Other juniors we see are Ivan Lendl and Robbie Venter. We arrive shortly before the ladies' final begins and there is still room for fans. We only watch five games as Evert forges ahead but then leave to watch Hewitt/McMillan beat Alexander/Dent 9-7, 7-5, 6-4 in a lively match. They finish just after Navratilova beats Evert 2-6, 6-4, 7-5. We watch 16-year-old Pam Shriver beat Barbara Hallquist in a plate match and Kerry Reid/Wendy Turnbull beat Jausovec/Ruzici 4-6, 9-8, 6-3 in the doubles final after saving two match points. The match of the day is Fleming/McEnroe beating Okker/Wojciech Fibak 1-6, 6-3, 9-7, 6-4. At 7-7 in the third, Fibak is broken and the next game goes many deuces with several break points and set points before Fleming/McEnroe prevail. After breaking Fibak early in the fourth set, our boys overcome several break points to hold serve each time and win the match. No more tennis today so Jackie and I have Indian food and Helen gets some needed sleep.

Saturday is the final day at Wimbledon with the men's final between Borg and Connors. We get to a surprisingly short queue at 10.30am and get good spots in standing room after the gates are opened at noon. I watch a bit of Bob Carmichael

IVAN LENDL

playing Dale Collings in the plate semi before returning to Centre before the 2pm start. Connors is blasted by Borg, who counters Jimbo's best shots with forcing topspin returns. The result: 6-2, 6-2, 6-3. The junior boys' final plays the same time with Lendl beating Turpin. I do see a few games of the finish of that and the start of Tracy Austin beating Hana Mandlikova in the junior girls' final but then it's time to see Fleming/McEnroe take on Hewitt/McMillan in the men's doubles final. It's a bit disappointing as Fleming/McEnroe are outclassed in three easy sets but still enjoyable to see how doubles is played by a master team.

Our final match is the mixed final where McMillan/Stove beat Ruffels/King in two quick sets to prevent BJK from getting her 20th title. I played junior tennis at the same time as Billie Jean Moffitt, now King. She was quite a talker then and one of the top junior players in California. I recall her talking about Karen Hantze Susman in hushed and respectful tones. Karen won Wimbledon in 1962.

What a wonderful experience that first Wimbledon is for me and my family. It portends the promise of many future visits to my favorite tennis tournament in the world. The three of us spend another two weeks exploring much of the UK in a drive to the far northern point of Scotland and back with many interesting visits along the way.

1980

My First Trip to Wimbledon

Chris Foulkes, COVENTRY

My chances to go to The Championships were the highlight of the year when I was younger. Usually I went with either my parents or a fellow friend who like tennis as well as myself. We didn't go much to any finals days but on the first Tuesday made a point to see the previous year's Women's Champion starting her defence of the title.

Dad recalls on our first visit we had tried for many years in the ballot to get tickets. Then when we did we parked our car and right away we were approached by ticket touts who wanted to buy our tickets from us. I know this goes on but we would never miss the chance to see top players in action.

The one thing I did do was to take some photographs. Although only a basic camera the best time to catch the player was on serve. I recall John McEnroe and Chrissie Evert in my first shots, two great champions of their time. The doubles events were more played by the top players then. John McEnroe teamed with Peter Fleming. Women's top ones were Billie Jean King with Rosie Casals.

The British for me started with Tim Henman, with the 1977 winner Ginnie Wade always favourite with the crowds. Jo Durie also pulled the British women's game along at this time. You could always tell when there was a top seed playing. The amount of fans particularly on the outside courts were making a lot of sound with large numbers. Sometimes the scoreboard would bring up a result that would catch your attention.

The crowds were usually busy getting around the courts so taking time to sit for lunch was a welcome break. We took our own sandwiches, but we had to try some strawberries as you should, taken from the stalls on the grounds. I always used to visit the LTA and BTCA stalls which were useful for getting the latest details on tennis such as equipment and coaching matters.

Autographs were hard to come by. I do recall us getting one from South African Frew McMillan along with a short but friendly chat with

Chrissie Evert

him as well. The British players at that time were very popular with the Wimbledon followers of course.

As for the most important thing, the weather I am pretty sure was good that we had no rain on our day so we saw no hold-ups of play and no splashing groundsmen. It was always good to watch the Juniors and the famous Veterans who had their events too.

The last recall would be the first Tuesday look at the previous year's women's Champion. I am pretty sure on my visit it was Steffi Graf of Germany. I took some photos of her I still have and shall not part with!

We are Here!

Audrey Green, BALDOCK

My first visit to Wimbledon was in 1980, when my youngest daughter Shirley and I came along by train from Cambridge. We had no idea where to go – went to Wimbledon Station (didn't know about Southfields then), bus to the tennis – where we found people very helpful, directing us to Court One.

I remember standing on top of the steps and saying 'We are here!' Such a great feeling! Also seeing two of my favourites – Evonne Goolagong (Cawley) and Stan Smith was just great!

Then later found our way to an outside court, where John McEnroe

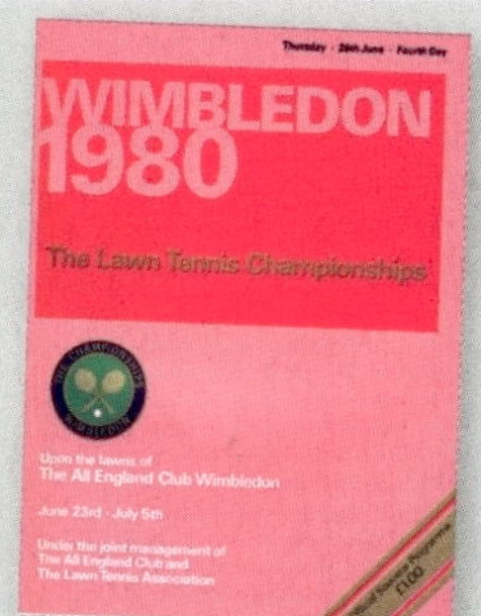

was playing, spent a great time there too! A lovely day altogether!

The first visit of many, over 30 years, have been lucky with tickets on the whole! (But will always remember the excitement of the first time!)

1981

It Had Changed So Much, Yet Not at All

Terry Brady, HARTFORD, CONNECTICUT

arrived in SW19 in the summer of 1981 by a circuitous path. I was living in Palm Beach, Florida and was a caretaker of a mansion owned by a British ex-pat. A friend had his 48' yacht docked outside about to take a transatlantic trip back to Gosport, UK and needed some help. So as a young and foolish lad, I jumped on board with my sea bag and headed out to blue beyond. Knowing I was an avid sports fan, my friend and former employer John Christlieb said don't forget to stop by Wimbledon. I was off to explore Europe and my first stop was London.

After a few days of exploration, I took the train out to SW19 and followed the masses to the Somerset Rd queue. I stepped thru gate 13 on to the grounds and knew I was in a hallowed icon of sports. Somehow I managed to find my way to Court 1 and watched a gentleman and future colleague, if you could call him that then, John McEnroe melt down in his famous rant match. I still have a few photos of that day. I came back the next day and took in several more matches and had my fill of Pimm's.

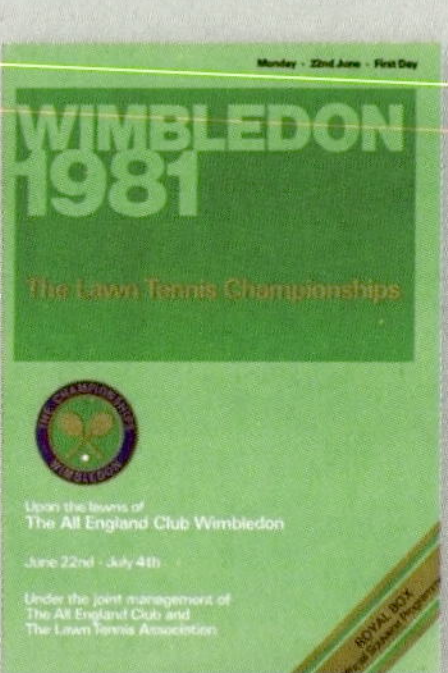

Fast forward 30 years and I am now the Director of Remote Operations for ESPN overseeing tennis. As I walked up Marryat Road to the venue I immediately recognized the famous walls and the gate I entered so many years before. Walking up to the broadcast gate 16 and into the venue and it had changed so much but yet not at all. It is the true center of the tennis universe and one of the iconic sporting venues in the world. For the next six years I had the honor of visiting in November for planning meetings

John McEnroe approaches the umpire to contest a call in 1981. He continued to argue with him and attempted to break his racket in frustration before going on to beat Tim Gullikson (USA) 7-6, 7-5, 6-3.

and coming back in June for the fortnight. My desk looking out at Court 18 was the envy of every tennis and sports fan. I wonder how I ever got any work done?

Through my job I have had the pleasure of visiting over 30 countries and covered all four tennis majors, ATP Finals, Davis Cup and many more world-class events but nothing compares to the green and purple of Wimbledon. I am honored to be part of the Wimbledon experience and feel my first trip back in 1981 was the beginning of a magical journey that has been my sports broadcasting career. I have met so many wonderful people and share so many fond memories of Wimbledon, the village and the many beers I consumed at the Crooked Billet. It is truly a magical and wonderful place, one that forever will remain in my heart.

1982

In the Free Standing Room

Kani Bawa, NOTTINGHAM

It was Sunday 4 July 1982, American Independence Day and Wimbledon men's finals day, an all-American affair. I had queued with my sister Meena for a few days to guarantee front row standing positions. This was the year the last four days were sold in advance. Earlier in the week, I had been into the grounds to watch the second-round match featuring Jimmy Connors and Aussie John Alexander, who took a set before losing in four. Jimmy Connors was playing well, and it was all so exciting.

The gates opened at 12 noon, then there was a two-hour wait time before play. Meena was a McEnroe fan and I a Connors fan. We'd got to know the people we queued with outside the grounds and those we stood with on Centre Court. We were a rowdy bunch. We were shouting the players' names. I shouted 'C'mon Jimmy'. He looked up at us and put his finger to lips asking us to shhh. We giggled.

After the final, we dashed over to Court One standing to watch Aussies, the late Peter McNamara and Paul McNamee play against Peter Fleming and John McEnroe (final number two for McEnroe). I loved Peter McNamara and Paul McNamee. Not only were they good-looking, they were an excellent doubles pair and fun to watch. They were fighters and determined to win. The SuperMacs won the Wimbledon doubles title that year. They were the Golden Age of tennis, along with Raul Ramirez and Brian Gottfried.

I was studying at Huddersfield Poly that year and went back for the end of term. Lecturers and other students and friends were telling me they had seen me at Wimbledon. One said he'd seen me whilst watching the final in Spain! I thought yeah, they'd seen me when the Beeb scanned the crowd. I'd been at Wimbledon for two weeks and always managed to get a front row standing position, just as in previous years. Of course, they would have seen me. Later, I found out, my face filled the whole TV screen! To this day, I still haven't seen that image.

When it rained, in the days before multiscreen and live pause, highlights from previous years were repeated. The 1982 men's final was one of them, and when that was shown my work colleagues and friends used to tell me they'd seen me on TV. I knew which match they were talking about!

When we used to queue overnight, we were given a queuing ticket every morning (a raffle ticket with a number), so we could go back to where we were staying, take a shower and change. We had to return to the queue by a certain time to be checked off. One year in the 1980s, my sister and I started queuing about a week before for the men's final. (We had been into the grounds during the first week.) The stewards made our queue the 'Official Men's Final queue'. It rained one night, so we walked up the road to Southfields, carrying our heavy sleeping bags to dry them out at the launderette. The atmosphere in the queue was electrifying. We'd hardly get any sleep during the night. Sometimes the only way to catch up was to sleep in the car park on the golf course for part of the day.

Gone are the days of standing room. My days of overnight queuing may be over, but I can treasure them from my photos and memories. These days, I attend with my sister on the days we are successful in the ballot and tennis club draws. We still attend every year for at least a day. It's a luxury to us now.

The Wimbledon Championships have often been played against a backdrop of political turmoil, economic strife and, on occasions, the dark clouds of military conflict. When Jimmy Connors won his second title in 1982, British forces had only weeks earlier been engaged in battle with Argentine troops in the Falkland Islands, but what tennis fans remember of that summer is how the indefatigable Connors refused to be bested by the upstart New Yorker. Without those gallant troops, however, and millions of others before and since, there would be no Championships and there would be no Wimbledon.

1982

What a Small World!

Julia Freeman, WARGRAVE

I have always been a keen tennis fan, going to Wimbledon as often as I could during my nursing days at Guys Hospital! Then I went down to Bristol to do my midwifery, met my husband, married and proceeded to have three children! We travelled around living in Hong Kong, Germany and North Wales before returning to our flat in Battersea where Anna, our youngest daughter, was born in April 1982.

We were planning our next move when, during The Championships in June, I said I must take the children to Wimbledon before we leave, so I packed them all in the car and set off with Sarah (seven years), Mark (four years) and Anna (three months). We got in and made a beeline for Court 2 where Anne Hobbs and Jo Durie were playing Pam Shriver and Martina Navratilova. I parked Anna in the pram with the security guard (she was sleeping!) and took the other two up the steps to the free standing room. We watched some of the game and as it neared the end, I said, 'Come on, let's go down to the entrance used by the players' which we did and as the players left the court, Martina patted Mark on the head – he is now a good Club player which I knew he would be with Martina's blessing!!

I started Umpiring in 1992 and my first Wimbledon was 1994. In 1996, I was sitting on Court 4 at the change of ends and chatted to the scorer who was standing next to me. I asked her how she got into that job as I had a daughter and son at University who would be interested in doing it. She said her father was a professional tennis player so I asked his name. She replied 'Frew McMillan'. 'Oh,' I said 'were you by any chance born at Southmead Hospital in about 1981?' At this, her jaw dropped and she said, 'Yes' to which I replied that I had admitted her mother and was in on her birth!!

In about 1998 or 99, I was sitting in my chair (between matches) in the corner of Court 2 when this lady tapped me on the shoulder and said, 'Are you Julia Burtenshaw from Hailsham?' I was quite amazed and said 'Yes' as I didn't recognise her, to which she replied that we were at Junior school together! In those early days, I only worked ten days at Wimbledon so when I had finished, I went down to spend a few days with my father who still lived in Hailsham and as usual went to church with him, and another very old school friend was helping with the service. Afterwards, I went up to him and asked if he remembered Sylvia from our Junior School days to which he replied, of course – she was my first 'girlfriend'!! What a small world!

Martina Navratilova

Julia Freeman is a familiar figure to British tennis fans, having officiated at many UK tournaments over the last three decades. She is pictured on page 59 of the 2019 Wimbledon Official Annual, sharing smiles with Stan Wawrinka after he accidentally hit her with his racket whilst chasing a wide ball.

1984

A Wimbledon Odyssey

David Rutherford, CROMLIX

first walked through the gates of The All England Club on Sunday 8 July 1984. I was 19 years old, it was a very hot sunny day and it made a big impression on me.

I had arrived in London in the very early morning of the previous day having come down from Scotland on an overnight bus. It was my first time out of Scotland and I found the sheer size of London quite overwhelming. Fortunately for me my elder sister had lived there for three years and had already been to Wimbledon on a couple of occasions. She knew of the procedure for obtaining tickets – the public ballot – and knew that it was much easier to get tickets for the standing enclosures of the Centre Court than for the seated section. In the ballot for that year's championships she had been allocated two tickets for the east standing enclosure of the Centre Court on the final day – hence how I found myself in London that day.

By the time I left Stirling bus station on the Friday night I knew that I was going to see John McEnroe play Jimmy Connors, the two biggest names in men's tennis at that time. I had been to some football matches in Glasgow by that time of my life, but nothing on this scale. This was something else altogether and I was very excited. On the day of the final we left Highgate in north London very early in the morning to travel by underground to Wimbledon. My sister knew that to get the best vantage point inside the Centre Court it was important to arrive at the grounds as early as possible and get as far ahead as possible in a succession of queues. This was to be my first experience of queuing at Wimbledon.

The train suddenly got much busier at Earl's Court and almost everyone, including me, alighted at Southfields. As we walked to The All England Club, retail and catering stalls were being set up in front gardens along the way despite the early hour.

The first queue was along the pavement beside Church Road outside the grounds of The All England Club. As we queued here a series of well-spoken elderly gentlemen in straw hats and striped ties walked up and down making sure that all those queuing had tickets and knew exactly where to go and what to do once inside the grounds. It all seemed terribly civilised to me – this didn't happen at Hampden Park in Glasgow!

These men contrasted markedly with other individuals walking up and down the line, some of whom would furtively mutter under their breaths from time to time words such as 'who needs tickets I'll buy any spare' or similar – my first experience of ticket touting.

At 11am the main gates to the complex were opened. Once inside we immediately made our way to our next queue which was behind a set of large iron gates on an area known as the 'lawn' even though it was paved in concrete. By this time the significance of the queuing was apparent to me. The first few people to reach the entry points into the standing enclosures of the Centre Court were allowed to take their places on the enclosure immediately. Once a certain number of people were in each section subsequent ticket holders arriving had to queue outside the court underneath the stands and weren't allowed in until shortly before the action started.

This system ensured that people on the enclosures weren't packed in tightly for any longer than was necessary – particularly important on a hot day. It also meant that those admitted into the court first of all got the choice viewing spots, so I knew that as soon as the gates opened at midday I had to get to entrance G in the South East Hall as quickly as possible. As the clock neared 12 the photographers inside lined up to capture the ensuing dash to the Centre Court. They weren't disappointed, despite the best endeavours of the stewards to keep things as orderly as possible.

Unfortunately, we didn't run fast enough and weren't permitted inside the Centre Court when we reached our entrance point, but we were at the very front of the queue to be allowed in just before 2pm; I wasn't terribly bothered. I was at Wimbledon, it was a lovely day and I was about to see John McEnroe and Jimmy Connors. What could be better? I had, however, learned an important lesson for the future.

One thing which seemed quite odd to me was the presence of so many military personnel in uniform acting as stewards until my sister explained that this was a Wimbledon tradition.

Shortly before two o'clock we were admitted into the Centre Court, which seemed to me much smaller than it appeared on television but which nevertheless was a very impressive arena. Despite not being part of the first group of spectators into the enclosure we still managed to get an excellent vantage point at the extreme end of the east standing enclosure, immediately beneath the seats where the players' families and coaches sit. The benefit of being on this side of the court was that the umpire's chair wouldn't obscure our view.

At 2pm precisely the players walked onto court behind a man in a white coat carrying their racquets. The crowd rose and gave rapturous applause, even those in the Royal Box. Soon after, following the warm-up and the preliminaries, the match was underway on what by that time was a very hot day – not something I was accustomed to in Scotland.

I was hoping for two things in particular. Firstly, that the match would be an epic five setter that would last for hours on end just as the final between the same two players had done two years previously. Secondly, I was hoping to witness in person one

of John McEnroe's renowned temperamental outbursts. In the event I was to be disappointed on both fronts.

The match simply flew by and was finished in just over an hour – one of the shortest men's singles finals of all time. I had, however, been lucky enough to witness a masterclass in tennis by McEnroe who simply blew the aging Connors away in three very short sets. Not only that but John behaved like a perfect gentleman throughout the match. It was a truly marvellous spectacle nevertheless.

When the trophy presentation was finished and the players had left the arena much of the crowd did likewise, so much so that by the time the mixed doubles final started the stands were still half empty. The final was between Britain's John Lloyd and Australia's Wendy Turnbull and America's Kathy Jordan and Steve Denton. The crowd steadily returned to the court at each break in play and was almost at full complement again by the time the match was over. That John Lloyd was part of the winning duo pleased the crowd.

Unlike the trophy presentation for the singles events, the doubles winners had to go up to the Royal Box to collect their prizes. The Mixed Doubles champions were followed by the winners of some of the lesser events including a young English girl by the name of Annabel Croft who had won the Junior Girls Singles Championship. Her final had been played on Court No.1 at the same time as the main event had been on the Centre Court.

As we made our way out of the Centre Court one of the military stewards was handing back tickets to any spectators who wanted

these as souvenirs. After such a memorable occasion I was pleased to get mine back. My sister then gave me a guided tour of the complex pointing out the Fred Perry statue, the giant scoreboard, the outside courts, and, of course, the strawberries and cream stall.

We visited a kiosk which sold postcards of all the top players, most of which I bought, along with other souvenirs such as pens, pencils and posters. I also purchased a copy of the official programme which I considered very important to have – as I also had these for all of the football matches I had seen.

There was a food court at raised level in Aorangi Park next to the Short Tennis arena, and we ate fish and chips from conical-shaped containers and had half a pint of Oranjeboom lager each from the bar.

As we caught a bus from the adjacent bus park back to Southfields station I knew that I had enjoyed a memorable day. What I didn't know, however, was that it had been my first of 11 consecutive years of spending at least one day at The Championships in what was to become an annual ritual for me.

ROLEX
16
MISS Z. GARRISON
2
v
3
MISS M. NAVRATILOVA

CHAPTER 5
Wimbledon Gets Serious
1985-2000

In 1984 a 16-year-old boy made his Wimbledon debut, reaching the third round of the men's singles before being forced to retire due to injury. In the following year, at just 17, Germany's Boris Becker became the youngest male champion in Wimbledon's history. He went on to reach a total of seven finals, winning three titles.

By the time of Boris's victory in 1985, his 16-year-old compatriot Steffi Graf had already played at Wimbledon three times, twice reaching the fourth round. In 1989, still a teenager, Steffi won the first of her seven Wimbledon singles titles. The success of these two young stars triggered a golden era for tennis in Germany, similar to the one Borg had started in Sweden a decade earlier.

Becker was shrewdly managed by Ilie Nastase's former Davis Cup doubles partner Ion Tiriac. From his base in the tax haven of Monte Carlo, Tiriac took player sponsorship to a new level, clinching a series of lucrative deals for the 'Wunderkind', as Becker was known in the press, with Ellesse, Puma and various other companies. The sums involved dwarfed the earnings of the pioneers of Open Tennis little more than a decade earlier.

Germany's Steffi Graf and Boris Becker reached a combined total of 16 Wimbledon singles finals between 1985 and 1999, winning ten titles

The 1986 Championships were Wimbledon's 100th and Boris Becker, at 18 now an experienced campaigner, won his second title. He was succeeded as champion in 1987 by Australia's Pat Cash, whose spontaneous celebration delighted all who saw it. David Rutherford was in the East Open Stand on that scorching hot Sunday afternoon in 1987: 'I was at The Championships at least one day for 11 consecutive years (1984–1994) and was lucky enough to witness some momentous events, including the shortest men's singles final of the 20th century (1984, McEnroe/Connors), Boris Becker's first Wimbledon success in 1985 and the day when Pat Cash climbed over the crowd, myself included, to reach his family and coach in the players' box.' Commentating for BBC Television, John Barrett, like everyone else, was taken completely by surprise. 'I've never seen anything like this before,' he remarked, adding, 'I'm quite sure this has never happened on Wimbledon's Centre Court before.' Speaking to *The Times* on Monday, 6 July 1987, Cash said: 'I didn't think it would be so difficult to get up there. Eventually I had to stand on some poor guy's head to make it.'

In the next three Wimbledon finals Boris Becker faced blond serve-and-volley exponent Stefan Edberg, the popular Swede coming out on top in 1988 and 1990 with the German's third title sandwiched in between.

In 1990 significant changes were made at The All England Club to increase spectator safety, following three tragic incidents at football grounds during the previous decade. On 11 May 1985 a fire had broken out during a football match at Bradford City's Valley Parade stadium. Fifty-six people were killed and more than 250 injured. Later that same month, 39 football fans were killed and 600 injured in a crush before the start of the European Cup Final between Liverpool and Juventus at the Heysel Stadium in Brussels. In April 1989, 96 people died and more than 750 were injured in a crush at Sheffield Wednesday's Hillsborough Stadium shortly after the start of an FA Cup semi-final match between Liverpool and Nottingham Forest.

As a result of these awful incidents, legislation was passed requiring all covered grandstands accommodating more than 500 people to receive a safety certificate from the local authority. To get a certificate, Wimbledon had to lose a number of popular features. All the courts with grandstands became all-ticketed, apart from the standing area at the back of No.2 Court, and only ticket holders could gain access to the Centre and No.1 Court complex. As a result it was no longer possible for people who had paid for ground admission to view the action on No.1 Court from the passageway separating it from the Centre Court. Also lost was the popular view over the outside courts from the openings above the Centre Court Clubhouse balcony. Most lamented of all, however, was the removal of the standing areas on the east and west sides of Centre Court. For a long time free and only recently ticketed, these standing areas had given countless fans their first glimpse of action on the world's most famous tennis court. ⓘ

The Club House during LTA Centenary year, 1988

Nineteen-ninety-one saw a Wimbledon 'first' as play was required on the Middle Sunday due to heavy rain on the first four days. Alan Little takes up the story in the *Wimbledon Compendium*: 'The Sunday became a unique day in Wimbledon's history. There was a queue stretching for one and a half miles outside the grounds. When the gates were opened at 10am, 11,000 Centre Court and 7,000 No.1 Court tickets at the flat rate of £10 and ground passes at £5 were available, on a first-come basis. By the start of play at 12 noon the Centre Court was full of excited spectators who created a carnival atmosphere.'

Middle Sunday was a great success, enabling the tournament to be completed on time, and the exercise was later repeated when rain interrupted The Championships in 1997 and 2004.

Ninety ninety-one also saw Andre Agassi's conversion from Wimbledon-hater to Centre Court favourite. He had played at Wimbledon once before, losing badly to France's Henri Leconte in the first round as a 16-year-old in 1987. After that chastening experience he stayed away for three years, perhaps agreeing with 1966 champion Manuel Santana that, in tennis at least, 'grass is just for cows'.

In his three years away from Wimbledon Agassi had become a tennis superstar, known as much for his flamboyant dress sense as his fine two-handed baseline game. At a time when new racket technology was threatening to turn tennis into an unappealing slugfest, Andre Agassi kept public interest high. Clad in pink bicycle shorts and with shoulder-length hair, the teenager from Las Vegas started out as an outspoken critic of Wimbledon's staid traditions. When he walked out onto Centre Court for his first match in 1991, there was great excitement about what he would be wearing. To the crowd's delight, Agassi removed his tracksuit to reveal his regular Nike apparel, including bicycle shorts, but all in white! The crowd roared its approval, and a love affair began that continues to the present day.

Despite his game not being ideally suited to grass, Agassi battled his way to the quarter-finals where he lost to fellow-American David Wheaton. The tournament was won by German outsider Michael Stich, but Agassi was back the following year and this time went all the way, defeating Goran Ivanisevic of newly independent Croatia to win his first Grand Slam singles title. The 1992 Championships finished on a high note when, on an extra 'People's Monday', John McEnroe and Michael Stich teamed up to win the Men's Doubles Final by clinching the fifth set of the final 19-17 against Jim Grabb and Richey Reneberg. McEnroe's regular partner Peter Fleming, with whom he had won four Wimbledon doubles titles, had retired five years earlier. ☉

Chris Evert, Martina Navratilova and Steffi Graf were three of the finest players and most popular champions in Wimbledon's history, and during the mid to late 1980s their Wimbledon careers overlapped. The rivalry between Chris and Martina was legendary and did much to elevate tennis in the public consciousness around the world.

Chris Evert played at Wimbledon every year from 1972 to 1989, and only once, in 1983, failed to reach the semi-finals. Despite her double-handed baseline game being better suited to clay courts, she reached the Wimbledon final ten times, winning in 1974, 1976 and 1981. Of her seven final losses, five came against the remarkable Martina Navratilova, who won her record-breaking ninth and last singles title in 1990. Thirteen years later, in 2003, Martina won the Mixed Doubles in partnership with India's Leander Paes to clinch a record-equalling 20th Wimbledon title.

1992 champion Andre Agassi was hugely popular with the Centre Court crowd

As Chris and Martina neared the twilight of their careers, Germany's Steffi Graf was approaching the peak of hers. She won her maiden Grand Slam singles title at Roland Garros in 1987 and in the same year reached her first Wimbledon final, losing to Martina Navratilova. A year later, Steffi reigned supreme, gaining revenge over Navratilova at Wimbledon on her way to a unique 'Golden Slam' – the big four titles plus a gold medal in Seoul as tennis returned to the Olympic Games for the first time in 64 years.

Between 1988 and 1996 Steffi was the dominant force at Wimbledon, winning the Ladies' Singles title seven times in nine years. Her only failures were both against Americans, a 1990 semi-final loss to Zina Garrison and a shock first-round defeat against Lori McNeil in 1994.

Yugoslavia's Monica Seles brought youthful exuberance to Wimbledon in the early 1990s, but in 1993 her progress was halted when a crazed Steffi fan stabbed her on court in Hamburg. Other women to shine in the last decade of the 20th century were Conchita Martinez, Martina Hingis, Jana Novotna and Lindsay Davenport. Novotna's victory in 1998 was warmly received, for she had been in floods of tears five years earlier after leading Steffi 4-1 in the final set of the 1993 final. ☉

Pete Sampras from Washington DC won Wimbledon seven times in eight years between 1993 and 2000, but his utter dominance over his main rivals coupled with his self-effacing manner did little to ignite the passions of the Centre Court crowd. Whether saving a break point with a second-serve ace, hitting a murderous passing shot or diving to make a seemingly impossible volley, as he did against Andre Agassi in the 1999 Wimbledon final, Sampras's reaction was always the same: eyes down, a quick adjustment of his racket strings and on to the next point. His modesty was admirable but, when combined with the lightning-fast courts and balls of his era, his matches were often dull fare for the watching millions.

The 1990s was a difficult period for Wimbledon's authorities, too. Matches involving tall, big servers such as Sampras, Goran Ivanisevic, Boris Becker, Todd Martin, Guy Forget and Richard Krajicek, who served his way to the title in 1996, often consisted of little more than a constant barrage of aces. The 1992 semi-final between Sampras and Ivanisevic, played on No.1 Court, was mind-numbing, and things got even worse when the two men met again in the 1994 final in 116- degree heat. Writing in the *Wimbledon Official Annual*, John Parsons of *The Daily Telegraph* drily observed: 'Brilliantly though both players served, especially in the first two sets before Ivanisevic lost heart, you can have too much of a good thing. This was such an occasion.'

Parsons was in no doubt about the cause of the problem: 'The players themselves can hardly be blamed. Their job is to win and to take advantage of everything at their disposal, be it their own skills, the weaknesses in their opponents, the high-tech rackets or balls which fly through the air faster, it sometimes seems, than ever.'

Wimbledon had to act, and within a few years the grass and the balls were slowed down considerably, eventually leading to the situation where clay-court specialists such as Gustavo Kuerten and Rafael Nadal could compete on equal terms with the big servers on the lawns of SW19. ⊘

In 1995 22-year-old Tim Henman accidentally hit a ball girl in a fit of pique during a first-round doubles match, resulting in him and his partner Jeremy Bates being defaulted. This was the first disqualification in Wimbledon's 118-year history, and was followed just three days later by the second when America's Jeff Tarango, coincidentally one of Henman's opponents in that fateful doubles match, stormed off Court 13 after verbally abusing French umpire Bruno Rebeuh.

A year later and a lot more mature, Tim Henman came to national prominence when he beat fifth-seeded Yevgeny Kafelnikov in a gripping five-set encounter en route to the Wimbledon quarter-finals. In a further boost for the home nation, big-serving Greg Rusedski had recently switched allegiances from Canada to Britain, greatly increasing the chances of Wimbledon success. For a decade from 1996 it seemed only a matter of time before a British man ended a long barren spell stretching back to 1936 when Fred Perry had won his third and last Wimbledon title. Perry, who had died whilst on a visit to the 1995 Australian Open, never did get to see his successor crowned.

Henman came closest, reaching four semi-finals in five years, the first two of which he lost in four sets to Sampras, the eventual champion. Subsequent last-four defeats to Goran Ivanisevic and Australia's Lleyton Hewitt finally put paid to Tim's Wimbledon dream. Despite having the ideal game for grass, Rusedski fared less well, his best effort being a solitary quarter-final appearance in 1997. The list of players he lost to at The Championships includes Stefan Edberg, Pete Sampras, Andy Roddick, Mark Philippoussis and Goran Ivanisevic, a veritable Who's Who of fine grass-court players.

The much-loved old No.1 Court was used for the last time in 1996, and on the first day of the 1997 Championships a parade of Wimbledon champions who had won three or more singles titles marked the opening of its magnificent replacement. The hundreds who had queued overnight for tickets were rewarded by seeing Wimbledon greats including Louise Brough, Margaret Court, Rod Laver, Chris Evert and Martina Navratilova

Tim Henman

Britain's Tim Henman was a Wimbledon semi-finalist on four occasions between 1998 and 2002

receive commemorative medals from the Duke of Kent, followed by Tim Henman 'christening' the new court with a straight-sets victory over Canada's Daniel Nestor.

Serena and Venus Williams, two of Wimbledon's greatest-ever champions

During the mid-1990s word spread around the tennis world of a pair of young girls from California who looked set for tennis stardom. These rumours were not misplaced, for the Williams sisters, Venus and Serena, have between them proven to be the dominant force in women's tennis up to the present day. Venus first played at Wimbledon in 1997, just after her 17th birthday, losing in the first round to Poland's Magdalena Grzybowska, but by the 2000 Millennium Championships she had matured sufficiently to win the first of her five singles titles. Serena, the younger of the two by a year, made her debut in 1998 and immediately became a champion, winning the Mixed Doubles in partnership with Max Mirnyi of Belarus. On the same day, 16-year-old Roger Federer from Switzerland got his first taste of the Centre Court, ascending the steps of the Royal Box twice to receive the Junior Boys' Singles and Doubles trophies.

Wimbledon celebrated the dawning of the new Millennium in grand style. The striking Millennium Building, containing state-of-the art facilities for players, officials, the media and All England Club members was opened by the Duke of Kent, and on the middle Saturday of the 2000 Championships 64 players, including many past champions, paraded on the Centre Court. As Master of Ceremonies John Barrett introduced each player in turn, memories flooded back for the packed Centre Court crowd and the millions watching on TV. At 94 Britain's Bunny Austin was the oldest former player present. The men's singles finalist of 1932 and 1938 was particularly warmly received, but sadly passed away a few weeks later. A particularly poignant moment came when John Barrett introduced his wife Angela Mortimer, the 1961 Ladies' champion. ◓

Bunny Austin took part in the Millennium Champions' Parade, 74 years after his Wimbledon debut in 1926

My First Wimbledon

Amisha Savani, LONDON

My very first Wimbledon was the precursor to what can only be described as my annual fortnightly obsession. I wish I still had the very first programme from that day, as I was too young to recall the exact date other than to say it was in the 1980s. A very interesting time in tennis, both in terms of characters (players and commentators), fashion and the game itself.

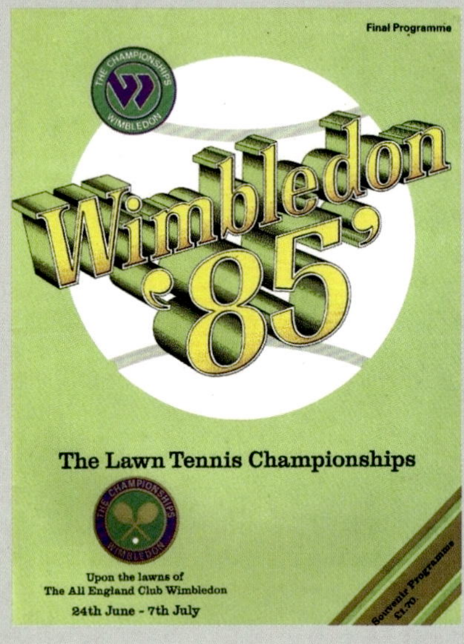

I was a small child so was accompanied by an older relative. My father had been given two tickets by a friend who had links to Wimbledon. I remember being excited for weeks before the visit, having watched the Wimbledon fortnight at home on TV coming home from school. For me, Wimbledon heralded the start of my summer and happy days playing tennis in the sunshine, whether on a court or hitting against a wall outside. Who can forget that memorable theme tune, Dan Maskell's infamous 'Oh I say' commentary, pristine green courts and the traditional all-white dress code. I cannot recall the exact date or year. I must have been very little because I do remember having to be lifted up to be able to get a view of the matches being played.

We travelled by District Line to Southfields. There was a shared taxi service available which took you straight to The All England Lawn Tennis Club. We joined some others in the taxi, and I recall queues and queues of people on the other side of the road with tents set up. That was in the days where people could camp out on the streets for a ticket.

I recall that McEnroe was playing. The biggest player at the time. Big hair, headband and a big attitude to match! And that we had some standing room tickets. I got a glimpse of the man when I was lifted up. My first live Wimbledon tennis match. Centre Court felt huge to me. People often say it seems smaller than on television. For me at the time I recall that it seemed bigger, probably as

I was a small child so everything was bigger then! I recall sampling some strawberries and cream with caster sugar sprinkled on top. The weather was gorgeous, we strolled past the outside courts. Looking at the court maps now, I can actually recall where we were walking – it was between the outside courts 5 and 9 when a white (yes they were white then!) tennis ball came rolling towards me from one of the courts (8, 9 or 10). I grabbed it and kept it – the perfect souvenir! Upon walking around the court to see who had been playing, I noted that it was the former Ladies' Champion, Virginia Wade! The ball I had kept had been used by a former Wimbledon champion – what better souvenir and on my very first visit! That started my passion for Wimbledon and for tennis. Over the years, I loved watching Navratilova, Graf, Seles, Agassi, Becker.

I take two weeks off work just for my annual Wimbledon pilgrimage. Everyone who knows me well, knows that that is where they will find me during that fortnight. My recent visits to the AELTC over the past few years have involved some fabulous experiences thanks to my being a guest of an esteemed tennis journalist who has invited me as her guest to the Broadcast/ media centre where I have been fortunate to have witnessed the behind-the-scenes set-up of the radio and television journalists from around the world. I have also been gifted debenture tickets, most recently for the Sam Querrey v Rafael Nadal quarter-final match, won by Nadal. I walked into the Debentures lounge after the match to be greeted by none other than Grace Jones, looking resplendent in one of her signature Issey Miyake hats. We had a long chat about Nadal (both of us being huge fans of his beautifully aggressive topspin groundstrokes, the man off court and what he has done for players and his charities, and the physique that is like no other player), amongst other amusing and varied topics. Ms Jones invited me to join her in sharing a glass of Rosé wine to celebrate Nadal's win! I was also lucky enough to have courtside seats for the first doubles match pairing of Serena Williams and Andy Murray. After their win, when they were both signing autographs for the fans that had rushed over, my two neighbours offered Andy a pint of beer to celebrate. He actually looked tempted for a second, before politely declining, laughing with them, and continued to sign autographs and pose for selfies with fans. Ever the gentleman.

Anyone who has ever attended The Championships will remember that visit forever. It is undoubtedly my happy place.

White balls were used at Wimbledon for the last time in 1985. In that year South Africa's Kevin Curren recorded straight-sets wins over Stefan Edberg, John McEnroe and Jimmy Connors in consecutive rounds before losing to 17-year-old Boris Becker in a closely contested final.

1985

A Different World

Stuart Peskett, FELTHAM

My first visit to Wimbledon was in 1985. It was the year of my CSEs, my first part-time job, the year EastEnders started and the year Bobby Ewing was killed off in Dallas (before coming back a few years later very much alive having a shower).

I remember being asked if I wanted to go to Wimbledon that year and having been a tennis fan for five years I was not sure, as I did not want to spoil the illusion of what my feelings for Wimbledon were. I was happy just to sit at home and watch on TV and hear the smack of tennis balls, the clapping from the crowds, Dan Maskell, Virginia Wade and Ann Jones commentating and the players berating themselves for losing a point. But a few days or so later I made the decision to take up the offer and go as I may later have had many regrets on not seeing these great characters of tennis before they retired. A few days later I was excited and ready to go but hoped it would not rain and that there would be no train strikes.

The day I went was Tuesday, 2 July 1985 which was in the second week. We arrived at Wimbledon station and queued for the bus for a short ride to the grounds at SW19. I remember coming down the hill along Marryat Road and seeing Wimbledon for the first time; it was a mouth-opening feeling of shock and I couldn't make out if the grounds were big or small – it was like an illusion. I was just overwhelmed by what I saw.

We got off the bus and the atmosphere was fantastic – the Union Jack flags, different accents, people rushing around, some looking smart, others looking not so but who cared – I was at Wimbledon, a dream come true for me a teenager thinking I have done the most brilliant thing ever.

The next hour was spent queuing up. I think it was in Somerset Road but I can definitely remember walking in past the gates and into the grounds after being checked and going into a different world. Play had already started and we bought a programme which I still have today and marked on the matches I had seen or glided past. We walked past the old Court 2 but that was hidden so we walked past Court 3 and the first player I ever saw in the flesh was the Czech great Helena Sukova playing Paradis from France. I couldn't believe what I was seeing – a player in flesh, yes, she was real tall and rangy, hit a good forehand. Everything seemed strange. Was this for real I thought to myself? But it was and did I enjoy it ... yes of course. The only thing that I was not keen on was getting pushed in the gangways of the outside courts. We walked around the other courts in that area and saw glimpses of former British number one Roger Taylor playing a Veteran's match and still playing good, also Anne White from the

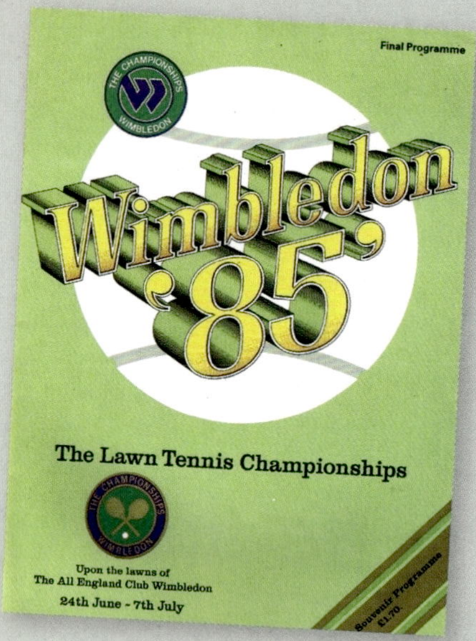

USA who had caused a stir for wearing an all-in-one white tight body suit; she was pretty hot-looking in the flesh. She was playing doubles with Betsy 'Boots' Nagelsen, a smiling tall player with a good forehand. We then decided to go to Court 13 as we knew one of my favourites was playing – the American Pam Shriver playing a young Steffi Graf. We queued up for a bit and then suddenly we were let in, me thinking I was not going to see much but boy was I wrong. 'Alrighty OK' as the Americans used to say, and I was, because we got ushered down to the second row near to the court ... fantastic. What I remember was how hot it was around the court, the atmosphere, the cheering, the smell of food and Pam Shriver's hot language ... was I shocked ... yes ... did I enjoy ... of course I had never had from a lady so much swearing but good on her, she was there to play, not to let Graf win and she had the most wonderful slice shots and service action and she was a joy to watch ... Graf was OK, her forehand was good.

After that match we went around the grounds and towards the Church Road end and suddenly it was like going into a different room; there was a band playing, the cluttering of knives and forks, the smell of food, drink and cigarettes, people looking and buying from the Merchandising area, fantastic and unreal. We then bought our fish and chips and drink of water (no alcohol or Pimm's; this I was to experience in a good few later years). I didn't want the strawberries and cream; it was not for me but it looked nice, fresh and well presented like everything at Wimbledon. We walked back to the scoreboard to see what was going on and you could hear the cheers from Centre Court; it was like an explosion but a good one and made me have goose pimples. Ivan Lendl and Henri Leconte from France had just walked on, but as we didn't have tickets we couldn't see them play. Well that's what we thought but that changed later in the day. We walked around back to Court 2 and the other courts in that area and saw Britain's David Felgate and Nick Brown playing doubles.

On Court 13 there was a women's doubles match involving two of my personal favourites – the great Aussie Wendy Turnbull and the great Czech Hana Mandlikova. We ran and queued which seemed like forever as the court was packed and people were not getting up from their seats as these two ladies seemed very popular. As I waited in anticipation I could hear a lot of Aussies cheering for Miss Turnbull. I was not disappointed. We got seated in the middle and there they were sitting during a changeover. It was strange to see them in the flesh like all the players we had seen at that time, both smaller in height but boy could they hit a shot. Mandlikova had a brilliant backhand and Turnbull had quick

court speed with a big volley. The crowd loved it and so did they both, smiling to the crowds.

When they won we went over to Centre Court and realised you could queue to watch the match but only standing. The Lendl and Leconte match was still going on and within minutes I was being ushered into Centre Court. What an experience, goose pimples again and this great arena, small but compact. The play was excellent. Lendl, one of my heroes, was stern and tall, Leconte smaller but with good hands and these two men played hard and quick. The crowd were loud and I was quite wary of too many people around me and I couldn't always see too much as I was smaller than them. Again I remember people smoking and drinking beer but I loved it; the atmosphere was again hot, sticky and armpits of not a nice fragrance but, I was in luck, I got on Centre Court. We went back there late in the evening to watch a mixed doubles match involving Kathy Jordan of the USA and the Aussie Mark Edmondson. This time I felt I could breathe as seats were available and I had the chance to sit on a green Wimbledon chair on Centre Court – the crowd subdued but still enjoying the entertaining play.

I saw Lendl again a bit later in the day this time on the old Court One and again standing but right up at the top. I was not good with heights and I didn't feel safe although I probably was. Lendl was playing doubles with the Aussie

Fancutt. They looked very small from where I was. When their match finished they stayed on as their next opponents were McEnroe and Fleming. Another favourite of mine; in the flesh McEnroe was smaller but he was a fantastic mover on the court and had good volleys but to much disappointment there were no tantrums that I saw but there was an atmosphere of competitiveness, not just with the players but the crowd getting involved as well. We saw the first set and decided that was enough. It was getting late and time to leave but I could have stayed all night; nothing else was important at that time. We saw a mixed doubles on Court 3 involving another favourite Martina Navratilova with Paul McNamee of Australia. It was a packed court but I managed to squeeze through the flock of people and see them play. Navratilova was slimmer in the flesh, more toned and smaller but she was tough, one great server for a woman at the time, while McNamee was fast with a brilliant backhand. Both were popular with the crowd.

Walking out of those grounds back into the real world, that day was an experience I will never forget. For a boy who was not originally interested in sport, this day made me love and respect tennis and I would encourage anyone to go to Wimbledon whether they like the game or not. The atmosphere is fantastic and once you are let in and walk into those grounds it's a different world … a better one.

1986

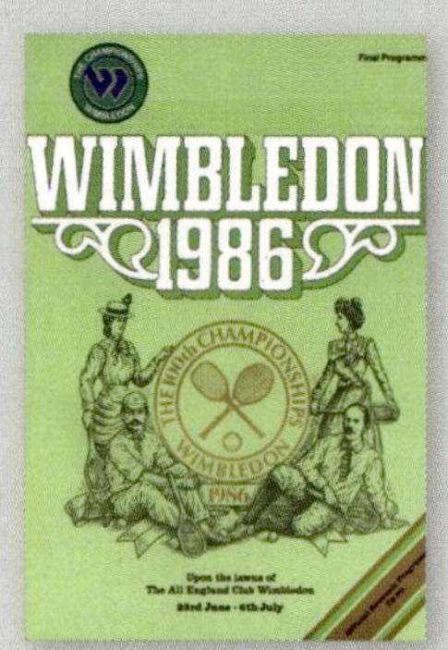

Wimbledon Tennis Story

Jim Puhl, EAU CLAIRE, WISCONSIN

As background for this story, I am an American male who was raised in Colfax, Wisconsin, a small village located about 100 miles east of Minneapolis, Minnesota. I was a three-sport athlete in high school, participating in baseball, basketball, and football, but I also had an interest in tennis. However, there was no real opportunity in Colfax at that time (1950s–60s) to develop my skills in that sport.

Later in life (1971), I earned a PhD in organic chemistry from the University of Minnesota, after which I was employed in industry as a research chemist and later as a manager of a research group before starting my own consulting business. My career led my family and me to Kansas City, Missouri in 1974, where my wife, Shirley, and I began playing recreational tennis on a regular basis and developed into accomplished club-level players. We became tennis 'addicts' and also began collecting tennis-related memorabilia. After moving to Madison, Wisconsin in 1984, we were members at the John Powless Tennis Center, owned and operated by John Powless, internationally renowned for his success in senior competitions.

In July 1986, on a business trip, I attended a scientific conference at the University of Surrey in Guildford, England, traveling alone. I arrived at London Gatwick in early morning, Sunday, 6 July, and traveled to Guildford by train. After registering at the conference in Guildford, I boarded a train to Wimbledon, as finals matches for the 100th Championships were being played that day at The All England Club. (I still have my train ticket for my journey between Guildford and Wimbledon.)

This was my first time at The Championships and I didn't expect to get tickets for finals matches, but I was hoping to at least tour the grounds so as to experience the atmosphere during such an event. Upon arrival at the Club, I was excited to learn that I was not only able to obtain a grounds pass, but that tickets were available for the Ladies' and Gentlemen's doubles finals. I purchased tickets for both and was thrilled to have the opportunity to witness those matches!

While on the grounds, I recall hearing the crowd noise from the Becker-Lendl finals match on Centre Court. I also recall watching some of the Ladies' consolation finals match, won by Pam Shriver. That match was on a side court, so I could be very close to the court. At one moment, between points, Pam and I made brief eye contact and it appeared, in that instant, that she may have recognized me, which is possible (but unlikely) as we had met briefly a year earlier at a social event in Florida in conjunction with the Ford National Mixed Doubles Championships, where I photographed her with our daughter, Liz, and friend.

At another time during the day, as I was standing near Centre Court, a gentlemen asked if I'd be interested in attending the Mixed Doubles Final. He said he had a ticket that he wasn't going to use and was so kind to offer it to me at no cost. Needless to say, I jumped at the opportunity and witnessed the Mixed Doubles Final on Centre Court.

I purchased a very nice 'coffee table' book while on the grounds: The Championships Wimbledon 1985, the Official Annual. Later, as I was touring the grounds, I noticed Ken Rosewall coming my way. I approached him and asked if he would autograph the book, which he did very graciously, and he added the date, 'July 86'.

I still have my ticket stubs for the Ground Pass, No.1 Court, and Centre Court for that day and a postcard showing an aerial view of The All England Club. I also bought a program for the day, but it did not, of course, have the final results from the tournament. At a later date, I bought, on eBay, a 'Final Programme' for 1986, which had been presented to Mr P. Harffey in appreciation for his services as an Umpire at the 1986 Championships. This program had results from all matches.

It was an amazing day for me at The Championships at Wimbledon, 6 July 1986!

1987

My First Wimbledon

Michael Stone, BATTERSEA

Tuesday, 30 June 1987 **was a gorgeous sunny day in the middle of a very hot and relatively rain-free Wimbledon.**

Greatly enthusiastic, but totally naïve as to the dos and don'ts of anyone hoping to see the top players in singles action, my friend and I ambled along to join the queue at around 11am!! Even in 1987, this resulted in standing in a very long line all afternoon in scorching heat, listening to the roars of excitement emanating from within the grounds and via the radios that the better prepared had brought with them.

The Wimbledon queue is, almost always, friendly and helpful and a number of people took pity on our totally unprepared pairing. Mention was made of a 'resale queue' which sounded like the ideal opportunity to get to see my idol, Jimmy Connors, in the last match of the day on Centre Court against Mikael Pernfors. (The fact that Pernfors and I were born on the same day in the same year did nothing to reduce my desire to see Jimmy win, nor my conviction that he would.)

Finally, at around 6pm, we got in on returned tickets and made for the resale queue, noting that Connors and Pernfors were already in battle and Jimmy was in trouble and in need of our support. Others had the same information though and the same plan. The resale queue was scarcely shorter than the line we had spent the previous seven hours in!

Frustrated, we sat on an outside court watching Tony Roche among others in a Veteran's Doubles. (Roche is a legend of the game, but he became a legend before I was born and in my early childhood and for all his status in the game, this was not the match we wanted to see.) We were sufficiently close to Centre Court, however, to hear the ever-louder roars of approval as Jimmy came back to win from two sets and 1-4 down in one of the great Wimbledon matches.

Though pleased with the result, we were intensely frustrated to have been so near and yet so far. We decided to head home, get sleeping bags and head straight back to join the overnight queue in order to get on to Centre Court for the men's quarter-finals the following day. In those days, one night on the pavement (it precedes the use of the park) was enough to do this. Indeed, we got on the front row to see Ivan Lendl beat Henri Leconte and the eventual champion Pat Cash beating Mats Wilander.

I fell in love with Wimbledon that day (1 July 1987) and love it still. I have attended every year since bar one (1990) and now have 74 Slams to my name. My ambition is to have attended 100 Slams by the time of my 65th birthday.

Jimmy Connors, Wimbledon, 1987

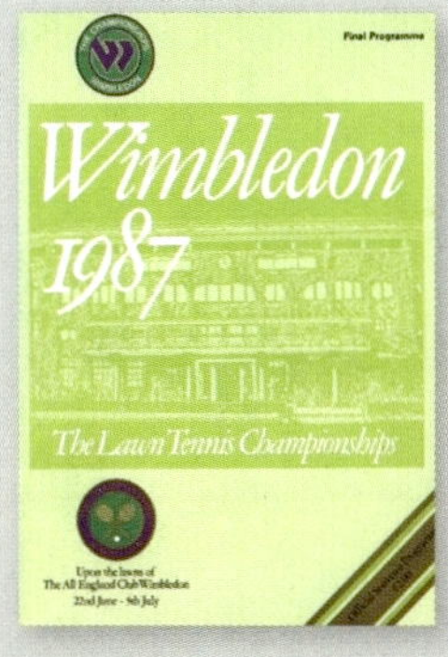

Ivan Lendl

The Connors v Pernfors match is part of Wimbledon folklore. In under an hour and a half, the 34-year-old American had found himself 1-6, 1-6, 1-4 down on the Centre Court to a Swedish player 11 years his junior. Two hours later, one of the most remarkable comebacks in Wimbledon history was complete, with Jimmy winning 1-6, 1-6, 7-5, 6-4, 6-2.

1986

IN THE HOT SEAT

George Grime, HAM

Between 1981 and 1996 Wing Commander George Grime umpired 13 semi-finals and finals at Wimbledon. He umpired finals in each of the five Championships singles and doubles events, including the 1986 men's singles final between Boris Becker and Ivan Lendl. Earlier in his career George had been on the receiving end of one of John McEnroe's outbursts at Wimbledon but had been well prepared, as he explains.

'One of my fellow umpires had got rather tongue-tied dealing with John, and I was determined not to let that happen to me, so, whenever I was listed to umpire one of his matches I used to practise my warning speech in the car on the way to Wimbledon.'

One of George's strongest Wimbledon memories, however, is of his own playing days. 'During the Wimbledon Championships there used to be an umpire's tournament called the Browning Cup. Matches were played across the road at the Wimbledon Lawn Tennis Club in Church Road. We played on grass courts, from 10am each day until about one o'clock. That was in the days when play in The Championships didn't start until 2pm.

'In 1977, Wimbledon's Centenary Year, Ernest Otto and I won the Browning Cup. A year or two later, the tournament was discontinued and I believe the Browning Cup trophy went to the Wimbledon Lawn Tennis Museum. Ernest once said to me it would be nice for our names to be engraved on the trophy. Sadly he has passed away now, but it would be nice to find the trophy and get it engraved, if the Museum still has it.'

1987

Jimmy's Great Comeback

Doreen Prangell, PUTNEY

Wimbledon 30 June 1987. My visit was an evening one. As I lived nearby I came to Wimbledon after work. As I remember, it was a lovely evening.

A colleague from work had tickets that day and he left early as he was watching Mikael Pernfors v Jimmy Connors and the match was so one-sided in Pernfors's favour that he left the match. Little did I know or he know till the next day that we were both at Wimbledon the previous evening. If so he would have let me use his ticket, as what followed in the match was incredible. Jimmy was 4-1 down in the third set but came back to win 1-6, 1-6, 7-5, 6-4, 6-2.

It was so exciting I was standing outside the court just listening to the score. The atmosphere was amazing. Very excited fans, most wanting Jimmy to win. After the win I hung around the grounds in hope of seeing Jimmy and was fortunate to see Jimmy getting into his car. My camera was held above my head and aimed for a photo. And wow it was a good one. Remember leaving Wimbledon a very happy young lady who was fortunate to say 'I was at Wimbledon the day Jimmy Connors came back from two sets down and won.' A great hero of mine.

1987

No Beginner's Luck

John Rowlinson, LAMBOURN

Everything was ready in the BBC compound on 22 June 1987. We were celebrating the 50th year of television coverage of Wimbledon. In the studio Harry Carpenter, composed as ever, would shortly voice defending champion Boris Becker's entry onto Centre Court. In the huge outside broadcast vehicle nearby, producer Martin Hopkins and Penny Wood, for years the architects of the BBC's Wimbledon coverage, were about to run the opening titles. It was my first day as the editor of the live programmes. Previously I had been entrusted with the evening highlights, a lively hour in the company of the sparkling Des Lynam and Gerald Williams.

There was only one small problem on that Monday afternoon. It was raining, and the forecast was worse. We were still, remember, two decades away from a roof on Centre Court. The call went out to the videotape area for the first of the 'standbys': the Borg/McEnroe tiebreak of 1980. Not for the first time I recalled that the BBC's main commentator Dan Maskell was never happy keeping track of tiebreaks, which is why John Barrett's voice is all you really hear on that famous recording.

As the rain continued, Harry Carpenter found yet new ways of promising viewers that play was still possible. We were running out of standbys. Our last throw was the recent final of the French Open. Ivan Lendl beat Mats Wilander in four sets and it lasted for hours! Just as well, for at Wimbledon on that opening day neither Boris Becker, nor anyone else for that matter, hit a ball in earnest. No beginner's luck for me: play was completely washed out.

Normal service for BBC viewers was soon restored. As with all championships the stories and great matches then came thick and fast. After the unseeded Peter Doohan beat Becker, the latter famously observed – in our tiny interview room – that he had not lost a war but merely a tennis match. Nineteen eighty-seven was also the year Steffi Graf reached her first of many finals, and the champion Pat Cash – in that black and white headband – surprised the Centre Court spectators by clambering over many of them to reach his supporters.

There were many more years when I felt fortunate to be involved in the coverage. Not least 'People's Sunday' in 1991. I still have my pink programme from that great day. But whoever is presenting the shows, the wonderful Sue Barker being the latest, and whoever is doing my old job – and thanking his lucky stars for the roof – the BBC's relationship with The All England Club remains close. It has meant The Championships are still free to air, and the winners of course are those watching, and listening, at home.

1987

A Wimbledon Odyssey - Part 2

David Rutherford, CROMLIX

When Wimbledon 1987 came along I was 22 and had finished college. The ballot had been kind to my sister and I and we had been allocated a pair of Centre Court standing enclosure tickets for each of the final two days of the tournament. The tickets were for my favourite area – section J of the east standing enclosure – in the corner beside one of the scoreboards and immediately below the area where the players' families and coaches sat.

As I was already in London when The Championships began I went down to Wimbledon on the opening day and bought a ground ticket. I didn't see a single ball hit in anger as it rained all day, but I took the opportunity to visit

the museum for the first time. Thankfully the tournament soon got back on track and my next trip down to SW19 was for the Ladies' Singles Final on the final Saturday. It was to be the first time that my sister and I would see Steffi Graf who by that time was starting to rival Martina Navratilova for the number one spot in the women's game which she had dominated for so long up until then. The final between the two of them would be a good 'litmus test' as to their respective positions at that time.

It was another very warm finals day and we watched the match from the east standing enclosure in line with the net and opposite the umpire's chair. I can still recall just how hard Graf hit the ball and how low over the net most of her shots were but unfortunately this still wasn't enough for her to win. Martina proved that she was still no.1 although given the ages of both players it seemed obvious that it wouldn't be too long before Steffi became top dog.

On Sunday, 4 July 1987 I awoke very early in the morning in north London with the sun already high in the sky and with the prospect of being in the Centre Court for my third men's singles final in four years. I got up, had breakfast, and prepared the picnic for me and my sister who was still asleep. I left a note for her saying that I was leaving early to get down to Wimbledon as soon as possible in order to get as far ahead as I could in the queue to get inside the grounds. I told her to make sure

that she got down to join me in the queue before 11am when the gates opened. This was still some years away from the mobile phone era!

I arrived at Southfields station well before 8am and ten minutes later took my place in a very advanced position in the queue on Church Road. The whole area was already a hive of activity and the impending final was an intriguing one. Ivan Lendl was clearly ahead of Pat Cash in terms of his standing in world tennis at that time, but grass was his least favourite surface. Cash was the more enigmatic of the two and seemed to be nearing his best form after lengthy injuries earlier in his career. It was a difficult match to call. My sister joined me in the queue in ample time and once inside the grounds we were quick enough to be admitted straight into the Centre Court at midday where I was able to take up my favoured position.

For the best part of two hours we watched all the familiar preparations for the match: the net being put in position, the umpire's chair being wheeled out, and programmes being placed on the seats in the Royal Box, while the band on the court entertained us and the other early arrivals.

Neither player lost a service game in the first set, but it was obvious that Lendl was having to work much the harder of the two. Cash took the first set in a tiebreak and the second more straightforwardly. Lendl's back was against the wall and it probably didn't help him that the majority of the crowd seemed to be favouring the Australian. The third set went the same way as the first two and for the second year in succession Lendl had been beaten in straight sets in the final by a player whose game was better suited to grass.

It was difficult not to feel sorry for him but that was probably the last thing on Pat Cash's mind. He held his arms aloft as he accepted the wild applause of the crowd after such a fantastic performance and for a brief moment he seemed overcome by the occasion. That didn't last long, however, and his impromptu behaviour in the next few minutes would become one of the most memorable acts of celebration in the history of not just tennis but of world sport in general. And I was to be at the very heart of it!

Standing beside his seat below the umpire's chair Pat looked up at his entourage who were all sat immediately above where I was standing. He then jogged across the court and stepped over the short wall into the crowd in the lower seated area. It was obvious by this time that he was attempting to join his coach, his father and his girlfriend to share the moment with them, but there was no obvious route for him to take.

In an instant I and the others around me realised that we were at the centre of a drama which was being watched live on television throughout the world by hundreds of millions of people. There is no preparation in life for such an occurrence and instinct kicks in.

Realising my closer proximity to the action my sister passed me her camera and ordered me to take as many pictures of the unfolding drama as I possibly could.

Meanwhile Pat had made his way up through the lower seated section and was at the bottom corner of the standing enclosure. For a moment he seemed unsure how to continue his journey, but then he placed his hands on the roof of the commentary box and managed to climb onto it with the help of some of the spectators next to me who cupped their hands under his feet and pushed him upwards. Those who weren't assisting him or taking photographs cheered and clapped wildly. Finally he climbed over the wall above the commentary box with the help of his father, and one by one he embraced everyone in his team to wild applause. And all the while I was clicking away to try and capture as much as I could of such a monumental event. Thankfully for Pat an official accompanied him back down onto the court via a route underneath the stand which avoided him having to retrace his steps.

When he came back out onto court the applause began again. This had truly been a unique celebration.

I could scarcely believe what I had just witnessed, never mind at such close quarters.

The trophy presentation and Mixed Doubles Final which followed almost paled into insignificance by comparison. As we left Wimbledon that evening it probably didn't occur to me that I had reached an apex in my Wimbledon career. How could anything top that for sheer raw excitement? At another level, however, it only served to strengthen my desire to be at The Championships in future years if possible. The following day my sister had the film developed and thankfully I had managed to get a few half-decent shots which would remind us forever just how close we had been to the event. It may not have lasted for 15 minutes as Andy Warhol once prophesised, but for two or three minutes Pat Cash had enabled me to be at the centre of the sporting universe!

More than 30 years on I am still occasionally reminded of the incident. It pops up on television every so often, or comes up in conversation with people I didn't know back in 1987 – usually when Pat appears on television. I got quite a pleasant surprise a few years ago after buying John Barrett and Ian Hewitt's book *Centre Court – The Jewel in Wimbledon's Crown*. I was leafing through the book when I came across a photograph of the incident in which I appear quite clearly.

1989

My First Wimbledon

Julia Kilby, HOVE

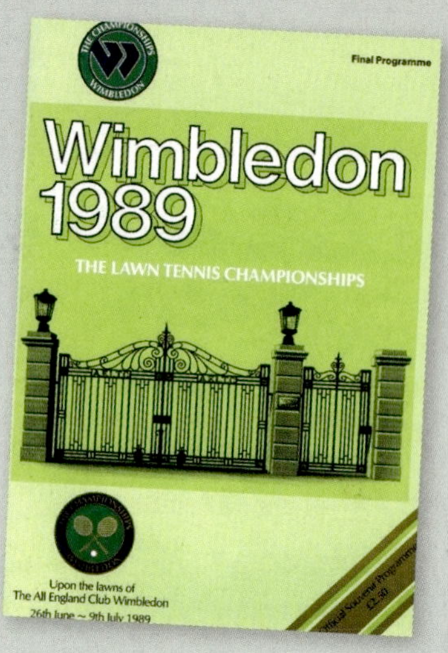

I first became aware of Wimbledon when I came home from school to find my mum in a deckchair in the garden intensely listening to the tennis on the radio. There seemed to always be a three-set match being closely contested by Virginia Wade. Mum was not keen on being interrupted.

When our school sports day was held on a hot Friday afternoon in 1978 I can remember mothers listening to the Ladies' Singles Final on their hand-held radios whilst we ran our races. They seemed to be upset about Martina Navratilova beating Chris Evert.

During the 1980 men's final between Bjorn Borg and John McEnroe I sat at the kitchen table listening to the match on the radio. While listening I wrote down every score given by the umpire on a paper roll including the famous 16-18 fourth-set tiebreak, which meant I learnt everything to know about the tennis scoring system. It was a very thrilling match; I was captivated.

When I started to play tennis regularly at a club, my auntie suggested a trip to the Wimbledon Championships in June 1989. With much excitement I caught the train from Portslade to Redhill where my auntie picked me up in her car then drove us to Wimbledon. We parked in the St Mary's Church car park and then walked down the hill to The All England Club. We joined the queue at 8am. It was Tuesday, 27 June, and whilst in the queue I was given an 'I Queued at Wimbledon' sticker, which I still have today.

When the gates opened the queue slowly started to move.

I found the last part of queuing very scary as you were in a mass of people filing around a zigzag of metal fencing. Then you emerged from the crush and chose a ticket from a wooden table for the court you required. This ticket was then taken to a kiosk were you paid in cash and received your actual ticket. We managed to get Court 1 row V seats but they had an obscured view behind a pillar. The ticket had been hand stamped 'obscured view' and the reduced price altered by ball pen!

Just when play was about to start it began to lightly drizzle. A huge disappointment but luckily we did not have long to wait before we saw Martina Navratilova beat Jill Hetherington 6-3, 6-3, then Kevin Curren beat Andrew Castle followed by Chris Evert beating Peanut Harper. Then much to my delight we managed to get into the standing area on Centre Court. I could hardly see much of the play peering around people's heads, but was thrilled to see Gabriela Sabatini play and experience Centre Court for the first time. This was to be the last year of standing on Centre Court as a consequence of the Hillsborough and Bradford tragedies.

I was so taken by Wimbledon I was back queuing the following year and my love of Wimbledon has never faded. I have been many years since and encountered many changes from that year when merchandise was sold in a marquee.

The crowds at Wimbledon can get very emotional. On Tuesday, 26 June 1990 I was lucky enough to get front-row seats on Court 2 when Gilles Muller beat Tim Mayotte. After the match we took a break and visited the ladies by the ivy-clad water tower and there we found women in floods of tears and also some attempting to disguise the fact they were crying because Tim Mayotte had lost.

I was thrilled to have the opportunity of going to the Ladies' Singles Final in 1993. It was a close-fought match between Steffi Graff and Jana Novotna. Steffi Graf prevailed but at the trophy ceremony Jana Novotna cried on the Duchess of Kent's shoulder. It nearly made me cry too.

The crowd roaring and cheering on Centre Court is phenomenal. On one such occasion it was unbelievable when Tim Henman played Mark Philippoussis on 28 June 2004. A young man in the crowd near me stood up and sang 'Henman we love you, Henman we do' between every single point. The familiar shout of 'come on Tim'' could also be heard. We left feeling totally uplifted after Tim Henman's victory.

1991

Flowers for Martina

Colin Lelliott, WEST WORTHING

I am an OAP now but I wrote down about my seeing Martina in an exercise book a few years ago so that I would not forget.

I guess we all know about Wimbledon growing up and watching the finals on TV, as with the FA Cup, but I never really thought about actually going. I went to my first football match at Brighton in 1964, taken by my dad, and I also went to watch Sussex play cricket.

I only had a passing interest in other sports but that all changed in 1978 when I read the story of this tennis player who left Czechoslovakia for America in 1975, Martina Navratilova. The more I read about her the more I admired her and at Wimbledon 1978 I wrote to her and told her so and sent her a bouquet of flowers to arrive on Ladies Day. I had started something that I was to continue to do into the 90s.

Martina won that Wimbledon and so when 1979 came around I did the same again, and about three weeks later I received a letter signed by Martina thanking me for the flowers, and saying that she greatly appreciated me taking the time to think of her.

I saw Martina play in the 1979 and 1980 Daihatsu Challenge finals at the Brighton Centre, but I was not able to get tickets for Wimbledon. In 1985 I received a lovely handwritten postcard from Martina, sent from her home in Dallas, again thanking me for all the flowers and cards. That

I never expected but it was nice to know what I sent did reach her.

Success in 1987 as I managed to get tickets for the first Tuesday on Centre Court, Ladies Day, and as defending champion Martina would be the opening match. However, the opening Monday was a complete washout and the referee and committee decided to put the day one line-up on day two. I was not pleased

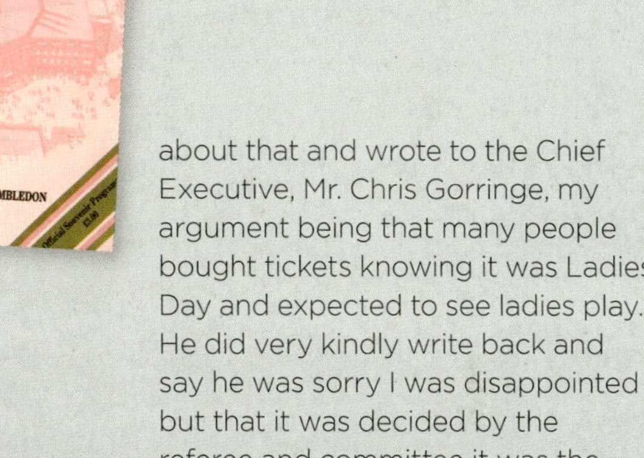

about that and wrote to the Chief Executive, Mr. Chris Gorringe, my argument being that many people bought tickets knowing it was Ladies Day and expected to see ladies play. He did very kindly write back and say he was sorry I was disappointed but that it was decided by the referee and committee it was the best way to proceed.

I was back in 1988, again with Centre Court tickets on Ladies Day, this time no problem as Martina took to the grass again as defending title holder. In less than an hour she was gone again having won her opening match. I left my seat as well going down to the front of the complex beneath the ivy-covered walls. I wanted to see Martina if I could but after waiting for a couple of hours I was beginning to think that was not going to happen. Then I saw Judy Nelson walking through the crowd toward the exit and I asked her if Martina had left yet. She pointed to the exit and there was Martina waiting on the other side of the road having already made it through the gates. I headed out, having got my hand stamped so that I could get back in, and started walking up the hill to catch up with Martina who had by now been joined by Judy. Now I don't know if my nerve went, or some good old-fashioned manners took over, but as Martina and Judy were deep in conversation I wasn't prepared to butt in. I walked back

down the hill, a little disappointed I had got so close, but feeling good that I held back and didn't barge in.

I thought there might be another day and, luckily for me, there was. However, it was not to be 1989 but 1990 when I was next able to get Centre Court tickets for Ladies Day. Sadly for me Martina was opening on No.1 Court that day but good fortune was to smile on me. As I was walking between the two main courts, which were side by side back then, there were two people looking toward Centre Court clearly speaking in German. Maybe cheekily I asked if they had tickets for that court to see Steffi Graf and, in English, they said no, they had tickets for No.1 Court. I produced my Centre Court tickets and asked them if they wanted to swap. They had the more expensive Centre Court tickets but I had another chance to watch Martina. The match was quickly over and I was away out of my seat in the hope of seeing Martina go back to her rented house nearby. I waited outside the grounds and after the usual delay I saw Martina come out of the gate, walk across the road, and start up the hill toward me but being followed by a sizeable crowd. I was able to get a picture signed but as more and more people surrounded Martina thrusting books, programmes and pictures in front of her to sign I backed off and went back down the hill.

The Wimbledon ballot system was kind to me again in 1991 with Centre Court tickets for Ladies Day where Martina would be back as defending champion having won her ninth singles crown in 1990. As it did in 1987 rain had washed out play on the opening day but this time the referee and committee decided to put Martina first up. Her opponent was Elna Reinach and it turned out to be a tough match for Martina and for me. Martina lost the first set, won the second, but at one stage in the third was 3-4 and 0-30 down. As a British crowd does they were cheering for the underdog and I have never felt so lonely in a crowd in my life. It was as though I was the only person willing Martina to win.

Martina got it back to 30-30 and then a Martina return hit the tape on the top of the net so hard it appeared to hang in mid-air for a few seconds before dropping stone dead on Elna's side of the court. That was the turning point and Martina went on to win and record her 100th singles win at Wimbledon. I was drained, I left the court to go and be on my own for a while to calm down and to dry out. As the match had finished late in the afternoon it would be early evening before Martina would leave the ground; I didn't realise it at the time but that was going to be to my advantage. As before I left the ground and waited in the road opposite the gate. It was a long wait but finally Martina came through the gate, all on her own, and, to my complete surprise, so was I. Walking toward her I congratulated her on a gutsy performance to which Martina smiled and said 'thank you'. I then asked her if she would mind signing a picture for me.

Martina apologised that her hands were full and indeed there were tennis rackets in her left hand and flowers in her right. I offered to hold the flowers for her, introduced myself, and suggested they may have been flowers I had sent to her. I was amazed when Martina said they were as she had just put the card that came with them in her shoulder bag. With that Martina leaned over, took my pen and picture, and signed it for me.

It is only a short walk up the hill to the home Martina rented and we were almost there. I wished her all the best for the rest of the tournament at the front gate and, as I turned to go back, Martina said 'Oh Colin, thank you again for the flowers'. With that she walked up the steps to the front door and went inside.

I walked back down the hill in absolute dreamland, I doubted anyone would believe me if I told them I had just walked home with Martina Navratilova. I didn't get to see Martina play at Wimbledon again but I did receive a further letter in 1992 from her Aspen, Colorado address. This was not signed by Martina but by her assistant. In it she says Martina has asked her to thank me for the beautiful flowers I sent on Ladies Day which Martina promptly placed in a vase and put them on the dining room table.

There are some things in life you wish could go on forever but time catches up with us all.

For me Martina Navratilova is the greatest female tennis player ever and I have been lucky enough to watch her play. Thank you Martina, and thank you Wimbledon, it has been a pleasure.

1992

Memories of Wimbledon

Susan Halliday, FELIXSTOWE

My earliest memory of Wimbledon tennis was when an elderly neighbour invited myself and a friend of mine into her house to watch her TV as she was rather excited because two British ladies were in the final. Of course I now know this was Angela Mortimer and Christine Truman but at the time I had never seen a tennis match as we didn't have TV. After that match I was hooked and by the following year we also had a television set installed in our house.

Although I watched Wimbledon for years after that I didn't have the opportunity to go myself until sometime in the early 1990s when myself and daughters were working in Nottingham; we were watching on telly again, a good match (probably Andre Agassi, as my girls idolised him), then one of the girls said something like 'oh, I wish we could go'; then suddenly we looked at each and said why don't we, what's stopping us so that night we jumped into the car and set off for Wimbledon.

That started a yearly ritual of camping in the road and the delights of queuing for a ticket or just getting a ground pass. I have to say it was great fun as the crowd were all good-humoured, although we didn't get much sleep, sometimes we were so tired we would have to have a nap on the grass picnic area. A few years later after we moved back to Suffolk we joined the local tennis club and were able to get tickets most years in the club draws so rarely camped any more although we did it a couple more times later just for fun. Friends couldn't understand how queuing several hours or camping overnight could be fun.

> **"***A yearly ritual of camping in the road and the delights of queuing for a ticket or just getting a ground pass.* **"**

Standing in Line by Ben Chatfield, Illustrated by Zebedee Helm

CENTRE COURT WIMBLEDON

Miles MacLagan on Court Five

Robbie Williams, MOSCOW

My first trip to Wimbledon in 1993 was an experience that lived up to my expectations. It was everything I hoped it would be. Arriving at Southfields Underground Station and walking to the Church Road queue with countless other people was a thrill in itself. It wasn't the only queue back then as there was also the old Somerset Road queue.

We arrived at the queue very late - about 10.30am - in the park adjacent to the golf course but my friend who had been to Wimbledon once before thought we would still get in before they closed the gates. We got out of the park and were on the street - when that was still allowed. Even seeing the famous Centre Court was a thrill. Just seeing it in 'real life'!

We finally got to the entrance - which I think was Gate 3. We were let in along with another couple. Then the security guard announced that the grounds were at full capacity and it was then a case of a 'one out - one in' basis. We breathed a sigh of relief!

I was struck by the beautiful yet imposing structure that is Centre Court. It was truly a magnificent site. There were tears in my eyes after seeing this court on television every year since I was five years old and to finally see it with my own eyes was overwhelming.

My friend gave me a tour of the grounds - including the 'underpass' by Centre Court where they had photos of past champions - singles and doubles champions dating back to 1922 (as I remember).

We went to the outside courts to the South of the grounds - what was then Courts No.2 to 13. I was surprised by the sheer number of people and it felt a little claustrophobic. We queued to get into the old No.2 Court to see Krajicek v Eltingh. We were high up in the standing room but it was great.

I also remember seeing the Brit Miles Maclagan on Court 5. He had unexpectedly got to the second round.

I LOVED the old Players Office - which no longer exists. It was a place to see so many players and get autographs. That year I think I got autographs from Steffi Graf, Aranxta Sanchez Vicario, Todd Woodbridge and many others who I can't remember now unless I looked at my old 1993 Programme.

It became my annual holiday ever since. There have been a few years I missed but I still try to go there every year.

> **❝ *There were tears in my eyes after seeing this court on television every year since I was five years old and to finally see it with my own eyes was overwhelming.* ❞**

Steffi's Flower Girl

Christina San, NEW MALDEN

My original name is Nhi Mui, and my English name is Christina. I was born in March 1978. My family lived in Croydon and I attended Garth High School in Morden. Our school was invited to send some pupils to train as ball boys and ball girls for the 1993 Wimbledon Championships, and I was one of the lucky ones selected.

Practice was in South Wimbledon, after school. We did two hours practice each week. The training consisted of throwing, ball rolling and stamina. We did star jumps, burpees and lots of circuit training. Fitness exercises took up the first hour of each training session. Wally Wonfor was the trainer and we were taught when to change ends and when to change the balls.

After three months you are told if you have been selected. I was the only person from my school selected that year.

I never used to play tennis, although I eventually took up the game around 2010 at Westside Tennis Club in Wimbledon. My husband Richard and I have two children, Oliver, born in 2014, and Valentina, born in 2015. Both have had tennis lessons and enjoy playing.

At Wimbledon, the coach stopped at Gate 13. We were kitted out in non-branded clothing and Hi-Tec shoes. The taller ball boys and ball girls were at the ends of the court, the shorter ones at the net. They gave us a Mars bar every afternoon, as a treat.

You are put in a team with people you don't know. You're all together

as a team. As a ball girl you are constantly on your feet. You could be on court for two hours without a break, in the hot sun; 1993 was a heatwave year, and there were no hats then.

Teams A to F were the top teams working on the show courts. It was different working on the outside courts, where it could be quite relaxing. It was much tougher on the show courts.

After play finished on the evening of the middle Saturday all the ball kids went out together to McDonald's in Wimbledon.

There were fewer ball girls towards the end of the fortnight. I was chosen as one of the two ball girls to carry the flowers for the players when they came onto court for the Ladies' Singles Final. 'We chose you because you always had a smile on your face!'

I was assigned to Steffi Graf and another ball girl called Annette was assigned to Steffi's opponent Jana Novotna. Annette said to me, 'Do you mind if we swap?' I replied 'Not a chance!'

I got Steffi's autograph during the practice earlier. She was nice, but shy. We didn't make eye contact. Before the final we were introduced to the players in the Ladies' Changing Room. The players talked to us, just chit-chat. Jana Novotna was the more talkative.

Going on court the clapping was thunderous. When you are on court it really comes down on you. So much I nearly forgot to curtsey to the Duchess of Kent.

> **❝** *Going on court the clapping was thunderous. When you are on court it really comes down on you. So much I nearly forgot to curtsey to the Duchess of Kent.* **❞**

Annette and I carried bouquets of flowers and the players' towels. We watched the match on TV in our canteen. There were no ball-girl duties for us that day.

I met Jana Novotna again at Wimbledon in 2013 and we had our photograph taken together.

It was one of the most memorable experiences of my life, meeting Steffi Graf and walking onto Centre Court. I feel very lucky and privileged to have been chosen as a flower girl.

Steffi Graf

1994

My First Wimbledon

Louise Mansergh, CAMBERLEY

I first went to Wimbledon in 1994. We lived in St Albans in Hertfordshire, and my dad picked me up from school and drove down to The All England Club. We queued up and got in about 5pm.

I was desperate to see my favourite player at the time, Goran Ivanisevic, but he was due to play on Court 1 and we didn't have tickets for there; we just had a ground pass. Once we were in we saw lots of people rushing to Court 14, so we joined them and found a couple of seats. The next match hadn't started so I turned to the person next to me and said, 'Do you know who's going to be playing on here?' Her answer? 'Goran Ivanisevic.' So the first match I saw there was watching my favourite player win in straight sets. It was brilliant.

I've been to Wimbledon almost every year since. I've seen some amazing matches, including three finals – all of which are classics. I watched Goran Ivanisevic (yes, him again!) win in 2001 against Pat Rafter. What a match! The atmosphere was amazing, and it was a privilege to watch him win his only Grand Slam.

I was also at the 2008 final between Roger Federer and Rafael Nadal – the one that finished in the dark. That was another fantastic match. The drama in that match was unlike any other match I've been to. At the end I was exhausted, goodness knows how the players felt!

I was lucky enough to go to the final again the following year in 2009 where Roger Federer defeated Andy Roddick 16-14 in the fifth set. That was such a tight match where Federer managed to sneak the win at the end.

Wimbledon has changed enormously over the 25 years I've been going. Many of the courts have got bigger, or moved places, and it feels smarter and more commercially astute, but that may just be my perspective as I've got older too. The Pimm's and strawberries haven't changed though, and I doubt they ever will. It will always feel like tennis in an English country garden.

1996

Breakfast at Wimbledon

Nick McCarvel, NEW YORK CITY

Wimbledon to me, growing up, was early mornings. The alarm would go off at 5 or 6 in the morning and I would wearily slip out of bed and into layers for the mountain cold awaiting me: I was 11, 12, 13 in what I remember, and I was a paper boy, one summer with my own route, but the others helping my older brother, J.P., who had his route for years and years.

But on Wimbledon mornings there would be a sense of urgency to our daily routine. After escaping bed and dressing for what was sure to be dark morning cold, I would make my way downstairs and to the waiting stacks of papers, tied with an unglamorous plastic twine that would only budge with scissors. No fingers could do the trick.

I mention the chilly mountain air because I was nowhere near Wimbledon, actually. I was in Helena, Montana, where I grew up with my family in a house built in the 1880s in a gold rush town set up against Mt. Helena, amidst the Rocky Mountains. This was as far away from Wimbledon as you could get, and also as far from the tennis world as possible, too: Here was a place of farming, ranching, state government and highways that ran for stretches of hundreds of miles without a town. Montana is known as 'Big Sky Country' because the sky stretches as far as you look.

'Somewhere Wimbledon is under the same sky,' I convinced myself.

We'd walk the route: sometimes together, sometimes alone. I was always in a hurry as a kid, but especially those Wimbledon days. The morning TV schedule was thrown into chaos on HBO, TNT or NBC (the networks that carried the event when I was young) when Wimbledon came around. And I wanted to see as much of the action as I could.

That was the lens you had in the 1990s, watching from afar. There was no social media or Twitter or breaking news alerts or streams to choose from. Instead, it was Bud Collins or Mary Carillo or Chris Evert or Ted Robinson telling you which matches were most important. And I loved them for that.

I would plunk myself in front of the couch post-paper route and be enraptured by the coverage. There was Monica Seles, making her post-stabbing comeback. There was Pete Sampras, losing on the famed Graveyard Court, No.2. There was Andre and Steffi and Conchita and Todd and Hingis ... They lived in what we called our TV room, just off the kitchen, and I would escape on commercial breaks for a bowl of cereal, granola bar or banana. Anything fast to get me back to the tennis.

Wimbledon was like a world I didn't know. I loved the grass and how pristine it was. I loved Centre Court and the privileged American TV booth courtside, just over the court. John McEnroe would peer through it on some of the TV shots, almost squinting to see the camera and it him. It was linear TV at its height, before the Internet made us that much more curious. I loved it for its pure simplicity. 'Breakfast at Wimbledon,' as NBC called it, was just that, American-time zone breakfast-time and tennis on TV. No hashtags about it.

But that wasn't where Wimbledon stopped for me. I would watch through much of the morning, or then just get too restless and head outside. Because outside was where Wimbledon was, too: in the back alley, against the barnyard wall that I essentially learned to play tennis against, I would become Andre, Steffi, Conchita, Todd...

I'd play for hours. Matches, tiebreaks, best-of-three, a fifth-set at 4-all. There would be commentary and line calls. There would be backstories and disputes. Oftentimes I was the wild card from the States, or a young Irish or English kid who somehow made his way into the third round. I remember being fascinated with Jelena Dokic's win over Martina Hingis in the first round in 1999. Tim Henman was always a personal favorite. Serve-and-volleying isn't easy against a wall, though, I have to say.

Eventually I grew out of the habit. The paper routes were abandoned as summer gigs, and instead I worked in a cafe and a restaurant as a waiter. Wimbledon mornings were still special, but now there was this thing called Yahoo and I could check results there before the matches had even started on tape-delay TV.

There was still that golden-green glow about summer Wimbledon mornings, the back door open to the kitchen as NBC played out its coverage, but it wasn't the same. Not until I made my first trip there in person, in 2009, did it feel like that magic of my childhood was recaptured. And then the place was even more than I expected it to be. How did they keep it so pristine? Was Henman Hill really real? Oh, that's where the Graveyard Court used to be!

I can still see the newspaper ink smeared all over my fingers as I watched for hours on end. Then I went out and won Wimbledon myself in the alley. That's Wimbledon to me.

Nick McCarvel is a host, commentator and sports writer. The old No.2 Court, the 'Graveyard Court' where so many top players were humbled, was on the site where the new No.3 Court now stands.

1997

That Magical Part of London that is SW19

Finlay MacKinnon, OUTER HEBRIDES

For years I dreamed of going to The Championships ... the oldest tennis tournament in the world and by far the most prestigious. Wimbledon is one of the premier sporting events in the world. It evokes so many wonderful images. A garden party atmosphere, strawberries and cream and glasses of Pimm's. The tradition, umpires, blazers, rules, dress code, and Royal Box and the very long queues waiting in line.

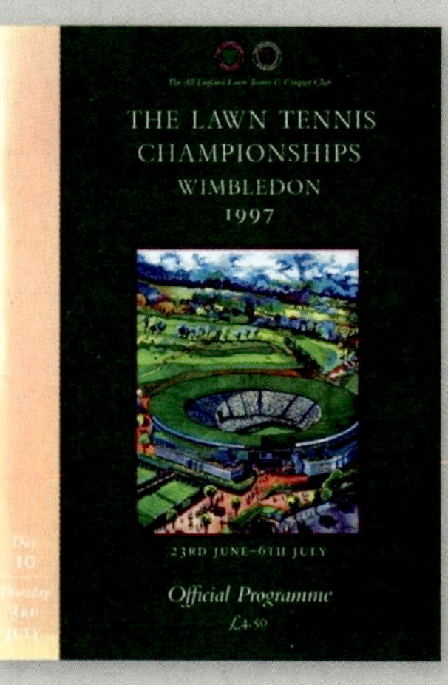

I was thrilled to be in London with my brother and sister to be at The Championships. We had travelled from a remote Hebridean island on the west coast of Scotland to Heathrow Airport. We were staying at the Gloucester Hotel in Kensington. We had a 15-minute walk from Southfields tube station and joined the queue for the sale of tickets at the Gate 3 turnstiles.

We were ushered into Centre Court an hour later and got seated across from the umpire's chair. I looked at the Royal Box which is grand with dark green wicker chairs. British Royals and VIP guests looked very well dressed. The scoreboard on Centre Court is instantly recognisable and has the names of the players and the score in green lighting.

Pete Sampras, the American who had won three Wimbledon titles in a row and one of the great serve and volleyers of all time, came onto court with German Boris Becker, another three-time champion. The very long-standing tradition of players bowing in front of the Royal Box was very nice to see. The players in their pristine classic white outfits and Boris wearing a skip cap. The players warmed-up and stretched their legs for five minutes and gave each other some eye contact. There were few rallies in this match with both serving many booming aces and the occasional double fault. There was a rain delay and the covers came on dragged on by the groundsmen. The weather at SW19 was a gentle breeze and some rain showers. Pete won in four sets to progress to the semi-final.

> **" We had travelled from a remote Hebridean island on the west coast of Scotland. "**

Next on court came two of the youngest women in professional tennis – world No.1 Martina Hingis and her rival, Russian 16-year-old Anna Kournikova. A different match altogether to the men's – many long baseline rallies with the two players grooving their strokes from the backcourt and using the whole court. Martina 'Swiss Miss' twirling her racquet before receiving serve and always jumping about with a smile on her face. She was full of confidence having only lost one match all year. She won the match to progress to the finals. There was a real switch from raw power to touch and finesse in this lovely match.

In the break before the next match on Centre, the three of us walked in the main grounds and had some afternoon lunch and tea from one of the many cafes and restaurants. Everywhere there were queues.

Tim Henman and Greg Rusedski were playing on Court No.1 on that afternoon against German Michael Stich and France's Cedric Pioline. British spirit and expectations were dashed as Tim Henman had just lost his match to Stich. Disappointment for the British public! I loved the Fred Perry sculpture. Perry was the last male British champion in the 1930s.

We walked to the outside courts – the old No.2 Court – called the 'Graveyard of Champions' where former champions such as John McEnroe and Jimmy Connors suffered surprise defeats. On court No.3 British heroine Virginia Wade champion in 1977 was playing with Australian Wendy Turnbull in the Senior Ladies' Invitational Doubles. We watched a few games of the match played in really good spirits. We then headed to the Wimbledon Shop in the south-east corner. The shop was full of people – bustling Americans and so many foreigners. We bought the Wimbledon towels which were white cotton in design and a white T-shirt – Adidas – and some postcards of our favourite players.

We walked back to Centre Court and took our seats in the Stands. The last match on was Spain's Arantxa Sanchez-Vicario playing a sentimental crowd favourite Jana Novotna, a former runner-up. It was a classic match between a serve and volleyer – one of the finest – and a baseliner. Jana's chipping and charging and her delightful low volleys impressed me. The weather was looking gloomy with dark clouds but play was completed.

I love Wimbledon… I felt so privileged, lucky to be at The All England Club – the huge crowds, the tradition, the grass courts, the flowers, the gates, the Clubhouse, the manic fans in their bright fancy-dress costumes and soaking up the incredible atmosphere! That magical part of London that is SW19.

1999

A Coach Trip to Wimbledon

Margo Fitzsimons, BOURNEMOUTH

Always watched Wimbledon on the TV as a kid with my mum. First chance to go, many, many years later, was on a coach trip from Bournemouth with my sister, staying overnight in London and being taken to Wimbledon on Sunday men's final day 1999, but our tickets are on Court 1.

Still a wonderful experience, loved the shop, the atmosphere and saw some great matches, Lleyton Hewitt, Kim Clijsters. Had my super swish camera (not phone) but the players were miles away down on the court.

Next year did the same trip again with my sister in 2000. Sampras to play Rafter in the final. Same tickets for Court 1. Decided NO point in taking my camera, far too far away.

But, discovered the practice courts (not seen before) and Sampras practising. WOW, fabulous BUT NO camera! Then found Rafter too, my real favourite … but NO camera. GUTTED. But still a wonderful experience, never to be forgotten.

In 2003, 2005 and 2006 I went to Australia to Melbourne, had the time of my life for seven days each time, seeing all the fabulous stars including childhood memories seeing Roche, Rosewall, Wilander and John Lloyd to name just a few. Got their autographs to be treasured, even Andy Murray who came in to watch Tim Henman play and I spoke to him and got his FULL autograph.

2000

My First Wimbledon

James Reed, WIMBLEDON

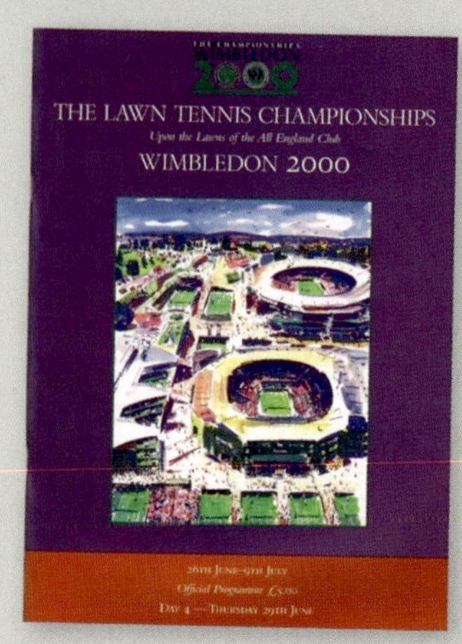

That first day at Wimbledon changed my life! It was Thursday 29 June 2000. I was 25 and despite growing up in Wimbledon I'd never actually been to the tennis. We'd always watched it on the BBC, especially the final, but it was one of those things that when you live there, you just don't seem to do. I'd just left a job working in a bank and was spending the summer not doing much really, other than watching *Neighbours* and the tennis.

One day my dad suggested why don't I go 'up there' and see if I could see Pete Sampras. He knew that since the early 90s I'd become a big fan of the man with the super serve. I'd even bought a pair of Sampras shorts when they first came out! So, that afternoon, I walked up to Wimbledon station, caught the special open-top 'Championships' bus and joined the fabled queue.

Back then there were less people or maybe it was the time of day that helped, but I made it to the entrance gates remarkably quickly. I remember buying a ticket, walking into the grounds and standing facing what is now Court 17. You could immediately sense the atmosphere and I'd never known anything like it. The buzz of the crowds, the serene surroundings, the sounds of racquets hitting tennis balls, the quietness, followed by cheers and the odd clink of a wine glass, it was very exciting. I adventurously explored the outside courts, fascinated by how you could see everything so close-up and how

> *"The buzz of the crowds, the serene surroundings, the sounds of racquets hitting tennis balls, the quietness, followed by cheers and the odd clink of a wine glass, it was very exciting."*

there were names on scoreboards that I recognised from the TV – names like Navratilova, Capriati and even Anna Kournikova!

It was a learning experience too. I roughly knew how the scoring system worked, but figuring out tiebreaks needed a couple of matches. Also, it sounds funny now, but it took me a while to get used to there being no action replay either! When somebody played a great shot and got a round of applause, I guess I just expected a replay to happen somehow.

A bit later I found myself scaling the stairs of the Court One building. I peered in through one of the entrances, spotting the pristine green court in the distance, only for the guard to stop me! I timidly asked him if I needed a ticket and he replied, 'Yeah!' Rather incredibly though, he then looked at me again, hesitated and said 'oh! go on' and let me in! This really was the best introduction ever and

it must've been my first-time enthusiasm, as that has never happened again. A guy called Mark Philippoussis was playing and he remains one of my favourite players of all time, along with Court One as my favourite court on which to watch tennis.

A few days later, I was back again and was indeed lucky enough to see Sampras play. That year he went on to win the final – his historic, record-breaking 13th Grand Slam. Tennis soon took over a lot of my time.

I joined and became an active member of my local tennis club, learning to play the game from scratch, reading numerous tennis books in the library and playing whenever I could, which I still do. I've made amazing friends and had countless, wonderful tennis-related experiences. I've even coached, worked and travelled the world for tennis, all thanks to that first day at Wimbledon.

Mark Philippoussis

Pete Sampras

In Pursuit of Greatness
2001–2019

Roger Federer

By the start of the 2001 Championships the enlarged footprint of the Wimbledon grounds stretching into Aorangi Park was largely as it is today, including the new No.1 Court and the grass bank known as Henman Hill which became the daily destination for hundreds of ground ticket holders.

The old No.2 Court was still in use, and would not be replaced for a further eight years. As a result of all the changes, Wimbledon's spectator capacity had increased considerably, and a record 476,711 attended the 13 scheduled days of The Championships.

Many of those spectators were armed with second-generation mobile phones, texting news of their day at Wimbledon to friends and relatives all over the world. In the next few years advancing technology would enable people to access the World Wide Web through their mobile devices, join social networks such as Facebook and Instagram, and turn their visit to SW19 into a truly shared experience. Most important of all, spectators had instant access to Wimbledon's daily Order of Play, results and latest scores of matches currently on court without leaving their seats.

Two thousand and one was a watershed year in men's tennis, with 19-year-old Roger Federer beating seven-times champion Pete Sampras in the fourth round in five dazzling sets to put an end to Sampras's last serious challenge for the Wimbledon title. Tim Henman then beat Federer in the quarter-finals and it appeared his time for championship glory had come at last. When rain caused play to be curtailed in his semi-final with Goran Ivanisevic on Friday afternoon, Tim had just won the third set 6-0 to go ahead, and already held a break of service in the fourth when the British weather cruelly intervened, with him only needing another ten minutes or so to reach his first Wimbledon final. The force was with him, and he would surely not be denied.

Saturday was another wet day, but the force was gone. There was just enough time for the Croatian wild card to break back and win the fourth set on a tiebreak. On the following day, Sunday, the inevitable happened, with Goran taking the fifth set to reach his fourth Wimbledon final. On a fine sunny 'People's Monday' afternoon, he beat the popular Australian Pat Rafter who had also been runner-up to Sampras in a rain-affected final a year earlier. Britain's hopes were dashed, and Ivanisevic became the first wild card to win a singles

Championship at Wimbledon. Goran was much loved by the Wimbledon crowd, and his victory was warmly welcomed despite the heartbreak he had inflicted on 'Our Tim'.

Henman's cruel loss reignited the long-running debate about putting a closing roof on the Centre Court, leading eventually to a major project which reached its culmination eight years later. Ivanisevic's win was an isolated triumph as injury marred the final years of his career, although he did return to Wimbledon one more time in 2004, reaching the third round. Pugnacious Australian baseliner Lleyton Hewitt was World No.1 in 2001 and 2002, winning Wimbledon in the latter year, before a new era of Wimbledon domination began. ✇

In women's tennis, the era of Steffi Graf had ended with her loss to Lindsay Davenport in the 1999 final. Steffi had carried herself with dignity for 15 wonderful years, and her retirement was closely followed by that of Arantxa Sanchez Vicario, the popular little Spaniard who had given her two very tough battles in the 1995 and 1996 Wimbledon finals. Steffi's other great rival, Gabriela Sabatini, had made her last Wimbledon challenge in 1995. Steffi had beaten the glamorous Argentinian three times at Wimbledon, including an epic win in the 1991 final. The two had also teamed up to win the Ladies' Doubles in 1988. Gabriela will always be remembered for her groundstrokes which always landed incredibly short but with a huge amount of topspin, enabling her to wear down all but the very top players.

At the start of the 21st century Belgium's Justine Henin and Kim Clijsters, along with America's Jennifer Capriati, all looked like potential Wimbledon winners, but it was 17-year-old newcomer Maria Sharapova who beat them all to it when she brushed aside Serena Williams in straight sets in the 2004 final. Setting this and Amelie Mauresmo's win for France in 2006 aside, the Williams sisters reigned supreme on the lawns of SW19 from 2000 to 2010, and they are still challenging for more titles today in their fourth decade of competition at Wimbledon.

Russia's Anna Kournikova ranks alongside Suzanne Lenglen and Maria Bueno as one of the most glamorous and attractive women ever to play at Wimbledon. During her brief career from 1997 to 2002 she reached one Wimbledon singles semi-final, losing to her friend and rival Martina Hingis, in partnership with whom she won two Grand Slam doubles titles. Anna's early departure from tennis was partly caused by injury but also by the incredible demand for her services as a model and media celebrity. At The Championships, posters and postcards featuring Kournikova flew off the shelves, and in Wimbledon town centre a giant-sized Anna modelling a leading brand of underwear stared down at passers-by making their way to The All England Club. 🎾

Amelie Mauresmo of France beat Belgium's Justine Henin-Hardenne in the 2006 Wimbledon singles final

Anna Kournikova reached four Wimbledon semi-finals in singles and doubles between 1997 and 2002

The promise Roger Federer had shown by beating Pete Sampras in 2001 came to full fruition two years later when he beat Australia's Mark Philippoussis to win his first Wimbledon title. He became World No.1 a few months later and stayed there for four years. Between 2003 and 2012 Roger won 17 Grand Slam singles titles, including seven at Wimbledon. In Wimbledon finals Federer beat Andy Roddick three times, including a five-set marathon in 2009, Rafael Nadal twice, and Andy Murray and Philippoussis once each.

Federer's five-set victory over Nadal in 2007 was played on a Centre Court completely open to the elements, the fixed roof having been removed to prepare the way for its retractable replacement. After beating Nadal in the 2006 and 2007 finals, Federer lost a five-set epic to the Spaniard in 2008. The match was interrupted several times by rain, eventually finishing just before dusk.

After having things pretty much his own way at the top of world tennis, Federer was challenged from 2007 onwards by Rafael Nadal, Novak Djokovic and Britain's Andy Murray.

Spain's Rafael Nadal was a teenage sensation, winning his first Grand Slam singles title at Roland Garros in 2005. Unlike most clay-court experts, Rafa was also brilliant on Wimbledon's grass, reaching five finals between 2006 and 2011, winning in 2008 against Federer and 2010 against Tomas Berdych of the Czech Republic. Despite his extraordinary successes at Roland Garros where, up to 2019, Nadal had won a record-breaking

12 French Open titles, his career has often been punctuated by injuries, and these have resulted in some surprising early losses at Wimbledon; 2012 saw him beaten in five sets in the second round by an inspired Lukas Rosol of the Czech Republic. In his next four Wimbledon campaigns, knee trouble dogged Nadal's progress and he suffered unexpected losses to Belgium's Steve Darcis, Australian teenager Nick Kyrgios, Germany's Dustin Brown and Gilles Muller of Luxembourg. In 2018 and 2019 Rafa was back to something near his Wimbledon best, reaching the semi-finals where he lost tight matches against Djokovic and Federer respectively.

Rafael Nadal of Spain celebrates against Gilles Muller of Luxembourg during their second-round match at the 119th Wimbledon Tennis Championships in 2005

Serbia's Novak Djokovic first made an impact at Wimbledon in 2007, reaching the semi-finals where he was forced to withdraw due to injury. He suffered from health and fitness problems early in his career, but put these behind him by altering his training and adopting a gluten-free diet. After winning his first Wimbledon title in 2011, Novak reached five more finals in the next eight years, losing only to Britain's Andy Murray in 2013. Djokovic has been the dominant force in men's tennis during the 2010s, but his career has run parallel with that of the great Roger Federer, and he has not enjoyed the same level of popularity as his Swiss rival. ◑

When Andy Murray won the US Open Boys' Singles Championship in 2004 the British public became aware of a very special talent. At Wimbledon the following year he led former finalist David Nalbandian by two sets to love before a lack of conditioning caught him out. Rapid progress saw him beat Roger Federer several times on the ATP Tour and reach his first Grand Slam final at Flushing Meadows in 2008. After a number of runner-up finishes in Grand Slam tournaments, Andy hired Ivan Lendl as his coach in 2012. In that year he reached the Wimbledon final, losing to Federer, but got his revenge by beating the same player to win the London 2012 Olympic gold medal a few weeks later. Andy's year was rounded off when he won the US Open singles title in September and was named BBC TV's Sports Personality of the Year.

In 2013 Andy beat Novak Djokovic to become Britain's first male Wimbledon singles champion since Fred Perry 77 years earlier. In 2016 he won Wimbledon again, this time beating Canada's Milos Raonic in the final. Andy was not the first member of the Murray family to win a Wimbledon title, however, for in 2007 his older brother Jamie won the Mixed Doubles Championship in partnership with Serbia's Jelena Jankovic.

Inspired as a junior by Tim Henman's achievements, Andy Murray had taken British tennis right back to the top of the world game, and for more than a decade there was a good possibility of a British victory at the start of each Grand Slam tournament. A serious hip injury kept Andy out of Wimbledon in 2018 and 2019, but not before he had become the first British player of the modern era to be ranked World No.1.

Between 2010 and 2019 12 players reached the Wimbledon Ladies' Singles Final, and there were six different champions. Serena Williams won four titles in six final appearances, and Petra Kvitova won in 2011 and 2014, before her hand was seriously injured by an intruder to her home at the end of the 2016 season. Angelique Kerber and Garbine Muguruza both reached two finals during the decade, winning the title once each, as did Marion Bartoli in her only final appearance in 2013. Other one-time finalists were Vera Zvonareva, Agnieszka Radwanska, Sabine Lisicki and Eugenie Bouchard, but the failure of these players to establish themselves in the public consciousness by reaching the latter stages more regularly made women's tennis less appealing than it had been in the great days of Evonne Goolagong, Chris Evert, Martina Navratilova and Steffi Graf. Simona Halep of Romania was the popular winner in 2019 in her first final appearance.

Another impediment to the women's game was the excessive grunting by some of the top players, and the failure of the Wimbledon authorities to take action to curb it. Players such as Maria Sharapova and Victoria Azarenka alienated large sections of Wimbledon's audience, and the women's game suffered as a result.

Novak Djokovic and Roger Federer with Omar Popal, Wimbledon 2019

In the modern era, all the great Wimbledon champions have eventually reached a point at which the physical and emotional toll of their achievements finally catches up with them. When Rod Laver won his fourth and last Wimbledon singles titles in 1969, he was a month short of his 31st birthday. Five-time champion Bjorn Borg lost the 1981 final to John McEnroe just after turning 25. Pete Sampras was not yet 29 when he won Wimbledon for the seventh and last time in 2000. None of these greats ever reached another final. When they were done, they were done.

Roger Federer, however, is different. He was just under 31 when he won his seventh Wimbledon title in 2012 and, by all precedents, that should have been it for Roger, particularly when he endured an injury-plagued and unsuccessful year in 2013. Rather than slip into graceful and well-earned retirement, though, he reinvented himself by changing his coaches, his racket and his game. At the beginning of 2014, Severin Luthi and Stefan Edberg persuaded Roger to switch to a new racket with a bigger head, and Edberg taught Roger the secrets of the serve-and-volley game that had won him two Wimbledon Championships. Edberg's appointment had initially been for just one year, but the two got on so well that he stayed on for a further 12 months before being succeeded by former top-five player Ivan Ljubicic. The Croatian remodelled Federer's backhand, making it a real attacking weapon. Federer had always been a delight to watch, but now he was a virtuoso performer, and every match was a masterclass. The game had reached a new level.

Some people wanted Roger to keep winning so that he could capture more titles and set new records, others so he could keep the younger generation of great champions at bay. Most, however, just loved to watch him perform. After losing the 2014 and 2015 finals to Novak Djokovic, Roger became Wimbledon champion for the eighth time in 2017 and was runner-up to Novak by the narrowest of margins in 2019. ✪

The first two decades of the 21st century contained many important Wimbledon milestones. In 2009 the new retractable roof over the Centre Court was unveiled during a special public demonstration event a few weeks before The Championships. Exhibition matches were played beneath the closed roof, with Andre Agassi partnering his wife Steffi Graf. Also on court were Tim Henman and Kim Clijsters, the latter enjoying the experience so much she decided to come out of retirement and compete once again on the WTA Tour.

Two thousand and ten saw Her Majesty Queen Elizabeth II make one of her rare visits to Wimbledon, and on a gloriously sunny day she was introduced to a line of great champions including Serena Williams, Roger Federer and Martina Navratilova. Also in that year a Wimbledon record was set that can now never be broken, when America's John Isner beat Nicolas Mahut of France 6-4, 3-6, 6-7, 7-6, 70-68 in a first-round match lasting 11 hours five minutes and played over three days. A plaque was later unveiled on Court 18 to commemorate Wimbledon's longest-ever match.

In 2012 the Olympic Games tennis event was staged at The All England Club, with the traditional green court surrounds replaced for one week only with bright purple. Serena Williams won the women's singles gold medal, brushing aside all her opponents. Andy Murray won the men's gold medal, a title he successfully defended in Rio four years later. Also in 2012, BBC TV's *Antiques Roadshow* was recorded at The All England Lawn Tennis Club. The programme was presented by Fiona Bruce, and items brought in for expert appraisal included a tennis racket smashed by John McEnroe.

In 2018 the two men's singles semi-finals lasted a combined total of 11 hours and 51 minutes. In the first match, which commenced shortly after 1pm on Friday, South Africa's Kevin Anderson beat USA's John Isner 7-6, 6-7, 6-7, 6-4, 26-24. This match lasted six hours and 36 minutes and was completed at 7.46pm, following which the decision was taken to start the second semi-final despite the lateness of the hour. With the Centre Court roof closed, Novak Djokovic took a two sets to one lead over Rafael Nadal before play was suspended at 11pm.

The following day was fine, but Djokovic and Nadal continued their semi-final with the roof closed. The agreement of both players had been required for it to be opened, but the Serbian player had declined. This led to a change in Wimbledon's roof protocols the following year. Djokovic eventually won the match 6-4, 3-6, 7-6, 3-6, 10-8 after five hours and 15 minutes' play spread over two days.

Novak Djokovic beat a tired Kevin Anderson in straight sets in the final, and after the tournament it was decided that tiebreaks would in future be played at 12-12 in the fifth set of all men's matches at Wimbledon. In an extraordinary twist of fate, the first singles match in which the final-set tiebreak came into operation was the 2019 final between Novak Djokovic and Roger Federer, when the Serbian player came out on top by seven points to three after earlier saving two Championship points. ◎

Two thousand and nineteen had also seen the unveiling of the new retractable roof over No.1 Court, and for the first time in Wimbledon's 143-year history everyone who queued overnight for a ticket to the main two show courts was guaranteed to see a full day's play. The honour of playing in the very first match on Wimbledon's new-look second stadium went to Romania's seventh-seeded Simona Halep and unseeded Aliaksandra Sasnovich of Belarus, the former going on to repay the Committee's kindness by lifting the Ladies' Singles trophy a little under a fortnight later. Fifteen-year-old Coco Gauff was also in action, beating Venus Williams, 24 years and five singles titles her senior, proving, as Billie Jean King has said: 'Wimbledon is a continuum, to cherish and to honour.' ◎

2001

Croatia's Golden Year

Davor Margetic, ZAGREB

In 2018 two Croatian sports lovers achieved a lifetime's ambition when they met one of their country's greatest sporting heroes, 2001 Wimbledon champion Goran Ivanisevic.

My first Wimbledon was beyond any expectation, it was like a dream come true. Two friends on the same journey, two friends sharing the same passion, two friends who grow up in the 90s watching and idolizing one man, a national hero, Goran Ivanisevic.

Who would have thought that during the last five years we would become so close to him? Some magical force united us and brought us to the gate of holiness/sanctuary, to the gate of Wimbledon.

It was a beautiful Monday morning, start of the second week, we came early to the gates, our accreditations were there and we could finally enter the gates of paradise. In that paradise there was only one king for us, Goran of course!! He approached us, hugged us and showed us his kingdom. We couldn't believe that we were on the empty central court alone with him. Lots of things went through my mind, all that pain that we felt after his finals against Sampras, I even remembered Pat Cash climbing through the crowd, but most of all I remembered that amazing Goran triumph over Pat Rafter in 2001. I mean, we were in a dream!!

While we were walking around the court I asked Goran to tell me his first memories of Wimbledon. He told me that it was in junior Wimbledon in 1988 and that he was playing with a pain in his stomach and that he almost died on the court because he injured his stomach muscle. Afterwards we went for the lunch in the players lounge and there he was, another king, Roger Federer. Goran introduced us and then he took a picture of us. That day I also met Gabriela Sabatini, my childhood crush. In the next few days we met Novak, Rafa, Stefan Edberg and Queen of Wimbledon Martina Navratilova. All those days the weather was perfect, it was sunny and unbelievably hot. Icing on the cake was Croatia's victory over the England soccer team in the semi-final of the World Championship in Russia. It was magical, we were celebrating deep into the night. What more could you ask for? What a first Wimbledon!

Wimbledon favourites, 2001

2005

My First Visit to Wimbledon

Sheila Chambers, CROSBY

On Wednesday 29 June 2005 my friend and I left home at 6.15am to get the 7am train from Lime Street Station Liverpool to Euston. Then the underground to Southfields. We stopped for a cup of tea at a nice little cafe nearly opposite the station (unfortunately next to a fish market not so nice).

We then got the bus up to Wimbledon which was, due to the traffic and the crowds, a very slow journey but it gave us a chance to look at the obviously large and expensive houses along the way and the vendors selling different things in the gateways of some of the houses. On arrival we joined a fairly large queue but it moved pretty quickly. I think they did a very cursory check of handbags but as this was a week before the London Underground bombs I don't think it was as stringent as it is now.

It was men's quarter-finals day but unfortunately we did not have Centre or No.1 Court tickets. Our tickets were for Court 2 East Stand Row N Seats 39 and 40. These looked along the net. The first thing I was aware of was the power behind the shots going across the net. You get an impression of this on television but the reality is it is played at an incredible pace with tremendous power. You are far more aware of this when you are actually sitting close to the court. Being on Court 2 for the doubles matches meant we saw more players than we would have done on the main courts. We watched Kuznetsova and Mauresmo beat McShea and Spears 7-6, 6-2 and Groenefeld and Navratilova beat Douchevina and Peer 7-6 (7-5), 6-4. In this match I remember Martina encouraging her partner all the time. We also watched Olivier Rochus and Kim Clijsters beat Knowles and Venus Williams in the third round of the mixed doubles. It was a warm day but it rained twice although they only stopped for a few minutes each time.

Eventually we decided to have a look round and as we walked round we went to the Court 11 cafe for a drink. No queue and no queue for the ladies either. We eventually came to the queue for the Strawberries and Cream but we didn't want to stand for half an hour!! We walked along to Henman Hill and up round the top. My friend suggested as it was around 7pm we might be able to get onto Centre Court as the main matches had finished so we walked up to the back of the court and they allowed us in and we watched Black and Huber, who eventually won the Ladies' Doubles that year,

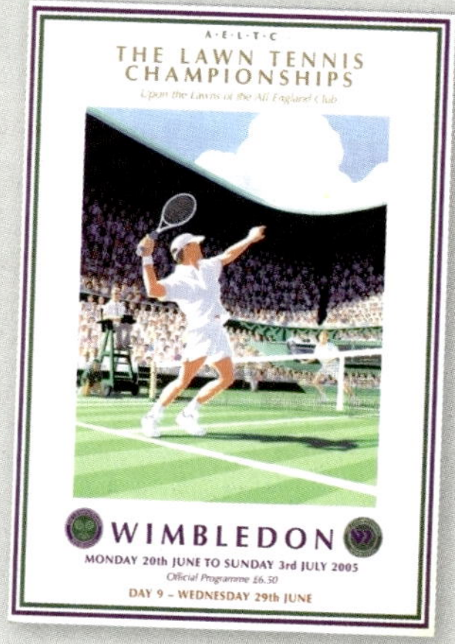

beat Hantuchova and Sugiyama in the quarter-finals 6-3, 6-2. I was disappointed with the view from the seats as it was very dark and I had to peer round pillars and it was quite difficult to see what was going on. Quite a contrast to the clear view on Court 2.

We thoroughly enjoyed our first visit to Wimbledon. Yes there was a lot of people but being on Court 2 we kept away from the crowds and also the queues. It was time to get a taxi to our hotel to enjoy a nice meal and an even nicer bottle of wine. A lovely end to a good day.

My First Visit to Wimbledon

Denise Paddock, SHREWSBURY

My first visit to Wimbledon was for my 50th birthday with my twin sister Diane. We arrived with a coach company and had tickets for Court No.1.

We enjoyed our games we watched, but during the afternoon we did pop on 'Henman Hill' to watch the big screen. The final was between Andy Roddick and Roger Federer.

I have been several times since but have never been on Centre Court.

Always a lovely place to visit, clean, lovely colourful displays of white, purple and green, especially the flowers.

2005

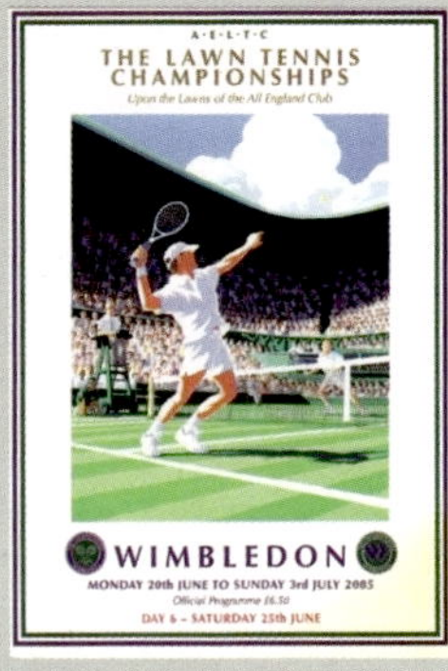

My First Visit to Wimbledon

Jamie Thomas, BASINGSTOKE

I was 11 years old for my first visit to Wimbledon, so I don't really remember the details of the day as a whole. But there are four people who really made my first Wimbledon experience a memorable one – Hammond, Redgrave, Federer and Murray.

The first two aren't tennis related but they really stand out in my mind. I remember walking around the grounds and noticing a very familiar face in the crowd – Richard Hammond from *Top Gear*. I asked my dad if it was him and he said it was, so I went over with programme and pen in hand and asked for his autograph. Ever since that moment I've always made sure I had a programme and pen ready for the next time I see someone famous; whether it's a tennis player or a celebrity, I'm now always on the lookout!

The second person was Sir Steve Redgrave. I recall seeing a mass of people on the move; there were autograph hunters, bodyguards and in the centre, Sir Steve Redgrave, one of the greatest Olympians of all time. Somehow I managed to squeeze my way in between the pile of bodies to get close to him so he could sign my programme. Later I found out why he was there – it was People's Saturday at Wimbledon; a tradition where selected sportsmen and sportswomen come together and watch some world-class tennis in the Royal Box on Centre Court.

We were fortunate enough to have Centre Court tickets, and the order of play for that day featured Roger Federer, Kim Clijsters, Andy Murray and Serena Williams. For me, nothing in tennis beats watching Roger Federer play. I've been lucky enough to watch him live numerous times, and when he's on court the whole atmosphere changes. He has this aura which means people stop what they're doing and watch him. No player causes the crowd to gasp in amazement quite as much as he does, so for me to have been able to watch him in my very first Wimbledon match was special.

Lastly, there was Andrew Murray, Britain's next big hope. The thing I remember most from his match against David Nalbandian was the atmosphere – it was incredible! There were 15,000 people willing on this 18-year-old Scot against one of the best players in the world at the time, a former Wimbledon finalist. It was Murray's debut on Centre Court and he relished being there on a stage where many have crumbled under the spotlight.

It's only now looking back that I really appreciate what a talented player he was. To compete at that level at such a young age takes something very special; and as it turns out, he is special. While he may have lost that match having been two sets up, it's still one of my favourite matches to have seen live at Wimbledon.

Hammond, Redgrave, Federer and Murray; these four people made my first visit to Wimbledon one to remember.

2006

Caught on Camera

Tim Edson, LEICESTER

On Tuesday, 4 July 2006 I took my wife Carolyn to Wimbledon for her first visit. As far as I can recall it was a very hot day. We bought ground tickets and after viewing inside Centre Court we went to Court 18. It was full so we decided to go down the side of the court where the press and players' entrance was.

I had recently obtained my bus pass and had it on me – on the spur of the moment I decided to flash my bus pass at the same time telling the security man I was from the *Leicester Mercury* sport dept (our local daily paper). He checked to see if there were any seats in the press area and to my amazement beckoned us both in to sit down. We ended up with a brilliant view and sat right behind Ilie Nastase!!!! The match was between McNamara and McNamee playing Lloyd and Fitzgerald. If I remember rightly the Aussie pair won. A few days later a friend of mine asked me if I had been at Wimbledon that day; I said 'yes' but queried why he had asked, only to be told we were both caught bang to rights by the TV cameras!

2008

Wimbledon at Last

Bendou Zhang, SHANGHAI

For many people, Wimbledon is the FIRST tennis tournament they want to visit. Surprisingly, as a tennis journalist, Wimbledon is actually the LAST grand slam tournament that I paid a visit.

That was in 2008. I was a guest of Rolex. They organised a small media group from China and I am one of them. Business flight and great food. Of course we did some journalism job, interviewing Mr Ian Ritchie and some players who were sponsored by Rolex, but it was not like super-serious journalism job with a media accreditation.

I still remember that I asked for a WIFI code in the Rolex VIP box on the first day. They give me a small piece of paper, and that was the longest and most complicated WIFI code that I had ever seen in my life. 'Why not make it simpler?' I asked. The lady answered, with a pleasant smile, 'But this is Wimbledon.'

For me, it was not like 'love at first sight' with Wimbledon, not like you can love Paris or Melbourne very easily. For my first visit and even the second visit, I felt a little uncomfortable and difficult. There are just so many traditions and rules. For instance, there are four or five different kinds of media accreditations, I guess it just reflects the hierarchy of the society.

However, after learning all these rules, get used to these rules and even be part of these rules, I start to appreciate these rules, the tournament and the city. Now that Wimbledon has become one of my favourite tournaments, I seldom miss it after the year of 2008. And I also enjoy London, with ATP London Finals. I spend almost one month every year in London all these years. For 2012 with Olympics, I spend two months.

For me, the city London, the tournament Wimbledon, and even British people, they are all keep distance with you when you first meet each other. It takes time for you to know them, to understand them, to appreciate them and to love them. And after you have love with them, the connections are stronger than ever.

AELTC Members' enclosure admission badges, 2009

Special Sundays

On Sunday, 17 May 2009 a capacity 15,000 crowd was present to celebrate the formal opening of the Centre Court's new retractable roof. Musical entertainment was provided by Katherine Jenkins, Faryl Smith and Blake, whilst on court Andre Agassi, Steffi Graf, Tim Henman and Kim Clijsters played a series of exhibition singles and doubles matches.

A decade later almost to the day, on 19 May 2019, another roof opening was celebrated on a damp Sunday afternoon in SW19. This time the No.1 Court was the centre of attention, and the players in action were Pat Cash, Martina Navratilova, John McEnroe, Venus Williams, Lleyton Hewitt, Kim Clijsters, Jamie Murray and Goran Ivanisevic. Music was provided by Paloma Faith and Joseph Calleja, accompanied by the BBC Concert Orchestra and the Grange Park Opera chorus. Not all of the 12,345 seats were occupied, but with tickets costing a cool £110 each this was not surprising. The proceeds went to a good cause, however: the Wimbledon Foundation's newly established homeless fund.

2008

No Place Like Wimbledon

Richard Hillway, COLORADO SPRINGS

About 2002, I became a good friend of Alan Little, Honorary Librarian of the Kenneth Ritchie Wimbledon Library, the best tennis library in the world. Alan (1928–2017) had been in charge of that Library since its beginning in 1977.

He was writing a biography of the fabulous tennis star, Suzanne Lenglen of France, and needed assistance to research the very first professional tennis tour which occurred in America during 1926 and 1927. So he turned to America's leading tennis historian, Frank Phelps, for help. Frank was in his eighties, and he recruited me to research the tour. During the next year-and-a-half, I sent Alan the results from 39 of the 40 series of matches. This turned into a 15-year correspondence in which Alan and I exchanged about 400 letters concerning tennis history. He educated me about Wimbledon tennis, while I gave him information on American players.

In 2008, Alan invited me to The Championships and I have enjoyed visiting Wimbledon for ten years since then, attending the matches for nine or ten days each year. Alan and the Museum staff have treated me royally, providing me with a grounds pass for each day, a Centre Court seat for at least two days yearly, and always lunch in the Members' Enclosure on the first Saturday. This included a Centre Court seat on the day Queen Elizabeth II visited Wimbledon to watch Andy Murray compete. To a tennis player, coach and historian this was a dream come true. Wimbledon was sacred to me, in the same way that the Vatican is sacred to a devoted Catholic, or the Sistine Chapel to an artist. The matches were terrific but I found equal enjoyment in my daily visits to the Wimbledon Library during which Alan Little and I discussed the earlier days of lawn tennis.

The day in 2008 finally arrived. My first visit to Wimbledon. The Championships had just started. I arrived early in the morning at Heathrow, took the underground to my housing in a college dorm, showered, put on a coat and tie, took the underground to Victoria Station, changed trains, and continued on the District line to the Wimbledon Park Station where I disembarked. Very near to that station I discovered The Tennis Gallery, a wonderful tennis bookstore that sold old and new tennis books. It is owned by two of the kindest and friendliest individuals in the world, Richard and Chris Jones. I consider them the unofficial hosts of The Championships, since they give a hearty welcome to numerous visitors from all walks of life who drop in on their way to the matches. In their shop I have met Rod Laver, Ken Rosewall, Christine Truman, Jenny Hoad, Gordon Forbes and other ex-champions, as well as celebrated tennis authors and journalists. My first day, I spent about an hour there over a cup of tea while talking tennis. In ensuing

years, I have repeated this exercise scores of times. Richard and Chris Jones have become friends for life.

Then I walked downhill across beautiful Wimbledon Park which was inhabited by ducks and swans from the nearby lake. I found Gate 5 of The All England Club on Church Road, showed my grounds' pass, and was in. The courts looked perfect – pristine, emerald green and surrounded by beautiful flowers all through the grounds. First I located the Museum and Library where, at long last, I met Alan Little for the first time after all the letters we had written to each other. I received a warm welcome and was introduced to the staff who were not only pleasant but also knowledgeable on the history of the game. American tennis historian and collector, the late Jeanne Cherry, author of *Tennis Antiques and Collectibles*, and more recently, *Helen Wills – Tennis, Art, Life*, had told me that she had received more respect as a tennis historian and interest in her work from Wimbledon than from any American tournament that she had visited. She was right.

The weather was perfect and I spent the rest of the day watching matches and returning occasionally to the Library. I enjoyed the first week of matches the most since every court was filled daily, although the second week brought the introduction of junior and veteran matches. I liked watching on the outer courts where I could be so close to the action. Sometimes I went to a random vacant court, sat down in the front row, and waited a few minutes until the ball kids, line people, umpires and players arrived. Then I would find out who was competing on that court. There were no bad players here.

I found out that Wimbledon was just as great as everyone had said it was. I searched out the Doherty gates, named after Reggie and Laurie Doherty and donated by their older brother, and also found the old pony roller still on the grounds. When hungry, I ordered fish and chips or Chinese food, and occasionally strawberries and cream. Twice during my initial visit I was given Centre Courts seats where I viewed the ultimate in tennis – Federer, Nadal, the Williams sisters, and others. Every seat in that stadium was a good one. I was surprised that, generally, much larger crowds turned out to watch the men's matches than the women's competition. The excellent Museum took me back to 1874, the first year of lawn tennis. It included a Major Wingfield set with the original lawn tennis rackets, trophies and rackets of early champions, and other glorious displays, including some of the modern players.

Honor Godfrey, the Wimbledon Museum Curator, has become a dear friend of mine. I bought a Wimbledon tie and a cap at one of the shops there, and bought a program on the grounds. I spoke with Alan Chalmers, the internationally known English dealer of rare and scarce real tennis and lawn tennis books. Occasionally, there was a great match on Centre Court to which I had no ticket. Then I'd watch the big screen on Henman Hill, or wait in line within the grounds to buy resold tickets left by spectators who exited early. Tickets were resold for all of the stadium courts, and became available by mid-afternoon and later. Luckily, the sun stayed out quite late in England, permitting spectators to witness matches until 9.30pm or later.

London had much to offer, and during my initial trip to Wimbledon I discovered many tennis-related adventures and treasures. I spent mornings exploring the city, and afternoons and evenings at the matches. I searched for rare old tennis books in London's bookshops, some on Charing Cross Road. Three of lawn tennis inventor Major Walter Clopton Wingfield's row houses were located and photographed. These were at 112 Belgrave Road, 33 St. Georges Square, and 83 Wimpole Street. His French & Company location at 46 Churton Street was also found. Unfortunately, his house

at 100 Buckingham Palace Road was missing, likely destroyed by German bombs during World War II.

I found the building in which the Doherty brothers lived as children, now a bookstore in the town of Wimbledon, and the apartment where Reggie Doherty died in 1910, right next to Albert's Hall. Ernest Renshaw's home was also located, near where James Buchanan had sold lawn tennis implements from his sporting goods store during the 19th century. One morning, I explored the original site of The All England Club (1869–1921) on Nursery Road near Worple Road. It is now the site of a girl's high school. Attila Szabo, likely the world's most expert tennis bibliophile, introduced me to the French restaurant, Le Gavroche, perhaps the top-rated restaurant in London.

On the middle Sunday, I took a pleasant train trip through Constable country to visit the renowned tennis collector Gerald Gurney and his wife Joan. Gerald owns a large collection of tennis memorabilia and founded the Tennis Collectors' Society in 1987. In subsequent trips, I have sometimes taken the train from London to Wolverhampton on the middle Sunday. There I have visited the tennis historian Bob Everitt and his fine tennis collection. In 2018, we co-authored the book, *The Birth of Lawn Tennis*.

All in all, I have come to one conclusion and it is this. There is no place like Wimbledon. It is the best.

2009

Wimbledon Days

Apphia and Daniel Parsons, DULWICH

grew up watching Wimbledon on TV. In the US, because of the time difference, the finals were always 'Breakfast at Wimbledon' – a favorite part of the summer. I moved to London when I was in my mid 30s to pursue a Master's degree.

I arrived in London in September 2008, and my first visit to Wimbledon was for the exhibition matches to test the new roof on Centre Court. That was a good year for me – I had entered the ballot, my first time, and received a pair of tickets for Court 1. In addition, a few days before the day my tickets were for, I queued with friends, for my very first experience of The Championship itself.

My date to the May 2009 roof closing event became my husband two years later, and together we have attended nine out of the last 11 years of Wimbledon, through a combination of ballot success, queuing, and last-minute tickets via Ticketmaster. Some years our visit has been in the first few days, exploring the outside courts; one year we got the men's final on Centre Court. One year we were almost entirely rained out, but we have had mostly good luck weather-wise. We enjoy the matches, of course, but also the atmosphere – the ball boys and girls and line judges marching on and off the court; finding a shady corner to sit and absorb it all; often a bottle of champagne; always strawberries and cream. A tradition we hope to continue for many years to come!

I keep in regular email contact with my family in the US, and here are some of my descriptions of Wimbledon:

Monday, May 18 2009

The event yesterday was really fun. The new roof worked well, and we had off and on rain all afternoon to truly test it. It lets in a lot of light, so it feels like you are outdoors, just not windy (or rainy) and a little warmer than the outside temp. We got there around 1.30pm and had sandwiches (cheddar and pickle) and Pimm's – very Brit! Then the roof closing started at 2.30pm. It takes about eight minutes for the roof to fully close. They had some classical singers there who sang 'Amazing Grace', among other songs. Then Agassi, Graf, Clijsters and Henman played mixed doubles (H and C won in a tiebreak), Agassi and Henman played men's singles (Agassi won 6-4) and Graf and Clijsters played women's singles (Clijsters won 6-4). All were only one set, since it wasn't a real match. The Duke and Duchess of Windsor were in the audience (in the Royal Box), as was Boris Becker. Quite a day! I kept saying 'I can't believe I'm at Centre Court'. We had really good seats (which I bought online as soon as they went on sale), about 15 rows back, in one corner, which I at first thought wouldn't be as good as on the side, but it was great, and you didn't have to keep turning your head to follow the ball.

Thank goodness I have tickets to go back for the real tournament, or I'd be in Wimbledon withdrawal!

Tuesday, June 23 2009

I had my strawberries and cream at Wimbledon yesterday, and thought of you! Am attaching a photo. Very tasty (although the cream isn't whipped, which was rather surprising – just poured cream). I 'queued' for four and a half hours to get tickets yesterday morning, with Anne and a few other friends. For Thursday, I have tickets already, that I got through the ticket lottery that I entered in the fall, which I am glad of. It's great that one can get tickets last minute, but four and a half hours is a long time in line!

Tuesday, June 28 2011

We are organizing a picnic this weekend. We decided to do the 4th of July picnic on the 3rd of July, so we can watch the Wimbledon final on the big screen, and have a midday picnic rather than an evening one. So far four friends are coming, so that will be nice. I am planning to make strawberry shortcake, to celebrate July 4th with something American, and to celebrate Wimbledon with the traditional strawberries and cream!

Thursday, June 28 2012

Well, I have succeeded, in the 11th hour, so to speak, to secure reserved seats for Wimbledon tomorrow. They have a few tickets that they put on sale 24 hours in advance of each day, and I was at my computer at 9am exactly and got two. So, Daniel and I will go tomorrow early afternoon. We have friends visiting from Geneva (the ones I have been to several tennis tournaments with), and they are planning to queue at 7.30am for grounds tickets, but I was not looking forward to getting up that early. So, we will be able to meet up with them, but sleep in a bit as well. It is quiet at work, as my boss is still away, so a good day to take off. We will be on Court 3, so you probably won't see us on TV – that tends to be Centre Court, I think.

Thursday, June 26 2014

Daniel and I had a great day at Wimbledon yesterday. We had four matches on our court, starting at 11.30am and finishing around 9.15pm! So, it was a full day of tennis. We had three singles matches and one doubles. In the doubles, we go to see Venus and Serena Williams against a Ukranian/ Georgian team. It was really something to see Venus and Serena together on court. The tickets we got were returns, and we did not know the exact seats until we picked up the tickets yesterday morning, and we ended up in the front row, on the side opposite the players. It was really fun to be so close. We also had good leg room, and were sitting right next to the press photographers. The weather was beautiful, with some sun and some cloud. If it had been sunny the whole day, it would have been too hot.

Apphia Parsons was born in Ann Arbour, Michigan and moved to London in 2008 to study for a Master's Degree in Translation and Linguistics.

Memories that will Last a Lifetime

Jeff Anthony, WEST HARTFORD, CONNECTICUT

grew up in a big family that all loved and played tennis. One of my sisters was a two-time state doubles champion and I was a captain and 4-year letter winner on my high-school tennis team in Connecticut. Wimbledon was always our favorite family sporting event to watch, and we never missed a Breakfast at Wimbledon and the likes of McEnroe, Lendl and Connors.

In 2009, I started working on tennis at ESPN and was fortunate to work my first Wimbledon – needless to say, I was overjoyed as Wimbledon to me was the 'cathedral' of tennis and a 'bucket list' sporting moment in my life. The way the shifts worked is each person had a day (in addition to the middle Sunday) off. My closest friends and I worked through the Saturday women's championship and had the Sunday gentlemen's championship off.

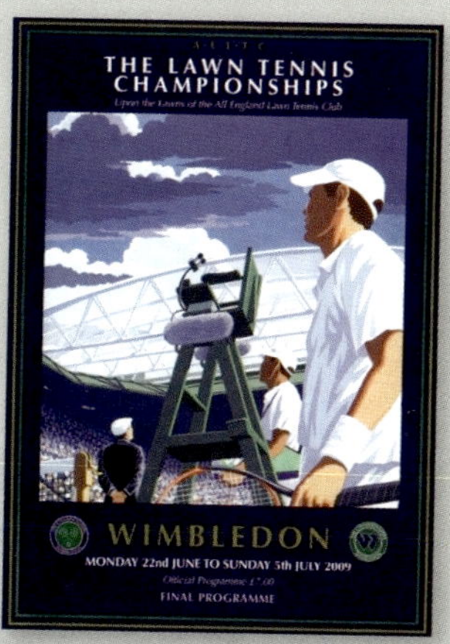

Late that morning, Caroline Davis called us to say that she had tickets to the final and asked if we wanted to go. This wasn't your average final in 2009, it was American Andy Roddick taking on Roger Federer. Federer was going for his record-breaking 15th Major title. As you know this match was a classic, as Roddick played the best tennis of his life (even better than his 2003 US Open Title). Almost the entire crowd was rooting for Federer to get his record Major title and my three friends and I were rooting for our countryman (even though we are all Federer fans). There was so much drama and excitement on Centre Court which was even smaller and more intimate than I ever imagined. Federer won 16-14 in the fifth set but memories of that day will last a lifetime.

That was my first time on Centre Court and I will never forget it, a memory of a lifetime.

Jeff Anthony is a Senior Associate Producer at ESPN.

2012

A People's Wimbledon

Richard Jones, WIMBLEDON

t is Wednesday, 1 August 2012, and today I have a ground pass for the Olympic Games tennis at Wimbledon! It is a day I never thought would come, and I am EXCITED!

My wife Chris and I arrive at Wimbledon station using our free Olympic Travelcards. These are a great idea, preventing ticket queues and speeding thousands of spectators through London's busy stations.

The free shuttle bus goes from close to Wimbledon station and drops you off at the apex of the grounds at the southern end, where Somerset Road and Church Road meet. You enter through the historic Doherty Gates, a privilege in itself as they are not usually used during The Championships.

Security is fast and easy, and then it's a short walk along the pavement of Somerset Road to enter the main grounds at Gate 10. It has the feel of a people's tournament, with no place for wealth and privilege. It is like everyone is going to Wimbledon for the first time, which of course many are. People are wearing their national colours in the form of football shirts, scarves and flags, and there are lots of blue Union Flag tee shirts of various types, utilising Stella McCartney's innovative design.

Instinct suggests a tour of the grounds to take in all the sights and spot all the differences from 'regular Wimbledon', but practicality for ground pass holders dictates that we head straight to our chosen court and secure the best seats possible. In our case that is Court 18, where Kim Clijsters is set to play Ana Ivanovic in the first match. It is 10.30am when we take our courtside seats, and the court only fills up a few minutes before the scheduled 11.30am start time.

I say scheduled, because in inimitable Wimbledon fashion it starts to drizzle just as the players are completing their warm-up. It is not raining much, and if the match was in progress, they would probably keep playing. But nobody likes to start a grass court match in the rain, so the court is covered, albeit far more slowly and less efficiently than it would be during The Championships. I learn later that it's the same court coverers that do the job during The Championships, but there are fewer of them, so it all takes longer.

During the rain delay I borrow a friend's Centre Court ticket. It has been a small sporting ambition of mine to see players in coloured clothing on the world's most famous tennis court. When I arrive Serena Williams is 3-1 up on Vera Zvonareva. The last time I saw these two meet was at Eastbourne 2011, when Serena was playing her second match following a year out through injury and life-threatening illness. Vera won that day in a tense three-hour struggle, but Serena's short-term goal of getting match practice on grass before Wimbledon had been amply achieved.

Thirteen months on, Vera has no chance. Now she's the one who's not played much, and Serena is playing like Superwoman, serving ace after ace and pummelling groundstroke winners. Serena looks like Superwoman too in her dark blue USA dress trimmed with white and red, and her wild hair kept away from her eyes by a bright red headband. Vera is a big strong woman attractively dressed in light blue and wearing a trademark white sun visor, but next to Serena she looks lightweight and most of the time she can barely get her racket on the ball.

Speeding serves deflect into the colourful crowd off the frame of her racket, and she throws it to the ground twice in rapid succession, eliciting surprised gasps from the spectators who are not the usual Centre Court crowd. I leave after about 15 minutes with Serena having won all five games I watched. She did not lose another in the match.

After an hour and a half delay, the players return to Court 18. Kim starts the second warm-up the same way she did the first by belting a forehand at about 80 miles an hour. On this frustrating day of weather they are to warm up three times in all, and each time Kim starts with the Exocet forehand. I feel a bit sorry for Ana, but she takes it in her stride.

After around three and a half hours including rain interruptions Kim closes out a 6-3, 6-4 win, and they are followed onto court by Jo-Wilfried Tsonga and Feliciano Lopez. A day earlier Tsonga had been involved in the longest match in Olympic history, beating Canada's emerging star Milos Raonic 6-3, 3-6, 25-23.

During the Tsonga versus Raonic match I had travelled from Wimbledon to Wembley for the GB v Brazil Women's football match, and I kept in touch with the Tsonga score through the excellent Olympic Tennis app on my mobile phone. As I left Wimbledon Park it was 7-7 in the third set, and by Waterloo it was 16-16. My next Central London update showed 19-19, and by the time I emerged from the underground at Wembley Park it was all over, 25-23 to Tsonga. Today it is much easier for the popular Frenchman and he sweeps aside the handsome Spaniard whose incredible talent seldom seems to bring its just reward.

Then comes the match we've all been looking forward to as Switzerland's reigning Olympic champions Roger Federer and Stan Wawrinka take on Israelis Jonathan Erlich and Andy Ram. Federer has just won the Wimbledon men's singles title for a record-equalling seventh time, but that is not why everyone wants to see him. At 30 he has reached a rare place for a top tennis player, having suffered no apparent loss of strength, stamina or agility but having gained an uncanny ability to anticipate his opponents' shots

and improvise his own. When pressured around the baseline, he improvises with groundstrokes that are almost half-volleys but are unerring in their accuracy.

Add to these qualities the fact that he comes across as a likeable guy who is neither egotistical nor falsely modest, and you have a player who will fill far bigger arenas than Court 18 at Wimbledon.

Sadly, Federer and Wawrinka lose. After taking a severe battering in the first set, the more experienced Israeli pair rally to win 1-6, 7-6, 6-3. Roger looks genuinely sad for his partner that they could not repeat their Beijing success. For Federer there is the singles to play but, for Wawrinka, London 2012 is over.

Last on court is an interesting men's doubles match which provides the best entertainment of the whole day. It's between France and India, with noisy and good-humoured support from fans of both countries. Tsonga returns to the court where he played singles earlier, this time partnered by Michael Llodra, a strong left-hander with a wonderful leftie serve. They are up against a tall Indian newcomer called Vishnu Vardhan who is partnered by the

experienced Leander Paes, playing in a record sixth Olympic tennis tournament. Tsonga is clearly very tired, and the Indians quickly gel into a solid partnership. Paes smiles a lot but competes hard, and he is very supportive of his young partner who responds with some great tennis. Unusually tall for one of his nationality, at only 22 he could be a star in the making.

Second seeds Tsonga and Llodra close out the match in three tight sets, and afterwards Tsonga is too exhausted to do his customary victory jig. So Llodra does a funny impersonation of it for him, much to the amusement of the still large crowd.

It's 8.30pm and the last half hour of August daylight. Having spent all day in an unreserved seat, there has been no time to look around the grounds or visit the London 2012 shop. But it has been a great day, and the volunteers ushering passengers onto the Shuttle bus to Wimbledon station are still good-humoured after a long work shift. That's the abiding memory of the London 2012 Olympics at Wimbledon – a top-class sporting event in a fun atmosphere. Quite an achievement amid all the highly visible security outside the grounds.

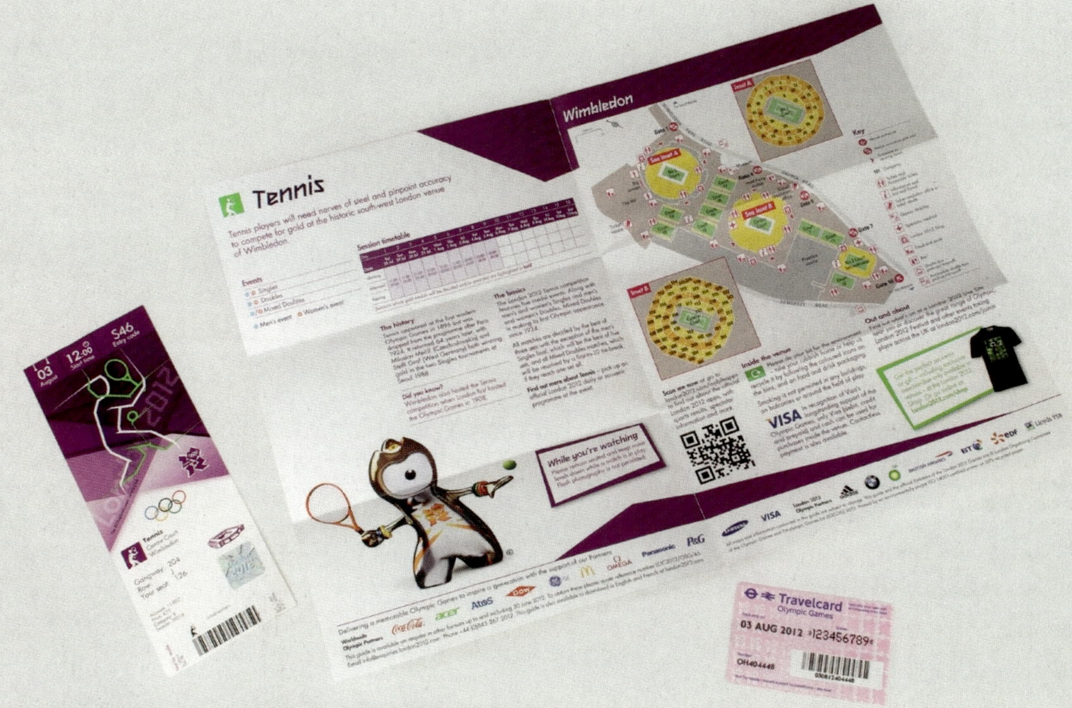

Olympic tennis ephemera, 2012

2012

Finals Day

Paul Strudwick, BRENTWOOD

I went on the Wimbledon tennis tour in 2011. I enjoyed it so much and they mentioned that the ballot opened a few weeks later. I applied and then waited until February the following year when a ticket offer came. It was for £105 per ticket. I was about to decline the tickets when I saw the date: 7th July 2012, women's finals day. I paid for the tickets and when they arrived a few weeks later I went online to check the view from the seats. They were on the baseline, so I was satisfied I had a good view.

The day of the women's final arrived and all the talk was of Andy Murray getting to the men's final. On route I met my friend and we travelled from Southfields by bus even though I knew it was walkable. Just as we arrived the heavens opened but as the roof had been installed we were guaranteed play.

On entry to the ground we headed to Court 1 for the shop and the toilets. During this time I lost my friend and after eating my sandwiches outside Centre Court in a small alleyway with another court adjacent I went to find my seat. It was in the front row, exactly how the picture on the internet had shown, and very close to the Royal Box. People were taking pictures by the scoreboard and I was thinking: is this really my seat? The Centre Court stewards were really pleasant. One was from the Royal Navy and another from the RAF.

It was almost time for the television coverage to start. Sue Barker was briefly seen, but as the heavens opened again she quickly disappeared. The roof was still open but the covers were placed on the court. All the seats got wet but my seat had some protection from the rain due to the new roof protruding over me. The rain stopped and a group of people came out to clean the

seats. As people started to gather, the covers were removed and you could sense the atmosphere building. By this time my friend had joined me and I had my picture taken against the scoreboard. The BBC camera crew arrived at the court in force, but there was still no sign of Sue Barker doing on-court interviews like previous years. The ball boys and girls appeared followed by the umpire and line judges. And then, after a brief wait, the players, Serena Williams and Agnieszka Radwanska. Serena looked nicer in real life than she appeared on the TV.

As usual the crowd supported the underdog but I just knew Williams would win. The first set was over very quickly. At some point during this set I had received a few text messages saying 'I can see you on the telly.' It turned out that even my sister was watching me and she lives in Australia. It was the first time she had seen me for 11 years.

At some point during this match one of the players questioned whether the ball was in or out. As I was on the baseline I already knew the verdict. At one point a fast ball

Serena Williams beat Poland's Agnieszka Radwanska in the 2012 Wimbledon Ladies' Singles Final. The unseeded pairing of Britain's Jonny Marray and Frederik Nielsen of Denmark won the Gentlemen's Doubles title, defeating Robert Lindstedt and Horia Tecau 4-6, 6-4, 7-6, 6-7, 6-3 in the final.

headed in our direction. My friend ducked and it just missed him.

The second set took longer and went to Agnieszka. I was thinking maybe she can win after all. It was not to be, the third set was another quick round with Serena winning. The final result was 6-1, 5-7, 6-2. Serena climbed the stand near to us to see her family which had recently become a tradition for the winner of the tournament. After the presentation and speeches the trophy was held up in all directions apart from towards me so I did not get a good picture face-on.

The next match was the men's doubles which featured a British man called Marray (not to be confused with Murray). The court lacked spectators at first especially in the Royal Box. This match was a lot longer than the Ladies' Singles Final so I left for a few minutes to stretch my legs. I was unlucky as I timed it for the start of a tiebreak. I was stuck outside the court unable to see what was going on but the Royal Navy guy at the court entrance was giving me a commentary. I got back on the court and the players came off either for rain or bad light. The roof was going to be used for the first time that day.

Once the roof was closed the atmosphere felt completely different. It was dark outside and I felt it was time to leave. I took a vintage bus to Southfields, and when I got home and turned on the TV to find out the result I discovered the third match, the women's doubles, including the Williams sisters, was still on!

2013

The Physio's View

Carlos Costa, PORTUGAL

As a private physio for ATP/WTA Tour players there are two moments at the Wimbledon Championships that I will never forget.

The first one was with Tommy Haas in 2013. A former No.2 ranked player, he made a comeback at the age of 35 to No.11, becoming the oldest player on tour with a ranking this high. This comeback came together with a presence on the big stages, and one of them was when he advanced to the fourth round in Wimbledon against Djokovic, where he played at the Centre Court. A sense of belonging was felt both in and out of the court and, although the result was not ideal, going so far in such an event represented a great achievement for himself and our team. It is only in those moments that we can fully understand how sacrifices and passion can surpass our expectations, making the impossible possible.

Seeing for the first time the Centre Court with such a crowd made me wonder if I would be there again and whether next time it could be any closer to the final. To my surprise, it was not that long after ... only five years later, when it happened again.

At that time I was working with Kevin Anderson and in beating the 'King of Grass', Federer at the quarter-finals, then Isner at the semi-final, with the second-longest Wimbledon match and the third-longest singles match in history, a marathon of six hours 36 minutes, there were many challenges to overcome – the constant replacement of fluids and electrolytes to re-establish their balance, to a post-match emotional gather and a wake-up call at 4am to help him relieve some of the excruciating pain on the feet. It was all worth it in the end and reaching the finals was like a wish come true.

The finals by coincidence happened to be again against Djokovic; however, that moment had a different taste in the air and I took the time to appreciate such a traditional event. That tennis began on grass and that Wimbledon is the only Grand Slam which has always been played on the same surface, that has an all-white dress code to demonstrate signs of cleanness, to the presence of a Royal Box at the Centre Court, shows how old traditions are still contemporary and it is still considered one of the most beautiful events of the world tour.

Through the years I have come to realize that those are the memories we live for, to witness at firsthand and be able to contribute for both to express is always a great honor and I feel very lucky to take part in them.

Carlos Costa is a physiotherapist on the ATP and WTA Tours and is the Head Therapist for Portugal's Davis Cup and Fed Cup teams.

Tommy Haas

The People's Wimbledon – Heaven on Earth

Simon Etheridge, BISHOP'S STORTFORD

I t is always an emotional moment when the Wimbledon Championships are completed for another year. Memories last a lifetime but there is a slight tinge of sadness even though 'the days are long but the years are short'. Just as the Club and The Championships have 'The List' of enhancements compiled each year, so we have our own personal and collective moments of humble reflection and giving goals for the future months.

But Wimbledon is not just for two weeks in July. As the yellows, blues and greens of summer give way to the reds, oranges and pinks of autumn, the purple and green of Wimbledon shines brightly all year round in all four seasons. Wimbledon is special to visit at any time of year, history and 'the pursuit of greatness' is sensed beneath the stillness, whilst the on-going meticulous preparations and outreach promise more memorable stories in the future. Moreover, there is also wonderful and warm wider local community around and beyond the Club and The Championships.

Every year since the autumn of 2013, Year 7 students of The Bishop's Stortford High School have visited Wimbledon Park. This educational visit is connected to the subject of Religious Studies and Citizenship. Students enjoy visiting The Buddhapadipa Buddhist Temple and The Wimbledon Mosque where they learn to respect and thoughtfully reflect upon theological beliefs, practices and values from wonderful, wise and welcoming guides and hosts.

The year group also enjoy visiting The All England Lawn Tennis Club, the landscape of which is overlooked and blessed by Saint Mary's Church, Wimbledon's own church seen every night on the BBC during The Championships and the place of many a moving tennis tribute.

Tennis began in monasteries of Northern France in the 1100s whilst, in history, a play depicted Jesus being given a tennis ball at The Nativity. Like tennis and sport as a whole, these outstanding tours also teach us about, and are a mirror of, life – ethos, standards, respect, character, preparation, uniform, sportspersonship, grace, integrity, humility values and equality in sport and life. Guides are insightful, illuminating, informative, enthusiastic and enlightening as students are inspired by the courts, the museum, the trophies, 'If', the media and broadcast areas and the hill and the beautiful grounds generally. A love of the game, life and timeless values is nurtured. 'The Tennis Gallery', which does so much to share an appreciation of tennis and life, very kindly and characteristically provide souvenir tennis balls and programmes for the students, all of whom have been a credit to themselves and their families.

Such an experience lives out 'The People's Wimbledon'. The inclusiveness of the Club and The Championships is evidenced by the promotion of equality for all in sport, the Queue, the Hill, charity ticket returns and the balcony trophy presentation to those in the grounds on fabulous finals days. School visit days live long in the memories and in the photographs but, like the story-makers and story-tellers of *The People's Wimbledon*, also in people's hearts and souls.

3D-printed trophies made on-site by IBM Wimbledon, 2013

2014

Catching the Bug

Amy Lundy, WESTPORT, CONNECTICUT

For fans, one of the great things about professional tennis is 'catching the bug' – watching the sport sparks an intense desire to pick up a racquet yourself and get out there. Tennis is one of the great pursuits that can be enjoyed as a spectator and a participant.

As an American, my first time at The Championships, I was thrilled to have a week in London to visit the tournament as well as surrounding areas. It was absolutely magical getting on the Tube on the way to Wimbledon and seeing young competitors sitting right alongside us fans as we all headed toward the tournament on the same train. Some players were entered in the doubles competition. Others were in the juniors event, traveling with their parents. It was fun sneaking a glance at the tags on their racquet bags to find out which country they represented.

I happened to be with a tour group that had a special agreement with a delightful little grass-court club tucked a short walk across the street from The All England Club. This allowed us fans to play for a bit on the grass courts before changing clothes in their locker room and heading across the street to The Championships to enjoy the action for the rest of the day. Pretty much a perfect day for any tennis enthusiast and a dream come true! Just like The All England Club, the other club required all-white attire. I'd been staying at a hotel in London, so I carefully chose my white tennis dress and packed my racquet bag neatly to honor the small club that was giving me this special opportunity. It would be my first time playing on grass. I paid special attention to my hair and makeup to look like a proper competitor – quite a bit of effort for a mom of two in her 40s!

On the Tube out to Wimbledon, I felt slightly embarrassed to be dressed in all-white tennis attire – obviously not a competitor at The Championships because of my age! Still, any feelings of conspicuousness or seeing inquisitive looks from fellow passengers were easily quashed by my excitement for the day ahead.

One thing I have always observed about British people is their joviality and enjoyment of a good laugh, especially the men. A few minutes into my journey on the train, I noticed two British guys joking with each other and generally 'cutting up', as we say in America. Rascals. Overhearing a few of their jokes, I could not help but turn my head to the side and smile. It turns out they were tennis coaches living somewhere a few hours from London. Armed with grounds passes, they were headed for a day of revelry and Pimm's on Henman Hill. Catching my amusement, one of them took a step toward me and said loudly in the most proper British voice he could muster, 'Excuse me, Miss. Are you entered in the Junior Championships at Wimbledon?' The entire train burst into laughter, including me. The two of them continued to playfully joke with me about my outfit and racquets. It was my very own British comedy routine – all centered on the sport I love – at my much-welcomed expense. I loved every minute of it.

I enjoyed getting to know them, learning that they coached mainly recreational players just like me. As I got off the train, surrounded by laughs and funny comments from fellow passengers and fans, I felt the flush of happiness and excitement. We shook hands and parted ways – all off to enjoy an exquisite day at Wimbledon.

Wimbledon Championships wristbands 2012-2014

2015

Wimbledon Recollections

Bruce Ryan, SYDNEY

t is 1956. I am 13 years old, sprawled on the lounge room floor, ears tuned to the radio broadcast of the Wimbledon men's singles final.

'Hoad serves, follows to the net backhand return down the line by Rosewall Hoad crosscourt forehand volley Rosewall is across, goes for the pass down the line Hoad lunges, backhand volley crosscourt for a winner.'

From this time onwards, the last week of June and the first week of July we follow the exploits of our champions including Margaret Court, Evonne Goolagong, Pat Cash and Lleyton Hewitt.

And, of course, the unique Monday final between Pat Rafter and Goran Ivanisevic. During a press interview in his rain-delayed semi-final Goran introduces us to the three Gorans: Good Goran, Bad Goran and Dial 999 Emergency Goran. What a lovable eccentric.

Finally in 2015 my wife and I are to be in London for a day during the Wimbledon tournament, and we are armed with ground passes.

Friday of the first week is a perfect English summer day, clear blue sky and no wind. On entering the grounds we are struck by the beautiful green of the courts, the players in white and the slightly olde world but immaculate dress of the linespersons. This is how tennis should be!

Surrounding a tea area there are tubs filled with hydrangeas, not blue or pink; no, the groundsmen have tweaked the alkalinity of

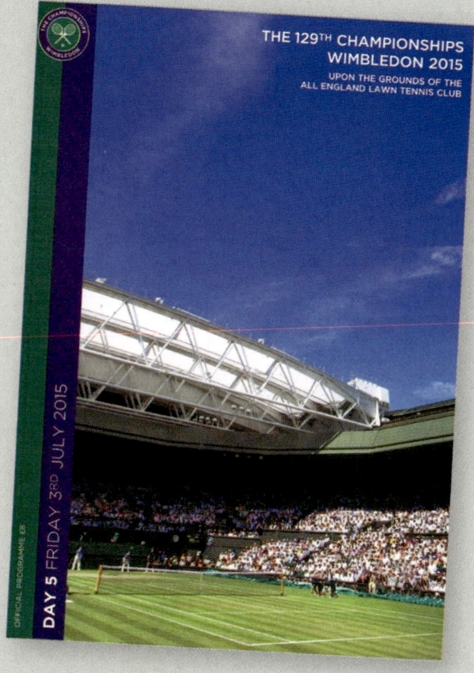

> ❝On entering the grounds we are struck by the beautiful green of the courts, the players in white and the slightly olde world but immaculate dress of the linespersons. This is how tennis should be!❞

the soil so there are green leaves with purple flowers, echoing the Wimbledon club colours.

We queue patiently (as the British do) for over an hour to gain entry to Court 3 and are rewarded with some exquisite baseline rallies between David Goffin of Belgium and Marcos Baghdatis of Cyprus.

But the main aim here is the next match, Aussie Sam Stosur taking on the aggressive American Coco Vandeweghe. The American opens up hitting the ball fiercely and Stosur's answer is to try to hit even harder, a strategy which fails dismally. At the end of the first set with no sign of a Plan B from Stosur I leave my wife to endure the agony and retreat to the field courts where a number of men's doubles matches are in progress.

I find a seat on the bench at the low fence of Court 6. Tecau and Rojer have clawed their way back from two sets to love down to level the match against Begemann and Knowle. As I join, it is five games all in the fifth set. All four men have powerful serves and each holds comfortably until the score reaches 13 all.

First point of the next game Rojer strikes a strong return down the forehand line. The ball catches the tape, hesitates and drops over for a dead winner. Love-15. Tecau nails the next return on the shoetops of the incoming volleyer. Love-30. At last, a chance. The game seesaws but the break of serve is achieved. Tecau comes around and easily holds serve to close out the match 15-13 in the fifth set.

To emphasize the importance of that dead net-cord winner, Tecau and Rojer go on to win the men's doubles championship of 2015.

Bruce Ryan is a dedicated supporter of the Australian Tennis Museum in Sydney, where tennis legend Ken Rosewall is the Patron.

2015

A Special Place

Antonio Demasi, MERIDEN

have been a tennis fan since 1994 and since watching Arantxa win the 1994 US Open I was hooked. Never missing a Grand Slam on TV, and yes even waking up at 3am to watch the Australian Open, to cheer on my favourite players.

In those years of watching tennis I would always admire the beauty of Wimbledon. The look, feel and tradition had me glued to the programme. Realizing how difficult it would be to score a ticket to Centre Court it felt far-fetched to think of ever actually visiting SW19.

Fast forward 20 years later and I begin job hunting after my company was moving its HQ outside the state of Connecticut. I applied at ESPN, amongst other companies, and landed a job in an admin position. Seven months into the job a colleague tells me a position has opened up in Tennis. Realizing I had no Operations experience I wasn't going to get my hopes up too high but nevertheless I applied. Three months after my application and a series of interviews I was offered the job!

Surreal is putting it mildly as I could not believe I was about to live in the tennis world. And the best part is Wimbledon would be my first assignment, June 2015, as the Operations Coordinator.

At the same time I was in this euphoric state of personal career achievement I was also in a personal low. My best friend, Nicole, of 20 years was battling Stage IV Ovarian cancer. She had been diagnosed back in May 2013.

Things seemed to be routine with her chemo visits and the doctors had given us a lot of hope. In early May 2015 she took a turn and started to feel worse. Still not thinking, or wanting to believe, it would only get poorer we stayed optimistic. A few weeks had passed and we eventually had to check into Yale hospital for around-the-clock care. She lost her battle on June 15th, 2015.

I was slated to travel to London on June 19th, 2015 but had a lot of doubts about leaving home. I am fortunate to have an amazing support system, both at work and at home, and we all felt it was best to get away.

I arrived to the Club a week before play would start as we would need to set up the operation. It was hard to be away from home and family and in an area where no-one knew Nicole. I kept myself busy and luckily in Operations you work long days so I could just go home and go to sleep.

Once play started and I walked outside to the grounds something small but magical happened. I'm still not sure what it was but a slight inner peace came into my mind, body and soul.

I walked into Centre Court and could not believe I was inside the holy grail of Tennis. At first I wanted to text Nikki a picture and as I reached into my pocket I remembered I was carrying her

> **"***Wimbledon will always hold a special place in my life. I do believe there is magic in the grounds.***"**

picture with me. I instantly snapped a pic of her and I in Centre Court and it happened again. This amazing feeling of peace transcended in me while inside.

I would go on for the next year and take along the picture with me to all my travels. It was a way of keeping her with me and sharing my experiences in this new Tennis world.

And every time I return to Centre Court – it has been three visits so far – I always walk into that same spot and still have that feeling of love and happiness rush through my body.

Wimbledon will always hold a special place in my life. I do believe there is magic in the grounds.

2016

Lleyton, Thanasi and Nick

Raphael Iberg, LAUSANNE

Martina Hingis, Roger Federer and Stan Wawrinka are my fellow citizens, and former Wimbledon Junior Champion Belinda Bencic shares the Swiss flag with me, but I've only ever had one tennis idol, Australia's Lleyton Hewitt.

In 2015 I had just flown into Gatwick Airport and made my way to Southfields, where my former host family – and now adopted family – lives and where I usually stay during The Championships. I've spent most of my summers in the SW19 area since 2008, the first ones as a student. It was Lleyton's final Wimbledon as a singles player, but on that day he was due to play doubles. He had already bowed out in singles, narrowly edged in the first round by Finn Jarkko Nieminen 11-9 in the fifth, in typical Hewitt fighting fashion. Doubles with highly talented fellow Australian Thanasi Kokkinakis was the only thing left in his Wimbledon career.

So there I was, hoping against hope that I might catch a glimpse of my childhood hero. I had seen him play 'for real' before, in Newport in 2012 and at Queen's Club in 2013, but I had never seen him play at Wimbledon. I got inside quite quickly, looking for the right outside court (Court 15 or 16, if memory serves). It was already packed, so I watched from a neighboring court. Hewitt and Kokkinakis were grinding their way back into the match against 15th seeds Kontinen and Draganja.

The Aussies ended up winning 8-6 in the fifth from two sets down, but the best part of that encounter didn't occur on the court. It took place in the alley between the court where Hewitt was playing and the court where I was standing, craning my neck to see. Nick Kyrgios suddenly (and very casually) showed up, sporting his aggressively pink headphones, and climbed onto the court's fence to watch his mentor. It took all of 30 seconds for a member of staff to tell him off, and I remember thinking that these hallowed grounds were probably the only place in the world where a celebrity (albeit minor) would get a slap on the wrist as if they were, well, one of us mortals. Rules are rules. I went on to be lucky enough to see Hewitt play twice more that year (in men's doubles but also mixed doubles, partnering Casey Dellacqua), but this 'incident' really stands out in my mind.

2016

Alisha's Big Day

Sarita Sharma, SURBITON

Wimbledon 2016 was the first year my daughter Alisha and I were lucky enough to win tickets at the ballot at our respective tennis clubs. She was beside herself and talked incessantly about it till the big day arrived.

Alisha, who was ten years old then, is a big tennis fan. She's the whole reason I picked up a racquet for the first time three years ago.

She got special permission to miss school that day. Everyone at her school knows that she's a tennis nut so resistance was futile.

She was so excited the night before our trip to Wimbledon that it took her awhile to drop off to sleep.

The morning broke, the birds were chirping, the sun was out, we packed our picnic and, like two teenagers heading off to a music  festival, we were ready for game, set and match!

We saw Dustin Brown play, but the highlight was watching Andy Murray which was awesome. Our fellow spectators were exceptionally friendly. They all made a fuss of Alisha and were impressed by her extensive tennis knowledge!

We indulged in the perfunctory exercise of queuing for autographs which was the cherry on top for Alisha.

It was truly a fantastic, fabulously memorable day and one we'll reflect on in years to come.

2017

Caring for Bethanie

Sandra 'Taff' Roberts, WIMBLEDON

'**M**y first experience of Wimbledon was watching on television as Virginia Wade beat Betty Stove in 1977, with the Queen present,' Taff recalls. 'That really caught my imagination, and from then on I was hooked on the game.'

Taff was on the spot when the popular US player Bethanie Mattek-Sands suffered a serious injury during the 2017 Championships.

'I more or less saw it happen,' she recalls. 'I was in the Ambulance Control Room high up in the North West Corner of Centre Court, and Bethanie was playing on Court 17 when she suffered a severe dislocation of her right knee. I rushed down to the court and called the Tournament

Doctor who quickly administered painkillers. We could have put the knee back in place, but Bethanie had experience of a previous injury and asked us not to.

'The Doctor was Fenella Wrigley, Medical Director of the London Ambulance Service. Nowadays she is also The Championships' Chief Medical Officer. We were able to bring an ambulance in through Gate 4 and then reverse right up to Court 17. Bethanie was taken to St. George's Hospital in Tooting where she received excellent treatment.'

This tale has a happy ending, for Bethanie and Taff renewed their acquaintance, albeit in much happier circumstances, during the 2019 Nature Valley International tournament at Devonshire Park, Eastbourne. Bethanie was delighted to meet up with the person who had helped her on that fateful day two years earlier, and the two were photographed together.

Taff has been watching tennis at Devonshire Park for 40 years, and relishes her annual visits to Eastbourne. 'I always stay at the same hotel, and it's a week I really look forward to.'

Taff had moved from Wales in 1987, working first at New Malden Ambulance Station before moving to Wimbledon in 1990. She has now been working in the Ambulance Service for 32 years.

She has for many years been responsible for the deployment of London Ambulance Service staff and vehicles at The Championships during Wimbledon Fortnight. Planning meetings are held at The All England Club a week before each year's tournament.

'One year I took a fortnight's leave and drove one of the player's courtesy cars instead. It was a wonderful experience, and I'd like to do it again after I retire. Amongst those I drove were Pete Sampras, Martina Navratilova and Gabriela Sabatini.

'Another person I drove was Jana Novotna, who sadly died recently. In the year I drove her, she had not expected to do well at Wimbledon and only had a visa for one week. I drove her to Croydon so she could get her visa extended. On the way back she said: "Are you a tennis fan, and do you have tickets for Wimbledon?" I replied "Yes" and "No", so she gave me a ticket to sit in her players box.'

At the rear of the women's changing rooms at Wimbledon Ambulance Station there is a small enclosed patio with a view out across the hockey pitch belonging to the Wimbledon High School for Girls. From there you can see where the original Centre Court used to be, just 50 yards away. Suzanne Lenglen won her first Wimbledon title there, exactly a century ago, and she would surely be pleased to know that Taff Roberts is there today, perpetuating her love of this beautiful game.

Sandra Roberts works at Wimbledon Ambulance Station which is located in Nursery Road right next to The All England Lawn Tennis Club's original ground. Sandra hails from the Swansea Valley and is affectionately known to her friends and colleagues as 'Taff'.

Virginia Wade receives her trophy from Her Majesty the Queen, 1977

2017

The Best Birthday Present Ever

Anne Comerford, WEXFORD

On Monday, 3 July 2017, I walked through the gates of The All England Lawn Tennis and Croquet Club, on my first-ever visit to the Wimbledon Championships. I was excited, emotional and armed with a ticket for Centre Court – a big-roundy birthday present from my family. It had taken me years to get to those gates (and I'm not talking about the Queue!).

My birthday present was an all-in package which included a return flight from Dublin, tickets for the Centre Court, and one night's hotel accommodation in London. Best birthday present ever!

On the previous day, Sunday, 2 July, my sister and I had travelled from our hometown of Wexford, in the sunny south-east of Ireland, famous for its Opera Festival, its sunshine and its strawberries! We had taken a crack-of-dawn flight from Dublin to London on the morning of the 3rd. We were tired, but we were here!! I couldn't stop smiling! I couldn't stop crying! (I had been tearful since arriving at Southfields station onto a platform decorated like a tennis court!)

The sun was shining.

The crowds were incredible – thousands of shiny, happy people looking forward to a great day. For years I'd been hearing about the garden-party atmosphere, the intimacy of the event, the traditional feel of an old-fashioned tennis club – and I had never believed it could still be possible, in 2017, at the world's top tennis tournament. Yet, here I was, among the glorious purple and green blooms, the bronze of Fred Perry, the signposts for the Tea Lawn and the Rose Arbour, the people enjoying picnics on Henman Hill, Club members in their striped jackets and boaters, and Centre Court resplendent in its coat of Virginia creeper.

I would imagine that's the experience for every tennis fan walking through those gates, while all the time being aware that there is no room for sentiment when it comes to organising the huge, behind-the-scenes industry that is Wimbledon, an industry that has expanded hugely and successfully in recent years and continues to do so.

Billie Jean King was right when she said: 'Tennis is a perfect combination of violent action taking place in an atmosphere of total tranquility.'

In Ireland, tennis has always struggled. It has never really been encouraged, supported or popular enough to make its mark on the world stage, though we have had many talented, hard-working Irish players over the years. Incredibly, we do have a Wimbledon Ladies' Champion – Lena Rice, from County Tipperary, won the title in 1890, beating May Jacks 6-4, 6-1. Lena Rice remains the only Irish female to win Wimbledon.

I have always loved tennis. I loved the cracked, concrete court in the village of Rosslare Harbour where I grew up, and where, at best, we had two working rackets

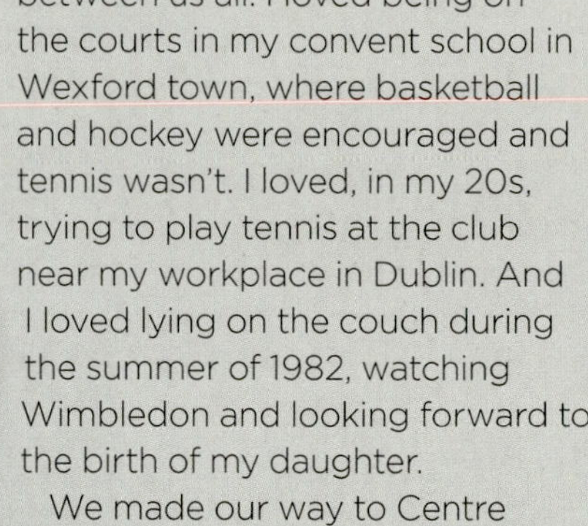

between us all. I loved being on the courts in my convent school in Wexford town, where basketball and hockey were encouraged and tennis wasn't. I loved, in my 20s, trying to play tennis at the club near my workplace in Dublin. And I loved lying on the couch during the summer of 1982, watching Wimbledon and looking forward to the birth of my daughter.

We made our way to Centre Court, myself, my sister and a bottle of Moet, a treat from my daughter, born in that summer of 1982. The summer of Jimmy Connors, John McEnroe, Vitas Gerulaitis, Mats Wilander, John Lloyd, of Martina Navratilova, Chris Evert, Tracy Austin, Pam Shriver, Billy Jean King – the summer when Pat Cash lifted the Junior boys' trophy!

So – Centre Court! A fabulous, perfectly manicured lawn. A stage for the best in the world. It shouldn't have looked so intimate, so local, with 15,000 people seated and ready for action, but amazingly, it did! We had great seats, great views and great fun trying to celebrity-spot. We sipped our Moet. When reigning champion, Britain's Andy Murray, and Kazakhstan's Alexander Bublik arrived on court, I was off again, wiping grateful, happy tears away!

It was strange at first, watching the match without the live commentary and analysis I was always used to at home – where was Sue Barker, or John Lloyd and Andrew Castle? And the ball seemed so much faster from court side – how could the lines people follow it at such speed!

But, oh, it was magic! Murray was in charge from the start, and the crowd were, of course, behind him. The atmosphere was alive. Murray, sadly, had been having hip problems. He had been beaten in the first round at Queen's a few weeks previously, and he was very obviously limping. However, he won the first set 6-1, the second 6-4, and at the beginning of the third, just after breaking Bublik, the rain came – not serious enough for the roof to be rolled out, just the covers – quickly and efficiently.

In a very short time play was resumed – for one game, before the rain returned and the players were off again and the covers back on!

We decided to get something to eat, so off we went in search of burgers or hot dogs – us and 15,000 other people from Centre Court, and probably the same number again from the other courts, all out and about because of the rain delay. The queues were long, but organised. British people love to queue and are very good at it. After about 30 minutes, as we made our way along the queue, the announcement came that play was resuming. My kind sister offered to stay put, while I returned to Centre Court (well, it was my birthday!). The people in the seats around us were friendly and chatty, some were regular visitors to Wimbledon, some were first-timers like ourselves.

Andy, even with his dodgy hip, didn't seem to be too pressured by Bublik and was able to take charge and serve out the match 6-1, 6-4, 6-2. There had been some mindblowing, cross-court shots from him and lots of determined fist clenching. Shouting 'C'mon Andy!' to himself, Andy ensured the crowd got

louder in his support. It had been a privilege to see him play, and at Wimbledon. Murray would go on to beat Dustin Brown, Fabio Fognini and Benoit Paire before succumbing to Sam Querrey, in five sets, in the quarter-finals. Andy would also suffer repeated problems with his hip which would, sadly, see him take time away from tennis for treatment in the months that followed.

Not surprisingly, my sister didn't make it to the head of the queue before the end of the Murray/Bublik match. I found her outside Centre Court, chatting to the attendant, a very friendly young man in a new uniform and a too-big hat. We didn't realise that hot food wasn't permitted into the Court, so Helen ate her hot dog outside and stood chatting to her new friend while waiting for the match to finish.

The afternoon passed so quickly, too quickly. We wandered around the grounds and the outside courts, we drank tea, we took loads of photos, we shopped for keepsakes and souvenirs.

A little later, we wandered back to Centre Court to see Petra Kvitova beat the Swedish player, Johanna Larsson. Petra was, happily, back to the courts after an attack at her home in the Czech Republic the previous Christmas had left her with injuries to her left hand. Petra would lose to the American, Madison Brengle, in the second round.

We were privileged also, to be able to watch fifth-seed Stan Wawrinka play on that glorious sunny, opening evening. Stan's serve and backhand are brutal, and

stunning. It was a dream to watch him, though unfortunately Daniil Medvedev got the better of Stan the Man in four sets, ensuring that Stan's remaining elusive Grand Slam would continue to elude him in 2017. Medvedev lost to the Belgian, Ruben Bemelmans, in the second round.

That evening, as the sun began to set and the crowds were beginning to thin out slightly, we made our way to Henman Hill. It was warm, lively and full of atmosphere as the crowds sat around the big screen watching Aljaz Bedene play the huge-serving Croatian and 21st seed Ivo Karlovic. We ate fish and chips and cheered as Bedene won in five sets, a great win for him.

It was dusk as we reluctantly made our way back to the gates. The courts were quiet, the lights were on, we were floating. We stopped at Court 7 for a final photograph of a scoreboard that read: 'No More Play on This Court.'

I was in tears again and I couldn't stop smiling.

A Dream Come True

Olivia Langinger, LONDON

My first Wimbledon memory is very special to me. As founder and designer of a tennis clothing brand called Ivincia, I spend a lot of time designing tennis dresses and imagining where they'll be worn. Even though at the time my brand was new, I envisioned my latest white tennis dress design being worn at Wimbledon.

I had found a beautiful white piqué fabric from a family-run supplier in Spain and knew it would be perfect for a Wimbledon-inspired white tennis dress. Shortly after they were made, I had a popup shop at the Will To Win tennis centre in Hyde Park. This event nearly didn't happen because when I received the first production run of the tennis dresses, they had all been sewn inside out! Luckily, my factory was able to rush a second production order just in time for the popup event. Wimbledon had just started, and one of the tennis coaches passed by and mentioned that his daughter, Tanysha Dissanayake, would be competing in the Girls' Doubles at Wimbledon that week.

Olivia Langinger is a tennis fashion entrepreneur and the founder of the Ivincia clothing brand.

I ended up going to Wimbledon for the first time with Tanysha and her coach to see her train wearing my tennis dress. It was so inspiring to watch. I remember thinking the dress looked so elegant and powerful; it was wonderful to see my design come to life on the beautiful green grass courts at Wimbledon.

2019

Our Illustrious Neighbour

Julian Harding, WORCESTER PARK

The ground of the New Malden Sports Club, as we are now known, was officially opened on Saturday, 6 May 1922. The guest of honour was Australian-born tennis star Randolph Lycett who had been a quarter-finalist in the Gentlemen's Singles at Wimbledon a year earlier, and had been champion in both the men's doubles and mixed doubles events that year, too. Lycett took part in an exhibition match to christen the New Malden courts and the practice must have done him good as he reached the Gentlemen's Singles Final at Wimbledon a few weeks later.

Our club is less than five miles from The All England Club and our Annual Open Tournament has attracted some important Wimbledon players over the years, most notably the incomparable triple-Wimbledon champion Fred Perry. Perry won the Men's Open Doubles title at New Malden in 1928, in tandem with Davis Cup team-mate Harry Lee, before claiming our Singles and Mixed Doubles titles, the latter in partnership with Winifred Beamish, in 1929.

Well-respected Wimbledon Referee Alan Mills was our Open Singles champion in 1957 and his assistant Tony Gathercole won our club's closed doubles tournament in 1953 and 1959. In addition, the irrepressible Teddy Tinling, who famously designed the controversial ruffled undershorts for Gussie Moran in 1949 and who went on to become Master of Ceremonies at Wimbledon, won a Men's Open Doubles title at New Malden in 1939.

Other notable Wimbledon players who have been New Malden Open Singles champions have included Wai-Chuen Choy (1936–39), Czeslaw 'Spike' Spychala (1948–49 and 1952), Angela Buxton (1953), Billy Knight (1953 and 1955) and Gerry Oakley (1954 and 1958). Lorna Cornell was a glamour girl of British tennis in the 1950s. She won our Open Singles in 1950 and again in 1954 under her married name of Lorna Cawthorn. In the same year she partnered Britain's Georgie Woodgate to the New Malden Open Doubles title. In more recent times, local girl Melanie South has played at Wimbledon on several occasions.

These historical links with our famous neighbour are a source of pride and inspiration as our Club's present-day members look forward to the second century of tennis here in New Malden.

In June 1922 King George V officially opened The All England Lawn Tennis Club's new ground at Wimbledon Park. Six weeks earlier, and a few miles to the south, another tennis ground had opened which was to see many famous Wimbledon stars grace its courts. The New Malden Lawn Tennis Club is located just off the A3 at New Malden, and in researching its Centenary history Chairman Julian Harding has uncovered a number of interesting links with The All England Lawn Tennis Club.

2019

Wimbledon at Last!

David Brown, FARRINGTON GURNEY

The Wimbledon bug can bite at any time, as this little story shows.

My wife and I are both in our early 70s and yesterday was our very first visit to Wimbledon. We managed to obtain two tickets for Centre Court later in the day and sat next to two charming older ladies who told us that they had been coming to Wimbledon for the last 30 years and had always sat in exactly the same seats!

We always closely watch Wimbledon on TV. We just had never thought of visiting before but we had friends visiting from India and thought it would be nice to meet them there. We used to live next door to them in Dubai.

People's Day at The Championships

Mark A. Kuhn, CHARLES CITY, IOWA

Saturday, 6 July 2019. Today is 'People's Day' at Wimbledon and Londoners are flocking to SW19 in droves. Approximately 7,500 people will gain access to the grounds and show courts today having spent time in the Wimbledon Park Queue.

I arrive early with my credential in hand, enter at Gate 1, check the daily Order of Play sign next to Court 17, and quickly decide on two matches I want to see. It's my fifth and final day at The Championships and I want to watch as much good tennis as possible. Little do I know, the most harrowing and fascinating action of the day would not occur on any of The All England Club's 18 courts, but rather in the spectator stands and what happened after that in the Wimbledon Library.

Unseeded American Sam Querrey is on a hot streak, having knocked off number five seed Dominic Thiem of Austria in the first round. I race to the practice courts hoping to get a look at the lanky American and, to my delight, there he was finishing up his pre-match practice. He signed one of my books and I wished him well. Quickly, I scurried off to get a good seat for his match against John Millman from Australia.

I got a seat in the front row of Court 17 right on the service line where I watched 'Slammin' Sam' serve 135mph cannonballs one after another. Despite spirited play by Aussie John Millman, Querrey prevailed in three action-packed sets.

Next up was a fascinating match between two players with completely different styles.

Hard-hitting Jan-Lennard Struff from Germany v the all-court game of Mikhail Kukushkin from Kazakhstan. I hustled over to Court 12 and stood in the queue for a short while until seats opened up on the newly expanded court on the south end of the grounds. It just so happened that I ended up sitting directly behind Struff's parents and family. I watched the 6'6"-tall Struff win his first-round match on Tuesday and was very impressed with his grass-court game.

I had also watched Kukushkin (who I nicknamed '5K') outlast 6'10"-tall American John Isner on the 4th of July in five gruelling sets. So I knew 5K had the kind of game to win against a tall, power player. And that's just the way the match started, with the first set going quickly to Kukushkin. Struff fought back in the second set and won it in a tiebreaker.

The crowd settled in for what looked like a match that could go the distance. With Struff up a break early in the third set, everyone's focus was diverted from the match to the stands when a woman collapsed. I was sitting a mere 50 feet or so from the calamity. It was hard not to watch as the London Fire Brigade attended to

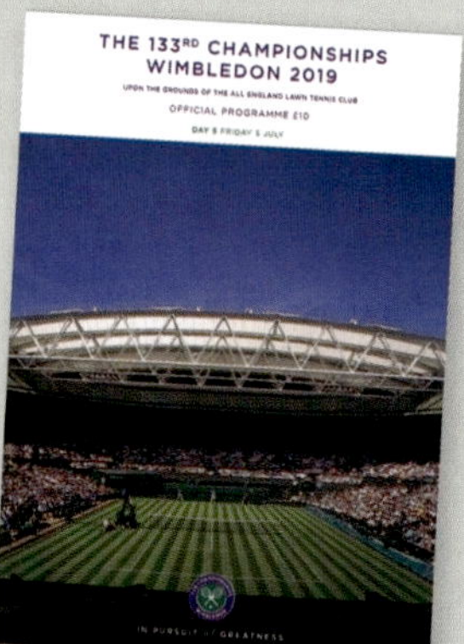

her. After attempts to revive her were unsuccessful, many of us in the crowd prayed for the best, but were fearful for her life. The chair umpire suspended play and the crowd was exited solemnly from the stands. Soon an ambulance arrived, and the emergency crew went to work with a defibrillator to restore her heartbeat. Like most everyone else in the stands, I left Court 12 not knowing if the emergency medical responders were successful or not.

It was a shocking end to the second match I had wanted to see. Without an appetite for any more tennis, I headed to the Wimbledon Museum for some solitude where I could clear my head and try to re-focus. And that's where the magic of Wimbledon happened once again. I was surprised and delighted to discover that the Kenneth Ritchie Wimbledon Library was open. I was greeted by librarian Mr Robert McNicol who made me feel very welcome. It was my second visit to the Library and I was thrilled to be there. The Wimbledon Library is, without a doubt, the most comprehensive tennis library in the world. It is home to some 6,000 tennis books and thousands more magazines, newspaper clippings and other publications from throughout the world.

On my first visit to the Library in 2016 I was honored to meet the late Alan Little, renowned tennis author and Wimbledon historian, who authored the first-ever Wimbledon Compendium in 1991. The current Compendium, edited by Robert McNicol, details in its 528 pages all the facts, figures and curiosities that make The Championships, Wimbledon a sporting event like no other in the world.

Upon arriving at the library Robert McNicol introduced me to two world-class gentleman tennis scholars: Mr Richard A. Hillway and Mr Attila Szabo, both guests of the Wimbledon Library during the first week of The Championships. Richard Hillway is the world's foremost authority on Maj. Walter Clopton Wingfield, who invented lawn tennis in 1874. Attila Szabo is the world's foremost authority on lawn tennis books, having a collection of more than 2,000 volumes.

I showed the esteemed gentleman a one-of-a-kind piece of Wimbledon history given to me by David Kramer, one of five sons of 1947 Champion Jack Kramer: The Champions Wimbledon tie given to 'Big Jake' by King George V in the Royal Box following his victory.

And that's all it took to get the Slazenger ball really rolling. Hillway and Szabo quickly pointed out that it was King George VI, not King George V, who would have presented the champion's tie to Kramer. With the help of librarian McNicol, they researched newspaper accounts from 1947 that showed Kramer receiving the Renshaw Cup from King George VI, with the Queen and Princess Margaret in attendance. Both Hillway and Szabo assumed Kramer was also given the champion's tie at that time, although it was not reported as such in the newspaper accounts.

With that issue now resolved, I was delighted to accept the invitation of Hillway and Szabo to visit another virtual Wimbledon museum, The Tennis Gallery bookstore in Wimbledon Park. Hillway was there the day before signing copies of the book, *The Birth of Lawn Tennis*, a seven-pound encyclopedia he co-authored with Robert T. Everitt. Hillway and Szabo introduced me to bookstore owners Richard and Chris Jones. The Tennis Gallery is a treasure trove of Wimbledon books and memorabilia of every kind and shape. Books, official Wimbledon posters, towels, balls and programs to name but a few items for sale in the massive collection.

Long after my new friends Hillway and Szabo left the store, the Jones's and I drank a cup of tea and continued to share stories about the hallowed ground on Church Road. Richard and Chris also put together a very special keepsake for me of the exquisite 2015 official Wimbledon poster. It was the year I visited The Championships with my late son, Alex. The keepsake is and will forever be on display at the Kuhn family farm in Iowa, home of the All Iowa Lawn Tennis Club.

Now completely drained from my long, exciting day at SW19 I had one more stop to make before heading to my rented flat near Southfields. So I hopped on the tube at Wimbledon Park and travelled one stop to Southfields Station. It was a short walk from there to my 'home away from home' while I'm visiting The Championships.

The Gardens Lawn Tennis Club, located halfway between the entrance to the Wimbledon Queue at Wimbledon Park and Southfields, is the perfect place to relax after a day at Wimbledon and share a drink and conversation with friends. I first found the Gardens Lawn Tennis Club quite by accident in 2013, and it is now a must stop after almost every glorious day I'm fortunate to be at The Championships. It is the ultimate people's place, a place where tennis fans and club members come to share their friendship and love of Wimbledon.

I was there to say goodbye for another year to my dear friends Chris Cohn, and soul sisters Suzanna and Mitch. As wonderful as that farewell always is, it was overshadowed by the news I received from a Wimbledon linesman, another regular at the Gardens, who told me the woman who suffered a massive heart attack earlier that day on Court 12 had survived and was doing OK.

My prayers were answered. The joy I felt was beyond description. I thought she was a goner. We all toasted the crew of emergency responders that brought her back to life. Power to the people! It was the perfect ending to 'People's Day' at The Championships, Wimbledon.

2019

Wimbledon Stopover

Chris Schruckmayr, ASHEVILLE, NORTH CAROLINA

Sunday, July 7 2019: my wife, Anne, and I, along with our two children, Zoe (14) and Michael (11), had the fortunate opportunity to vacation in England this summer. Our travels began shortly after the kids got out of school, which, here in the US, is just past mid-June. In planning our vacation, we didn't include a trip to Wimbledon in our itinerary, but, having been able to go to the 2018 and 2019 US-based Fed Cup competitions held in our hometown of Asheville, NC, we had thought it would be amazing to somehow experience Wimbledon during our holiday.

With our vacation coming to an end, we spent the final night prior to departing back to the US at a hotel near Heathrow airport. After talking it over a bit, my tennis-loving daughter and I decided that we needed to find a way to make it to Wimbledon the following morning before our flight. Anne and Michael decided not to join us but would help our efforts by getting everything ready for our departure from the hotel with the understanding that we would have a tight timeline upon our return. Having the challenge of getting from Heathrow to Wimbledon and back to the hotel, and then catching our flight in just a few short hours, was an aggressive proposition but perhaps maybe, with a little luck, we could make it happen. Knowing that it was Middle Sunday and no matches were set did not dampen our interest in any way.

The plan was as follows: wake up at 6.45, have a quick hotel breakfast, leave Heathrow by 7.30, get to Wimbledon by 9.00, leave by 9.30 and get back to the airport hotel by 11.00. Ready, set, go!

Without having an international SIM card on our mobile phone, we quickly realized that we very much needed to rely on the kindness of strangers during our adventure. A wonderfully kind lady on our train pulled up a local map on her phone and helped us answer the question of whether we should get off at Wimbledon Park or Wimbledon. After deciding on Wimbledon Park, the view of her map also seemed to indicate that the distance to the courts were equal whether we decided to cut through the park, or, if we were to follow the streets. We decided on the park route.

Upon getting off at Wimbledon Park station, Zoe and I weren't expecting a sign stating that the courts were a 30-minute walk away. Oh no! Would we still be able to see the courts given our tight timeline? Could we get back to the hotel for checkout, meet up with Anne and Michael, and then catch our flight back to America? There was only one way to find out. We started to run. And run and run. We passed the lawn tennis courts where volunteers were putting on a clinic for children as part of the Middle Sunday activities. We passed the ticket queueing area in the park and asked a security guard if we were close to the main courts. Could he tell that our question was also an excuse for us to stop running and catch our breath as well? I'm not sure, but he encouraged us on and said that we were close. We ran up the hill from the ticket queue and saw the golf course on the left.

Finally, we got to Court 1. Zoe in her Converse All-Star high-top sneakers and me in my sockless Teva sandals were 'feeling the burn' but we were now at the courts. After taking some pictures and spending a few moments of appreciation for the beauty and spectacle that is Wimbledon, we continued up the hill to the Rosewater Pavilion and then headed back to the tube station. We started to run again, took a break or two, and got directions along the way from a jogger and a delivery man.

The Wimbledon Park station was now in sight and we noticed that most shops in the surrounding area were closed. Just before the station, we gazed up on a green-signed storefront named 'The Tennis Gallery' which happened to be open this early Sunday morning. We couldn't leave without a souvenir so, out of breath and red-faced (and just a bit sweaty), we popped in the shop and had the pleasure of meeting a gentleman who was preparing to host a tennis radio show that afternoon. We spoke for a few minutes, bought some Wimbledon souvenirs and were back on our way. The waking up early, the combined two-hour and 40-minute tube ride, the running, and the help we received along the way made our adventure to Wimbledon one that Zoe and I will never forget.

Wimbledon is a special, magical place. I'm so glad that I was able to share this experience with my daughter even without seeing a single serve. And, yes, we made it back to the hotel a little late but in time for check-out and in time to catch our flight.

2019

The Boy Who Tossed the Coin

Omar Popal, LONDON

On Sunday, 14 July 2019 Omar Popal, a Year 10 student at Westminster School, performed the coin toss at the start of the Gentlemen's Singles Final between Novak Djokovic and Roger Federer. He wrote of his amazing experience for his school magazine:

On the morning of the final, my family and I were picked up in a Range Rover to arrive in style and in good time for the busy day ahead. We were given a tour around Centre Court and got to see all the trophies – it was really amazing. They told me how they polish the trophies every single week. Whilst on the court I got to help set up the nets ready for the match. I was also interviewed, which made me nervous at first but I became more comfortable as I answered questions. I learned more about the coins being used

table was none other than Roger Federer! I had a short conversation with him and I told him I wanted him to win. He said, 'Thanks but you need to be neutral for the game.' Ever professional! He told me that he wanted to win the coin toss to serve first.

After lunch we watched practice games on other courts, and then it was time for the big moment, the Wimbledon Gentlemen's Singles Final 2019. Going out onto the court in front of all those people – including royalty – was nerve-wracking, but as I went

" If I had just flipped 'tails' instead of 'heads' maybe Federer would have won. "

for the coin tosses at the Ladies' and Gentlemen's Singles finals this year; they were particularly special as they had travelled to space and back after NASA Astronauts Commander Drew Feustel and Tim Peake attended The Championships in 2017 and decided to take something from Wimbledon aboard the six-month-long mission.

At lunch we were given a reserved table, and on the adjacent

onto the court I felt the incredible atmosphere there and just went with it. I saw Commander Feustel and gave him a wave. I performed the coin toss and then it was over, just like that, but in the moment it felt phenomenal. Although the coin toss was over quickly, the match lasted four hours 57 minutes – the longest final in Wimbledon history. The final hour was definitely the most exciting.

My role in the event made me realise the importance of a coin toss. I thought to myself, if I had just flipped 'tails' instead of 'heads' maybe Federer would have won, maybe the match could have been a different story …

I would like to thank Mosaic and The Prince's Trust for allowing me the honour of representing them at such a special event.

The Great Final

Andrew Fulcher, SUTTON

Sunday, 14 July 2019 was one of my most memorable days at The Championships, dating back to 1992 when I first attended. A friend had won a pair of tickets in the public ballot and I had sweated for many months knowing that the second ticket was a toss-up between him taking his wife or myself.

My luck was in! Having studied the draw I could see no other final materialising other than Nadal v Djokovic or Federer v Djokovic. I knew either had the potential to be a blockbuster … and so it did prove! With this ticket being so precious to me, I carefully weakened the perforation on the ticket and detached a tiny portion on the very top and bottom of it to ensure that when the staff member detached it, it detached very smoothly which eliminated any risk of the ticket being torn.

We soon found Djokovic practising on Court 6 which was heaving with spectators and because we were on the court early we got there before security closed off the whole area for congestion purposes. Djokovic appeared relaxed but focused in the warm-up and after it had finished we made our way to our seats on Centre Court. Our seats were just ten rows from the very front diagonally behind Djokovic's chair and halfway between the service line and the baseline. The view was incredible and we could almost smell the grass. Even a full hour before play was due to commence the atmosphere was building and we were both buzzing. Pat Cash, John McEnroe and Sue Barker were right in front of us and we were almost close enough to hear them speaking. With the Centre Court gradually filling we saw numerous famous faces arriving in the Royal Box which was off to our right-hand side.

The most meaningful faces I saw were Rod Laver and Stefan Edberg, both such modest gentlemen, as well as tennis legends. On the stroke of 2pm the players walked out to enormous applause and everyone was buzzing. What unveiled was not only the longest-ever Wimbledon Singles Final but possibly the highest-quality final. Three minutes short of five hours of exceptionally high-standard tennis. If either player was nervous they did not show it, nor did either show any signs of physical tiredness, nor did either player appear to sweat throughout the whole contest. I saw no spectator leave their seat for toilet or refreshments, the

The Duchess of Cambridge presents the Gentlemen's Singles trophy to Novak Djokovic, Sunday, 14 July 2019

match was so intensely gripping. Federer was the clear fan's favourite but this did not rattle Djokovic, whose composure and belief was admirable. At 8-7 to Federer in the fifth set at 40-15 on his serve it appeared Federer had broken Djokovic's iron-man resilience. The crowd were gagging to leap up and celebrate but Djokovic, despite returning serve with the sun directly in his eyes at his end of the court, on the deuce side hit a heavy forehand return which Federer off balance hit wide to rescue the first match point. And on the second match point he hit a blistering forehand winner past Federer at the net. I cannot recall such tension at a live tennis match since the Murray v Djokovic 2013 Wimbledon men's final, where Murray too had multiple match points.

Throughout the entire fifth set my friend was punching the air at every point Federer won and I found myself doing the same. I was aware of the new fifth-set 12-12 tiebreak rule but many spectators around me were not and when the umpire announced it when the score reached 12-12 there was a surge of excitement and anticipation circulating around. Having won the other two tiebreaks Djokovic again won this one, this time more comfortably. After what was an absolute blockbuster encounter, Djokovic's celebration on winning match point was notably reserved. This could have been emotional tiredness but I put it down more to showing respect to his opponent in what was an outstanding match that indeed Federer probably should have won based on the opportunities. Djokovic had beaten the fans' hero and this mild celebration warmed him to spectators who had been so vocally supporting Federer.

Seeing the trophy presentation was highly memorable and I very much enjoyed taking photos throughout the match and the trophy presentation.

With this men's final being such pulsating tennis it was time for us to stretch our legs and head off in search of a celebratory drink!

Andrew Fulcher is not alone in taking great care of his sporting memorabilia. Dedicated fans have devised their own unique filing systems and even had special shelves built to house their collections. However, for Andrew and all other ardent 'Wimblephiles', it is the sport that comes first and Sunday, 14 July 2019, when Novak edged out Roger just as England and New Zealand were starting their cricket World Cup Final 'Super Over', was one of the most momentous days in modern sporting history.

2019

The Last Word

Gordon Forbes, BURGERSDORP

'You never know,' Gordon Forbes reflected, 'that may be my last ever visit to the Centre Court.' Hopefully he will be back, but what better way to take one's leave of The Championships than by witnessing Roger Federer and Novak Djokovic going head-to-head in one of the most remarkable finals in Wimbledon's illustrious history?

Gordon had been at Wimbledon 65 years earlier when Jaroslav Drobny beat Ken Rosewall in the 1954 final. Two decades later he wrote *A Handful of Summers*, a poignant memoir which captured the spirit and camaraderie of top tennis in the 1950s and 60s. Many people consider it the finest – and funniest – book ever written on tennis.

Federer is a virtuoso performer who appeals to the artist in Gordon's soul. As a boy growing up on a remote farm on the edge of South Africa's Karoo desert he lived an outdoor life, creating all kinds of madcap diversions with his elder brother Jack and a little black boy called Joseph who was often the unwitting victim of their dangerous pranks.

Gordon wrote about these escapades in diary notes, a habit he continued during his globetrotting tennis career. They provided him with a rich vein of memories as he documented what it was like to be a touring player in the years before Open Tennis changed the game from an adventure to a business.

A Handful of Summers is a helter-skelter journey, beginning in the apartheid South Africa of the 1940s and culminating with the psychedelic explosion of London's Kings Road in 1968, when the first Open Wimbledon reunited tennis

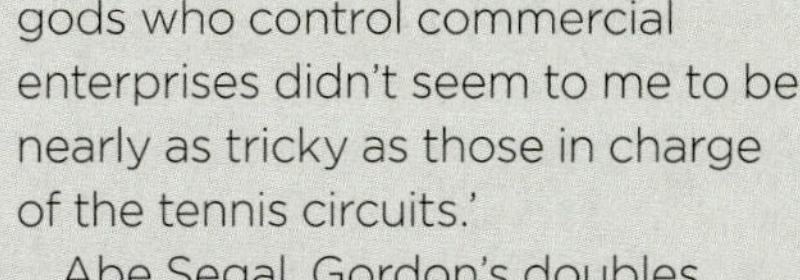

players past and present. 'If you remember the 1960s you weren't really there,' the saying goes, but Gordon was there, he did remember, and, thank goodness, he wrote it down. Well, some of it at least.

'The diaries which I kept during my playing days are dotted with the random beginnings of books,' he observes. The first diary note in the book describes a Forbes' family trip to their local tennis club. It is 1942, and the author is just eight. Thereafter the reader is taken on a meandering 26-year journey with Gordon as a knowledgeable, articulate and downright funny guide.

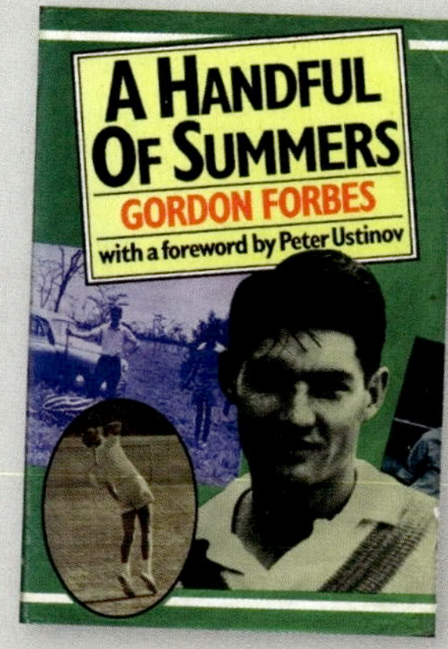

His writing style draws on a few simple and pleasing devices. The 'tennis gods' did not see fit for Gordon to become a major tennis star. Instead the 'crossroads gods' took his life in another direction. Various gods crop up in the book and Gordon writes of them in puzzled bemusement. When his amateur tennis career is nearing its end he gets a job selling lights, and on winning his first big contract reflects that 'the lighting gods had smiled on me'. On forming his own successful company a year or two later, he observes that 'The

gods who control commercial enterprises didn't seem to me to be nearly as tricky as those in charge of the tennis circuits.'

Abe Segal, Gordon's doubles partner and lifelong friend, is quoted at length. 'Abie' is the book's main character whose spirited bumbling belies a canny intelligence and leads the pair into all sorts of scrapes, not least when they are in pursuit of the fairer sex.

A Handful of Summers captures better than any other book the spirit of the game at a time when tennis players earned little money but banked a fortune in adventure, laughter, friendship and romance. Gordon Forbes did not win Wimbledon, or even come close, but by writing diary notes on napkins and retrieving them from the bottom of his sports bag decades later he has left a warm trail through its history, one that will be followed as long as tennis is played on the lawns of SW19.

The last word goes to Gordon himself: 'Roger Federer has the ultimate characteristics of the truly great – the ability to become stronger as the competition tightens. To play day after day with no fear at all, no sign of strain, but only the positive will to win. To acknowledge the skills of his opponents and to scorn the use of any form of trickery. He astounded the tennis world at Wimbledon with the mastery of his game.'

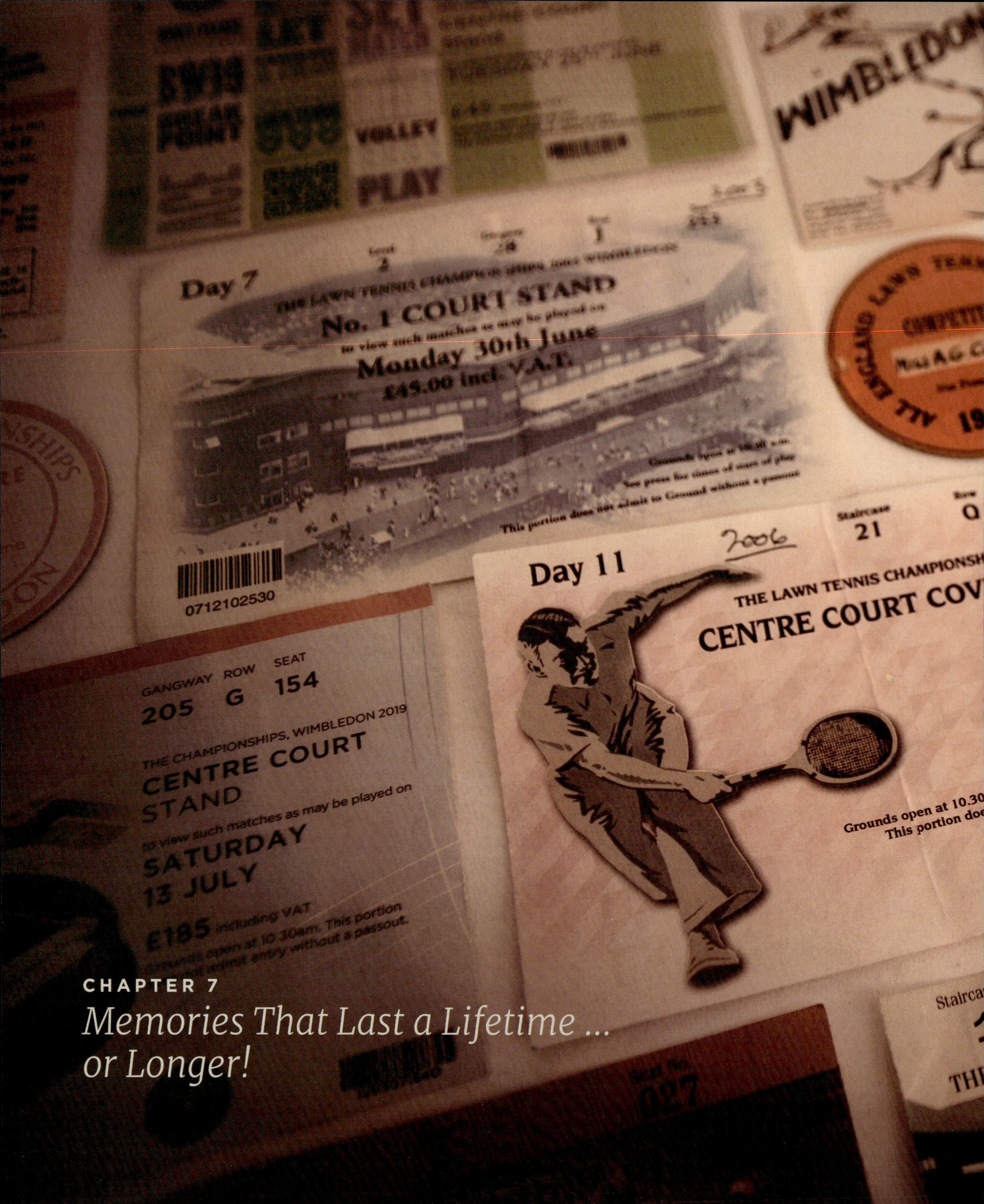

Memories That Last a Lifetime ... or Longer!

The All England Lawn Tennis Club
PASS OUT ONLY
Friday, July 7   154
THE LAWN TENNIS CHAMPIONSHIPS
WIMBLEDON
GROUND ONLY
to view such matches as may be played on
THURSDAY 4th JULY
£7.00 incl. V.A.T.
Grounds open at 10.30 a.m. See press for times of start of play
THE LAWN TENNIS CHAMPIONSHIPS 1984
DEBENTURE HOLDER
Friday June 29
to view such matches
as may be played on
Friday 7th July
£7.00 incl. V.A.T.
See press for times of start of play
admit to Ground without a passout
1103173620
Category 94
Row S
Seat No. 80
GROUND
Sunday
6 July
NOTICE
A.E.L.T.C.
Seat No.
213
Row
F
LAWN TENNIS CHAMPIONSHIPS 1993 WIMBLEDON
COVERED STAND
CENTRE COURT
SATURDAY 3rd JULY
Seat No.
054
Row
C
Entrance
M
THE LAWN TENNIS
CHAMPIONSHIPS 1991 WIMBLEDON
Lena Rice
EAST OPEN
CENTRE
to view such matches as
may be played on
WEDNESDAY

Cigarette card album, 1930s. Trade card collecting was a popular hobby during the first half of the 20th century

Players cigarette cards, 1936

Contributors to *Wimbledonia* have often been aided in their recollections by the souvenirs they kept of their visits to The Championships. Some of these storytellers are not just tennis lovers, they are also keen tennis collectors with particular collecting interests which they have pursued as serious hobbies. It was only in the late 1950s and early 1960s that television came into most family homes in Britain; before that hobbies were needed to alleviate the boredom of long winter evenings and interminable Sundays when shops and places of entertainment were shut. People needed pastimes, for there was a lot of free time to pass.

Up to the 1960s collecting was hugely popular. Stationers on every high street offered a wide range of autograph books, postcard albums and scrapbooks. Cigarette cards featuring movie stars and sports personalities were collected by millions, young and old. Other popular subjects included animals, birds, buses, flags of the world, classic motor vehicles, railway engines and royalty. Cigarette cards were tremendously popular, as were the trading cards contained in packets of tea made by such companies as Brooke Bond and PG Tips. Cards were usually issued in series of 30 or 50, and collectors could send away to the companies for albums to put them in. They were called trading cards as collectors would exchange duplicates or 'swaps' with friends to help complete their sets. For many people born before the 1960s, collecting was in their genes.

Collectors of Wimbledon tennis memorabilia fall into two groups. The vast majority simply hang onto their Wimbledon souvenirs for the memories they embody, but there are also some people who get just as much pleasure from their collecting as they do from Wimbledon itself. These specialist collectors become very knowledgeable, to the point that today some of the leading writers on tennis history are people who started out collecting tennis items just for the fun of it.

What is Wimbledonia?

The word 'Wimbledonia' was first coined on 28 June 1930 in a weekly magazine called *The Illustrated Sporting and Dramatic News*. The new word was used in the title of a photographic spread showing recent changes to The All England Lawn Tennis Club's grounds, along with pictures of some tennis celebrities. The full title of the piece was 'WIMBLEDONIA: INNOVATIONS AND ODD ITEMS OF INTEREST.' *Wimbledoni*a adapts the use of this delightful word, in the same way that 'Cricketana' and 'Golfiana' are the collective names given to the memorabilia of the sports to which they relate.

WIMBLEDONIA: objects and ephemera connected with the Wimbledon Lawn Tennis Championships; Wimbledon tennis memorabilia.

In the chapters that follow, attention is focused on items of Wimbledonia which have been created specifically to provide information about The Championships, to record its history and to evoke memories. Most are official products and publications, and nearly all were available to the public at one time or another on the grounds of The All England Club during The Fortnight. They are the main items which people collect, and there are separate chapters on Programmes, Postcards, Posters, Books and Films. Each of these has an interesting creative story behind it, featuring talented individuals and innovative independent companies. ✆

Official Programme, 1947. Continuing post-war austerity resulted in the programmes for all 12 days having the same coloured cover

Vinyl two-record set, 1986

Postcard Album, 1930s

Scrapbooks, Autographs and Photographs

During Wimbledon's first century, scrapbooks were a simple and popular way of keeping memories alive. A typical, lovingly compiled Wimbledon scrapbook contained daily reports of matches cut from the pages of *The Daily Telegraph* or another national newspaper along with black and white photographs carefully removed from one of Britain's popular periodicals such as *The Illustrated London News*. Sometimes used tickets and photo-postcards purchased at Wimbledon were included, too. When complete, the scrapbook was an illustrated diary of The Fortnight, much as the Wimbledon Official Annual is today.

Wimbledon was particularly fertile ground for autograph hunters. Many people had autograph books which they would carry with them everywhere just in case they should bump into a star of stage, screen or the sporting world. An autograph book was a very personal and nostalgic record of the owner's movements, likes, and the era in which they lived. Players would often write a personal message alongside their signature, thus making the brief encounter personal. The modern equivalent is when a player takes a 'selfie' from a fan's phone to get a shot of the two of them together.

Today, fans queue up at the exits of the outside courts at Wimbledon in the hope that their favourite player will stop and sign an autograph or pose for a selfie as they head back to the locker room. The autograph book has been replaced by a giant tennis ball, a cap, a tee shirt, a programme or a ticket. Often, there is a show of camaraderie, as a victorious player uses one fan's Sharpie pen to sign autographs for half a dozen others.

Amateur photography became increasingly popular during the 20th century, but the results were variable. Unlike today, when photographs are taken so easily and quickly on a smartphone, the photographer did not see the results – good or bad – until he or she had paid for the roll of film to be developed. There was no second chance.

Scrapbooks, autograph books and photograph albums were very personal records of their owners' Wimbledon experiences, but they have now largely been replaced by modern alternatives, as have popular items of Wimbledon tennis ephemera such as printed tickets and picture postcards stamped with the distinctive SW19 postmark. Programmes are still bought in large quantities at Wimbledon each year, but ironically their increased size and weight has made them more disposable and less collectable. 🎾

This 1931 autograph book belonged to Miss Cynthia Gladstone of 60 Somerset Road, just a few yards from The All England Club. The left-hand page bears the distinctive signature of eight-times Wimbledon champion Helen Wills Moody of the USA. The right-hand page has been signed by Colin Gregory, a leading British player who reached the Wimbledon men's doubles final in 1929 and beat Fred Perry in singles in 1930. Other autographs in the book include those of Perry himself, Dorothy Round and Bunny Austin.

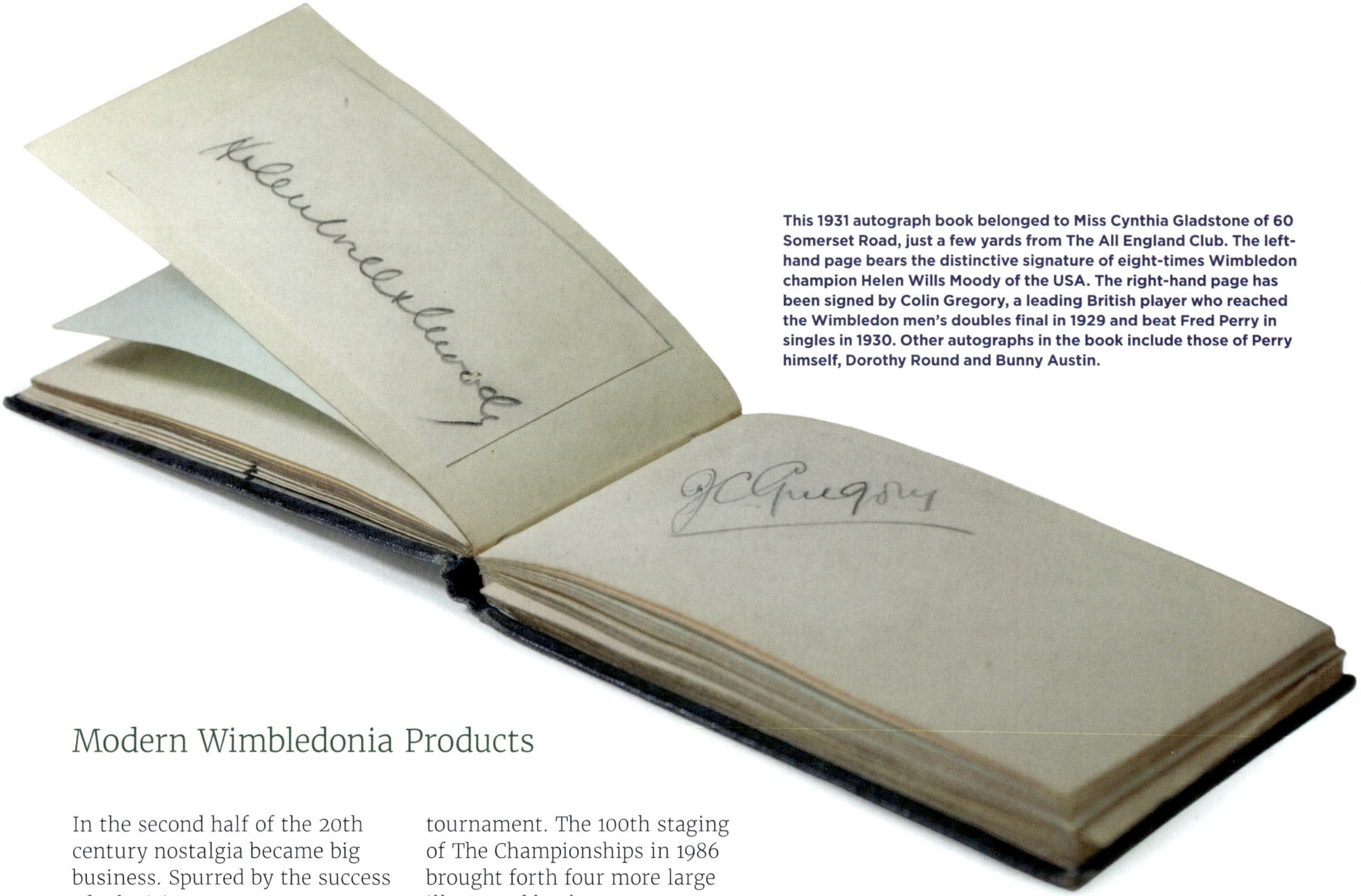

Modern Wimbledonia Products

In the second half of the 20th century nostalgia became big business. Spurred by the success of television programmes such as Granada TV's *All Our Yesterdays*, presented by Brian Inglis from 1961 to 1973, and the BBC's *100 Great Sporting Moments*, short snippets which aired between programmes during the 1980s, producers and publishers began to bombard the public with archive material relating to major historical, cultural and sporting events.

Wimbledon's Centenary in 1977 was marked by the release on video cassette of a 50-minute documentary film entitled *The Great English Garden Party*, presented by actor and Wimblephile Peter Ustinov, and the publication of three books about the history of the tournament. The 100th staging of The Championships in 1986 brought forth four more large illustrated books.

The first 'Open' Wimbledon in 1968 and the inauguration of the Wimbledon Lawn Tennis Museum in 1977 triggered a sharp acceleration in the commercialisation of The Championships. Happily this increase in merchandising activity led to the introduction of yearly Wimbledon Official Films in the 1970s and Wimbledon Official Annuals in the 1980s, both of which provided welcome reminders of The Championships in much the same way that scrapbooks had done in earlier times. Also, like scrapbooks, the films and books gave even greater enjoyment as the years passed.

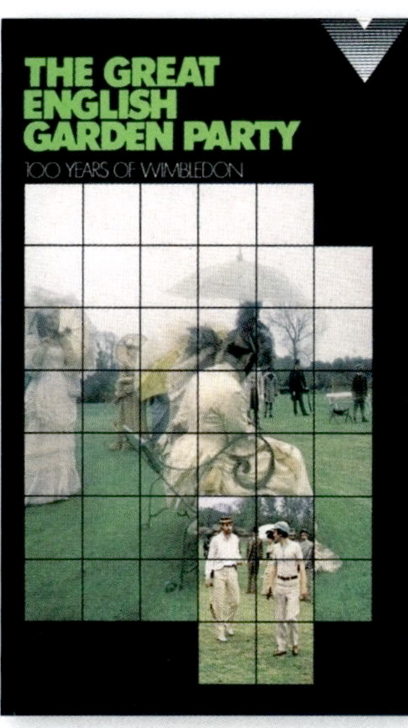

One of the earliest Wimbledon video releases

Programmes

Wimbledon is the only tennis tournament in the world to have consistently produced an updated official programme for each playing day, and many people have bought one for every day upon which they attended The Championships, particularly during the years between 1948 and 1976 when the entire editorial and pictorial content of the programme changed each day. Rich in information, contemporary imagery and design, these precisely dated souvenirs are by far Wimbledon's most popular collectables. ◎

Postcards

Technological advancements in photography and printing in the late 19th and early 20th centuries led to the launch of Wimbledon's first commercial product: the photo-postcard. Small, light and inexpensive, these cards featuring portraits of leading players and general views of the Wimbledon grounds have been on sale at Wimbledon since around 1905. The stories of the two leading producers of these cards, Edwin J. Trim and Co. of Wimbledon and Le-Roye Productions Ltd. of Beckenham, Kent, speak volumes about local life in the Wimbledon area and the metamorphosis of The Championships from a small local tournament to an iconic global event. ◎

Art and Posters

Wimbledon's alluring combination of athleticism, beauty, fashion, glamour and romance has long been appealing to artists, cartoonists and photographers. The attractive posters sold at Wimbledon between 1986 and 2019 only tell part of the story, for the art of Wimbledon is also found on tickets, book jackets, magazine covers, greeting cards and product advertising and packaging dating back more than a century. Nowadays The All England Club is very thoughtful about the commissioning of new works, recognising the importance of recording its visual history for future generations. ◎

Books

Nearly 200 books and booklets have been published about The Championships and The All England Club, plus countless thousands of column inches in magazines, newspapers and programmes. From all of this, the work of five fine writers stands out. Arthur Wallis Myers, Sir John Smyth, Lance Tingay, John Barrett and Alan Little have between them chronicled the stories and history of Wimbledon, from its Victorian origins through to the 21st century, enabling us to consider the merits of past luminaries such as Laurie Doherty and Suzanne Lenglen alongside those of Roger Federer, Martina Navratilova and other greats of the modern game.

A selected tennis bibliography has been included in this chapter, listing publications specifically about Wimbledon along with general tennis books containing valuable material relating to The Championships and The All England Club. ◐

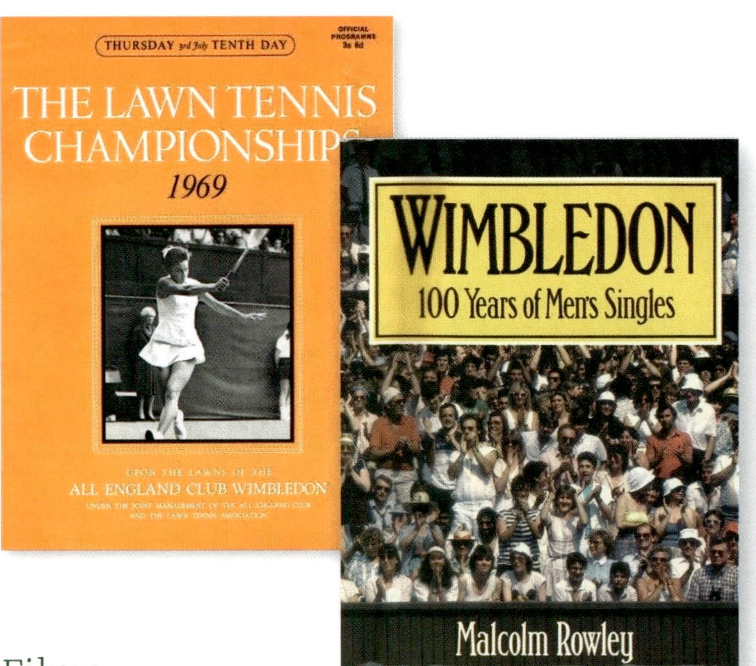

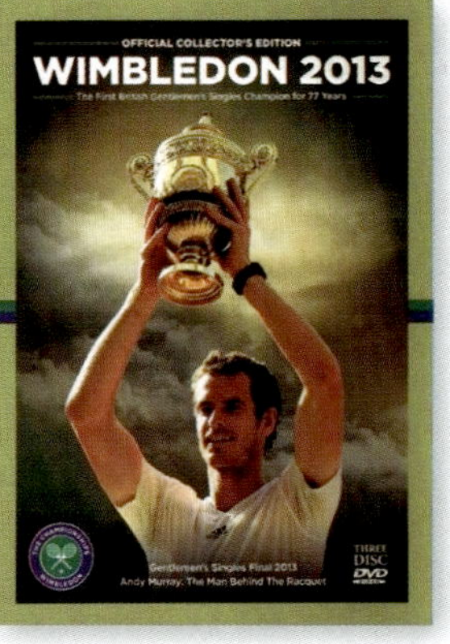

Films

The digital world in which we now live places great value on original archive footage of major events such as the Wimbledon Championships. Newsreel companies were filming at Wimbledon as early as the 1920s, and the BBC began broadcasting live pictures from the Centre Court in 1937. A lot of original footage has been lost over the years, but some has survived and snippets are included in Wimbledon's official video releases which commenced in the mid-1970s. Unlike programmes, postcards and books, the tennis public knows relatively little about Wimbledon's output on video and DVD. For this reason the 92 known official video releases have been catalogued in some detail to assist those interested in tracking them down. For movie buffs, brief information is also given about feature films shot on location at Wimbledon. ◐

Wimbledon Lawn Tennis Museum and Kenneth Ritchie Library

The world's finest collection of Wimbledon memorabilia, ephemera and publications is housed on-site at The All England Lawn Tennis and Croquet Club. As well as such familiar objects as champions' match-worn clothing and shoes, antique rackets and equipment, the Wimbledon Lawn Tennis Museum also has in its collection advertising signs, cigarette cards, gramophone records, locker room notices, queue stickers, wristbands and thousands of other miscellaneous items linked to Lawn Tennis and The Championships.

The Museum is open to visitors all year round, and the Kenneth Ritchie Library is available by appointment to those researching the game's history. From humble origins in the 1970s, the Museum has become a major attraction for visitors to London, and the Library is now a hub of tennis scholarship and research. ◐

Collecting Wimbledonia

There are two kinds of Wimbledonia collectors: those whose personal souvenirs mount up over the years, and those whose passion is to conscientiously seek out particular Wimbledon-related items. In the first category come many of the tennis lovers who have contributed memories and stories to this book. They would never give house-room to a Wimbledon programme other than one for a day when they were there, and they would probably not admit to being tennis collectors at all! In the second group come those who have spent decades compiling complete collections of such things as Wimbledon postcards, posters, programmes and annuals. ◓

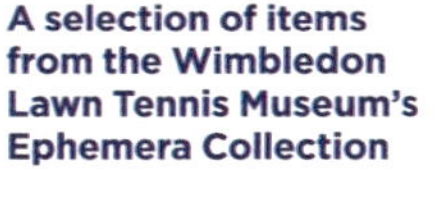

A selection of items from the Wimbledon Lawn Tennis Museum's Ephemera Collection

Perrier 'Wimbubbledon' Hand Fan, 1998. Only official suppliers and partners may distribute promotional items bearing the Wimbledon logo

Royal Gift Box, 2011. A small box of De Rosier Chocolates with a 125th Championships ribbon

Tiptree Preserves Box, circa 2011, made to resemble the Centre Court

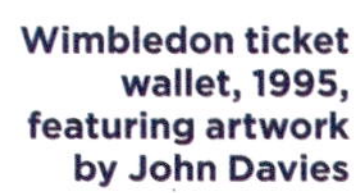

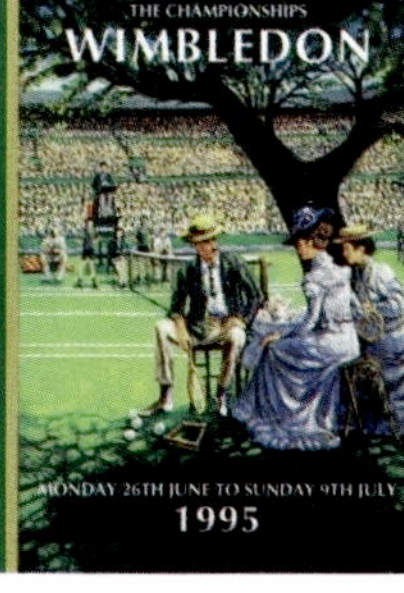

Wimbledon ticket wallet, 1995, featuring artwork by John Davies

Aubrey Jones

Lifelong tennis enthusiast **Aubrey Jones** (1926–2019) of Marlow in Buckinghamshire attended the Wimbledon Championships for 70 consecutive years from 1947 to 2016, and saw all the great champions in action on the Centre Court, from Maureen Connolly and Jaroslav Drobny in the early 1950s through to Roger Federer and Serena Williams in the New Millennium. He kept nearly all the Wimbledon programmes for the days he visited The Championships, and in many of those years he also purchased the completed Final Programmes with full printed results. In Aubrey's heyday these could be pre-ordered during the tournament from the Programme Office beneath the West Open Stand of the old No.2 Court, where purchasers were given a large manila envelope on which to write their name and address. The programmes were mailed out a week or two after The Championships.

In later years, Aubrey also began keeping his used Wimbledon tickets, noting down how he had obtained them. For example, 'Public Ballot', 'LTA Members' Ballot' or 'BLTA', the latter referring to the Buckinghamshire Lawn Tennis Association, which he served in an honorary capacity for more than 40 years, first as County Match Secretary and then as a Life Vice President. His meticulous records also show the location of the seats he was allotted, the names of the friends and relatives he went with, how much he paid for the tickets and other general observations. In 2015, for example, Aubrey – then nearly 90 – was in the Centre Court on Monday, 6 July and noted of his seats, 'about 8 rows down from entrance – too difficult for me to access. The attendant swapped them for ZF 267 and 268 (back row, next to entrance)'. Remarkably Aubrey also kept records of his successes and failures in the Wimbledon public ballot. In 1996 Aubrey's notes show that he 'missed the new app'n deadline of Dec 31' but in the 21 years thereafter no fewer than nine of his applications were successful, a remarkably high success rate.

Aubrey took lots of photographs at Wimbledon which he kept in an indexed filing system. He often visited The Bookstall, too, and his book collection included memoirs by Fred Perry, Helen Wills, Jaroslav Drobny, Angela Mortimer, Mike Davies, Gordon Forbes, Hana Mandlikova, Pete Sampras and many others, each one recounting a host of tennis experiences including halcyon summer days spent at Wimbledon. Every book had Aubrey's name, always in pencil, along with the year (and sometimes the month) of purchase. It was a collection carefully and thoughtfully compiled over a period of seven

Aubrey Jones attended Wimbledon for 70 consecutive years

decades, with every volume lovingly cared for and with all the dustjackets in as good condition as it was humanly possible to keep them.

Aubrey bought tickets because he wanted to see the tennis, programmes to enhance his enjoyment on the day, and books simply because he wanted to read them. His photographs captured happy memories. He never set out to build a fine collection of Wimbledon memorabilia, although that is exactly what he did. ◉

Jeanne Cherry

There are some tennis lovers who go to extraordinary lengths to track down rare tennis and Wimbledon collectables. Popular with dedicated collectors are antique wooden rackets, silverware, trophies and medals, along with many more obscure items. For three decades from the late 1980s **Jeanne Cherry** (1932–2017) of Santa Monica, California was one of the world's most knowledgeable and respected tennis collectors. Her book *Tennis Antiques and Collectibles* inspired many collectors all over the world and is still a key reference work.

Jeanne and her paediatrician husband Jim spent three one-year periods living in England, during which time they developed a deep love of Wimbledon. They attended the tournament whenever they could, and in 1988 Jeanne purchased her first item of tennis memorabilia, an antique wooden racket called 'The Bat' which she found at a local flea market. Wanting to find out how old it was, Jeanne looked around for a book on tennis collectables, and was surprised to find that none existed.

Jeanne Cherry (left) with Chris Jones, Wimbledon 2016

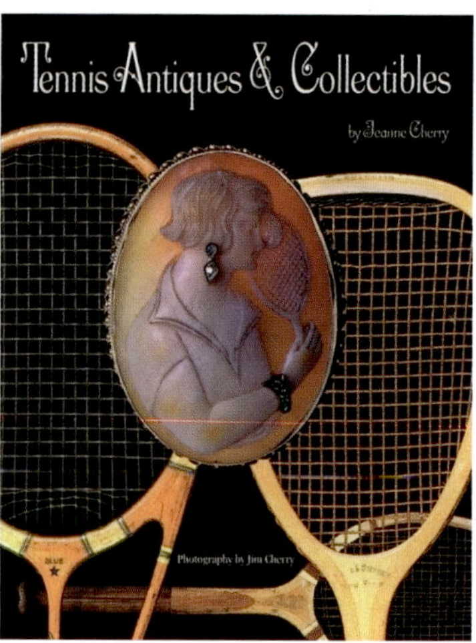

Jeanne particularly loved foraging for tennis items at the giant fleamarket in Brimfield, Massachusetts. When the eBay online auction site launched in 1995 she became an avid follower and a regular buyer and seller. Several times Jeanne travelled from her home in Santa Monica to attend sporting sales at London auction houses in search of one particular item: a Victorian skirt-lifter. This device, designed to aid ladies' freedom of movement on court in the days when long skirts were de rigueur, was very hard to find. Another of Jeanne's collecting passions was tennis sheet music, several examples of which are to be found in the Wimbledon Lawn Tennis Museum's Ephemera Collection.

One of the most unusual items in Jeanne's collection was a tennis-themed pinball machine which seven-times Wimbledon champion Pete Sampras liked to play on when he came to visit his fitness coach Brett 'Moose' Stephens, who for a period was the Cherry's long-term house guest.

Following the publication of *Tennis Antiques and Collectibles*

in 1995 Jeanne was contacted by Helen Wills Moody, the eight-times Wimbledon Ladies' Singles champion of the 1920s and 30s. Jeanne appraised and catalogued Helen's collection of tennis trophies, and these were later donated to the University of California at Berkeley. After Helen's death in 1998 Jeanne arranged for the remaining items in her collection to be sold at auction in California and London. Jeanne began collecting press agency photographs of Helen, many of which were included in her second book *Helen Wills – Tennis, Art, Life*, which was published in 2018, a year after her death.

Jeanne Cherry and Aubrey Jones shared a common love of tennis and Wimbledon, but represented opposite ends of the collecting spectrum. Jeanne loved beautiful things and pursued them with a true collector's zeal, whilst Aubrey's equally impressive collection was a happy by-product of his annual summer visits to The Championships.

Jeanne Cherry met Helen Wills three times during the 1990s

Wimbledonia at Auction

When Fiona Bruce and the BBC's *Antiques Roadshow* team recorded two programmes at The All England Lawn Tennis Club in the summer of 2011, it was surprising how few Wimbledon tennis-related items were brought in by the public for the team of experts to inspect. Those that were included a 1930s album containing a collection of player postcards published by Edwin Trim & Company of Wimbledon and, in complete contrast, a tennis racket smashed by John McEnroe. Wimbledon tennis memorabilia does, however, surface from time to time in general and specialist auctions throughout Britain, and monitoring the catalogues of upcoming sales can be both rewarding and fun.

Helen Wills auction catalogue, 1999

Two auctioneers specialising in sporting memorabilia are John Mullock of Church Stretton in Shropshire, whose auctions are held at Ludlow Racecourse several times each year, and Graham Budd, whose twice-yearly sporting sales are held at Sotheby's in London.

It is worth keeping an eye on generalist auctions in provincial towns and cities, too. In July 2017 a wonderful collection of Wimbledon signage and ephemera was sold by Tennants Auctioneers of Leyburn in North Yorkshire. The lots sold included some of the metal signs from the entrance halls to Centre and No.1 Courts prior to the demolition of the latter in 1997.

In the late 1990s Christie's auction house in London's South Kensington was the venue for two high-profile sales containing many items of Wimbledon tennis memorabilia. In June 1997 property formerly belonging to triple Wimbledon champion Fred Perry was sold, including the three Renshaw Cups he was given for his Wimbledon singles victories in 1934, 1935 and 1936. Each carried a pre-sale estimate of £15,000–25,000, and on the day they sold for £36,700, £35,600 and £25,300 respectively. In June 1999, the Helen Wills Collection, much of which had been painstakingly catalogued by Jeanne Cherry, went under the hammer. The lots offered included many of Helen's original etchings, sketches and paintings, some of which were of her Wimbledon contemporaries during her playing career.

Prior to the world financial crisis of 2008/09 the tennis collectables market was very strong, with discerning collectors around the world competing for rare items and willing to spend considerable sums to get them. Since then things have changed dramatically. There is less money around, mature collectors have mostly found the things they want, and very few younger collectors are entering this niche market. However, despite these factors, rare and high-quality items still command premium prices.

Other important tennis auctions in recent years have included the Jaroslav Drobny Collection (Sotheby's, London, July 2002), the Alan Little Collection (Graham Budd, London, May 2018) and the Jeanne Cherry Collection (Morphy Auctions, Denver, August 2018). Graham Budd's auction at Sotheby's in November 2019 included a remarkable collection of early 20th-century Wimbledon postcards published by Edwin Trim & Company. ✇

Fred Perry auction catalogue, 1997

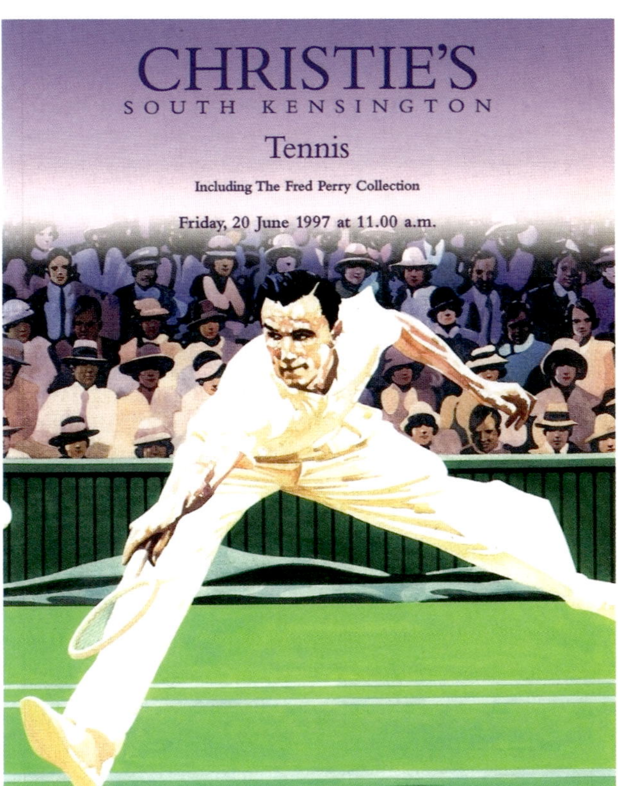

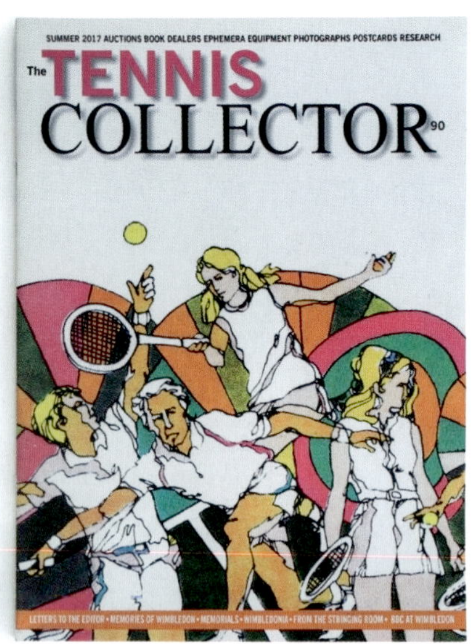

When Collectors Become Historians

Attention is increasingly switching to the historical rather than monetary value of tennis artefacts. Several prominent collectors have produced interesting illustrated books, and magazine articles written by tennis collectors now focus primarily on the stories behind the objects they collect.

The Tennis Collectors' Society was founded by avid Essex-based collector **Gerald Gurney** in 1987. Gerald's charming and informative booklet *Tennis, Squash and Badminton Bygones* (1984) is an excellent introduction to the world of tennis collectables. The Society's illustrated magazine *The Tennis Collector* is published three times a year and provides a forum for members to exchange information and share the findings of their historical research. Now approaching its 100th issue, *The Tennis Collector*'s back issues are a mine of information about the history of Lawn Tennis and Wimbledon. Of particular interest to collectors are the magazine's auction reports which have tracked the sales and values of Wimbledonia items over more than three decades.

The Tennis Collector is edited and designed by **Bob Everitt**, a leading tennis collector and historian. Bob is the author of *Racket Sports Collectibles* (2002), a superb 304-page illustrated guide to all types of lawn tennis, table tennis, squash and badminton collectables. Bob lives in Bilston in the West Midlands and was the researcher who uncovered the truth about the origins of Lawn Tennis, confirming Major Walter Wingfield's pioneering role in establishing the game in the early 1870s. Bob's compelling evidence led John Barrett to revise his account of the early years of Lawn Tennis in the most recent edition of his book *Wimbledon – The Official History*.

Another of the world's most dedicated tennis historians, and a regular contributor to *The Tennis Collector*, is **Richard A. Hillway** of Colorado Springs. Richard is the co-author, with Bob Everitt, of *The Birth of Lawn Tennis* (2018), an important history book focusing on the early years of the Wimbledon Championships and featuring illustrations of many items of Wimbledonia. Richard has written numerous articles on the

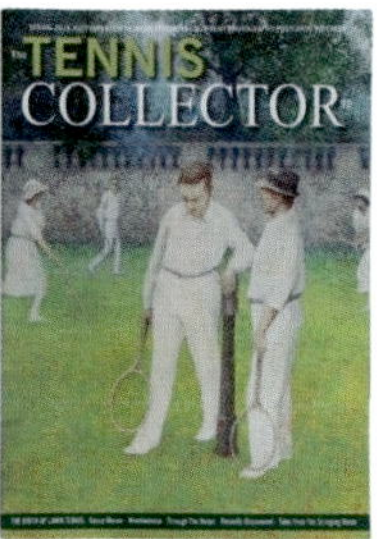

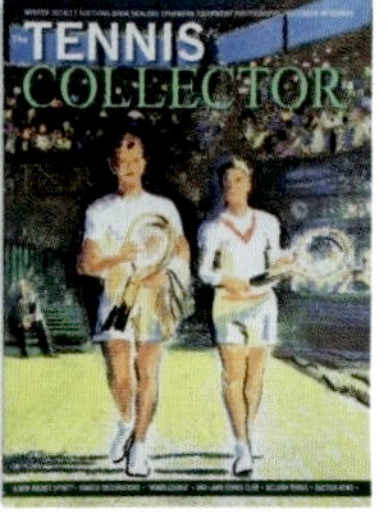

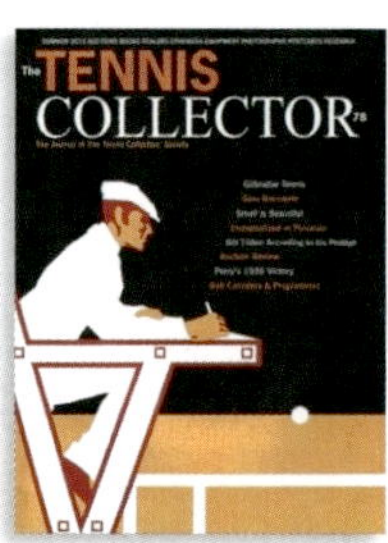

history of the game, and loves collecting letters written by tennis stars, officials and others involved with the sport. As he explains: 'Much may be learned from letters about the personality, the views, and the likes and dislikes of the writer. Information is found in letters that would never be published in books. Handwritten letters certainly trump typed ones. If one reads enough of these, he will eventually feel transported back in time, almost as one of the family of the writer.'

Collecting tennis letters is far from straightforward, however: 'I have not yet read a book on tennis collectables that listed tennis letters as a category. To me, they are the very best collectable. I search for tennis books and magazines as well, but tennis letters are my favorite items. Many tennis collectors hunt for tennis autographs. Some even cut the autographs off the bottom of letters, and throw the letters away. This is almost sacrilegious.'

You can learn a lot from letters, as some in Richard's collection illustrate. For example, Dwight Davis, in England for the 1901 Wimbledon Championships, wrote that he and partner Holcombe Ward 'are practicing hard but at present are playing very poorly so that our chances look rather slim'. They lost to Britain's Laurie and Reggie Doherty in the Challenge Round.

In 2022 *The Tennis Collector* was expanded to 48 pages and it's name changed to *The Tennis Historian*.

Digital Memories

History may record that the golden age of Wimbledon tennis ephemera ran from around 1922, when The All England Lawn Tennis Club moved from Worple Road to Wimbledon Park, until the Centenary Championships of 1977, or perhaps just a few years later. During this period Wimbledon's creative output reflected the mood, spirit and changing attitudes of the Jazz Era, Art Deco design, the post-war consumer boom, jet travel, the Swinging Sixties and the frenetic early years of Open Tennis.

This half-century of creativity had its roots in the emergence of Lawn Tennis as a spectator sport in the early 20th century, and saw the sport's stylish and aspirational image reinforced again and again in the public consciousness on printed greeting cards, postcards, travel posters, advertisements, product packaging, book and magazine covers, and of course on Wimbledon's own tickets, posters and programmes.

The door to this golden era of printed ephemera had been opened by French poster artist Jules Cheret's mastery of colour lithographic printing in late 19th-century Paris, and it was another technological advance a century later which finally brought it to a close. In 1990 British scientist Tim Berners-Lee invented what he called the World Wide Web, and the rest, as they say, is history. The future is digital, and the internet constantly spawns exciting new forms of creativity.

Londoner Amisha Savani fully embraces new technology: 'Instead of passing around a photo album when friends and family visit, I pass around my iPad. One advantage is that it is light, and you just swipe through photos and enlarge them if you want to see more. The device takes up very little space. The shortage of living space in an increasingly busy city has driven people to become more electronic. Bookshelves no longer hold books or DVDs, which are all now on Kindle and online downloadable software like Spotify.'

However, Amisha also has concerns about storage and navigation in years to come: 'Today when I go to Wimbledon I am armed with my mobile phone camera and I take lots of photographs, my personal mementos. These will be sent to friends and shared on Instagram or Facebook. A back-up will be on the cloud. But in fifty years' time, how will this information be accessed and shared? Instagram, Facebook and even the cloud may no longer exist. Another medium will come along, of course, but how can I be sure that today's precious digital memories will not be lost in the ether?'

Amisha foresees the relationship between players and fans at Wimbledon growing ever more distant. 'During the 2019 Championships The All England Club announced plans to build a tunnel to enable players to travel securely into and around the grounds without interruption from fans. The plans will certainly have taken into consideration both player and crowd security, but how will fans be able to get autographs from their favourite players in the future? How will they be able to get a selfie?'

As the digital world seeks to categorise, organise and pigeonhole us, and to anticipate – and then satisfy – our almost every need, many people look back with affection on simpler times when a trip to Wimbledon was often an impulse decision that led to an unforgettable summer day out, its memories rekindled by treasured mementos such as tickets, programmes and photographs, or a handwritten personal message in a pocket-sized autograph book. ✪

Attractively printed tickets may soon be a thing of the past

Resources for Collectors

In the UK, *The Tennis Historian* magazine gives regular news about forthcoming sporting auctions, and Tennis Gallery Wimbledon is an independent shop specialising in Wimbledon-related art, books and collectables. In the US an organisation called the Tennis Collectors of America provides a forum for collectors to meet and exchange information. ✪

CHAPTER 8

Wimbledon Programmes

The LAWN TENNIS
CHAMPIONSHIP MEETING
1927
SATURDAY, JULY 2nd

Upon the Lawns of the
All England Club, Church Road
Wimbledon

Patron - - HIS MAJESTY THE KING

President - - - - H. W. W. WILBERFORCE

Committee of Management:

VISCOUNT D'ABERNON, P.C., G.C.B., G.C.M.G., LORD DESBOROUGH, G.C.V.O., VISCOUNT DONERAILE, THE HON. P. BOWES-LYON, MAJOR C. H. L. CAZALET, D.S.O., MESSRS. W. BADDELEY, G. A. CARIDIA, G. COULSON, W. C. CRAWLEY, G. E. FOWLER, A. W. GORE, A. C. GRIFFITHS, G. C. BALL GREENE, S. A. E. HICKSON, F. C. LOHDEN, O.B.E., R. J. McNAIR, T. M. MAVROGORDATO, H. H. MONCKTON, G. H. MUSGRAVE, A. B. J. NORRIS, C. PFLAUM, G. R. D. PRITCHETT, H. A. SABELLI, A. STERRY, T. D. STOWARD, M.C., A. E. M. TAYLOR, M.B.E., C. B. WATSON, and H. W. W. WILBERFORCE.

Secretary and Manager: D. R. LARCOMBE.

Director of Championships

The first thing many visitors to The Championships do is make a beeline for the nearest vendor of the Wimbledon Official Programme containing the Order of Play on all courts. Programmes were first produced for the inaugural Championships in 1877, and have been Wimbledon's most popular collectables ever since.

The first known Wimbledon Programme was for Monday 16th July 1877 when the first-ever Wimbledon Gentlemen's Singles Final between Spencer Gore and William Marshall was set to take place at 3.30pm at The All England Croquet and Lawn Tennis Club's Worple Road ground. Entitled 'List of Players', it was a single sheet folded in half to make a four-page programme costing sixpence. In the event, the final fell foul of the weather and was not played until three days later.

Fast forward to the present day and official programmes have evolved into heavyweight colour magazines containing tournament information, feature articles, player profiles, photographs, maps, advertisements and much more besides. In 2019, 13 different daily editions of the programme were produced for The All England Club by Liverpool-based publisher PPL Sport: 11 daily editions, each updated overnight with the previous day's scores and the current day's Order of Play, along with special souvenir editions for the Ladies' and Gentlemen's Singles finals. A Final Programme with the complete results of all singles and doubles events was published a week or two after the tournament.

Royal Box programme with ribbon bookmark, 1937

The story of Wimbledon officialp rogrammes is the story of Wimbledon itself. Buying a programme and keeping it as a souvenir has been part of the Wimbledon tradition right from the start. The early programmes were simple folded cards, containing just the draw sheet and a plan showing the layout of the 12 courts. They may have been modelled on the cast lists given free to West End theatre-goers in those mid-Victorian days.

The Kenneth Ritchie Library at Wimbledon has a comprehensive collection of original programmes, and examining them reveals how Wimbledon has evolved over 143 years and 133 Championships. ✪

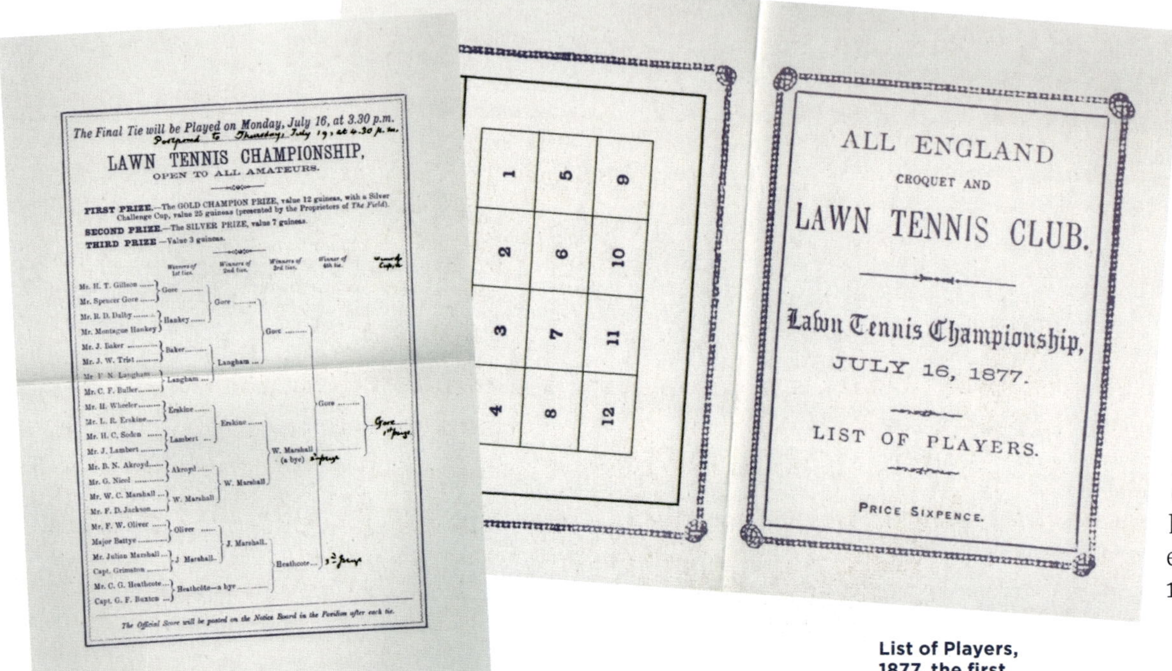

List of Players, 1877, the first Wimbledon collectable

1877 to 1904

The programmes for 1877 and 1878, the first two years The Championships were held, were folded sheets measuring 140 x 195 millimetres (5.5 x 7.75 inches). It is not known who printed them, or whether they were made of paper or card, although the latter seems most likely. The Library has photocopies of these programmes, but the whereabouts of the originals are not known. Nothing at all is known about the programmes for 1879 and 1880, but the Library has a copy of an 1881 programme which bears the footnote 'Printed on the grounds by the National Press Agency Limited', a very interesting development and somewhat reminiscent of the updated scorecards printed at Lord's and other major cricket grounds.

Little is known about the Wimbledon programmes for 1882 to 1893, for all the Library has is a photocopy of the inner pages of the 1884 programme. This is the same size as the earlier years and contains the draw sheets for the Gentlemen's and newly instituted Ladies' Singles Championships along with the Gentlemen's Doubles which was then called the 'Four-Handed Championship'. The absence of the front cover from the Library's copy means we do not know who printed the 1884 programme.

After a gap of nine years, the next programme in the Library's collection is for 1894, and my, how things have changed! Programmes are now clearly targeted at spectators rather than players, and entry fees and prizes have been dropped in favour of a Railway Time Table and information about press coverage of The Championships. The programmes have also become much smaller at just 70 x 105 millimetres (2.75 x 4 inches), comfortably fitting into a ladies' purse or a gentleman's jacket pocket. The updated daily editions are printed on a range of coloured cards, and the price has halved from sixpence to 3d. These attractive new-look programmes were printed by a firm called Neller & Co. of 4 Hill Road (later renamed Wimbledon Hill), just a few hundred yards from The All England Club's ground at Worple Road.

The Library has copies of these small-format programmes for every year from 1894 to 1898, although interestingly none have been folded. This suggests that these examples, unlike the majority of others in the Library's collection, were never actually sold or used, but rather kept in the Club's (or the printer's) archives.

There are no programmes for 1899 or 1900, but there is a photocopy of a 1901 programme which shows a return to the original large size of the 1870s. It may be assumed that the larger format was used in 1899 and 1900 also, as non-Championship Ladies' Doubles and Mixed Doubles events were introduced in those years.

The Library has original programmes for 1902, 1903 and 1904, all printed on stiff card by Neller and Co. in a taller, slimmer format of varying heights but just 125 millimetres (five inches) wide. There are also clear signs of commercialisation creeping into Wimbledon; 1902 was Slazengers' first year, and on page four is the simple but important footnote: 'Slazenger and Sons' Championship Balls were used throughout the Meeting.' A year later, in 1903, we find what is probably the programme's first-ever advertisement for the book *Lawn Tennis at Home & Abroad* by

Daily programmes, 1895

A. Wallis Myers. This was 'On Sale Everywhere priced ten shillings and sixpence.'

In 1904 63 gentlemen took part in the singles Championship, an increase of almost 50 percent, and the printers had to use a very small typeface to fit them all into the four-page official programme along with the entrants for the Ladies' Championship, the Gentlemen's and Ladies' Doubles, Mixed Doubles and the All-England Plate, a consolation event for those defeated early in the Gentlemen's Singles Championship. ◑

1905 to 1923

The record number of entries for the Gentlemen's Singles in 1904 signalled the end for Neller and Co. as Wimbledon's programme printers. Programmes were getting bigger, and in 1905 Wimbledon turned to another local firm, Edwin Trim & Co., which had premises at 20 Hill Road, just a few doors along from Neller and Co. Trim also had premises at 30 Homefield Road in Wimbledon Village, where the programmes were printed.

For the 1905 Championships the new printers produced an expanded six-page programme. It was still made of card, but now with two folds, and even though two extra pages had been added the players' names and match scores were still in quite small print. In their last few years Neller had added gold-leaf trim to the edges of the programmes they produced; ironically Edwin Trim ceased this expensive practice immediately.

The relationship between Edwin Trim and The All England Club was to prove an important one, for the firm also began taking photographs of the players and selling them as postcards on the grounds, a practice that continues to the present day, albeit in different hands.

Trim continued to produce tall, slim programmes for Wimbledon every year until 1923. Before the outbreak of World War I, these were all six-page, twice-folded cards of the same tall, slim format. The 1913 edition was a whopping 126 x 360 millimetres (5 inches wide, 14 inches high).

The size of the entry for the Gentlemen's Singles – traditionally Wimbledon's biggest event – dictated the size of the pages in each year's printed programme, as the entire draw sheet had to appear on a single page to make sense to the reader. This in turn dictated the size of the programme itself.

During the Trim years the number of players in the Gentlemen's Singles rose steadily, reaching a peak of 133 in 1923. The other Championship events were attracting more entries too, and when Wimbledon resumed after the war Trim switched to eight-page paper programmes folded three times to give the same tall slim appearance as before. When opened out the page size of the 1919 programme was 255 x 320 millimetres (10 inches by 12.5 inches), a size that has hardly changed since. These bigger programmes came with a price increase, from sixpence to one shilling.

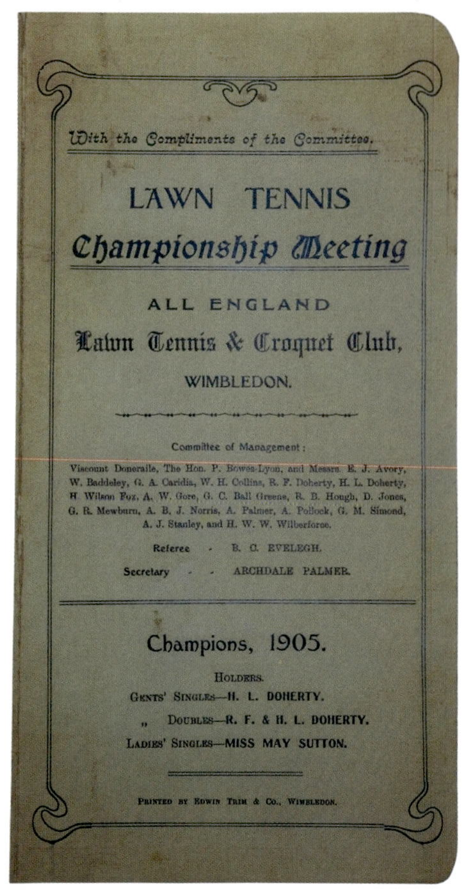

This eight-page, folded-paper format continued to be used until 1923, Wimbledon's second year at the new ground at Wimbledon Park, nowadays referred to as Church Road. ◑

 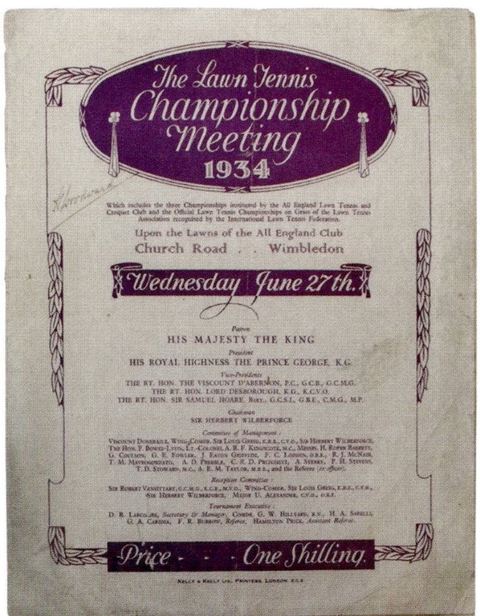 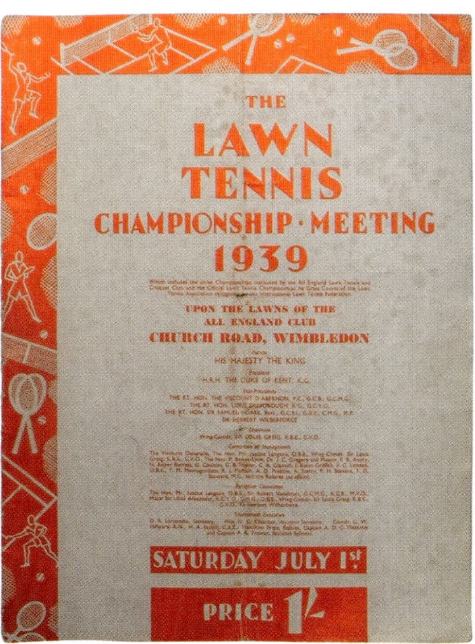

1924 to 1939

Although Edwin Trim's printing press could cope with the large Wimbledon programme pages, the hugely increased demand at The All England Club's new ground was apparently too much for a small local printer. Thousands of updated programmes had to be printed, bound and delivered to The All England Club each morning of The Championships, and to meet this challenge the Club now turned to Kelly and Kelly of Moor Lane, E.C.2, a major London-based printer, 'who specialize in quality work'.

The new firm made an immediate impact, turning the 1924 Wimbledon programme into an attractive, 20-page magazine. New features included a full page devoted to the 'Intended Order of Play', a half page of 'Official Announcements' and a page with 'The Championship Roll' showing the names of all Wimbledon Singles, Doubles and Mixed Doubles champions to date. It is interesting to note that Ladies' Doubles champions from 1885 to 1912 and Mixed Doubles champions from 1888 to 1912 were included in these lists, for these were 'non-Championship' events and they did not appear in the Roll of Honour in 1925 or subsequent years.

A little section entitled 'Hints To Spectators' included advice 'not to confine your applause to one competitor', and to 'give the other his or her due'. Applauding net-cord strokes was also frowned upon. The 1924 programme also contained no fewer than 31 advertisements, and ten of the 20 pages were given over entirely to advertising. Slazenger had a full-page advertisement on the outside back cover, and have occupied that position in every Wimbledon programme since. Other advertisers included Birmal, F.H. Ayres, Wisden and En-Tout-Cas, and some of the advertisements were illustrated, signalling the arrival of photographs in the Wimbledon programme.

During the 1920s and 30s programme covers became more decorative

Wimbledon celebrated its Jubilee in 1926, and the programme's front-cover artwork depicted players in 1870s and 1920s tennis costumes reaching out to shake hands. Six-time champion Suzanne Lenglen controversially defaulted from her third-round match, and the public was deprived of a potential fourth-round encounter with Spain's glamorous Lili de Alvarez. Sadly, Suzanne was never seen on court at Wimbledon again.

The Wimbledon programme's format and contents remained unchanged during the remainder of the 1920s and throughout the 1930s, although there were different and colourful cover designs each year during the latter decade. The 1938 programme carried an advertisement for Murphy Television Sets, enticing would-be owners with the prospect of watching Centre Court matches live 'as hundreds are doing on their Television Sets'. ⊘

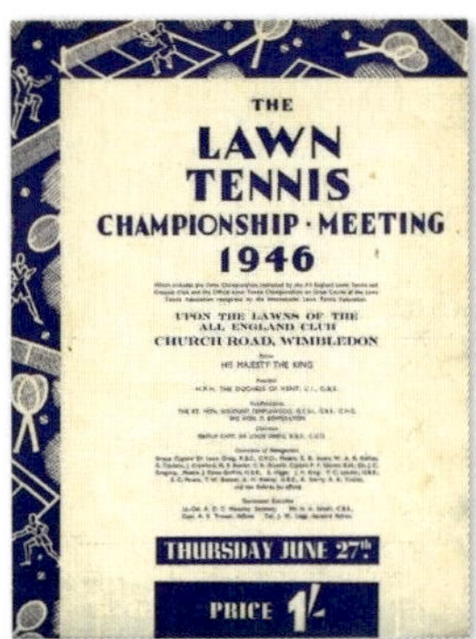 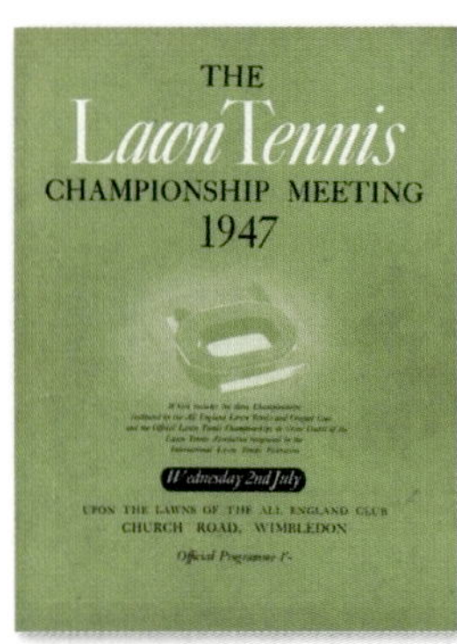  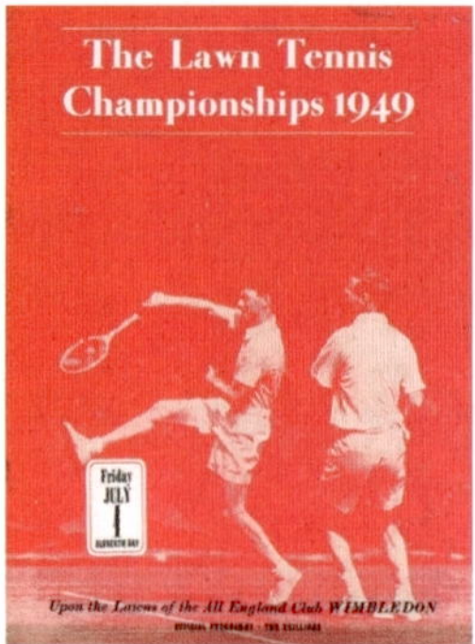 

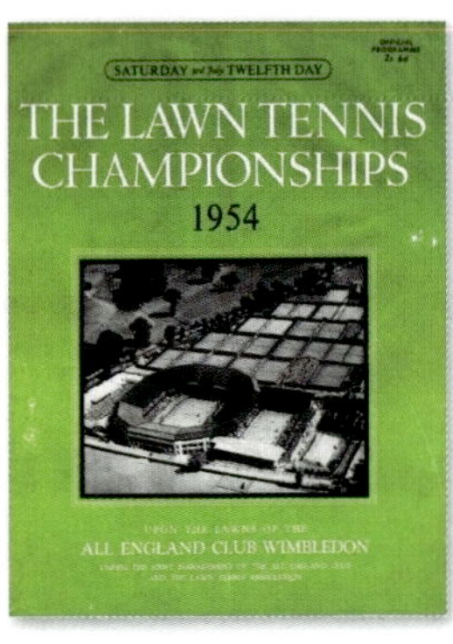 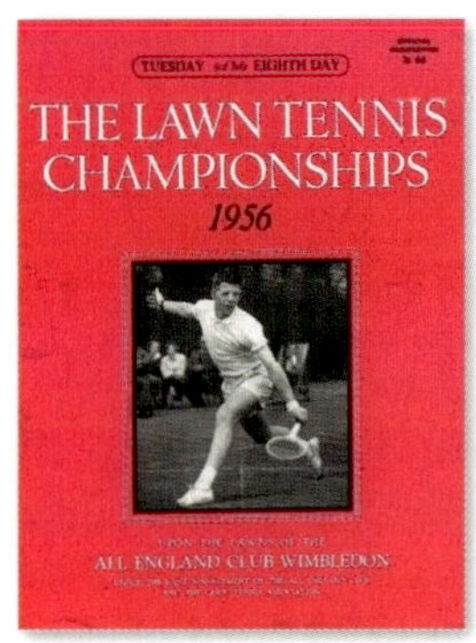 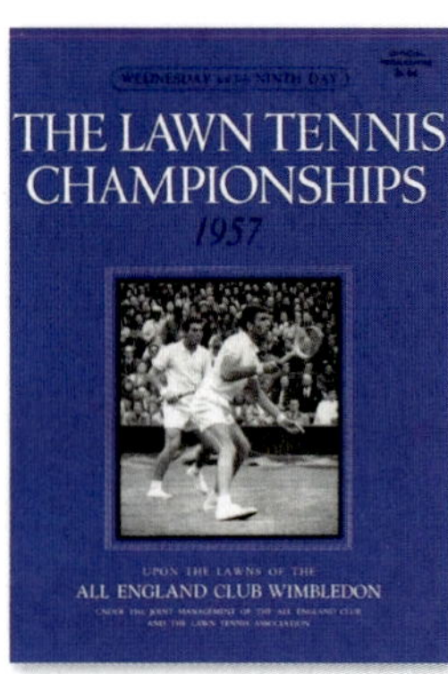 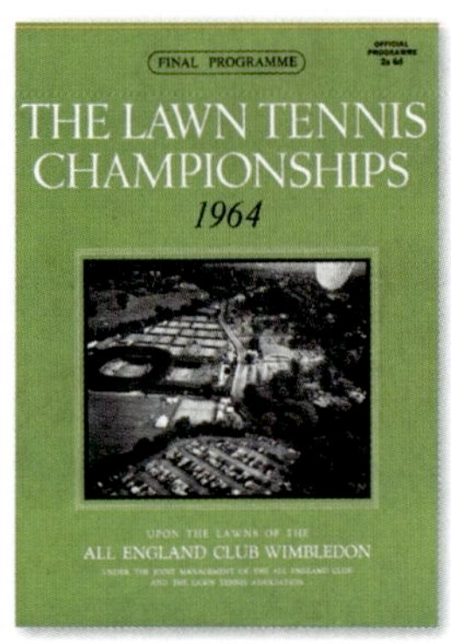 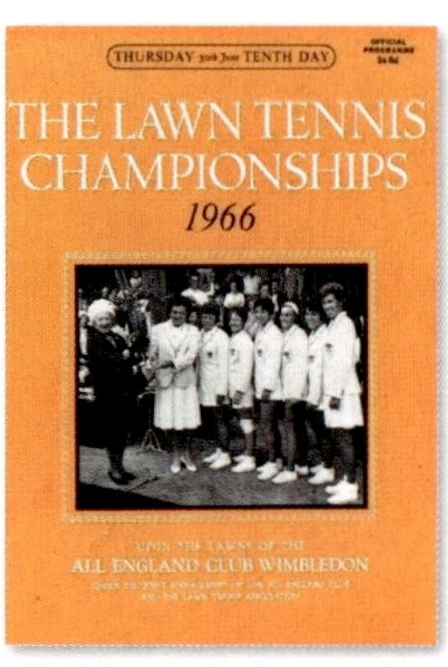

1946 to 1976

The three decades following the end of World War II were a golden period for the Wimbledon programme. During most of that time each day's programme had a different daily feature article and at least two sections of black and white photographs, and there were photographs of different stars on each day's front cover, the colour of which also changed day by day. The bright colours used were: Mondays green; Tuesdays pink; Wednesdays blue; Thursdays orange; Fridays purple; and Saturdays light green. This was clever marketing, for fans now had several good reasons to purchase a programme on each of their visits during The Fortnight.

In the immediate post-war years, however, the after-effects of six years of global conflict were apparent, and the 1946 Wimbledon Official Programme showed understandable signs of post-war austerity. It was printed on coarse paper, and the 1939 Art Deco front-cover design was reused. Food rationing was in force, and in the Official Announcements it was stated that 'Owing to current restrictions there will only be a limited number of Buffets at which light refreshments can be obtained'. A display box told of the damage caused to The All England Club on the night of Friday, 11 October 1940 when a 'stick' of five 500-pound bombs fell on the grounds and the surrounding area. The public were informed that 'The first bomb demolished the club tool house. The second fell on the roof of the Centre Court. The damage to the Centre Court means a loss of approximately 1,200 seats.'

The 1947 programme was printed as usual by Kelly & Kelly, but Programme Publications Ltd were brought in to look after distribution and the sale of advertising space, a relationship that continues to the present day. The programme was expanded to 24 pages, and one of the extra pages contained six black and white photographs from the previous year's Championships – the first time editorial use was made of photographs in the Wimbledon programme.

In 1948 another four pages were added, and there was a different coloured cover with a different player's photograph on the front each day. There were two inside photo spreads which were changed each day, and for the first time there was something to read: a daily article by Brigadier J.G. Smyth, V.C., M.C., the tennis correspondent of *The Sunday Times*. John 'Jackie' Smyth had served as an officer in both World Wars, and his straightforward writing style both informed and entertained Wimbledon spectators as they waited for play to start each day. He would go on to contribute over 300 daily articles until his retirement in 1973, and there was a photograph of him in the 1948 programme, alongside British player Kay Menzies. All these improvements to the programme came at a cost, however, and the price doubled to two shillings.

The year 1949 saw another four pages added, bringing the total to 32, and even more photographs were included, along with an 'Alphabetical List of Competitors' and a

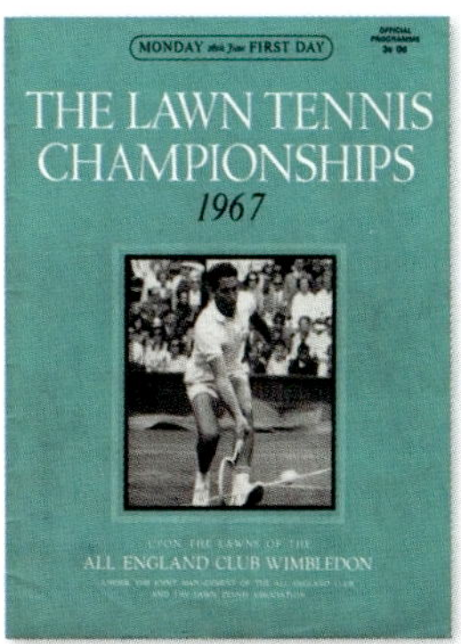 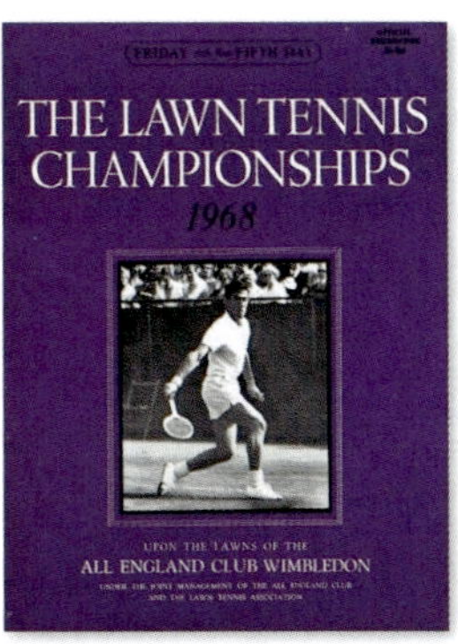 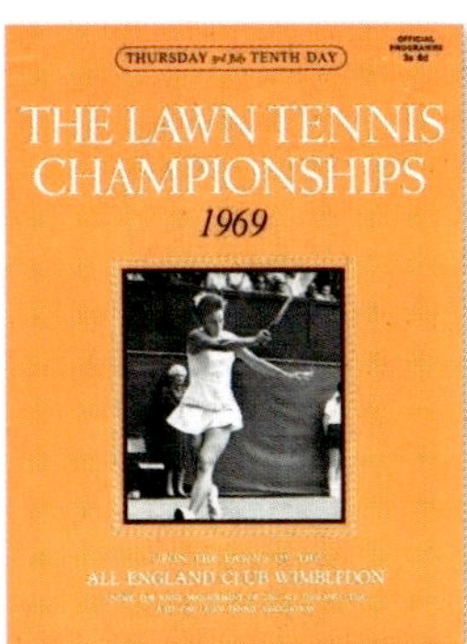 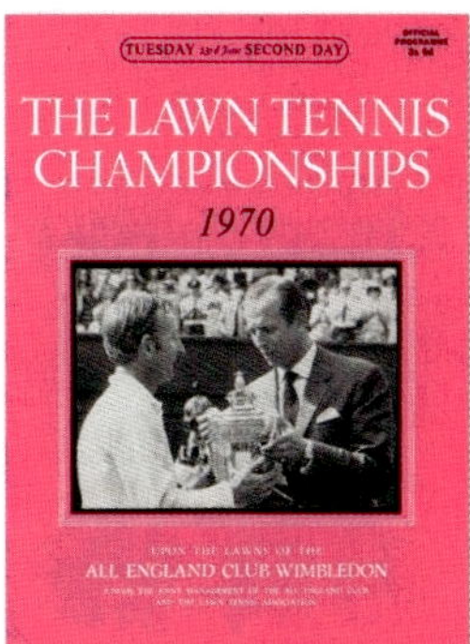 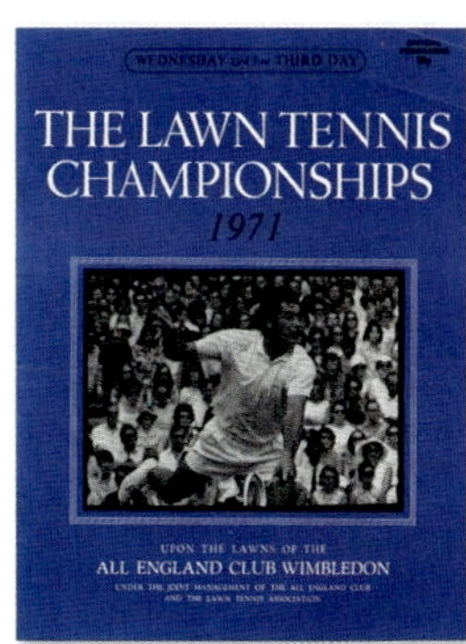

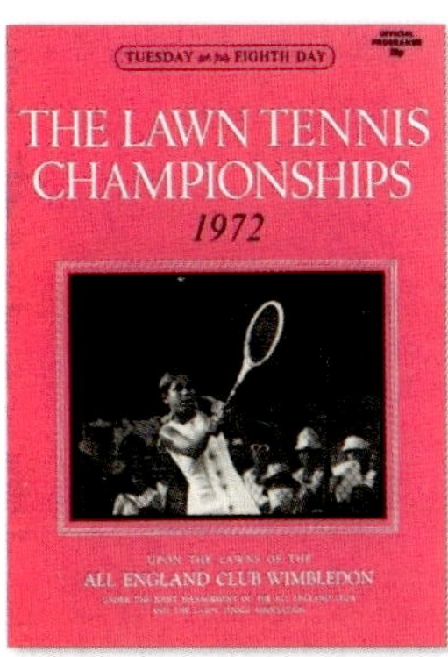 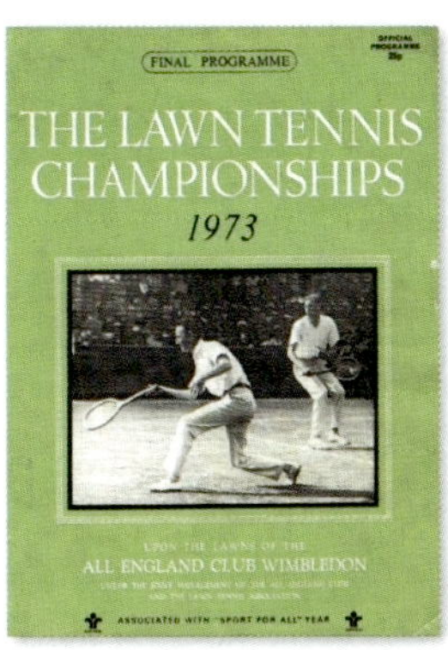 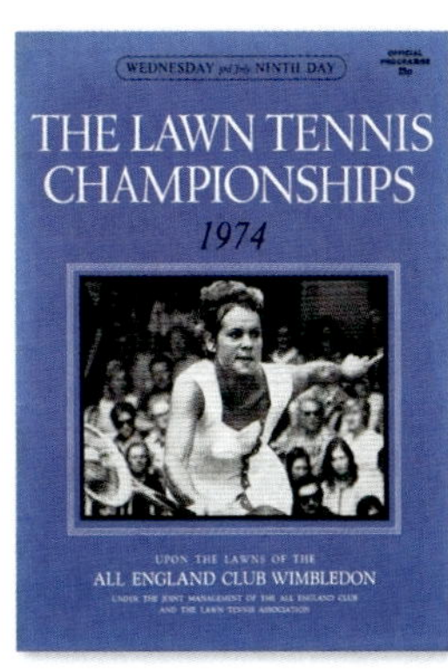  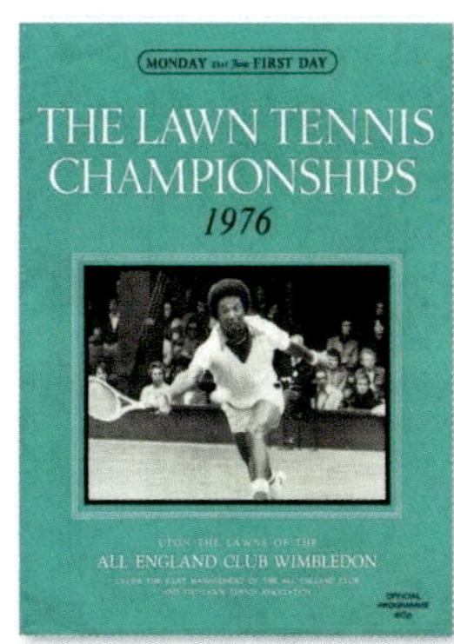

list of 'Maiden Names of Lady Competitors'. Colour also appeared inside the programme for the first time, with Dunlop and Grays of Cambridge taking full-page colour advertisements. The 1950 and 1951 programmes followed the same format, the latter having a special insignia to mark Festival of Britain Year, with the price increasing to two shillings and sixpence.

The 1952 programme advertised the availability of 'Wimbledon Final Programmes', which would be available by post shortly after The Championships, giving complete round-by-round results. Final Programmes had been produced before, but this was the first time they had been advertised in the programme itself.

The front cover of the 1953 programme featured a special crest to celebrate Coronation Year. Her Majesty Queen Elizabeth II had been crowned in Westminster Abbey on Tuesday, 2 June, just 20 days before the tournament began. To accommodate the increasing clamour for advertising space, a further four pages were added, bringing the total to 36, a successful format that would remain largely unchanged for the next 23 years.

Programme production did not always go smoothly, however, and in 1959 an industrial dispute prevented the inclusion of updated results and Daily Order of Play. These were supplied on a separate four-page insert.

The year 1963 was the 75th Anniversary of the Lawn Tennis Association, a fact celebrated on the front cover of the Wimbledon programme, and the following year the number of pages was increased to 40. The 1967 programme carried a small but significant announcement: The Wimbledon World Professional Lawn Tennis Championship would be staged from 25th to 28th August on the Centre Court. This event was a resounding success, and led directly to the start of Open Tennis the following year.

The 1968 programme had four extra pages, one of which contained Wimbledon's first-ever prize-money list. In 1966 the price of the programme had risen to three shillings; in 1969 it went up to three shillings and sixpence. When Britain switched to decimal currency in the early 1970s, price increases followed in rapid succession: 20p (equivalent to four shillings) in 1971; 25p (five shillings) in 1973; and 50p (ten shillings) in 1975. Eight more pages were added to the programme in 1976, bringing the total to 52, but purchasers were spared another price increase.

Nineteen seventy-six was the last year of the distinctive programmes of the post-war years. Peter Wilson had taken over responsibility for daily articles from Sir John Smyth in 1974, but this apart, the programme's format and content had basically remained the same for over a quarter of a century. Wimbledon's Centenary year was approaching, however, and the programme was about to change beyond all recognition. ✆

 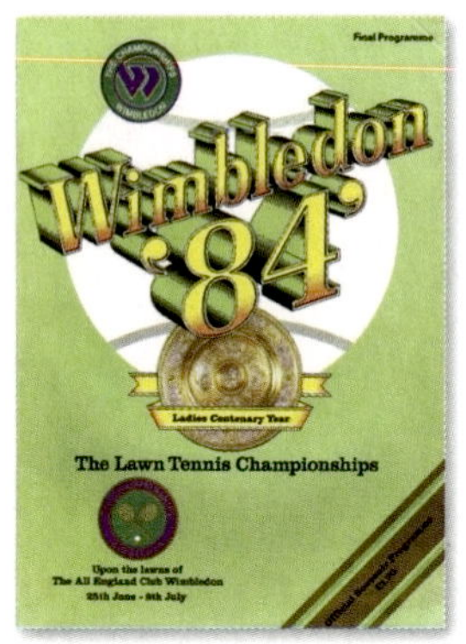  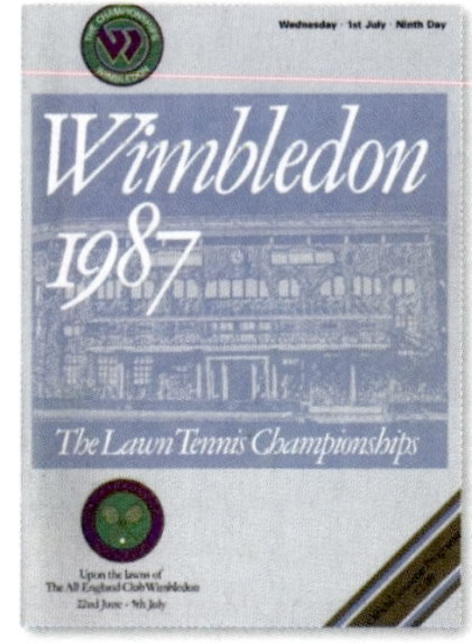 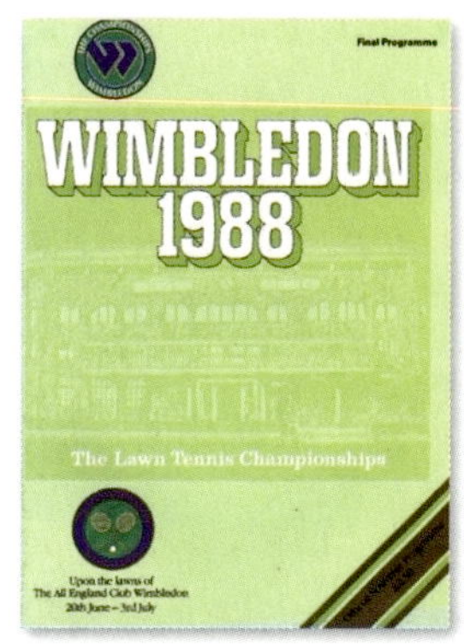

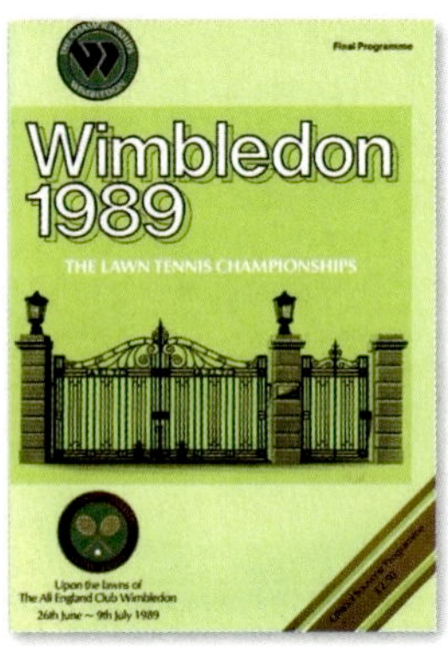 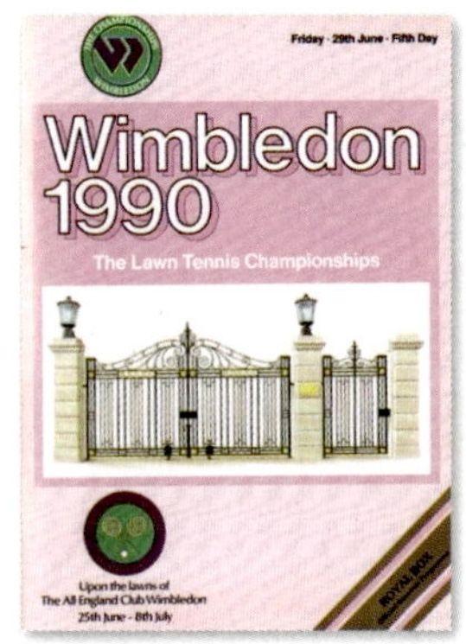 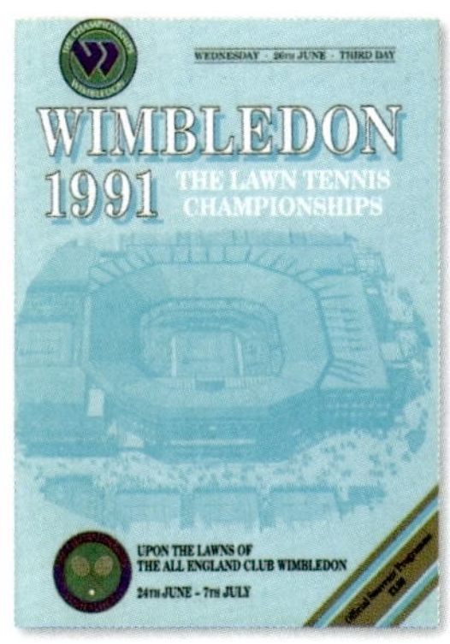  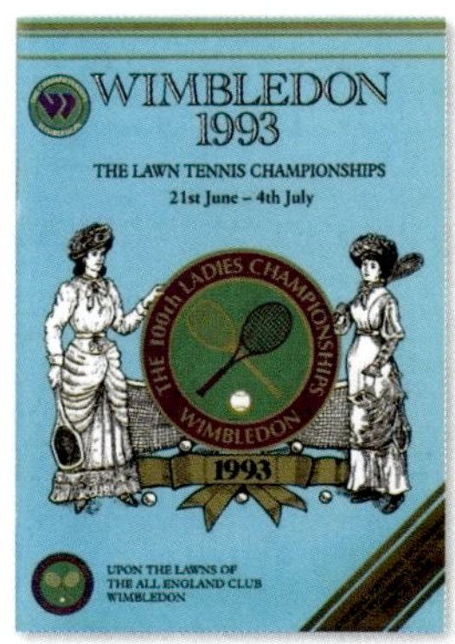

1977 to the Present Day

The first Wimbledon programme in 1877 was a small folded card. One hundred years on, a heavyweight 80-page glossy programme was produced with new content including player profiles with colour photographs and a second daily article in which David Gray of *The Guardian* looked at aspects of the history of lawn tennis to coincide with the opening of the Wimbledon Lawn Tennis Museum. The 1977 programme had 50 percent more pages than the previous year, and there was a commensurate price rise to 75p. Nineteen seventy-seven was also Queen Elizabeth II's Silver Jubilee, and her Majesty – not noted for her love of tennis – was at the Club on Ladies' Finals Day to present the trophy to Virginia Wade.

For the next 30 years, the Wimbledon programme just kept on growing in size and quality, and increasing in price. Ten pages were added in 1978, eight more in 1980, and the programme reached 100 pages in 1984. Perfect binding was introduced in 2010, allowing a printed spine, and by 2016 the programme had 144 pages and no fewer than 14 feature articles. The price rose steadily, too, from £1 in 1978 to £2 in 1986, £5 in 2000, £8 in 2010 and £10 in 2016. Programme Publications – now called PPL Group – is still responsible for production and advertising, and 2017 marked the 70th anniversary of the company's involvement with Wimbledon.

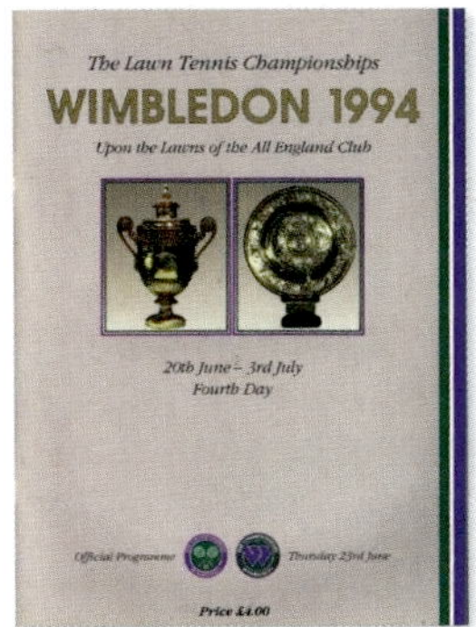

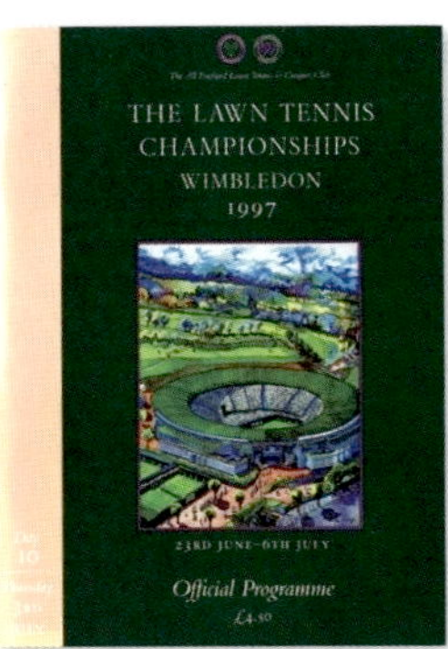
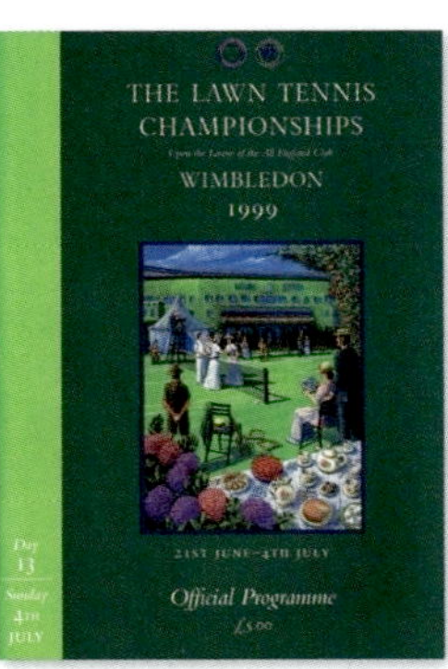
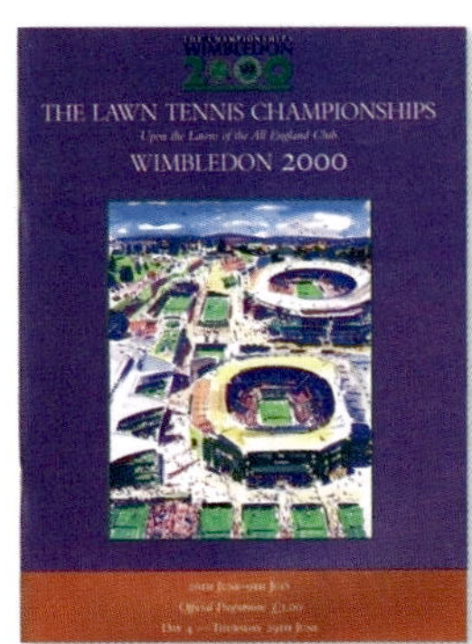

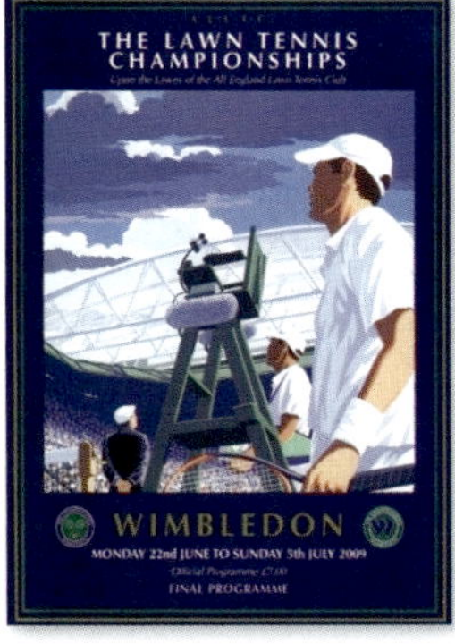
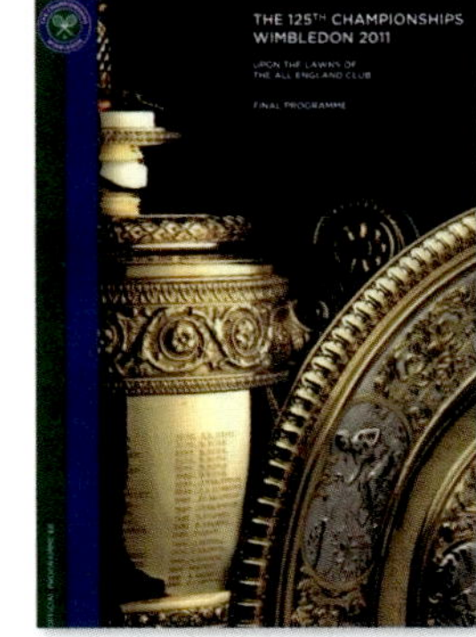
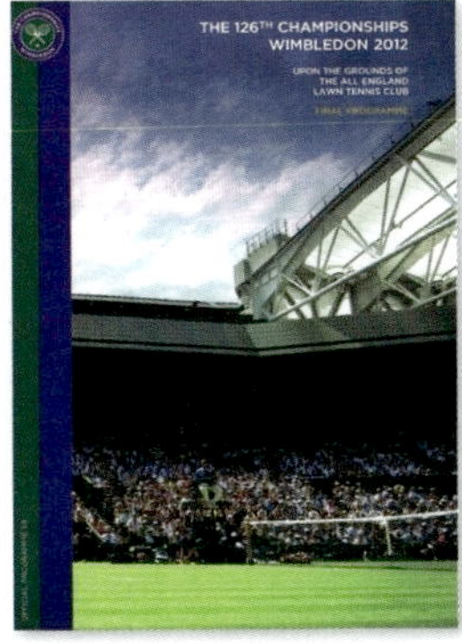
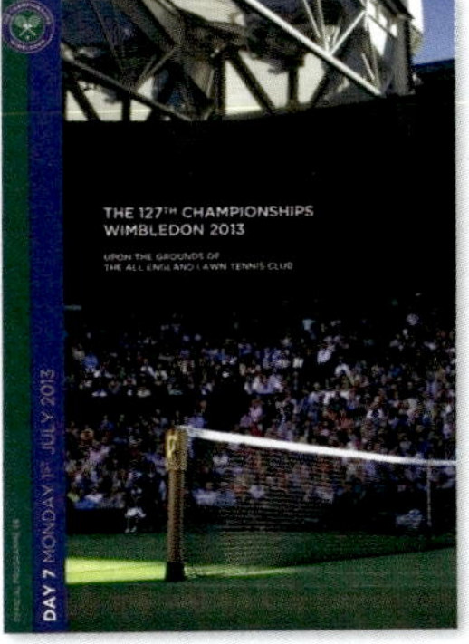
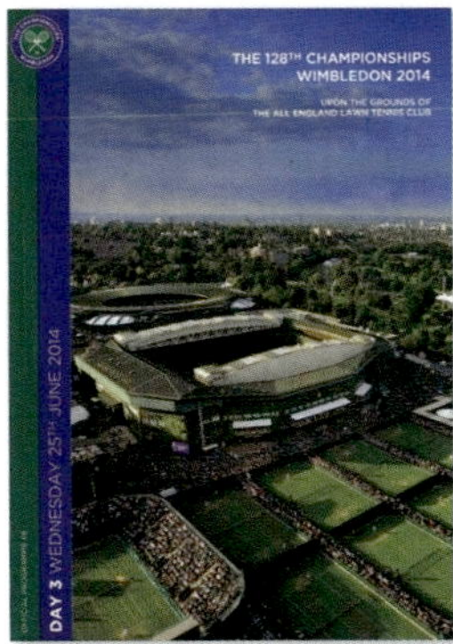
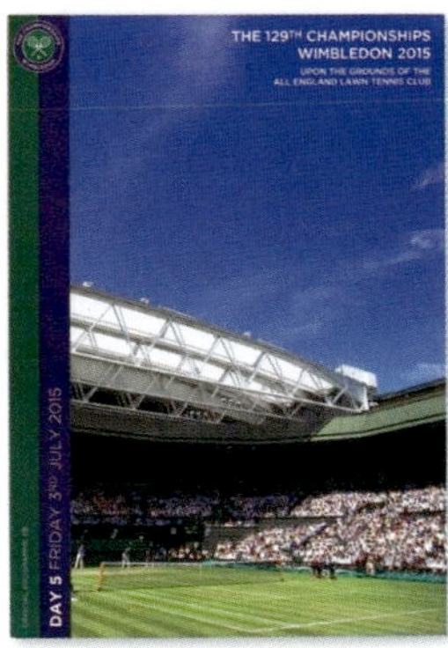

Collecting Wimbledon Programmes

The Official Programme is Wimbledon's most popular collectable. Spectators keep them as souvenirs, but their high sentimental value means people tend to hang onto them for their whole lives. Daily programmes are sought after as birthday and anniversary gifts, but it is Final Programmes with full printed results that are of most interest to collectors, along with special Royal Box editions which were first produced in the 1930s. To be of interest to a serious collector a programme must be in excellent or mint condition. The folded card and paper programmes produced up to 1923 rarely come onto the market; their truly ephemeral nature meaning few have survived.

As we move further into the digital age younger generations may not feel the same nostalgic affection for printed programmes. There are already some sporting events that have ceased to offer printed programmes to spectators, so the future of this much-loved British collectable is in some doubt. The hope is, however, that there will always be a place at major events such as the Wimbledon Championships for programmes which are chock-full of creativity in their editorial and advertising content, and which can trigger a lifetime of happy memories. ✪

CHAPTER 9

Postcards & Photographs

POSTCARDS
PHOTO POSTCARDS
PHOTO POSTCARDS
PHOTO
POST CARDS
PLAYERS
3
PHOTO
POSTCARDS
PLAYERS
PHOTO
POSTCARDS
OF ALL LEADING
PLAYERS
TRIM & Co.
Photo
2
Enlargements

When the first Wimbledon Championships were held in 1877, *The Illustrated London News* sent artist Horace Petherick along to The All England Croquet and Lawn Tennis Club to capture the scene. At the time that was the only way to do it, as photography was still in its infancy and limited to professionals mainly working in their own studios. It was not until well into the 20th century that members of the public would have come to Wimbledon in large numbers armed with Kodak Brownie box cameras and taken their own snapshots. In the intervening period, from the early 1880s through to the mid-1920s, the professional photographer held sway at Wimbledon.

Wimbledon's Postcard Tradition

In the first decade of the 20th century postcard-sized photographs of players and general views of The All England Club's grounds went on sale at Wimbledon during The Championships. It was the start of a Wimbledon tradition that now spans more than a century, and even today few communications are more welcome than a short greeting handwritten onto the back of a card bearing the evocative 'SW19' postmark.

Sometime between 1903 and 1910 the Wimbledon authorities allowed a professional photographer to work regularly inside the grounds at Worple Road, taking portrait photographs of players competing in the Lawn Tennis Championships, and general views of The All England Club's grounds. We know from the players' appearance and demeanour that the photographs were probably taken before rather than after their matches, but we do not know who the first regular Wimbledon photographer was, or indeed if the duties were shared amongst several photographers on a rota basis.

The resultant images were printed as photo-postcards by E. Trim & Co. of Wimbledon, a local printing and stationery firm based just a few hundred yards away from The All England Club in Wimbledon town centre, near the railway station. Picture postcards were hugely popular at the time, so much so that the Kodak company manufactured and distributed pre-printed postcard stationery, thus making local, small-scale production of photo-postcards relatively straightforward. Kodak had also just launched the soon-to-be iconic Brownie box camera, but in the age before amateur photography really took off postcards were still all the rage.

Advances in printing at that time had made it possible for postcards to be produced very quickly. It is quite possible that a photograph taken at Wimbledon one day could be on sale there as a high-quality photo-postcard the next.

It is not known what commercial arrangements the firm of E. Trim & Co. made with The All England Club, but these photo-postcards were, almost certainly, Wimbledon's first items of retail merchandise. It is probable that Trim sold his photo-postcards from a table inside the compact grounds at Worple Road, but the precise retailing arrangements and location are not known. Certainly some protection would have been needed against the rain.

It was not until 1922 when The All England Lawn Tennis Club moved to Church Road that dedicated space was set aside for a retail shop from which Edwin Trim and Co. sold 'Photographs of the Players' each year during Wimbledon fortnight. Even then, it was only a temporary structure. ◐

Early Photography at Wimbledon

The story of photography at Wimbledon dates back to the fourth staging of The Championships in 1880. The earliest known photograph appears on page 12 of the book *Fifty Years of Wimbledon: The Story of the Lawn Tennis Championships* by Arthur Wallis Myers, published by the proprietors of *The Field* on behalf of The All England Lawn Tennis and Croquet Club in 1926. It shows the scene during the 1880 Singles Challenge Round match between the Reverend John Hartley, the successful defending champion, and Herbert Lawford, who would go on to become champion himself seven years later.

The photograph is credited to 'A.H. Fry'. **Allen Hastings Fry** (1847–1931) was a Brighton-based professional photographer who made lengthy photographic trips by bicycle, including several visits to the National Rifle Association's annual meeting which was held on Wimbledon Common from 1860 to 1889, prior to the move to Bisley where it continues to the present day.

Close study of Fry's photograph of the scene around Wimbledon's Centre Court in 1880 reveals that it has been carefully composed and the image extensively retouched. At that time, when photography was still relatively new, it was normal practice for photographic studios to employ retouching artists as well as photographers.

Top left:
Dorothea Douglass
(later Mrs Lambert Chambers)

Top right:
Herbert Roper Barrett

Bottom right:
Laurie Doherty

Centre:
Cecil Parke

Bottom left:
Charlotte Sterry
(née Cooper)

Russells of Wimbledon

Fifty Years of Wimbledon is a wonderful illustrated record of the Worple Road years, and contains many interesting early photographs, of which two in particular are helpful in plotting the evolution of photography at Wimbledon. Both were taken in 1883, the first during the Challenge Round of The Championships and the second a few days later when Britain's William and Ernest Renshaw defeated another pair of brothers, America's C.M. and J.S. Clark, in what Wallis Myers described as 'The First International Match at Wimbledon'.

Both images show players poised for action near the net, and are shot from the same elevated position in a corner of the Centre Court, just outside the playing area. The players are clearly aware that their picture is being taken, and appear to be following the directions of the photographer. This high degree of professionalism bore fruit, as the resultant images are first class, both in quality and composition. Wallis Myers credits these photographs to 'Russell', which may well be a reference to the family firm of J. Russell and Sons of Chichester, founded in 1858 by James Russell (1809–1889).

James Russell was a pioneering photographer who founded his first studio in Chichester, West Sussex in 1858. His three sons joined the firm, and during the 1870s the business expanded steadily, opening further studios in various Sussex and Surrey towns including Bognor, Lewes, Littlehampton, Worthing and Petworth.

In 1881 Russell's youngest son **John Lemmon Russell** (1846–1915) travelled to London to look for

An early photocard by Russells of Wimbledon

opportunities to expand the business, and during the next decade he successfully opened new branches in Baker Street, Brecknock Road, Brompton Road, Tufnell Park and, in around 1883, a studio on the corner of Worple Road in Wimbledon. For this reason it is highly likely that he, or a member of his staff, took the two 1883 Wimbledon photographs which appear in *Fifty Years of Wimbledon*. It is also possible that Russell or his staff later went on to take some of the tennis photographs published as postcards by Edwin Trim, as the latter's premises at 20 Hill Road were only a few yards from Russell's studio.

Photographs were taken at Wimbledon throughout the 1880s and 1890s, but very few seem to have made it into print. Six photographs from the period appear in the book, including those credited to Fry and Russell, and *Black and White* magazine published an illustrated report with three photographs of The Championship matches in its issue of 28th July 1894. Apart from these images, most magazine covers and articles from the late 19th century are illustrated with sketches and cartoons rather than photographs.

J. Russell and Sons went on to operate Wimbledon's leading photographic studio for more than 120 years, and the company still exists today, based in nearby Morden. ◎

Edwin J. Trim & Co.

And so we come to the dawning of the 20th century, and here for the first time we encounter the name 'Trim', destined to forever be associated with the iconic series of photo-postcards sold at Wimbledon during the 1900s, 1910s, 1920s and 1930s. In *Fifty Years of Wimbledon*, a 1901 photograph of Arthur Gore and a 1902 photograph of Laurie Doherty, the Wimbledon champions in those years, are both credited to 'Trim', as are three other photographs later in the book. The style and composition of these images is very similar to early Wimbledon photo-postcards of players such as Doherty, Cecil Parke and Herbert Roper Barrett: a posed, full-body shot, rackets in hand, with the ivy-clad wall of the Worple Road clubhouse providing a contrasting backdrop to the player, who is invariably dressed in all-white tennis clothing.

Edwin James Trim (1863–1952) was a local printer and stationer who, on his father's death in 1888, took over the running of the family's printing and stationery business. The Wimbledon Printing Works at 30 Homefield Road, Wimbledon Village had originally been established by C.F. Haughton in 1862, with the Trim family taking it over two years later when they moved up to Wimbledon from Somerset. In the early years of the 20th century the firm had two premises: the steam print works at 30 Homefield Road, where the family also resided, and a stationer's shop at 20 Hill Road, in Wimbledon town centre.

Edwin J. Trim, printer and publisher

Edwin Trim was an early adopter of new technology and an energetic and imaginative entrepreneur who was well known and well liked in the Wimbledon local community. An active sportsman, ardent Methodist and a dedicated supporter of local charities, he published *Trim's Wimbledon and Merton Directory* from 1880 to 1909.

Trim's earliest known work for The All England Lawn Tennis Club was a large letterpress poster produced to advertise the 1893 Lawn Tennis Championships. The small print at the foot of the poster reads 'Printed by Edwin Trim at "The Wimbledon Printing Works"'. It is not known if printed tickets were issued for

Wimbledon at this time, but if they were it is highly likely that Trim would have printed them, for the company was printing tickets for other local community events as early as 1888.

Edwin Trim and Co. printed the official programmes for The Championships from 1905 to 1923. Around this time, the company also produced the first known Wimbledon photo-postcard, a view of a Ladies' Singles match played on the Centre Court during the 1903 Championships.

The Trim photo-postcard era lasted more than three decades, during which time hundreds of different designs were produced and many thousands of postcards sold. With just a few exceptions Trim's postcards nearly always featured photographs taken at Wimbledon, and almost always bore the company's name, either embossed on the front or printed on the front or back in order to assert copyright over the images used.

Many of Trim's postcards bore the featured player's name accompanied by a unique reference number with a single letter prefix, for example 'A9. Miss Joan Ridley', 'T90 D. Budge' and 'W103 Senorita De Alvarez', but despite extensive research no one has yet been able to understand exactly how this numbering system works. Some letters relate to particular years, but not all. It is a mystery.

There is no evidence that Edwin James Trim was actually a photographer himself. All Trim's advertising refers solely to the company's printing, publishing, bookbinding and stationery

Chaplin Jones of Kingston upon Thames

services, with no mention of photography, which suggests that he sourced his images from local photographers, possibly including John Lemmon Russell and his staff. Photographers are not credited on the postcards, which bear just the Trim company name.

In 1924 Edwin James Trim was approaching retirement and his only son Frank became a partner in the family firm. However, when Frank Trim died at just 51 years of age in May 1938 the company's long association with The All England Club came to an abrupt end. The Wimbledon tennis postcards produced in 1938 and 1939 came from a new supplier, City Press Photo Agency of 199, The Strand, London. The Trim era at Wimbledon was over, although the company continued to trade in the town until 1959.

Edwin James Trim died in 1952 at the age of 89. He had been the driving force behind the production of thousands of high-quality Wimbledon tennis posters, programmes and postcards, many of which survive to the present day in the hands of private collectors and in the collection of the Wimbledon Lawn Tennis Museum.

At his funeral a speaker paid this fulsome tribute: 'If ever there was a Wimbledon man it was he. He came to Wimbledon when he was a small boy, grew up with the town, and printed books about it. Wimbledon he loved, and would refer to it at all times as his little village, for a village he once knew it was.' ◓

For a brief period from around 1925 to 1927 the credit 'Chaplin-Jones, Kingston-Thames' appeared on the front of the photo-postcards sold at Wimbledon. **Chaplin Jones** was a portrait photographer and miniature painter whose studio was at 9 Surbiton Park Terrace, half a mile from Kingston town centre, where Edwin J. Trim and his brother Alfred Miller Trim had opened a second branch of their Wimbledon-based stationery business in 1896.

It seems that printer Trim and photographer Jones entered into a short-lived business relationship, and the Wimbledon postcards produced during that period are both distinctive in appearance and highly sought after by collectors. In the late 1920s the old order was restored, however, and the Trim name returned to the front of the cards.

World War II brought a six-year suspension of The Championships, and when play resumed in 1946 another new name appeared on Wimbledon's postcards: S.M.A. Photos. At first S.M.A.'s cards were printed onto postcard paper bearing the name and address of their pre-war predecessors City Press, but when this ran out S.M.A.'s cards were printed onto plain photographic card, signalling the start of a period when plain-backed postcard-sized photographs replaced postcards at Wimbledon. Many customers continued to use these photographs as postcards, however, by simply drawing a line down the middle of the plain side to separate the message from the address and popping them in the post as before. ◓

The Cole Family of Beckenham

The black and white photographs sold at Wimbledon during the 1950s and 60s were not just taken at Wimbledon, but also at other tournaments on the British summer grass-court circuit. These photographs bear no clues to the identities of the photographers and printers, but a strong possibility is that they were taken by **Arthur Cole** (1920–2001), one of the pioneers of tennis photography who reputedly took his first tennis shots when still a schoolboy in the mid-1930s. Nearly all of the photographs were taken at the pre-Wimbledon tournaments at Beckenham (where Arthur lived), Eastbourne, Hurlingham, Surbiton and Queen's Club, all of which Cole's meticulous records show he attended during the 1950s and 60s.

Arthur and his son **Michael Cole** definitely took the photographs that were sold at Wimbledon during the 1970s and 80s, first as black and white prints and then, from the late 1970s through to the mid-1980s,

Michael Cole

as lithographically printed colour postcards. These cards were published by Le-Roye Productions, the Cole family's photographic business. Michael explains the origin of the company's name: 'Arthur went to Roland Garros in the late 1950s or early 1960s and whilst out walking saw a shop called "Le-Roye". He took a photograph of the shop, liked the name, and then used it for his own business.' Photographs credited

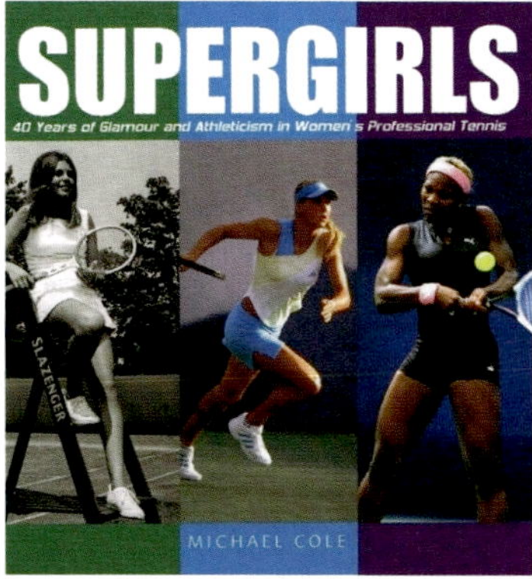

Supergirls book by Michael Cole, 2008

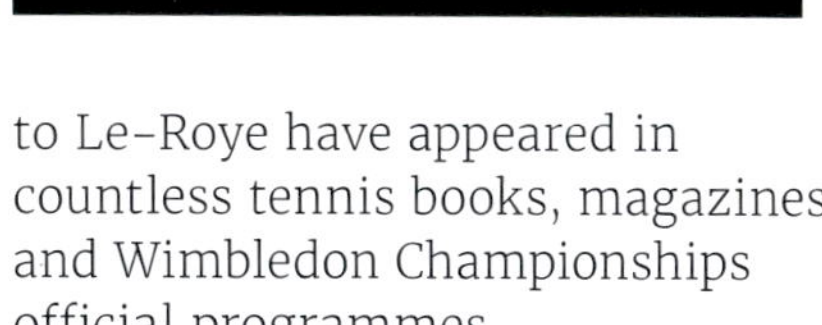

Arthur Cole, late 1940s

to Le-Roye have appeared in countless tennis books, magazines, and Wimbledon Championships official programmes.

Other members of the Cole family were involved at Wimbledon, too. Arthur's daughter **Suzie Cole** was a journalist for *Tennis World* magazine, founded by Arthur in the 1960s, and his wife **Hazel Cole** worked in the shop selling photographs, books and magazines each year during Wimbledon fortnight.

Arthur and Hazel Cole retired to Cornwall in the mid-1980s, at which point Le-Roye ceased to supply postcards to Wimbledon. Michael Cole continued to take photographs there, covering every Wimbledon Championships from 1969 until his retirement in 2014. Like his father before him, Michael became renowned as one of the world's leading tennis photographers. When the new Media Centre opened in 2000 at Wimbledon, Michael was given locker No.1. The Le-Roye photographic archive now resides at the Wimbledon Lawn Tennis Museum. 🎾

Hazel Cole and Stanley Hawkins

Recent Times

Up to the mid-1980s two families, the Trims and the Coles, provided most of the postcards and photographs sold at Wimbledon. After that time a number of publishers supplied Wimbledon with postcards, namely: Beric Tempest of St. Ives, Cornwall (1986); Leonard Lawrence of Hampton, Middlesex (1987); Clifford Frost Publications of Wimbledon (1988 to 1997); and Sporting Titles of London (1997 to 2004).

Several leading photographers took the pictures that were used including Tommy Hindley and Clive Brunskill, the latter working first for the Allsport agency and then Getty Images.

Since 2004 The All England Club has taken the production of postcards in-house, slimming down the range to just a few top stars and general views, and increasing the price gradually from 30p per postcard in 2004 to 90p in 2019.

In 2015 Vision Sports Publishing of Kingston upon Thames produced 'The Wimbledon Postcard Collection', a one-off set of 50 Wimbledon view postcards in an attractive presentation box.

The arrangements for selling postcards have changed considerably over the years. The original Edwin Trim shop continued in operation, in various guises, until the opening of the Wimbledon Lawn Tennis Museum in 1977, when it was replaced by a much larger retail shop next to the Tea Lawn. For a period during the 1990s and 2000s postcards were sold from a hexagonal wooden booth near the north-east corner of the Centre Court, opposite what is now Gate 4. This arrangement continued until 2005, when the new Wimbledon Lawn Tennis Museum opened along with various satellite shops around the grounds.

A visit to Wimbledon in December 2019 revealed that there were no postcards on sale other than the last few presentation boxes produced by Vision Sports. However, at the time of writing, a small new range is being produced, so the Wimbledon postcard tradition stretching back more than 110 years is still alive! ⚲

Wimbledon's Postcard Publishers 1905–1996

Beals Wright, USA, photographed in 1905,
1907 or 1910
Edwin Trim & Co., Wimbledon

Ray Casey, USA, photographed in 1925
Chaplin Jones, Kingston upon Thames

Kay Stammers, photographed in 1938 or 1939
City Press Photo Agency, The Strand

Betty Nuthall, photographed in 1946
SMA Photos

Hana Mandlikova, photographed in 1981
Le-Roye Productions, Beckenham

Conchita Martinez, photographed in 1994
Clifford Frost Publications, Wimbledon

CHAPTER 10
The Art of Wimbledon

KENNETH REED

T he Art of Wimbledon is not found on gallery walls, but in advertisements, on tournament posters and on the covers of books, catalogues, magazines and a host of other ephemeral publications. With its beguiling blend of athleticism, fashion and tradition, Wimbledon has from its earliest days been a compelling subject for artists and illustrators.

From the very first Championships in 1877 creative people have sought to capture the grace and style of the players who perform annually on the verdant lawns of The All England Lawn Tennis Club. From its origins in Victorian England, lawn tennis was seen as a symbol of aspiration, and as a result was seized upon by advertisers wishing to sell their products and services to the masses. Tennis is rare amongst the major sports in providing women and men the opportunity to play and socialise together, and tennis imagery is the perfect vehicle to advertise holiday destinations, hotels, and travel by rail and air.

The early days of the 20th century saw a surge of growth in travel and tourism, and railway stations were the ideal places in which to display promotional material. Whilst commuters waited for rush-hour trains, posters made them think longingly of trout fishing in the Scottish Highlands or winter skiing in the French Alps. Railway companies in Britain and abroad began to commission artists to create appealing designs for their advertising posters, and lawn tennis was a popular theme used to sell a diverse range of products from biscuits, brandy and bicycles through to car tyres, coffee and Coca-Cola.

In Britain, celebrated poster artist Tom Purvis produced a striking design entitled 'Harrogate – The British Spa' which featured an Edwardian couple playing mixed doubles whilst their fashionable friends looked on. At around the same time, leading Belgian poster artist Roger Broders produced a superb depiction of the Monte-Carlo Country Club for the Paris Lyon Méditerranée railway. Both these famous posters – like many others produced during the 1920s and 30s – featured a combination of leisurely exercise, sophisticated onlookers and an attractive resort backdrop. ⊘

Shop counter
advertisement,
circa 1930s

Early Posters

Wimbledon's first known advertising poster was produced in 1893 on a letterpress. Prior to the 20th century, letterpress printing was the primary means of printing and distributing information. Showing basic information such as dates, prices and travel information only, this poster bore no illustration. However, the early years of the Wimbledon Championships in the late-Victorian era coincided with advancements in lithographic printing which would soon make it possible for art images to be reproduced in print. French artists Jules Cheret and Henri de Toulouse Lautrec were the pioneers, and during the 1880s the streets of Paris were redecorated nightly with advertising posters bearing their work. So popular were these posters that people used to steal them under cover of darkness, before the paste was dry.

Cheret and Toulouse Lautrec influenced a generation of commercial artists across the globe, and in Britain the momentum for 'public art' received a huge boost in the early years of the 20th century from **Frank Pick** (1878–1941), Managing Director of the London Underground and later the first Chief Executive of London Transport. He fervently believed that the rapidly expanding network needed to communicate with and reassure the travelling public. This belief manifested itself in everything from the design of stations through to the provision of maps and

Letterpress poster printed by Edwin Trim of Wimbledon, 1893 by courtesy of the Wimbledon Lawn Tennis Museum

passenger information, and Pick commissioned some of the leading commercial artists of the day to design posters for the Underground. Amongst these were Tom Eckersley, Sybil Andrews and Herry Perry, each of whom designed numerous images for the Underground in the 1920s and 30s including posters advertising tube travel to the Wimbledon Championships.

For more than a quarter of a century Frank Pick was the leading commissioner of public art in Britain. His objective was to get everyone in London travelling by public transport, and through his patronage, the

early careers of many commercial artists flourished. Pick had the walls of stations to decorate, along with lifts, escalators, platforms and railway carriages. The subjects of his commissions included London's parks and theatres, West End shopping and major sporting events. The Derby at Epsom, Cricket at Lord's and The Oval, Rugby at Twickenham, the FA Cup Final at Wembley, the Boat Race – all were depicted on eye-catching colour posters that were seen every day by millions of travellers.

When The All England Club moved to Church Road in 1922, the recently electrified District Railway was the obvious choice for spectators wishing to travel to Wimbledon from the West End and the City, and Frank Pick's posters made this abundantly clear. They told travellers what they needed to know: the dates of the tournament and which stations to use. The imagery was alluring, and the graphics were simple and clear. The Lawn Tennis Championships, Davis Cup and Wightman Cup at Wimbledon were the subject of more than 20 original posters commissioned by Pick between 1922 and 1939. 🎾

Posters with a Purpose

Throughout the world, railway companies became major commissioners of poster art. In France, skilled artists such as Roger Broders, Pean and Cassandre produced innovative and colourful poster designs which not only succeeded in getting people to travel but also made the posters themselves immensely popular. In the 1920s and 30s, their posters became accepted as a legitimate form of art, in styles drawing on the best of Art Nouveau and Art Deco.

There was never any doubt about the artistic merit of London Transport's posters. From 1911 onwards Frank Pick regularly donated batches of new creations to London's Victoria and Albert Museum, which today holds a collection of 1800 London Transport posters. Many of the images are now considered design classics and are highly sought after by collectors. In 2012 an auction sale of nearly 400 original posters from the London Transport Museum's collection took place at Christie's in South Kensington. Entitled 'Posters With A Purpose', the auction offered duplicates from the Museum's collection to raise funds for conservation, restoration and new acquisitions. During the marathon seven-and-a-half-hour sale 326 posters were sold and over £740,000 was raised.

Of particular interest to tennis collectors were the posters advertising travel to the Wimbledon Championships. These urged spectators to go by Underground to Southfields or South Wimbledon stations, and 'thence by bus to the Ground'. Eleven of the tennis posters were of the small size used for advertising inside railway carriages, and the remaining three were of the larger size displayed at stations.

Of the 14 tennis posters offered, nine exemplified the classic characteristics now associated with the Art Deco period of the 1920s and 30s: contrasting blocks of vivid colour, strong geometric lines and stylish figures with featureless flat-colour faces. Images such as Andre Edouard Marty's 'Wimbledon Tennis' and Charles Burton's 'Wimbledon' are familiar to tennis aficionados having been reproduced many times over the years in postcard and greeting card form. When displayed together the original posters had a remarkable freshness, due in equal measure to the striking designs, vivid colours and distinctive period graphics. The Art Deco tennis posters in the auction had the highest pre-sale estimates and achieved considerably higher sale prices than the more traditional images.

The earliest tennis poster in the sale was Aldo Cosomati's 'Wimbledon Tournament' from 1922, the year of the inaugural Championship Meeting at The All England Lawn Tennis Club's new Church Road ground. This was also the first year in which the Underground was the most convenient way for spectators to travel to The Championships, the old Worple Road ground having been better served by the overground Southern Railway which ran within 100 yards of the Centre Court with a special halt for passengers to alight during the tournament. The text on Cosomati's poster is minimal, but even in this first year at the new location mentions the provision of 'Special Buses to & from the Station and Ground'.

Herry Perry's 1931 tube carriage poster measured just 10" x 13", but quickly sold for £2,400. Perry's image showed a grass tennis court viewed from the perspective of a uniformed ball boy, and employed the then-popular flat-colour technique pioneered by European poster artists such as Roger Broders, whose iconic 'Monte-Carlo' poster for the Paris Lyon Méditerranée railway had been produced just a year earlier.

Sybil Andrews's 1933 Wimbledon poster carried the highest pre-sale estimate of the tennis posters at £6,000–8,000, but was sold for a remarkable £20,000, possibly a world record for a tennis-themed poster.

'Posters With A Purpose' had brought together the Art Deco style of the jazz era, popular subjects such as sport, fashion and travel, and the skills of some of the 20th century's leading poster artists. 🎾

Postcard set published by Christie's auction house, 2012

Modern Posters

The outbreak of World War II in 1939 saw the end of the first golden era of Wimbledon posters, but the medium was revived in the 1980s when The All England Lawn Tennis Club began commissioning commercial artists to create artwork promoting The Championships. Between 1986 and 1993 a series of promotional posters was produced, and from 1994 until 2011 a superb series of annual posters on high-quality paper was available to the public in the Wimbledon Museum Shop.

With one or two exceptions these posters depicted the spirit of Wimbledon's garden-party origins in modern settings, a charming juxtaposition that really caught the public's imagination. The posters were of uniform size (20 x 28 inches or 50 x 70 centimetres) and were printed on the same heavy art paper each year, making them ideal for visitors to The Championships to collect and display. Contributing artists included John Davies (1992, 1993, 1995, 1996, 1999, 2001), Peter Welton (1997), Michael Whittlesea (1998), Andrew Bylo (2000), Matthew Cook (2002, 2003, 2007), Andrew Davidson (2005, 2009 and 2011), Alastair Taylor (2006), Christine Berrington (2008) and Eileen Hogan (2010).

Official tournament posters are still produced each year at Wimbledon, and since 2012 a series of innovative methods have been used to select the designers and create the imagery. Whilst individually interesting and often attractive, these posters have varied in size from year to year and have been produced on lighter paper, making them less attractive to collectors.

The 2013 official Wimbledon poster was designed by Priya Eardley, winner of a competition on BBC TV's *Blue Peter*. Part of Priya's prize was a guided tour of The All England Lawn Tennis Club with chairman Philip Brook, and millions of TV viewers saw the delighted eight-year-old standing next to her framed poster near the players' entrance to Centre Court. Such is the power of TV that all the posters disappeared from Wimbledon's on-site shops within days of the broadcast.

The 2015 Wimbledon poster was based on a 3-D 'paper graphic' entitled 'Wimbledon Awaits' by London-based Russian artist Yulia Brodskaya. This striking image had at its centre the date 29.06.15, emphasising

that The Championships had moved to a new position in the tennis calendar, one week later than before. The 2018 Wimbledon poster was designed by IBM 'Watson' technology which created a photo-mosaic from 8,400 smaller images to achieve an eye-catching visual effect.

Wimbledon 1993 official poster, with artwork by John Davies

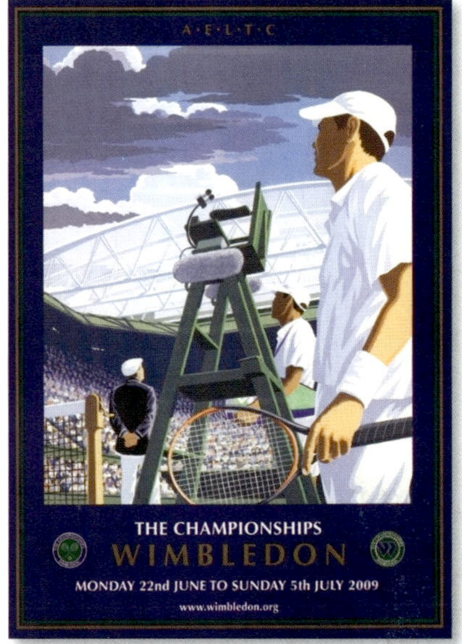

Wimbledon 2009 official poster, with artwork by Andrew Davidson

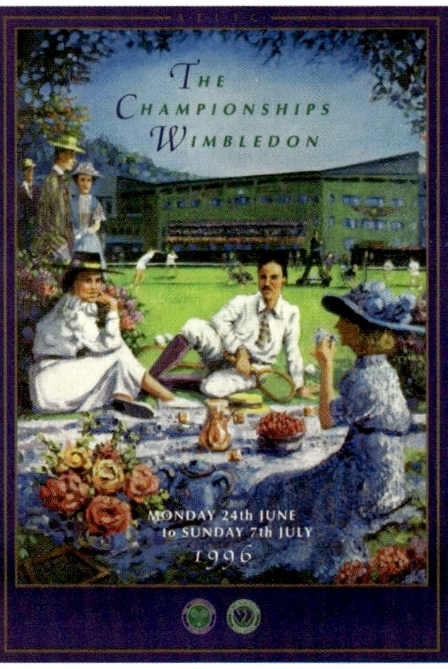

Wimbledon 1996 official poster, with artwork by John Davies

Powerful Posters

In 2016 the Wimbledon Lawn Tennis Museum mounted a special poster exhibition entitled 'Powerful Posters – Tennis and Advertising 1893–2015'. The Museum has a collection of 850 tennis-themed posters, and included in the exhibition were the famous Athena 'Tennis Girl' poster by Graham Elliott, displayed alongside the tennis dress designed by Carol Knotts and worn by her friend Fiona Butler in the original photograph, and an early Wimbledon Championships poster produced by Edwin Trim of Wimbledon in 1893. This rare letterpress poster was found behind an old mirror and sent in by a member of the public with the message, 'please throw this away if it is of no use to you!'

The exhibition was conceived and produced by Anna Renton, the Museum's Curator from 2014 to 2018. Anna was previously at the London Transport Museum in Covent Garden, home to one of the world's major poster collections.

'Powerful Posters' was the third poster exhibition staged by the Museum, following 'Continental Posters 1900–1939' in 1990 and 'Striking Images – The Golden Years of the Tennis Poster 1890–1940' in 2003.

Of all the imagery and ephemera spawned by the game of Lawn Tennis and the Wimbledon Championships, posters have had the greatest impact on the wider public consciousness. Iconic poster images live long in the memory, but by their transient nature the physical posters often have a very short lifespan, and those that do survive are difficult to store in perfect condition. 

Original Art

Midlands-based artist **Bob Everitt**'s depiction of the scene at Worple Road on the first day of the inaugural Wimbledon Championships in 1877 is one of the most recent additions to a strong tradition of original Wimbledon artworks. It is also one of the most unusual. Inspired by a contemporary sketch by Horace William Petherick (1839–1919), a Surrey-based artist, Everitt's painting is significant because, unlike most of Wimbledon's pictures, it is a present-day interpretation of a scene from the past. It brings Petherick's important pencil sketch to life in vibrant colour, thus revealing to the 21st-century observer the true gaiety and vitality of that first Championship meeting.

Bob has written several books on tennis history and collectables, and it was during the two decades spent working on his latest book *The Birth of Lawn Tennis*, co-written with fellow-historian Richard Hillway, that he had the idea to recreate Petherick's small pencil sketch as a large colour illustration. 'I developed a strong desire to create an image which might allow us to view a scene of that historic first day of the tournament in full colour, from the viewpoint of the original artist.'

Everitt started on his painting in 2008, working on it between professional assignments as a graphic illustrator. 'I resolved to attempt to reproduce the image as a large, full-colour oil on canvas illustration – in an attempt to capture the atmosphere and colour of the scene as though we were making a time-travelling visit to this historic event.' The large stretched canvas measures 31" x 24" (79 x 60 centimetres) and the painting took over 400 hours' work spread over ten years to complete. Finally, in 2018, the finished work was delivered to the Wimbledon Lawn Tennis Museum where it now resides, along with a framed copy of Petherick's original sketch.

Wimbledon, 1877 by Bob Everitt

Lawn Tennis,
acrylic on canvas,
1999
by Michael Copus

During the 19th century there was little photography at Wimbledon, so paintings and sketches of the early Championships provide a valuable historical record. 'The Lawn Tennis Championship Match at Wimbledon', circa 1888, by Arthur Hopkins, younger brother of the poet Gerard Manley Hopkins, is one such example (see pages 26 and 27).

From the early 20th century photographers captured the Wimbledon scene, although the Wimbledon Lawn Tennis Museum also has several paintings from this period in its art collection. Most of these depict scenes inside the Centre Court after the move to Church Road in 1922. ◍

Later in the 20th century one anonymous artist's work brought pleasure to thousands of visitors to The Championships and the Wimbledon Lawn Tennis Museum. **Michael Villeroy Copus** (1936–2000) was a mural painter who created the Victorian and Edwardian tennis scenes which were the backgrounds to the showcase displays at the original Wimbledon Museum, along with decorative wall panels in the Museum Tea Room, the Aorangi Pavilion and other locations within The All England Lawn Tennis Club.

Copus was a very talented artist who worked in his Wandsworth studio and in situ at Wimbledon.

During the 'off-season' Michael could sometimes be found on his hands and knees in the Wimbledon Museum, brush or scissors in hand, making final adjustments to one of his large canvasses. His work had a misty, ethereal quality, with white-clad lawn tennis players seeming to hover against backgrounds of green lawns, clusters of trees and pillared walls.

When the original Wimbledon Lawn Tennis Museum and Tea Room closed their doors in 2005 Michael Copus's murals were carefully taken down and placed in storage. ◍

Centre Court, 2006
by Luis Morris

Another skilled artist who has made an important contribution to the art of Wimbledon is Hampshire-based **Luis Morris**. A former banknote designer, he began his tennis art career in the 1990s, producing a series of portraits of tennis players during the golden era of Boris Becker, Tim Henman, Steffi Graf, Andre Agassi, Martina Hingis and Pete Sampras. These were reproduced as prints which Luis and his partner Jane Williams exhibited and sold at British tournament venues.

Early in the 21st century a number of his works were purchased by the Wimbledon Lawn Tennis Museum, following which Luis was commissioned to capture the scene inside the Centre Court prior to the commencement of the three-year project to fit a new retractable roof. He took photographs and made preparatory sketches during the 2006 Championships and the finished work, a giant red monochrome painting, brilliantly captured the atmosphere inside the Centre Court in the years prior to the opening of the new roof in 2009.

In the book *Four Artists and a Poet – Views of The Championships 2006–2010*, Luis talked about the work: 'My project fell naturally into two phases. Firstly, I had to help record for posterity the iconic old structure, which involved gaining an appreciation of how the roof was put together, and also trying to convey on canvas the feeling of what it was like to sit in that space. The end product, a red monochrome painting based on countless photographs as well as sketches done in situ, took on quite a romantic air.'

In addition to the main painting, Luis's commission involved creating a series of artistic 'snapshots' as construction of the new retractable roof progressed. The artist takes up the story: 'The second task was to draw the assembly of the new sliding roof. These drawings, scribbled down in pen as the giant components were hoisted and lowered into position, attempt to convey something of the urgency and excitement of how it felt to stand there and witness Centre Court assuming its new shape.'

Such was the success of the project, Luis Morris was back at Wimbledon a decade later to create an artistic record of the new No.1 Court roof construction. ◐

Limited Edition Prints

In the last quarter of the 20th century a number of artists painted appealing pictures of Wimbledon which were reproduced as signed limited edition prints. These included 'The Centre Court, Wimbledon' by Edward Dawson (1983), 'No.5 Court, Wimbledon' by Kenneth Reed, FRSA (1986, pictured on pages 242 and 243), and 'Centre Court, Wimbledon' by Peter Watson (1990).

Kenneth Reed of Ponteland in Northumberland visited Wimbledon with his wife during the 1985 Championships, the year of Boris Becker's first victory. Whilst walking around the outside courts the couple took some photographs, and on returning home Ken made his highly evocative painting using just the photographs for reference. Writing in 2011 Alan

Above
'The Centre Court, Wimbledon' by Edward Dawson, 1983

Below:
'Centre Court, Wimbledon' by Peter Watson, 1990

Reed, Ken's son, also an artist, said: 'My dad has been a constant influence throughout my life. He trained as a graphic designer but would often be working on paintings in watercolour at home, usually on the dining room table. For the last thirty years he has become recognised as the leading golf artist in the world, capable of painting in a number of different mediums, including watercolour, oils and an Art Deco poster style.'

Yorkshire-born Peter Watson's painting features a scene from the 1990 Wimbledon Ladies' Singles Final between Martina Navratilova and Zina Garrison which Martina won 6–4, 6–1. The painting was done the same year. Peter described how the work was created: 'It can be quite difficult sometimes getting permission but I had a friend who was a debenture holder who invited me into his box and I took a lot of photographs from

different angles of all aspects of the stadium to get the view and detail I wanted. I was not there for the final but managed to work from press cuttings of pictures of the players as this was pre internet days!'

In 1993 Scottish artist Graeme W. Baxter created an image remarkably similar to Kenneth Reed's 1986 painting. Baxter's work was reproduced in a signed limited edition entitled 'The Championships, Wimbledon' bearing the official logo of The Championships, and was sold in the Wimbledon Museum Shop. Reed and Baxter are best known as golf artists, and their Wimbledon paintings show play in progress on Court No.5 with the imposing ivy-clad façade of the Centre Court in the background.

During the 1996 Championships the BBC filmed a documentary about the old No.1 Court which was scheduled for demolition later that year. In the film, Twickenham-based artist Jill Storey was shown working on a watercolour painting of the much-loved old stadium, and in 1997 the finished work was issued as a signed limited edition print with the title 'No.1 Court Wimbledon, June 1996'. ◓

The Art of Helen Wills

Helen Wills Moody (1905–1998), eight-times Wimbledon Ladies' Singles champion between 1927 and 1938, was one of the finest players ever to grace the Centre Court. She was also a talented artist whose paintings and sketches were featured in one-woman shows in London and New York.

Between 1927 and 1933 Helen was unbeaten in singles anywhere in the world, and did not lose even a single set. Throughout this time she produced sketches of the world's leading tennis players as well as still life and landscape paintings. Her work was of sufficiently high quality to attract the interest of leading art dealers and a wealthy patron in former US Senator James Duval Phelan.

Thirty-four of Helen's sketches appeared in her book *Tennis*, published by Scribners of New York in 1928. These are highly competent action portraits of leading players of the day including Bill Tilden, Suzanne Lenglen and Kitty Godfree.

Helen's first one-woman art show was held at the Cooling Gallery in London's Bond Street in June 1929, and was a success. It was the first of five such exhibitions in London and New York.

In her book *Helen Wills – Tennis, Art, Life* historian Jeanne Cherry wrote of Helen's second public exhibition in the spring of 1930:

'The show at Grand Central Galleries, New York City, which took place April 16th to 25th, was a huge success.' Frank Crowninshield, Editor of *Vanity Fair*, observed: 'What is especially notable is her ability to convey the sensation of an authentic and continuing motion; there being in them nothing static or posed.' In her autobiography *Fifteen-Thirty* Helen simply remarked: 'To my surprise every sketch sold.'

There is no doubt that Helen Wills Moody's celebrity as a tennis champion helped propel her art career, but that diminishes neither her artistic ability nor the significance of her body of work. She was truly multi-talented, for in addition to her careers in art and tennis she was also a successful journalist, writing and sketching for numerous publications including the *Oakland Tribune*, *The Sketch* and the *London Daily Mail*. For a number of years her newspaper columns were syndicated throughout the US. ◓

The Cartoonist's Art

From the late 19th century through to the outbreak of World War II cartoons played a major role in bringing Wimbledon to the masses. With its strict codes of dress and etiquette, lawn tennis was fertile ground for the skilled cartoonist, and each year during Wimbledon fortnight caricatures of the sport's leading personalities featured prominently in newspapers and periodical magazines.

PUNCH, or *The London Charivari* to give its full title, was an illustrated satirical magazine published weekly in London from 1841 to 2002. From 1880 through to 1941 the magazine regularly included humorous lawn tennis-themed cartoons in its issues produced around the time of the Wimbledon fortnight. *Punch*'s cartoonists often focused on gender politics, with women either portrayed as hapless romantics or virile athletes whose tennis abilities far exceeded those of their inadequate male mixed doubles partners.

Tom Webster (1886–1962) of the *Daily Mail* produced cartoons at breakneck speed during the 1920s and 30s, although with Wimbledon's relatively early 2pm starts he was under less pressure there than at boxing matches and other evening sporting events. His cartoons consisted of a series of little sketches linked by narrative captions. Webster liked to pick out and exaggerate players' features, foibles, mannerisms and attire. Men's baggy shorts, ladies' hemlines, big noses, grunting and groaning during play; all were highlighted day after day by Webster until the player in question was knocked out of the tournament.

H.M. Bateman (1887–1970) was one of Britain's leading cartoonists of the 1920s and 1930s, his work appearing regularly in such magazines as *Punch*, *The Tatler*, and *The Bystander*. He started drawing for publication when still at school and his cartoons of the Edwardian era were immensely popular. His pioneering strip cartoons, and the work he produced during the First World War, made him a household name. But it was a series of cartoons that began just after the war that really cemented his fame and made him the most celebrated humorous artist of his day. The 'Man Who …' cartoons described social misdemeanours and embarrassing offences against accepted custom and behaviour. The predicaments he described passed into the folklore of the nation and became known as 'Bateman situations'. One of his most enduringly popular sketches is 'Discovery of a Dandelion on the Centre Court at Wimbledon' which shows the scene of panic as a weed is spotted on Wimbledon's pristine lawn. ◍

'Discovery of a Dandelion on the Centre Court at Wimbledon' by H.M. Bateman

Confectionery box, circa 1920s

Cover Art

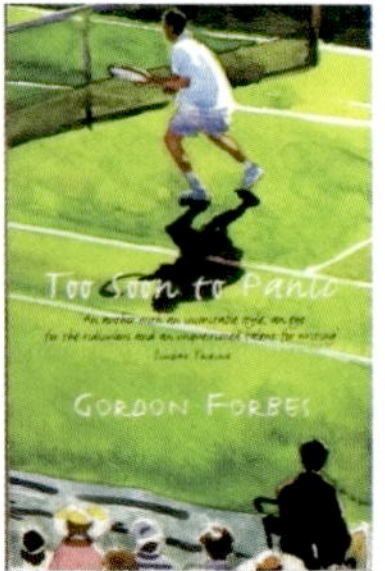

Cover artwork for *Too Soon to Panic* by Gordon Forbes (paperback edition, Harper Collins, 1997)

Some eye-catching original artworks have been created to decorate the covers of books, leaflets and magazines sold to the public at Wimbledon. These include the excellent front-cover paintings for Maurice Brady's book *Centre Court Story* (1957), and Dan Maskell's autobiography *From Where I Sit* (1988), the former by an unknown artist, the latter by Gwyn Hughes.

The front cover of the May 15, 2001 issue of the American magazine *Tennis Week*, edited by

Advertising and Packaging

The aspirational nature of tennis has resulted in many manufacturers and advertisers associating their products to lawn tennis in general and Wimbledon in particular. Wimbledon's pre-eminent position in the sporting world made it a byword for quality and excellence. For many years companies did not require a licence to exploit Wimbledon's name and good reputation, resulting in products with the word 'Wimbledon' being shown on their packaging and sometimes even included in their name. Examples include Huntley and Palmers 'Wimbledon Assorted Biscuits' and 'WIM-"BELL"-DON Flannels – The Trouser with a Guarantee'. The latter was produced around 1925, when traditional tennis flannels were facing competition from twill trousers which were said to be cooler and easier to launder.

Slazengers have been the official suppliers of the tennis balls used at the Wimbledon Championships since 1902, and as part of that long-running commercial relationship the company has occupied the prime advertising position on the outside back cover of the Wimbledon official programme every year since 1924. This has resulted in the creation of some imaginative original artworks which are highly evocative of the eras in which they were produced.

Another product closely associated with Wimbledon is Robinsons Barley Water. Reputedly first concocted by the Dressing Room staff at The All England Club in 1935 to ward off dehydration, the company's advertising for many years featured 'Old Hethers', a faithful retainer who would cheerfully deliver this most refreshing of summer drinks. This approach to advertising oozes traditional Britishness and the aspirational nature of lawn tennis.

Since World War II there has been a steady shift away from the use of original art in advertisements, modernity being better served by photography. ⊘

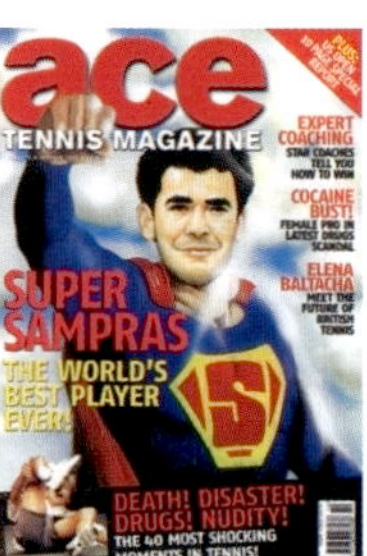

ACE Tennis magazine, UK, October 2002

Dust jacket illustration for Dan Maskell's autobiography (Willow Books, London, 1988)

Wimbledon Art Today

Tennis Week magazine, USA, May 2001

Eugene L. Scott, has a full-colour illustration of Wimbledon's new Millennium Building with Courts 3, 4 and 5 in the foreground. An unusual but eye-catching image was created for the front cover of *ACE Tennis* magazine (issue 70 October 2002). Seven-times Wimbledon champion Pete Sampras was depicted as Superman, which was highly appropriate as he had just won his 14th and final Grand Slam singles title at the 2002 US Open, a feat truly worthy of the original *Action Comics* hero. A more recent example of comic book art came when reigning Wimbledon champion Andy Murray guest-edited the 28th June 2014 issue of *The Beano*.

Under the direction of Club member Ian C. King, The All England Lawn Tennis Club is now very proactive in commissioning new works of art. An architect by profession, Ian became an All England Club member in 1967 and was a member of the Club's Long Term Planning Committee which conceived and oversaw the project to install a retractable roof over the Centre Court. As the roof construction proceeded the interior of the Centre Court was also refurbished, and Club Chairman Tim Phillips invited Ian to manage the internal decoration of the Clubhouse which is situated behind the Royal Box.

Ian King takes up the story: 'I was surprised by how few paintings and photographs of the Club's long history we had, especially compared with those comparable sports of cricket at Lord's and the collections at our famous golf clubs. The Museum has since been active in purchasing past works of art relevant to The Championships.

'We commenced to commission and purchase paintings and photographic wall hangings for the Clubhouse and throughout our Championship facilities, including several sculptures and other features.

'The artist Andrew Davidson designed the impressive glazed doors situated beneath Kipling's quotation which all players pass as they enter the Centre Court.

'Surprisingly, the Club had never celebrated the achievement of the five British ladies' singles champions so Ian Rank Broadley was commissioned to create the sculpture busts which are displayed either side of the Club entrance to join Fred Perry's statue by David Wynne displayed adjacent to the Debenture Holders' facilities.

'We introduced the concept of appointing each year a Championships Artist who produces paintings related to the tournament for display in the Club and helps create the Club's art collection. Many eminent artists' works are now displayed, along with engraved glassware and even some poetry!

'Matthew Cook started this project with a whole series of watercolours depicting aspects of our Championships. Eileen Hogan produced evocative oil paintings of our Members' Tea Lawn that now enhance our dining room. Andrew Fleming captured another special occasion, Roger Bannister handing to Tim Henman the Olympic torch surrounded by all the Club's executives and Committee Members.

'Many other talented artists now have their interpretations of the Wimbledon Championships displayed within our Pavilion and elsewhere in the Club. Sarah Frandsen manages our growing art collections which now includes many interesting wall displays and murals.'

Wimbledon in Print

WIMBLEDON 1993
WIMBLEDON 1994
WIMBLEDON 1995
WIMBLEDON 1996
HAZLL
HAZLL

Books are special. Books are important. In the case of books about tennis, they are a physical embodiment of a sport loved by millions. In the case of Wimbledon, printed books provide a tangible link between an illustrious past and a vibrant present, ensuring that the epic encounters and charismatic personalities of nearly a century and a half of tennis action on the lawns of SW19 will never be forgotten.

The books on Lawn Tennis published during the first three decades of the game's existence mainly contained information on the rules and how to play. It was not until 1903, when two of the most important books in the game's history, *R.F. and H.L. Doherty on Lawn Tennis* and *Lawn Tennis*

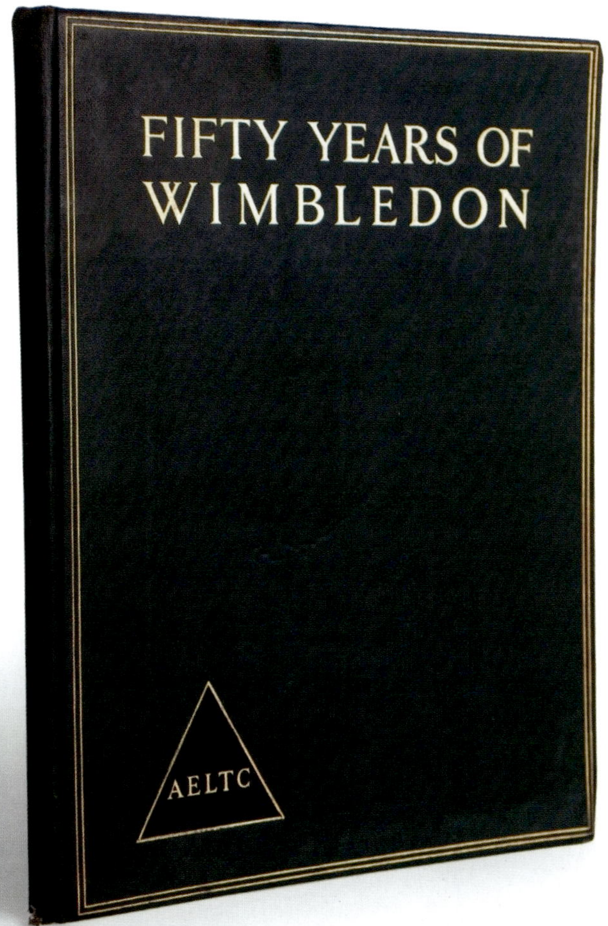

Fifty Years of Wimbledon by A. Wallis Myers. The first illustrated book about The Championships

at Home and Abroad by Arthur Wallis Myers, were published that Lawn Tennis began to build a strong bibliography. These were substantial volumes by well-known and respected authors, and they took the game to a broader readership than it had previously enjoyed. Reggie and Laurie Doherty won 17 Wimbledon Singles and Doubles titles between them, and rank high in the pantheon of Wimbledon's all-time greats. Arthur Wallis Myers was the Lawn Tennis Correspondent of *The Daily Telegraph*, and perhaps the finest wordsmith the game has known.

Anthony Wilding's *On the Court and Off*, published in 1912, marked the next stage of development as tennis literature approached adulthood. The twice-Wimbledon champion's book contained an entertaining mix of thoughts on playing the game and memories of tournaments and players he had encountered during his stellar career. Wilding's book must have sold in phenomenal numbers, for it was reprinted three times in the first year and seven times in all, although sadly the author did not live to see the last two of these editions as he had fallen whilst on active service in France during the First World War.

When peace was restored Lawn Tennis boomed, and there was huge growth in participation, both in clubs and on newly installed courts in public parks. The tennis books of the 1920s reflect this, with a considerable increase in the number of instructional books. Notable amongst these was *The Art of Lawn Tennis* by William T. Tilden, first published in Britain in 1920 and reprinted no fewer than nine times during the following 15 years. The author was of course the great 'Big Bill' Tilden, seven-times winner of the US National Singles title and Wimbledon champion in 1920, 1921 and 1930.

The 1920s also saw a considerable increase in the number of spectators attending the Wimbledon Championships, with three times as many people coming to the new ground at Church Road. With such a high level of interest, it was not surprising that books about the tournament started to appear. The first known book on the Wimbledon Championships is *The Lawn Tennis Championships Souvenir*, published in 1914. A copy of this is in the collection of the Kenneth Ritchie Library at The All England Lawn Tennis Club. Since 1914 more than 150 books have been written about Wimbledon, and from all these publications the works of five writers stand out. ◓

A. Wallis Myers

Arthur Wallis Myers (1878–1939), who liked to be known simply as Wallis Myers, was *The Daily Telegraph*'s Lawn Tennis Correspondent from 1909 to 1939. His detailed descriptive reports brought Wimbledon to life for thousands of devoted readers in the days before radio and television, and his annual player ranking lists were treated as de facto official world rankings. His work put *The Daily Telegraph* ahead of other newspapers in its coverage of The Championships, a status it retained throughout the 20th century.

In addition to his journalism, Wallis Myers edited *Ayres' Lawn Tennis Almanack* from 1908 to 1938 and wrote several important books on Lawn Tennis. These include *Lawn Tennis at Home and Abroad* (1903), *The Complete Lawn Tennis Player* (1908), *The Story of the Davis Cup* (1913), *Captain Anthony Wilding* (1916) and *Lawn Tennis: Its Principles and Practice* (1930). His finest work relating to Wimbledon is to be found in *Twenty Years of Lawn Tennis* (1921), *Fifty Years of Wimbledon* (1926) and *Great Lawn Tennis – Pen Pictures of Famous Matches* (1937).

Fifty Years of Wimbledon was commissioned by The All England Club to commemorate Wimbledon's 50th birthday. It is a fine illustrated work, produced in standard and deluxe editions, chronicling Wimbledon's first half-century year-by-year and setting these early Championships in their true social and historical context. This method was employed equally skilfully six decades later

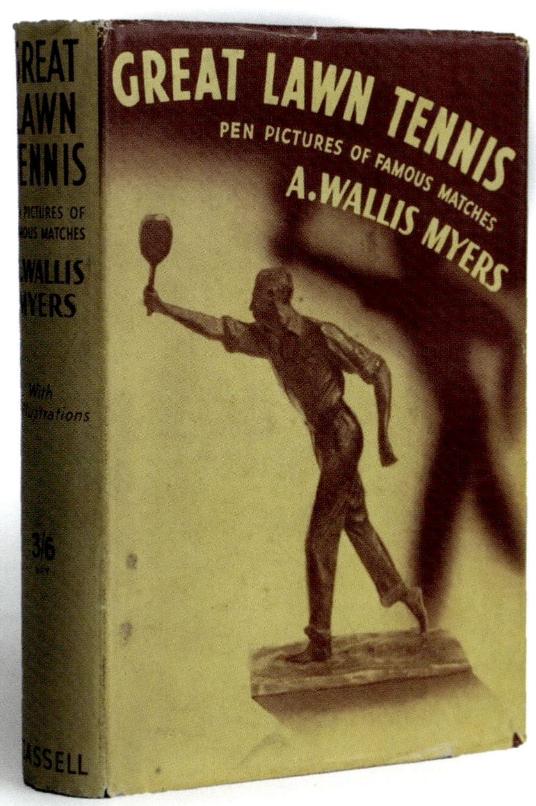

by John Barrett in his book *100 Wimbledon Championships – A Celebration*.

Memory's Parade (1932) is a fascinating autobiographical account of life in the first three decades of the 20th century. In 2004 his youngest daughter Prue published *A. Wallis Myers – A Testament to Tennis*, a charming little booklet sharing family stories and photographs. ◯

Lance Tingay's *Royalty and Lawn Tennis* was one of the Wimbledon Lawn Tennis Museum's first publications, in 1977

Lance Tingay

Lance Tingay (1915–1990) was *The Daily Telegraph*'s second distinguished Lawn Tennis Correspondent of the 20th century. He assumed the role when John Olliff, Wallis Myers's successor, died suddenly on his way to Wimbledon in June 1951 at the age of just 42.

Tingay's writing was very much in the Wallis Myers tradition, the hallmarks being a descriptive style and the confidence to express opinions based on his own deep knowledge of the game. When the tiebreak was first introduced at Wimbledon in 1971, Tingay, unimpressed, disdainfully described it as 'that sequence of abbreviated values'.

In addition to his journalism, Tingay wrote several books on lawn tennis, most notably *100 Years of Wimbledon* (1977). This fine illustrated history book contained more Wimbledon match results than had ever been published in a single volume before. His other books on the game included *Wimbledon Ladies – A Centenary Record* and *Wimbledon Men – A Hundred Championships 1877–1986*, both co-written with Alan Little, and *The Guinness Book of Tennis Facts and Feats* (1983).

Lance Tingay retired in 1981 and his complete Wimbledon reports are held in cuttings books at Wimbledon's Kenneth Ritchie Library. His career ran parallel with Dan Maskell's time in the BBC TV commentary box, and between them these two men did much to raise the profile and popularity of tennis in Britain. ◯

Sir John Smyth

If newspaper reports are set aside, **Sir John Smyth** (1893–1983) is probably the most-read author in Wimbledon's history. Between 1948 and 1973 he contributed over 300 Daily Articles to the Wimbledon Official Programme, at a time when it contained no other articles or features, just photographs, draw sheets and the Daily Order of Play. Smyth's articles were read by thousands of people each day as they queued for tickets and waited for play to start 'at 2p.m. precisely'.

Smyth also wrote about Lawn Tennis for *The Sunday Times* and was the author of four excellent books on the game, but it is his informative and entertaining articles in the Wimbledon Programme that earn his place amongst Wimbledon's most important writers. Many of the people who attended each year's Championships lost touch with the game during the intervening 50 weeks; Smyth's articles quickly brought them up to date. His recurring themes included 'It's Wimbledon Again' (on the First Monday), 'The World's Leading Women', (and Men), 'The Davis Cup', 'The Wightman Cup' and 'British Players at Wimbledon'. Despite the repetitiveness of the titles, the articles were always freshly written each year.

In addition to his regular subjects, Smyth also wrote about the history of the game in articles such as 'The Doherty Era' (Day 7, 1948), 'The Years of French Dominance at Wimbledon' (Day 10, 1973) and 'Comparing Yesterday with Today' (Day 11, 1974). Over a quarter of a century he wrote many times about the greats of the past, with the Doherty Brothers, Jean Borotra, Suzanne Lenglen and Bill Tilden appearing regularly in his articles.

Usually, but not always, the programme's front-cover photograph was of a player featured in Smyth's article that day. Smyth himself was pictured in the programme just once, in 1948 alongside British player Kay Menzies.

'Jackie' Smyth, as he was known to his friends, was a remarkable man: a hero in World War I; disgraced in World War II, but later exonerated; tennis correspondent for *The Sunday Times*; and a government minister under Winston Churchill and Anthony Eden during the 1950s. He was a man who, to paraphrase Rudyard Kipling, 'filled every unforgiving minute with sixty seconds' worth of distance run'.

When Duncan Macaulay retired as All England Club Secretary in 1963 he turned to his friend Jackie Smyth to help him produce an autobiography which for those times was quite candid. The book is called *Behind the Scenes at Wimbledon* (1965), and reveals much about the inner workings of The Championships in the years when 'Open' tennis was looming ever closer. Smyth's other books on the game were *Lawn Tennis* (1953) for which All England Club Chairman Sir Louis Greig wrote the foreword just a few weeks before his death, *The Game's The Same* (1956) and *Jean Borotra – The Bounding Basque* (1974), the latter written with the full involvement and co-operation of the much-loved Centre Court star of the 1920s.

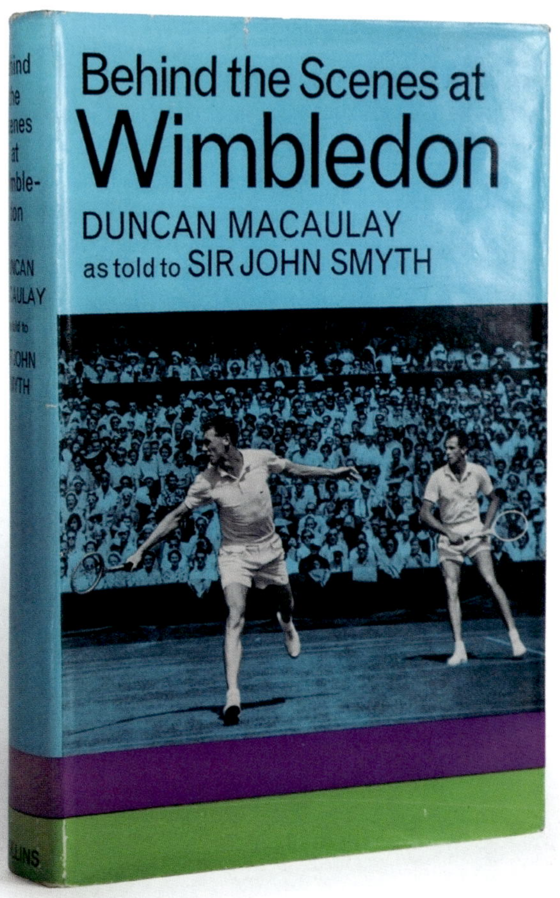

Sir John Smyth also published works on military history, a series of children's novels, and books about cats!

John Barrett

A Wimbledon player for 20 years; Davis Cup player and Captain; innovative coach; respected journalist; and a television commentator whose authoritative, friendly voice was for three decades one of the sounds of summer in households throughout Britain. Those activities and achievements would be a life's work for most people. However, that description of the career of London-born **John Barrett** is lacking in one key respect, for he is also a respected Lawn Tennis historian and the author of some of the most interesting and important books ever written about the Wimbledon Championships.

John began his journalistic career in 1963 as the Lawn Tennis Correspondent of the *Financial Times*, having previously written articles for magazines and programmes. In 1969 and 1970 he edited the *BP Year Book of World Tennis*, working with long-time friend and colleague Peter West. From 1971 onwards the year book was re-titled *World of Tennis*, and continued under that name until 2001, with John Barrett in the Editor's chair throughout.

Nineteen eighty-six saw the 100th staging of The Championships, and the publication of *100 Wimbledon Championships – A Celebration*, John Barrett's first major book about Wimbledon. He skilfully set the tournament in its true economic, political and social context, with the book's ten chapters broadly mirroring the ten decades of Wimbledon's history, supplemented by over 90 pages of information and results. A much-expanded second edition was published in 2001 under the new title of *Wimbledon – The Official History of the Championships*, and a third edition *Wimbledon – The Official History* followed in 2013, accompanied by a separate volume of results entitled *Wimbledon – The Singles Draws 1877–2012*.

Wimbledon – The Official History is an extraordinary tennis publishing achievement. The book's production values are first class, as is John Barrett's compelling narrative which tells the story of Wimbledon's evolution from Victorian garden-party pastime to world-leading 21st-century event. The author chronicles Wimbledon's history against the background of world affairs, and illustrates the story with many archive photographs. Barrett, along with Wimbledon's Honorary Librarian Alan Little, carried out years of painstaking research for the results volume, and the data they compiled was used to establish the Wimbledon online results archive.

In the late 1980s John assisted his fellow-BBC Television commentator Dan Maskell in the production of his autobiography *From Where I Sit* (1988). This was later released as a paperback with the more familiar title *Oh I Say!*

Wimbledon – Serving Through Time followed in 2003. This tall, slim volume contained a potted history of The Championships for visitors to the Wimbledon Lawn Tennis Museum. *Wimbledon – Ladies' Singles Champions 1884–2004* (2005) and *Wimbledon – Gentlemen's Singles Champions*

John Barrett and Ian Hewitt, May 2009

1877–2005 (2006), both co-written with Alan Little, were updated editions of books originally written by Little with Lance Tingay in the 1980s, and were subsequently updated twice more, most recently in 2015.

In 2009 John Barrett and fellow-historian and All England Club Member Ian Hewitt collaborated on *Centre Court – The Jewel in Wimbledon's Crown*. This beautifully produced coffee-table book was published by Vision Sports Publishing of Kingston upon Thames and was named Best Illustrated Book at the British Sports Book Awards. A second edition was published in 2010.

Wimbledon and its millions of devotees owe a huge debt of gratitude to John Barrett, and many will be hoping that his next published work will be his own long-awaited autobiography.

Alan Little

Alan Little (1928–2017) was Wimbledon's Honorary Librarian from 1977 until 2017 and during that time wrote, edited and compiled 114 tennis publications, the vast majority of which were about Wimbledon. Before Alan Little, Wimbledon was a tennis tournament. He turned it into a cultural institution.

Born in Greenwich, South East London, Alan was a keen tennis player in his teenage years, albeit of self-confessed modest ability. He played on public park courts with his friend and doubles partner Leslie Reeves, and one day Leslie gave Alan a copy of *Lawn Tennis and Badminton* magazine, which Alan promptly read from cover to cover. Wanting more, Alan paid a lunchtime visit to the magazine's office on the seventh floor of a building opposite the Houses of Parliament, near where he worked. The editor, a Mr Dorey, allowed Alan to purchase a couple of back issues of the magazine, and these lunchtime visits became more and more frequent until Alan had all the back issues.

When Dorey died, New Zealander Keith Dyer took over, and on visiting the office Alan Little got to know him. Dyer owned a guesthouse in South Norwood, and later Alan would visit him there every Wednesday evening to work on the magazine. Alan's life as a tennis journalist began by pure chance. One day he told Keith Dyer that he was planning a visit to Scarborough, and was promptly enlisted to write a report on a tournament going on there. Alan became a regular contributor to *Lawn Tennis and Badminton*, often compiling tournament reports by gleaning results and information from newspapers.

In addition to *Lawn Tennis and Badminton*, Alan also contributed to *Tennis Pictorial International* and *Tennis World*. In 1967 he used his regular monthly column in *Lawn Tennis and Badminton* to propose the establishment of a National Lawn Tennis Museum and Library at Wimbledon, and when this idea came to fruition ten years later Alan was appointed Honorary Librarian.

From that moment on, Alan was in his element. He donated many Lawn Tennis books to get the Library's collection started, then proceeded to acquire thousands more over the years that followed. In parallel with his work in the Kenneth Ritchie Library, as it was called, Alan also began writing books and booklets of his own. The opening of the Wimbledon Lawn Tennis Museum in 1977 led to a greater public interest in the history of the game, and Alan produced a series of informative and entertaining booklets about early Wimbledon champions and the evolution of The All England Lawn Tennis Club. Later, in 2002 and 2003, he produced three illustrated booklets to mark the 80th anniversary of the Club's move from Worple Road to Church Road in 1922. Alan researched and wrote a total of 16 Wimbledon history booklets.

Each year from 1980 to 2013 Alan edited the popular

Alan Little compiled and edited the *Wimbledon Compendium* each year from 1991 to 2017

information booklets sold in kiosks inside the Club's grounds along with the Official Daily Programme for The Championships. Initially titled *Know Your Wimbledon*, these were renamed *This is Wimbledon* from 1981 onwards. Over the years the number of pages increased from 24 in 1980 to 50 from 1987 to the present day. Black and white photographs were introduced in 1982, and colour photographs in 1990, with the images included changing from year to year. From 2014 responsibility for these booklets passed to another area of The All England Lawn Tennis Club.

In 1984 his first book *Wimbledon Ladies – A Centenary Record 1884–1984*, co-written with Lance Tingay, was published. The book contained Tingay's illuminating biographical essays on each champion, accompanied by their Wimbledon playing records and overall career achievements compiled by Alan, no easy task in pre-computerised days. A companion volume *Wimbledon Men – A Hundred Championships 1877–1986*, again co-written with Tingay, followed in 1986. Three later editions of these books, the most recent in 2015, saw John Barrett take over from the late Lance Tingay as Alan's co-author.

The first of Alan Little's major books was published in 1988. *Suzanne Lenglen – Tennis Idol of the Twenties* charts the turbulent life of the game's first global superstar who triggered a massive increase in the popularity of Lawn Tennis and the Wimbledon Championships. Alan's book tells the year-by-year story of her remarkable career and contains a complete list of the 241 open titles she won, along with the full results of all singles, doubles and mixed doubles matches she played at Wimbledon between 1919 and 1926. A much-expanded second edition was published in 2007 with an additional 77 pages giving the result of nearly every match played by Suzanne Lenglen during her adult career, painstakingly compiled by Alan with assistance from researchers all over the world.

Between 1980 and 1990 Alan produced a Media Guide for journalists and broadcasters covering the Wimbledon Championships, and in 1991 he turned this into a new-look *Wimbledon Compendium* of Championships facts, figures information and records. Each year from 1991 to 2017 Alan produced an updated edition of the *Wimbledon Compendium*, gradually turning it into an indispensable reference book. A particularly useful feature of the *Wimbledon Compendium* is the section entitled 'Wimbledon Year by Year' which charts changes to the arrangements for The Championships and to The All England Club's grounds, plus miscellaneous happenings such as heatwaves, floods, lightning strikes, player strikes, Royal visits and extensions to The Fortnight. This section now runs to nearly 100 pages and makes fascinating reading. It could easily be a book in its own right.

Whatever anyone wanted to know about Wimbledon, the answer was to be found in the *Compendium*. The first edition

in 1991 had 216 pages; by 2017 it had grown to a mammoth 642 pages. Assistant Librarian Audrey Snell worked on the *Compendium* for many years, and Alan's Sri Lankan-born friend Cuthbert James conducted countless hours of fact-checking to ensure that each new edition was as complete and accurate as possible. Current Wimbledon Librarian Robert McNicol has worked on the *Compendium* since 2016.

With the London 2012 Olympic Tennis event due to be played at Wimbledon, Alan produced a delightful illustrated history of Olympic tennis. *Tennis and the Olympic Games* (2009) gave a short description of each Olympic tennis tournament from Athens in 1896 through to Beijing in 2008, followed by the results and scores of every match in Olympic tennis history. At the conclusion of the London 2012 Games, Alan realised that a published record must be kept of Andy Murray's historic victory for Great Britain. *The Olympic Tennis Event at Wimbledon 2012* was written, designed and published in just ten weeks, but was not put on public sale until early 2013 due to administrative delays.

Alan's final book, apart from the *Wimbledon Compendium*, was *The Golden Days of Tennis on the French Riviera 1874–1939*. Published in 2014, this heavyweight volume told the story of the French Riviera tennis scene which had its heyday during the late-19th and early-20th centuries. It gave year-by-year descriptions of the tournaments at such places as Antibes, Menton, Beaulieu, Nice, Cannes and Monte

Cuthbert James (left) and Alan Little, 2005

Carlo, and concluded in typical Alan Little fashion with a 90-page results section.

Alan had a very modest opinion of his own ability as a writer. He felt he was a chronicler of facts, rather than a clever wordsmith, but he produced what the sport of Lawn Tennis needed more than anything: detailed and factual historical accounts. Journalism aside, his first published work was the 1977 booklet *The Changing Face of Wimbledon 1877 to 1977*. Over the years that followed he produced 14 history books, 27 compendiums, 16 history booklets, 34 information booklets, 11 media guides and 12 library catalogues. His most celebrated books were his biography of Suzanne Lenglen and his history of tennis on the French Riviera. Alan's final published work was the 2017 *Wimbledon Compendium*.

As his friend and fellow-historian Richard Hillway remarked: 'When it came to Wimbledon, Alan was an encyclopedia. There was little that he did not know.'

Between them, Wallis Myers, Sir John Smyth, Lance Tingay, John Barrett and Alan Little have created an enduring literary legacy for present and future generations of Wimblephiles to study and enjoy. ✲

Other Important Wimbledon Writers

In the 19th century **Henry Jones**, writing under the pseudonym 'Cavendish', did much to promote Lawn Tennis through his books on the new game and his articles in *The Field*. With Julian Marshall and John Moyer Heathcote, Jones had been a prime mover behind the first Wimbledon Championships in 1877.

George Hillyard, The All England Club's Secretary from 1907 to 1925, had first played at Wimbledon as early as 1888, when he partnered William Taylor in the Gentlemen's Doubles event. He made his final competitive Wimbledon appearance as a player in 1913. During his 26-year playing career he came up against all the early champions including Laurie Doherty, Arthur Gore, Anthony Wilding and Norman Brookes, and in his book *Forty Years of First Class Lawn Tennis* (1924) he described the styles and personalities of these and many other prominent players he had seen first-hand at Wimbledon since the 1880s. Hillyard was a fine player himself, and was married to six-times Wimbledon Ladies' Singles champion Blanche Bingley. They had a grass tennis court at their home in Thorpe Satchville, Leicestershire where they regularly played tennis against Wimbledon champions and other leading players of the day. Hillyard's book is doubly useful, for it also contains a long chapter entitled 'The Story of the All England Club' by **Herbert Wilberforce**, the Club's President.

Francis Russell Burrow was Wimbledon's much-respected Referee during the inter-war period from 1919 to 1936, and his book *The Centre Court and Others*, published in 1937, is a highly informative eye-witness account of the principal events at Wimbledon during the 50-year period from 1886 to 1936. In producing this book Burrow performed a great service to Wimbledon and to the game, and many years after his death he posthumously performed another when his comprehensive collection of press cuttings and cartoons was added to the Wimbledon Lawn Tennis Museum's Ephemera Collection.

When Arthur Wallis Myers died suddenly on the eve of the 1939 Championships he was succeeded as *The Daily Telegraph*'s Lawn Tennis Correspondent by another former Wimbledon player, **John Olliff**, whose book *Romance of Wimbledon* (1949) is a fascinating history covering the period from 1868, when The All England Club was founded, through to the 1948 Championships.

The first book about Wimbledon to be published after World War II was the excellent *Wimbledon Story* by **Norah Gordon Cleather**, The All England Club's Acting Secretary from 1939 to 1945. On her very first visit to Worple Road she saw Dorothea Lambert Chambers practising; on her second, reigning champion Norman Brookes saved her from being hit in the eye by a stray ball. Few observers were ever better qualified to write about Wimbledon, for Miss Cleather had been personally acquainted

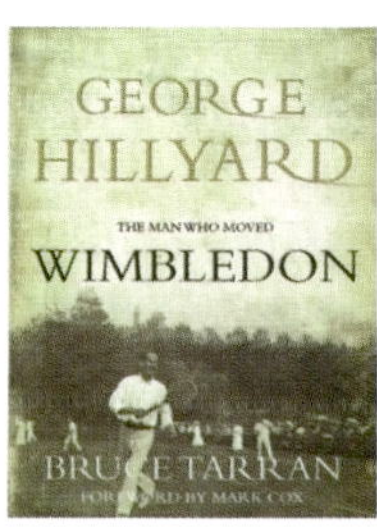

Bruce Tarran's excellent biography of George Hillyard was published in 2013

with Suzanne Lenglen, Jean Borotra, Helen Wills and many other top stars of the 1920s and 30s, and had almost single-handedly kept the Club afloat during World War II.

Unlike the books that preceded it, *The Centre Court Story* (1957) by **Maurice Brady** succeeds through the enthusiasm of a fan rather than the knowledge and experiences of a first-class player. The book comprises a series of linked essays about the personalities of the Centre Court from 1920s legends Suzanne Lenglen and Bill Tilden to 1950s teen sensations Maureen Connolly and Lew Hoad, and the front-cover painting showing a Gentlemen's Singles match in progress on the Centre Court is simply delightful.

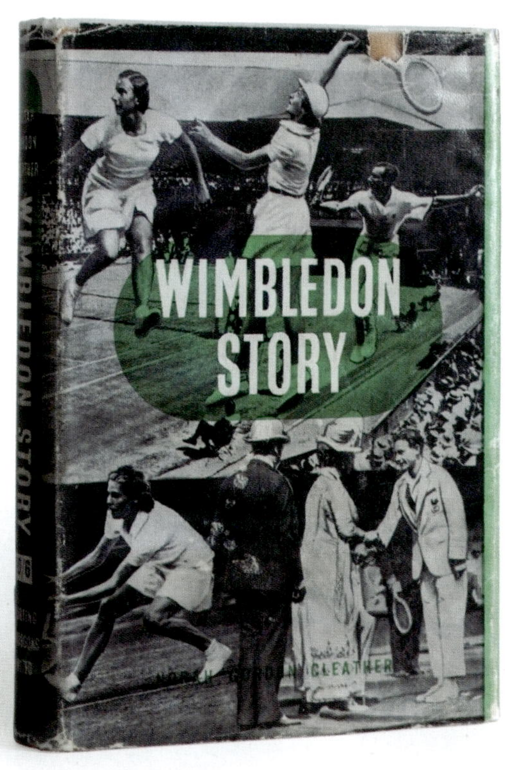

Couturier **Teddy Tinling** was famous for creating Gussie Moran's lace panties, but he had earlier umpired for Suzanne Lenglen on the French Riviera and served as player liaison officer at Wimbledon during the inter-war years. His book *White Ladies*, published in 1963, describes the challenges of dressing Wimbledon stars of the calibre of Maureen Connolly, Althea Gibson and Maria Bueno, and gives fascinating insights into the inner workings of The Championships. Tinling later published two more excellent volumes of memoirs, but in *White Ladies* the memories are still fresh.

Wimbledon – A Celebration by **Alfred Eisenstaedt** and **John McPhee** (1972) was completely different to any book about Wimbledon that had gone before. Photographer Eisenstaedt's abstract portfolio showed The Championships in an entirely fresh light, and author McPhee's text focused on often-overlooked details whilst paying homage to an unsung hero of Wimbledon, Head Groundsman Bob Twynam.

Max Robertson's *Wimbledon 1877–1977* is an excellent popular history of The Championships. Originally published in Wimbledon's Centenary year, the book was republished in new editions in 1981 and 1987. Max Robertson later produced an excellent history in verse entitled *The Ballad of Worple Road* (1997).

Of particular interest to Lawn Tennis historians is **Tom Todd**'s *The Tennis Players – From Pagan Rites to Strawberries and*

Cream which traces the modern game back to its earliest roots. The author wrongly credits Gem and Perera as the pioneers of the modern game, and Leamington as the first Lawn Tennis club, but with the limited information available to him back in the 1970s that is an understandable mistake and does not invalidate his other important research.

To get a look at Wimbledon from an overseas player's perspective one need look no further than *A Handful of Summers* (1978), by South African Davis Cup player **Gordon Forbes**. The fact that this book is still in print today tells its own story. The tales of Forbes's tennis travels with fellow-South African Abe Segal have become part of tennis folklore, and later extended into two further volumes, *Too Soon to Panic* (1995) and *I'll Take the Sunny Side* (2017).

In 2018 The All England Lawn Tennis and Croquet Club celebrated its 150th birthday, and the occasion was marked by the publication of a fine illustrated book entitled *The All England Lawn Tennis & Croquet Club – Celebrating 150 Years*. Edited by **Ian Hewitt**, the book uses timelines, reproductions of important documents and 'then and now' photographic comparisons to chart the evolution of the

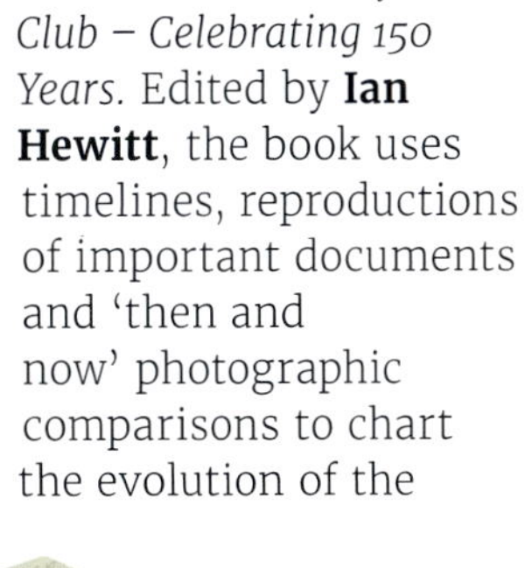

Club. The Foreword is by HRH The Duke of Kent, who in 2018 started his 50th year as the Club's President. This book fully lives up to the high standard set almost a century earlier in Wallis Myers's *Fifty Years of Wimbledon*.

Other important Wimbledon-related books published in 2018 were **Ben Chatfield**'s *Standing in Line – 30 Years of Obsessive Queuing at Wimbledon*, **Jeanne Cherry**'s *Helen Wills – Tennis, Art, Life*, and **Robert T. Everitt** and **Richard A. Hillway**'s *The Birth of Lawn Tennis – From the Origins of the Game to the First Championship at Wimbledon*.

The Birth of Lawn Tennis marked the culmination of 20 years of research by two of the world's most respected tennis historians. The book focuses on a short but crucial period in Lawn Tennis history, from the commercial launching of the game in 1874, and the events leading up to it, through to the first Wimbledon Championship in 1877. Its 568 illustrated pages examine the events of this period in forensic detail, and the results include the reaffirmation of Major Walter Wingfield's role as the pioneer of Lawn Tennis, the debunking of myths regarding Harry Gem, Augurio Perera and the Leamington Club, and fascinating profiles of the 22 competitors in the 1877 Championships. As John Barrett states in his Foreword: 'Every now and then a book appears that transforms our understanding of its subject. This is one of those seminal works.' ✇

Wimbledon – The Official History

John Barrett's superb Wimbledon history book has a very interesting history of its own. It was first published by Collins Willow in 1986 as *100 Wimbledon Championships – A Celebration* (ISBN 0 00 218220 3). The book contained the narrative history of Wimbledon along with the results of all Championships singles matches from 1877 to 1986. A new edition was produced by the same publisher in 2001, this time in association with The All England Lawn Tennis and Croquet Club, under the title *Wimbledon – The Official History of The Championships* (ISBN 9 780007 117079). The page count was increased from 287 to 468, and the first names of all singles competitors were included.

The third edition in 2013 had a new look, a new title and a new publisher, Vision Sports Publishing of Kingston upon Thames. *Wimbledon – The Official History* (ISBN 9 781907 637896) now had a massive 552 pages, and that was without the results, which had been moved into a 280-page companion volume entitled *Wimbledon – The Singles Draws 1877–2012* (ISBN 9 781909 534094).

Andy Murray's Wimbledon victory in 2013, the first by a British man for 77 years, led to a new fourth edition with an additional chapter '2013 – History In The Making' – in 2014 (ISBN 978 1909534 23 0). The fourth edition had 584 pages.

In 2016 Vision Sports Publishing produced a reprint of the 2014 edition under the same ISBN (9 781909 534230). It was not just a straightforward reprint, however, for it contained a key revision to the early history of Lawn Tennis. There were some small but extremely important differences between the books produced in 2014 and 2016. In the later book, previous references to Harry Gem and Augurio Perera as early pioneers of Lawn Tennis, and Leamington as the first Lawn Tennis Club, had been removed. John Barrett's telling paragraph is at the foot of page 50 of the 2016 reprinted book:

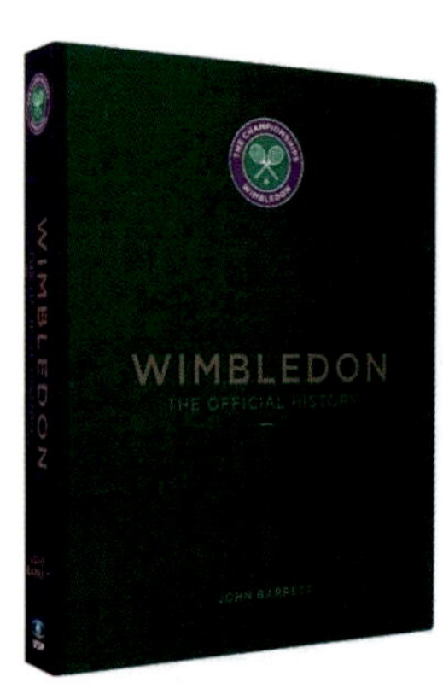

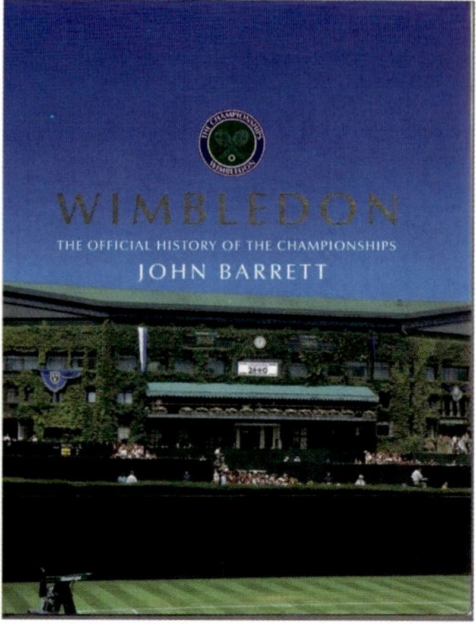

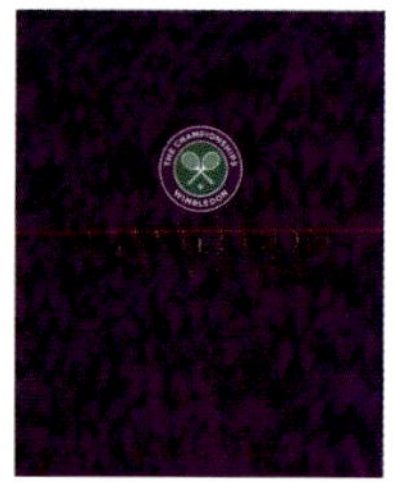

'It used to be thought that two Warwickshire men Harry Gem, a Birmingham solicitor, and his Spanish friend Augurio Perera, who were both keen rackets players, had been experimenting with an outdoor version of tennis since 1859. Furthermore it was claimed that as early as 1872, together with two young doctors, they had founded a tennis Club in Leamington, whence both had moved, in the grounds of The Manor House Hotel. However, detailed online research of local newspapers and contemporary archives by English tennis historian Bob Everitt, editor of *The Tennis Collector*, has proved conclusively that the Leamington Club had been founded in 1874, some months after the publication of Wingfield's patent of 23 February.'

This was an important revision of Lawn Tennis history, proving that Major Walter Wingfield was indeed the sole inventor of the game. In their 2018 book, *The Birth of Lawn Tennis – From the Origins of the Game to the First Championships at Wimbledon*, Everitt and his fellow-historian Richard Hillway explained the true facts. Gem and Perera had never claimed to have invented

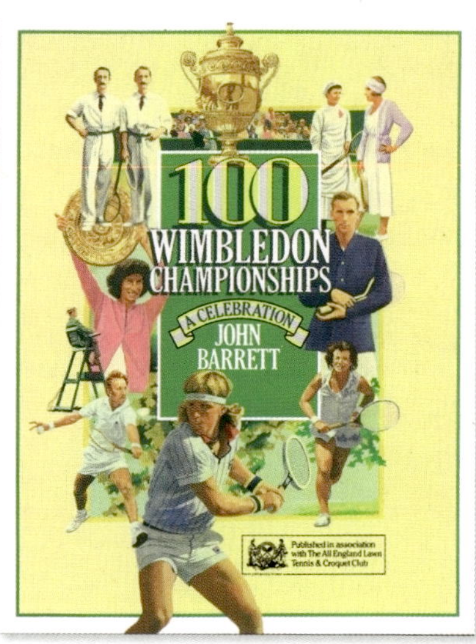

Lawn Tennis; that myth had been created by an over-enthusiastic local newspaper journalist when writing Harry Gem's obituary in 1881. The obituary had been used as source material by later writers and historians, and thus the myth of Gem and Perera as the founders of the game had been established and perpetuated.

In June 2020 an updated edition of *Wimbledon – The Official History* was published by Vision Sports Publishing (ISBN 9 781913 412005). John Barrett had recently celebrated his 89th birthday, and was assisted in the preparation of this new edition by Paul Newman of *The Independent*. ⛝

The Wimbledon Official Annual

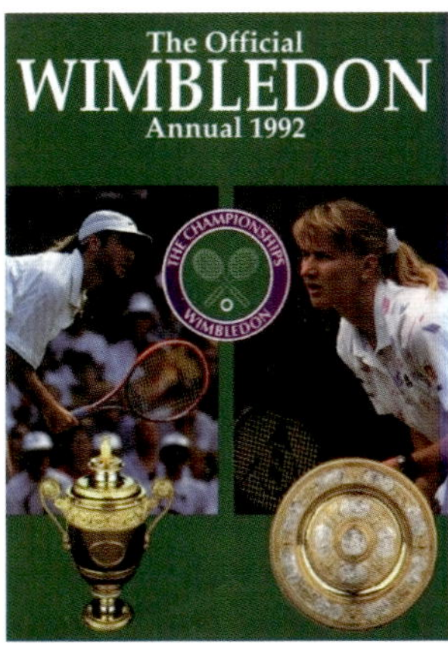 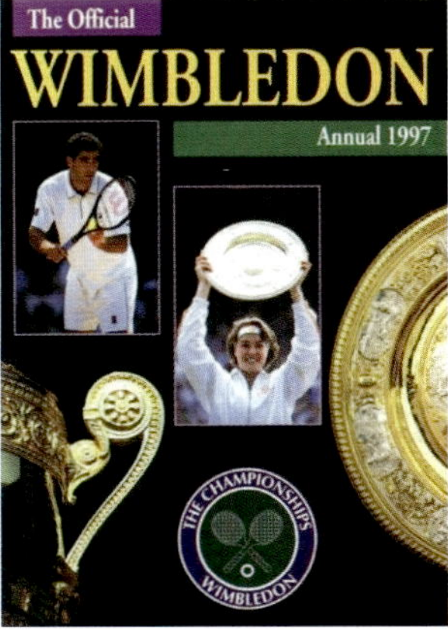  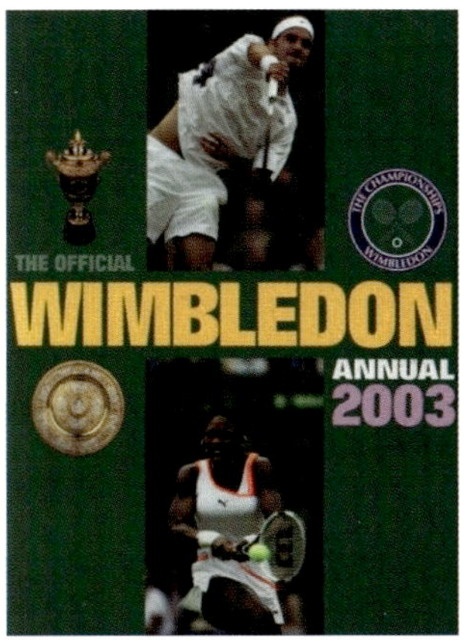

Since 1983 the Wimbledon Official Annual has provided a day-by-day diary of each year's Championships, with text written by a leading tennis journalist and accompanying photographs which become more evocative with each passing year. Thirty-seven annuals were published between 1983 and 2019, and there are quite a few collectors in Britain and worldwide who are known to have complete sets.

The first Wimbledon Official Annual was not a great success in sales terms, because the public were not expecting it and did not know it had been published until they went to Wimbledon the following year and found copies on sale at the reduced price of £2 in the Wimbledon Museum Shop. The print run was small, with only 2,000 copies produced, and the books were quickly snapped up. Since then hundreds of people have collected these annuals, and a full set of thirty-seven volumes from 1983 to 2019 now takes up a sizeable space on the tennis lover's bookshelf. That first edition back in 1983 has become an expensive and sought-after collectable.

From 1983 to 2003 the Annual was written by **John Parsons** of *The Daily Telegraph*. He was succeeded by **Neil Harman** of *The Times* (2004–2013). **Paul Newman** of *The Independent* is the current author, having taken over from Harman in 2014.

There have been six publishers: Pavilion Books (1983–1984), Aurum Press (1985–1989), Chapmans (1991–1993), Hazleton Publishing (1994–2005), PPL Sport and Leisure (2006–2011) and Vision Sports Publishing (2012–2019, continuing). The 1990 Annual was self-published by The All England Lawn Tennis Club.

The size and format of the Annuals has remained constant, although the number of pages has risen from 160 in 1983 to 204 in 2019. The number of copies printed has varied from year to year, the peak being 10,000. Andre Agassi's fans snapped up all copies of the 1992 book, and the Annuals for 2013, the year of Andy Murray's first Wimbledon victory, and 2017, when Roger Federer won for the eighth time, are equally hard to find.

The Future

Since the Wimbledon Lawn Tennis Museum opened in 1977 no fewer than 198 Wimbledon official books and booklets have been published either by the Museum or The All England Lawn Tennis Club. Wimbledon has become a major force in tennis publishing, due in no small measure to the efforts of John Barrett, Ian Hewitt and Alan Little.

As we move further into the digital age it is important that this print publishing tradition continues. Wimbledon's success is due in a large part to the public appeal of its history and traditions, and printed books remain an important vehicle for communicating this rich heritage.

A Selected Tennis Bibliography

THE LAWN TENNIS CHAMPIONSHIPS SOUVENIR
1914

FORTY YEARS OF FIRST-CLASS LAWN TENNIS
by G.W. Hillyard
Williams & Norgate, London, 1924

LAST EIGHTS AT WIMBLEDON 1877–1925
by F.R. Burrow
Lawn Tennis and Badminton magazine, London, 1st edition 1925, subsequent editions 1926, 1929, 1931

WIMBLEDON LAWN TENNIS ILLUSTRATED
Lillywhites, London, 1925

FIFTY YEARS OF WIMBLEDON
by A. Wallis Myers
The Field, London, 1926

WIMBLEDON CHAMPIONSHIP SOUVENIR
by A. Wallis Myers and others
E.T. Heron & Co. Ltd., London W.1, 1931

WIMBLEDON WHO'S WHO
Dunlop Rubber Company, 1934

PERRY WINS!
by Fred J. Perry
Hutchinson, London, 1934

THE CENTRE COURT AND OTHERS
by F.R. Burrow
Eyre & Spottiswoode, London, 1937

GREAT LAWN TENNIS
by A. Wallis Myers
Cassell, London, 1937

WIMBLEDON STORY
by Norah Gordon Cleather
Sporting Handbooks, London, 1947

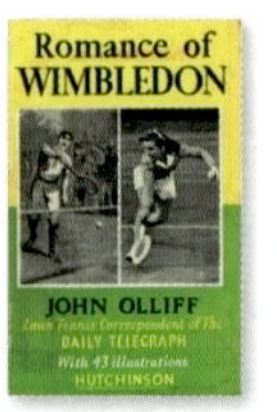

THE ROAD TO WIMBLEDON
by Alice Marble
W.H. Allen, London, 1947

ROMANCE OF WIMBLEDON
by John Olliff
Hutchinson, London, 1949

CAN YOU TELL ME?
Facts and figures about The Championships
AELTC, 1954, updated 1955, 1956, 1960, 1964, 1967, 1970

CHAMPION IN EXILE
by Jaroslav Drobny
Hodder and Stoughton, 1955

THE CENTRE COURT STORY
by Maurice Brady
W. Foulsham, London, 1957

FOREHAND DRIVE
by Maureen Connolly
MacGibbon and Kee, London, 1957

I ALWAYS WANTED TO BE SOMEBODY
by Althea Gibson
W.H. Allen, London, 1959

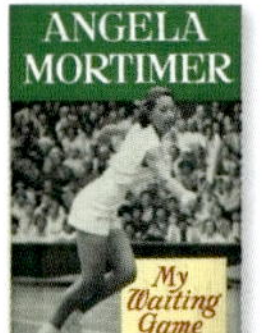

MY WAITING GAME
by Angela Mortimer
Frederick Muller, London, 1962

WHITE LADIES
by Teddy Tinling
Stanley Paul, London, 1963

BEHIND THE SCENES AT WIMBLEDON
by Duncan Macaulay and Sir John Smyth
Collins, London, 1965

LEVELS OF THE GAME
by John McPhee
MacDonald, London, 1970

THE EDUCATION OF A TENNIS PLAYER
by Rod Laver and Bud Collins
Pelham Books, London, 1971

A GAME TO LOVE
by Ann Jones
Stanley Paul, London, 1971

WIMBLEDON
A Celebration
by Alfred Eisenstaedt and John McPhee
Hamish Hamilton, London, 1972

WONDERFUL WIMBLEDON
by Alastair Revie
Pelham Books, London, 1972

WIMBLEDON:
The Hidden Drama
by Gwen Robyns
David and Charles, Newton Abbott, 1973

JEAN BOROTRA:
The Bounding Basque
by Sir John Smyth
Stanley Paul, London, 1974

PORTRAIT IN MOTION:
The Arthur Ashe Diary
by Arthur Ashe and Frank Deford
Stanley Paul, London, 1975

THE INNER GAME OF TENNIS
by W. Timothy Gallwey
Jonathan Cape, London, 1975

BEHIND THE SCENES IN WOMEN'S PRO TENNIS
by Grace Lichtenstein
Robson Books, London, 1975

KNOW YOUR WIMBLEDON
Facts and Figures About The Championships at Wimbledon
AELTC, 1976, updated 1978 and 1979

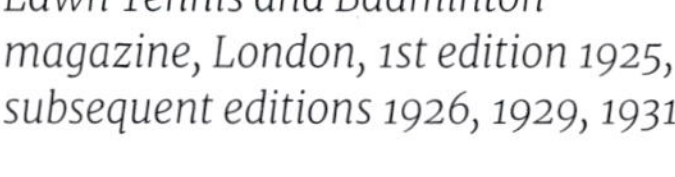

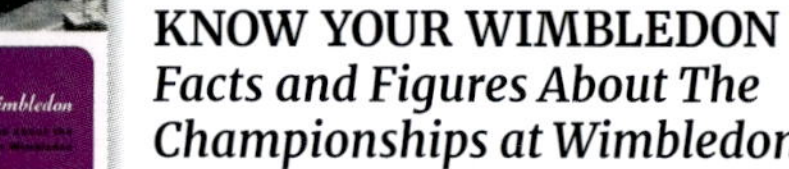

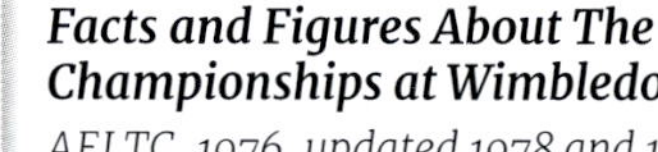

TENNIS
by Gianni Clerici
Octopus Books, London, 1976

100 YEARS OF WIMBLEDON
by Lance Tingay
Guinness Superlatives, London, 1977

WIMBLEDON 1877–1977
by Max Robertson
Arthur Barker, London, 1977

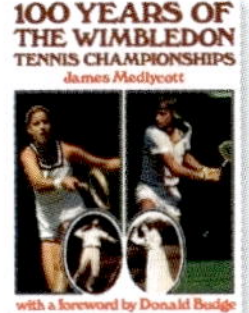

100 YEARS OF THE WIMBLEDON TENNIS CHAMPIONSHIPS
by James Medlycott
Hamlyn, London, 1977

BIG BILL TILDEN
by Frank Deford
Victor Gollancz, London, 1977

COURTING TRIUMPH
by Virginia Wade
Hodder and Stoughton, London, 1978

Wimbledon Centenary Booklets:

ROYALTY AND LAWN TENNIS
by Lance Tingay

THE CHANGING FACE OF WIMBLEDON, 1877–1977
by Alan Little

THE ROYAL AND ANCIENT GAME OF TENNIS
by Lord Aberdare

THE FIRST WIMBLEDON CHAMPION
by Michael Searle

IS IT A RECORD?
by Tom Todd

LOVE AND ALL THAT
by Roy McKelvie

THE STORY OF WOMEN'S TENNIS FASHION
by Ted Tinling
All published by Wimbledon Lawn Tennis Museum, London, 1977

A HANDFUL OF SUMMERS
by Gordon Forbes
Heinemann, London, 1978

THE KENNETH RITCHIE WIMBLEDON LIBRARY CATALOGUE, 1979
by Alan Little
1st edition 1979, updated editions 1982, 1986, 1989, 1992, 1995, 1998, 2001, 2004, 2007, 2010, 2015

THE TENNIS PLAYERS
by Tom Todd
Vallency Press, Guernsey, 1979

KNOW YOUR WIMBLEDON
Facts and Figures About The Championships, Wimbledon
Edited by Alan Little
All England Lawn Tennis Club, 1980

THIS IS WIMBLEDON
Facts and Figures About The Championships, Wimbledon
Edited by Alan Little
All England Lawn Tennis Club, 1981

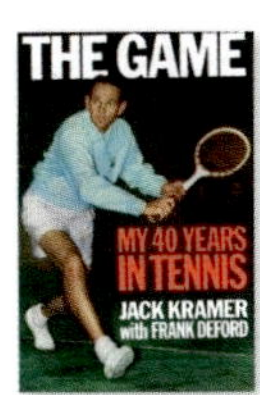

THE GAME
My Forty Years in Tennis
by Jack Kramer
Andre Deutsch, London, 1981

WIMBLEDON
Centre Court of The Game
by Max Robertson
British Broadcasting Corporation, London, 1981

WIMBLEDON ON CAMERA
by Arthur Cole
Rothman's Publications, London, 1981

THE BOOK OF WIMBLEDON
by Ronald Atkin
Heinemann/Quixote Press, London, 1981

WIMBLEDON
The Official Guide to The Championships
by Alan Little
All England Lawn Tennis Club, 1982

CLASSIC MOMENTS OF WIMBLEDON
by Charles Landon
Moorland Publishing, London, 1982

THE WIMBLEDON LAWN TENNIS MUSEUM GUIDE
by Valerie Warren
1982

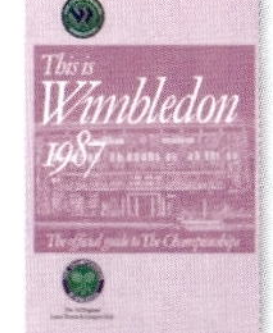

THIS IS WIMBLEDON
The Official Guide to The Championships
by Alan Little
AELTC, 31 annual editions, 1983–2013

TINLING
Sixty Years in Tennis
by Ted Tinling
Sidgwick & Jackson, London, 1983

LOTTIE DOD
Wimbledon Champion and All Rounder Extraordinary
by Alan Little
Wimbledon Lawn Tennis Museum, 1983

MAUD WATSON
The First Lady Wimbledon Champion
by Alan Little
Wimbledon Lawn Tennis Museum, 1st edition 1983, 2nd edition 2002

WIMBLEDON LADIES
A Centenary Record 1884–1984
by Alan Little and Lance Tingay *Wimbledon Lawn Tennis Museum, 1984*

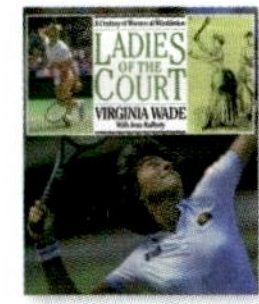

LADIES OF THE COURT
A Centenary of Women at Wimbledon
by Virginia Wade with Jean Rafferty
Pavilion Books, London, 1984

TENNIS MY WAY
by Martina Navratilova and Mary Carillo
Allen Lane, London, 1984

TENNIS, SQUASH AND BADMINTON BYGONES
by Gerald Gurney
Shire Publications, Princes Risborough, 1984

ST. LEGER GOOLD
A Tale of Two Courts
by Alan Little
Wimbledon Lawn Tennis Museum, 1984

KATHLEEN GODFREE
Wimbledon Champion of 1924 and 1926
by Alan Little
Wimbledon Lawn Tennis Museum, 1984

MAY SUTTON
The First Overseas Wimbledon Champion
by Alan Little
Wimbledon Lawn Tennis Museum, 1984

DOROTHEA CHAMBERS
Wimbledon Champion Seven Times
by Alan Little
Wimbledon Lawn Tennis Museum, 1985

LENA RICE
The Only Irish Wimbledon Lady Champion
by Alan Little
Wimbledon Lawn Tennis Museum, 1985

WIMBLEDON MEN
A Hundred Championships 1877–1986
by Alan Little and Lance Tingay
1986

100 WIMBLEDON CHAMPIONSHIPS
A Celebration
by John Barrett
Collins Willow, London, 1986

THE FIELD STORY OF WIMBLEDON
by Jeremy Alexander
Associated Magazines, London, 1986

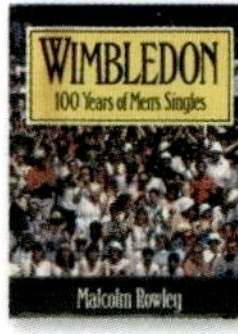

WIMBLEDON
100 Years of Men's Singles
by Malcolm Rowley
Sidgwick & Jackson, London, 1986

LE TENNIS A L'AFFICHE 1895–1986
by Jean-Pierre Chevallier
Albin Michel, Paris, 1986

THE CHANGING FACE OF WIMBLEDON
by Alan Little
Wimbledon Lawn Tennis Museum, 1st edition, 1986, subsequent editions 1987, 1989

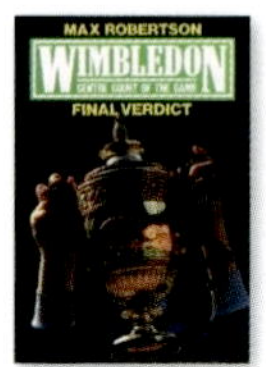

WIMBLEDON
Centre Court of The Game – Final Verdict
by Max Robertson
British Broadcasting Corporation, London, 1987

KITTY GODFREE
Lady of a Golden Age
by Geoffrey Green
Kingswood Press, London, 1987

STOP TALKING & GIVE THE SCORE
by Max Robertson
Kingswood Press, London, 1987

DAN MASKELL
From Where I Sit
by Dan Maskell with John Barrett
Willow Books, London, 1988

OPEN TENNIS
The First Twenty Years
by Richard Evans
Bloomsbury Publishing, London, 1988

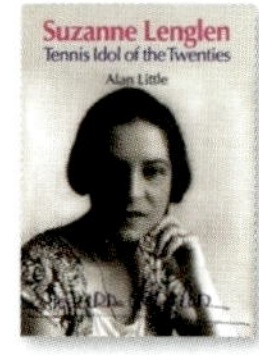

SUZANNE LENGLEN
Tennis Idol of the Twenties
by Alan Little
Wimbledon Lawn Tennis Museum, 1st edition 1988, updated edition 2007

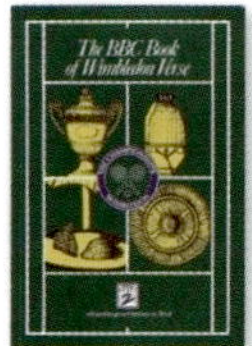

THE BBC BOOK OF WIMBLEDON VERSE
Edited by Joanne Watson
Wimbledon Lawn Tennis Museum, 1988

VIJAY
From Madras to Hollywood via Wimbledon
by Vijay Amritraj with Richard Evans
Libri Mundi, London, 1990

THE ART OF TENNIS 1874–1940
by Gary H. Schwartz
Wood River Publishing, Tiburon, 1990

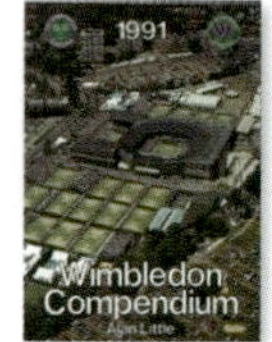

1991 WIMBLEDON COMPENDIUM
by Alan Little
All England Lawn Tennis Club, 1st edition 1991, updated annually 1992–2017

THE LAWNS OF WIMBLEDON
by Jim Thorn
All England Lawn Tennis Club, 1991

TENNIS FASHIONS
Over 100 Years of Costume Change
by Valerie Warren
Wimbledon Lawn Tennis Museum, 1st edition 1993, 2nd edition 2002

FORTY LOVE
Lawn Tennis Cigarette and Trade Cards
by Derek Hurst
Privately published, Billericay, 1993

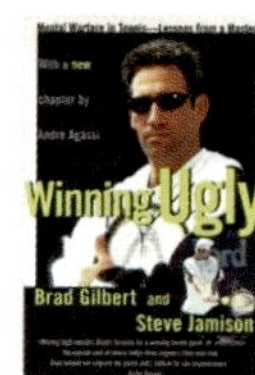

WINNING UGLY
by Brad Gilbert and Steve Jamison
Simon & Schuster, New York, 1994

TENNIS ANTIQUES & COLLECTIBLES
by Jeanne Cherry
Amaryllis Press, Santa Monica, 1995

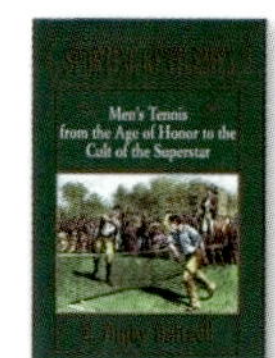

SPORTING GENTLEMEN
Men's Tennis From The Age of Honor to the Cult of the Superstar
by E. Digby Baltzell
Free Press, New York, 1995

TED AVORY
A Life in Tennis
by Huw D. Evans
All England Lawn Tennis Club, 1995

TOO SOON TO PANIC
by Gordon Forbes
Penguin Books, South Africa, 1995

THE BALLAD OF WORPLE ROAD
by Max Robertson
Queen Anne Press, London, 1997

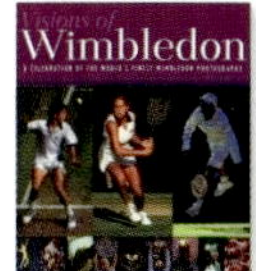

VISIONS OF WIMBLEDON
by Andrew Longmore
Andre Deutsch, London, 2000

THE HISTORY OF PROFESSIONAL TENNIS
by Joe McCauley
Short Run Books, Windsor, 2000

WIMBLEDON
The Official History of The Championships
by John Barrett
Collins Willow, London, 2001

WIMBLEDON 1922
The New Ground and Centre Court
by Alan Little
Wimbledon Lawn Tennis Museum, 1st edition 2002, 2nd edition 2005

WIMBLEDON 1922–2002
The Changing Face of Church Road
by Alan Little
Wimbledon Lawn Tennis Museum, 1st edition 2002, subsequent editions 2005, 2009, 2011, 2014

FRIENDS AT COURT
Wimbledon and Slazenger Since 1902
by Brian Simpson and Hugh Barty-King
Quiller Press, London, 2002

RACKET SPORTS COLLECTIBLES
by Robert T. Everitt
Schiffer Publishing, Atglen, USA, 2002

TENNIS STAMPS OF THE WORLD
by Douglas Dickson
Privately published, London, 2002

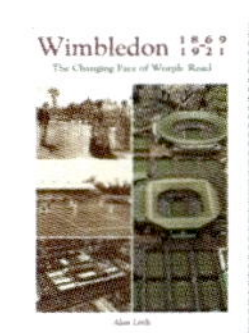

WIMBLEDON 1869–1921
The Changing Face of Worple Road
by Alan Little
Wimbledon Lawn Tennis Museum, 2003

WIMBLEDON
Serving Through Time
by John Barrett
Wimbledon Lawn Tennis Museum, 2003

A. WALLIS MYERS
A Testament to Tennis
by Prue Wallis Myers
Privately published, Manchester, 2004

TENNIS BIBLIOGRAPHY 1874–2000
by Frank Phelps & Gordy Sabine
Amaryllis Press, Santa Monica, 2004

WIMBLEDON
Facts, Figures & Fun
by Cameron Brown
Privately published, London, 2005

LIFTING THE COVERS
by Alan Mills
Headline Books, London, 2005

WIMBLEDON
Ladies' Singles Champions 1884–2015
by John Barrett and Alan Little
Wimbledon Lawn Tennis Museum, 1st edition 2005, updated 2012 and 2015

WIMBLEDON
Gentlemen's Singles Champions 1877-2015
by John Barrett and Alan Little
Wimbledon Lawn Tennis Museum, 1st edition 2006, updated 2011 and 2015

FANTASTIC FEDERER
by Chris Bowers
John Blake, London, 1st hardback edition 2006, subsequent paperback editions with various titles 2009, 2010, 2012, 2013, 2016

WIMBLEDON CONFIDENTIAL
by Patricia Edwards
Pen Press, Brighton, 2007

FROM PALM TO POWER
The Evolution of the Racket
by Peter Maxton
Wimbledon Lawn Tennis Museum, 2008

THE GAME OF SPHAIRISTIKE OR LAWN TENNIS:
Rules of Tennis
by Walter Wingfield
Wimbledon Society Museum Press, Wisley, 2008

CENTRE COURT
The Jewel in Wimbledon's Crown
Edited by John Barrett and Ian Hewitt
Vision Sports Publishing, 2009, 2nd edition 2010

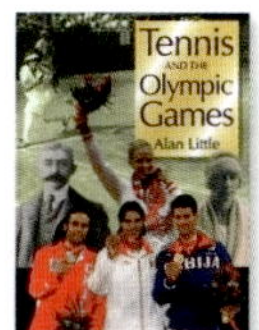

TENNIS AND THE OLYMPIC GAMES
by Alan Little
Wimbledon Lawn Tennis Museum, 2009

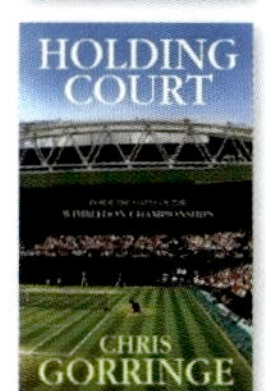

HOLDING COURT
Inside the Gates of the Wimbledon Championships
by Chris Gorringe
Century, London, 2009

A CENTRE COURT CELEBRATION
All England Lawn Tennis Club, Wimbledon, 2009

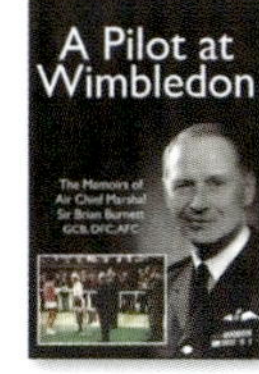

A PILOT AT WIMBLEDON
by Sir Brian Burnett
Blenheim Press, Codicote, 2009

THE LAST CHAMPION
The Life of Fred Perry
by Jon Henderson
Yellow Jersey Press, London, 2009

OPEN
An Autobiography
by Andre Agassi
Harper Collins, London, 2009

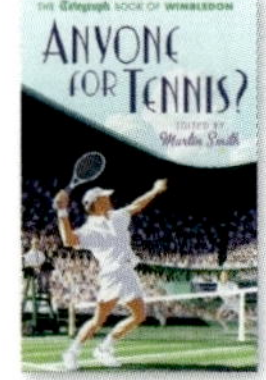

A TERRIBLE SPLENDOR
by Marshall Jon Fisher
Crown Publishers, New York, 2009

ANYONE FOR TENNIS?
*The Daily Telegraph Book
of Wimbledon*
Edited by Martin Smith
Aurum Press, London, 2010

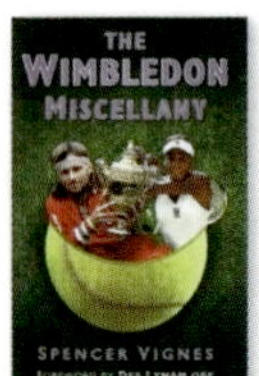

**THE WIMBLEDON
MISCELLANY**
by Spencer Vignes
History Press, Stroud, 2010

**THE ORIGINAL RULES
OF TENNIS**
*Bodleian Library, Oxford/
All England Lawn Tennis Club,
Wimbledon, 2010*

**HER MAJESTY THE QUEEN
VISITS WIMBLEDON,
24th JUNE 2010**
*All England Lawn Tennis Club,
Wimbledon, 2010*

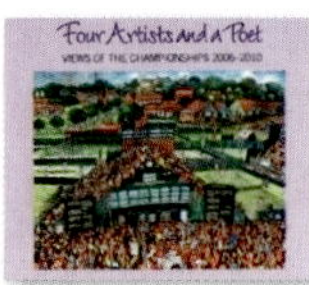

FOUR ARTISTS AND A POET
by Ian King, Rosabel
Richards and Honor Godfrey
AELTC, 2010

BALLS FROM THE QUEUE
by Poem Catcher
*Privately published, Edinburgh,
2010*

WIMBLEDON
Visions of The Championships
Edited by Ian Hewitt
and Bob Martin
Vision Sports Publishing, 2011

**THE WIMBLEDON JUNIOR
TENNIS INITIATIVE**
The First Ten Years
by Julian Tatum and Ian
Hewitt *AELTC, 2011*

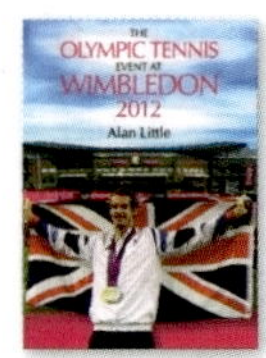

**THE OLYMPIC TENNIS
EVENT AT WIMBLEDON,
2012**
by Alan Little
*Wimbledon Lawn Tennis Museum,
2012*

WIMBLEDON
The Official History
by John Barrett
*Vision Sports Publishing, 2013,
updated 2014 and 2016*

WIMBLEDON
The Singles Draws
by John Barrett
Vision Sports Publishing, 2013

GEORGE HILLYARD
*The Man Who Moved
Wimbledon*
by Bruce Tarran
Matador, Leicester, 2013

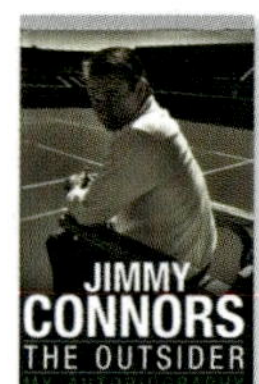

THE OUTSIDER
by Jimmy Connors
Bantam Press, London, 2013

ANDY MURRAY
Wimbledon Champion
by Mark Hodgkinson
Simon & Schuster, London, 2013

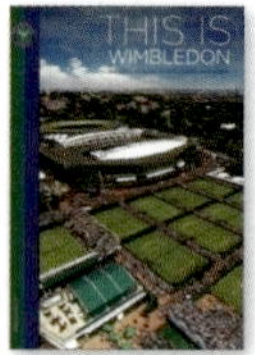

THIS IS WIMBLEDON
*The Official Guide to
The Championships*
by AELTC
Four annual editions, 2014–2017

ROD LAVER
An Autobiography
by Rod Laver with Larry
Writer
Harper Collins, London, 2014

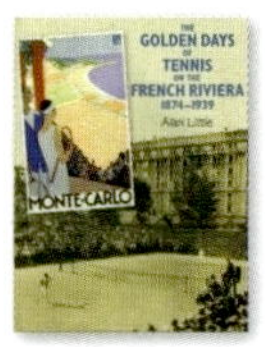

**THE GOLDEN DAYS OF
TENNIS ON THE FRENCH
RIVIERA, 1874–1939**
by Alan Little
*Wimbledon Lawn Tennis Museum,
2014*

**BORIS BECKER'S
WIMBLEDON**
with Chris Bowers
Blink Publishing, London, 2015

**WIMBLEDON LAWN
TENNIS MUSEUM
SOUVENIR HANDBOOK**
by Ian Hewitt, Anna Renton
and Hermione Crawford
2015

THE ROVING EYE
by Richard Evans
Clink Street Publishing, 2017

A PORTRAIT OF WIMBLEDON
by Jim Drewett and Bob Martin
Vision Sports Publishing, 2017

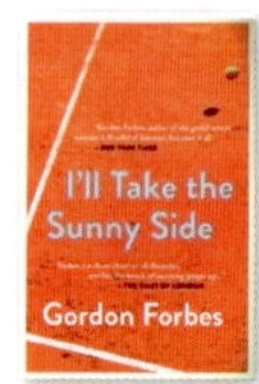

I'LL TAKE THE SUNNY SIDE
by Gordon Forbes
Bookstorm, South Africa, 2017

**2018 WIMBLEDON
COMPENDIUM**
compiled by Alan Little
and Robert McNicol
All England Lawn Tennis Club, 2018

**THE ALL ENGLAND LAWN
TENNIS & CROQUET CLUB**
Celebrating 150 Years
Edited by Ian Hewitt
AELTC/Vision Sports Publishing, 2018

STANDING IN LINE
*30 Years of Obsessive
Queuing at Wimbledon*
by Ben Chatfield
Pitch Publishing, Brighton, 2018

THE BIRTH OF LAWN TENNIS
*From the Origins of the Game
to the First Championship at
Wimbledon*
by Robert T. Everitt
and Richard A. Hillway
Vision Sports Publishing, 2018

AMERICAN COLOSSUS
*Big Bill Tilden and the Creation
of Modern Tennis*
by Allen M. Hornblum
University of Nebraska Press, 2018

HELEN WILLS
Tennis, Art, Life
by Jeanne Cherry
*Tennis Gallery Wimbledon, London,
2018*

**THE WIMBLEDON
COMPENDIUM 2019**
All England Lawn Tennis Club, 2019

THE PEOPLE'S WIMBLEDON
by Richard Jones
with Amisha Savani
Pitch Publishing, 2021

THE RACKET
by Conor Niland
Penguin Sandycove, 2024

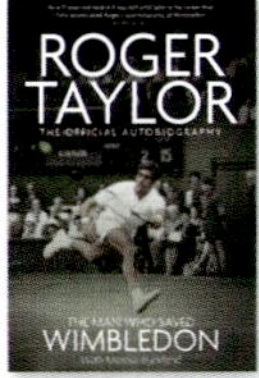

The Man Who Saved Wimbledon
Roger Taylor's Offical Biography
with Marcus Buckland
Pitch Publishing, 2025

MODERN TENNIS INSTRUCTION
A Historical Guide to Play Your Best Tennis
by John B. Carpenter
Privately published, 2023

WIMBLEDON
The Pinnacle of Sport
by Ian Hewitt and Bob Martin
All England Lawn Tennis Club, 2024

IT'S BEEN A BALL
A Memoir
by John Beddington
Tennis Gallery Wimbledon, London, 2026

Wimbledon Through the Ages

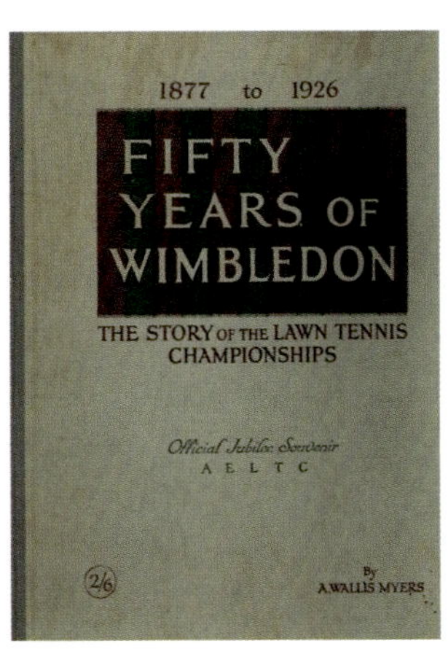

1926

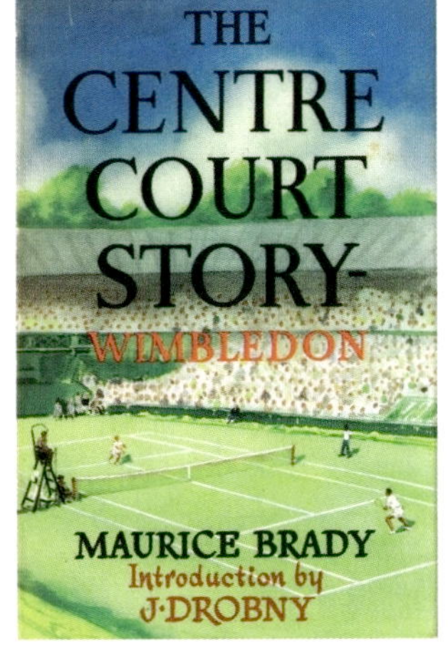

1957

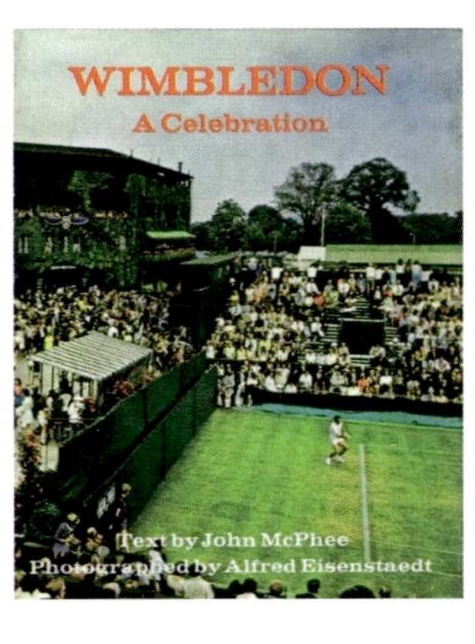

1972

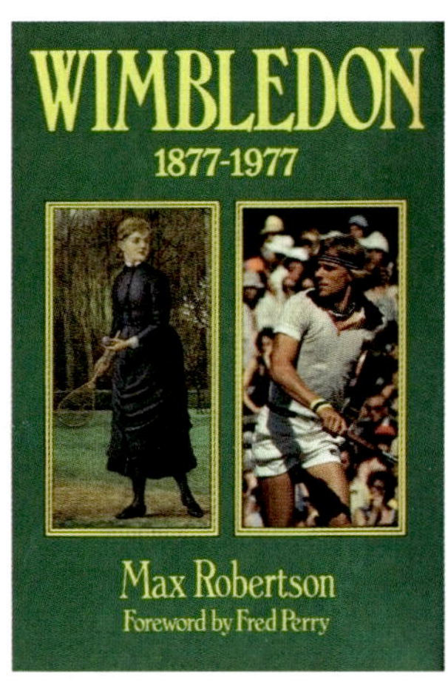

1977

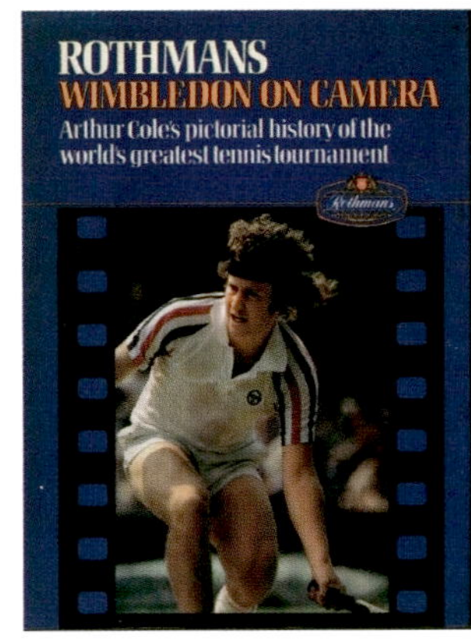

1981

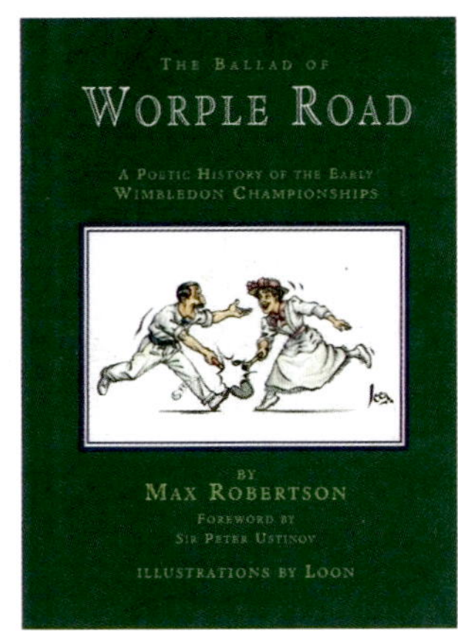

1997

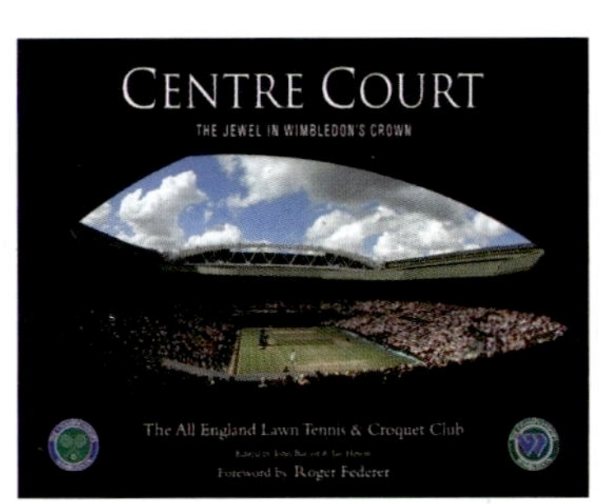

2009

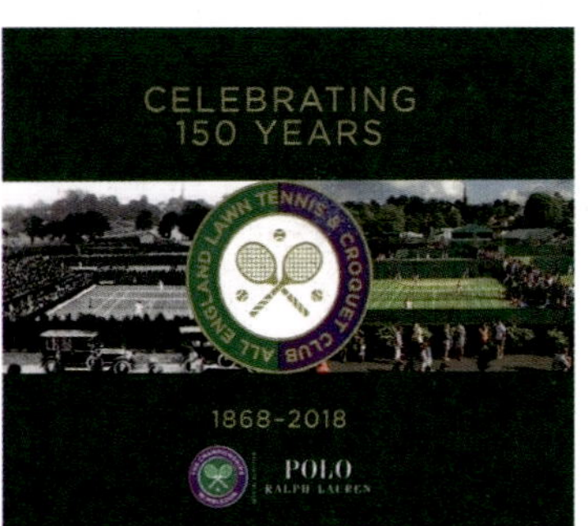

2018

CHAPTER 12
Wimbledon on Film

During the 1920s British cinema goers were able to watch the first moving pictures from the Wimbledon Championships courtesy of Pathé News. A decade later the BBC began live television broadcasts of selected Centre Court matches, but it was not until the widespread availability of video cassette players in the 1970s that viewers could watch recordings of Wimbledon tennis in the comfort of their own homes. Before that, the only way to make a home recording was to film the television set with an 8mm movie camera during a live tennis broadcast. Believe it or not, some people did that!

The video cassette player was one of the major consumer innovations of the early 1970s, but when the first Wimbledon tennis films were released in the mid-1970s pre-recorded video cassettes were still relatively new to the British public. They were available in high street shops, but at first they were very expensive. Mass production quickly led to better quality and lower prices, and for three decades the video industry boomed, with hundreds of feature films, TV programmes, sports events and concerts available to buy from retailers such as Woolworths and W.H. Smith or hire from chains such as Blockbuster Video. Blank tapes were also widely available, and home recording was a pastime the British public embraced with huge enthusiasm.

The annual Wimbledon Official Film was the brainchild of Mark McCormack, founder and CEO of the International Management Group (IMG). In the early 1970s McCormack was advising The All England Club on the sale of worldwide TV rights for The Championships, and suggested that a highlights package would increase revenue, as broadcasters could show it during rain breaks. Another of McCormack's companies, Trans World International (TWI), was awarded sole rights to produce all Wimbledon video content including official films, complete matches and documentaries.

TWI awarded licences to various UK distributors over the years, and two or three different versions of the same film were often produced. Early releases were packaged in large moulded plastic boxes which provided great protection to the video cassette inside, but as the years passed packaging became more compact and less robust. Companies involved in the distribution of Wimbledon video releases in Britain included IPC Video (1977–1980), EMI Video (1981), Mirror Vision (1983–1985), Castle Communications (1989–1995), Parkfield Entertainment (1990), Watchword Video (1991), Carlton (2004), Target Entertainment (2008) and Good Guys Media (2009–2018). In addition, the UK distribution rights to Wimbledon's back catalogue were awarded to Quadrant Video of Carshalton in Surrey during the 1990s, and this company repackaged the entire range of Wimbledon Official Films and kept them available for many years.

Amongst the first Wimbledon tennis films to be released on video cassette were *The Great English Garden Party*, a delightful documentary containing a theatrical recreation of the inaugural 1877 Championships presented by actor and 'Wimblephile' Peter Ustinov, and the 1977 *Wimbledon Official Film* celebrating Virginia Wade's historic victory. Wimbledon highlights films had been made once or twice before, but this was the first public release.

In the early years of the 21st century, video cassettes were replaced by Digital Versatile Discs or 'DVDs' as they became known. *The 2004 Wimbledon Official Film* was released on both video cassette and DVD, but from 2005 onwards all Wimbledon video content was released on DVD only. The final Wimbledon DVD release was in 2018, and The All England Club now uses YouTube and other digital channels to disseminate its video content.

The decision to discontinue these popular films was understandable in the digital age but came as a disappointment to those who used them to keep their happy memories of Wimbledon alive, including people with visual impairments who derived great pleasure from listening to the familiar voices of commentators such as Dan Maskell, Jack Kramer and John Barrett. ✍

Wimbledon Official Films

Between 1974 and 2018 these films captured the eras and exploits of Jimmy Connors, Chris Evert, Bjorn Borg, Martina Navratilova, John McEnroe, Steffi Graf, Boris Becker, Martina Hingis, Andre Agassi, the Williams sisters, Roger Federer, Rafael Nadal, Novak Djokovic, Andy Murray and many other Wimbledon champions and personalities.

It was not just the chronicling of iconic players and great matches that made the *Wimbledon Official Films* special, however. Match action and player interviews were interspersed with behind-the-scenes footage which showed the gradual transformation of The All England Lawn Tennis Club from a private members' institution which opened its doors to the public for a fortnight each year into the world-leading sporting venue it is today.

**WIMBLEDON 1974
Revolution in
Church Road**
*VHS video cassette, 52 minutes, colour
Trans World International/ Quadrant Video*

**WIMBLEDON 1975
with Peter Ustinov**
*VHS video cassette, 52 minutes, colour
Trans World International/ Quadrant Video*

**WIMBLEDON 1976
with James Mason**
*VHS video cassette & PAL DVD, 52 minutes, colour
Trans World International/ Quadrant Video*

WIMBLEDON 1977
*VHS video cassette, 52 minutes, colour
Trans World International/ IPC Video*

**WIMBLEDON 1978
Year Of The Exile**
*Narrator: John Newcombe
Commentator: Dan Maskell
VHS video cassette & PAL DVD, 52 minutes, colour
Trans World International/ Quadrant Video*

WIMBLEDON '79
*Narrator: Charlton Heston
VHS video cassette, 52 minutes, colour
Trans World International/ IPC Video*

**WIMBLEDON 1980
This Is Tennis**
*Narrator: Patrick Allen
Commentator: Dan Maskell
VHS video cassette, 52 minutes, colour
Trans World International/ IPC Video*

Wimbledon Official Films

WIMBLEDON 1981
All I Can Say Is That I Won Wimbledon
Narrator: James Hunt
Commentator: Dan Maskell
VHS video cassette, 52 minutes, colour
Trans World International/ Quadrant Video

WIMBLEDON '82
A Diamond Championship
Director: Jeff Harvey
VHS video cassette, 52 minutes, colour
Trans World International/ IPC Video

WIMBLEDON 1983
You've Got To Have Class
Narrator: Michael Smee
Commentator: Dan Maskell
VHS video cassette, 52 minutes, colour
Trans World International/ Quadrant Video

WIMBLEDON 1984
The Birthday Party With A Million Guests
Narrators: Keith Washington and Nigel Clarke
Commentator: Dan Maskell
VHS video cassette, 52 minutes, colour
Trans World International/ Quadrant Video

WIMBLEDON 1985
The Year Of The Thunderbolt
Narrator: Patrick Allen
Commentator: Dan Maskell
VHS video cassette, 52 minutes, colour
Trans World International/ Quadrant Video

WIMBLEDON 1986
More Than A Game
Narrator: Michael Jayston
Commentator: Dan Maskell
VHS video cassette, 52 minutes, colour
Trans World International/ Quadrant Video

WIMBLEDON 1987
'There's No Place Like This'
Narrator: J. Benedict
Commentator: John Barrett
VHS video cassette, 52 minutes, colour
Trans World International/ Quadrant Video

WIMBLEDON 1988
A Family Affair
Narrator: Peter Robertson
Commentator: John Barrett
VHS video cassette, 52 minutes, colour
Trans World International/ Quadrant Video

WIMBLEDON 1989
A Labour Of Love
VHS video cassette, 63 minutes, colour
Trans World International/ Quadrant Video

WIMBLEDON 1990
A Matter of Record
VHS video cassette, 60 minutes, colour
Trans World International/ Quadrant Video

WIMBLEDON 1991
The People's Championships
Narrator: Ian Wooldridge
VHS video cassette, 54 minutes, colour
Trans World International/ Quadrant Video

WIMBLEDON 1992
Not Just Rackets & Balls
Narrator: Tom Conti
VHS video cassette, 55 minutes, colour
Trans World International/ Quadrant Video

The Official Film Of WIMBLEDON 1993
VHS video cassette, 52 minutes, colour
Trans World International/ Quadrant Video

The Official Film Of WIMBLEDON 1994
VHS video cassette, 52 minutes, colour
Trans World International/ Castle Communications

The Official Film Of WIMBLEDON 1995
Narrator: Zoe Wanamaker
VHS video cassette, 52 minutes, colour
Trans World International/ Castle Communications

WIMBLEDON The 1996 Official Film
Narrator: John Nettles
VHS video cassette, 52 minutes, colour
Trans World International/ Wimbledon Video Collection

WIMBLEDON The 1997 Official Film
Narrator: Toyah Wilcox
VHS video cassette, 52 minutes, colour
Trans World International/ Wimbledon Video Collection

WIMBLEDON The 1998 Official Film
Narrator: Stephen Fry
VHS video cassette, 52 minutes, colour
Trans World International/ Wimbledon Video Collection

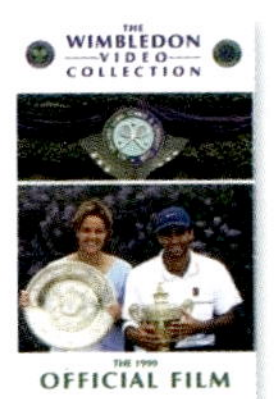

**WIMBLEDON
The 1999 Official Film**
*Narrator: Geoffrey Palmer
VHS video cassette, 52
minutes, colour
Trans World International/
Wimbledon Video Collection*

**WIMBLEDON
The 2000 Official Film**
*Narrator: Andrew Sachs
VHS video cassette, 52
minutes, colour
Trans World International/
Wimbledon Video Collection*

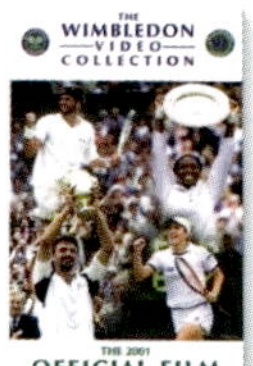

**WIMBLEDON
The 2001 Official Film**
*Narrator: Andrew Sachs
VHS video cassette, 52
minutes, colour
Trans World International/
Wimbledon Video Collection*

**WIMBLEDON
The 2002 Official Film**
*Narrator: Leslie Phillips
VHS video cassette, 52
minutes, colour
Trans World International/
Wimbledon Video Collection*

**WIMBLEDON
The 2003 Official Film**
*Narrator: Andrew Sachs
VHS video cassette, 52
minutes, colour
Trans World International/
Wimbledon Video Collection*

**WIMBLEDON
The 2004 Official Film**
*Narrator: Stephen Fry
VHS video cassette & PAL
DVD, 52 minutes, colour
Trans World International/
Wimbledon Video Collection*

**WIMBLEDON
The 2005 Official Film**
*Narrator: Greta Scacchi
PAL DVD, 65 minutes, colour
Trans World International/
Wimbledon Video Collection*

**WIMBLEDON
The 2006 Official Film**
*Narrator: Sam Hazeldine
PAL DVD, 60 minutes, colour
Trans World International/
Wimbledon Video Collection*

**WIMBLEDON
The 2007 Official Film**
*Narrator: Benedict Taylor
PAL DVD, 60 minutes, colour
Trans World International/
Wimbledon Video Collection*

**WIMBLEDON
The 2008 Official Film**
*Narrator: Sam Hazeldine
PAL DVD, 60 minutes, colour
IMG Sports Media/Target
Entertainment*

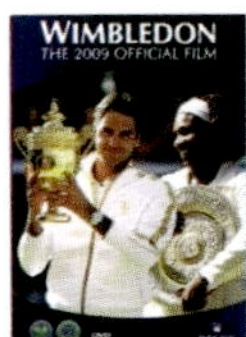

**WIMBLEDON
The 2009 Official Film**
*Narrator: Sam Hazeldine
PAL DVD, 60 minutes, colour
IMG Sports Media/Good Guys
Media*

**WIMBLEDON
The 2010 Official Film**
*Narrator: Sam Hazeldine
PAL DVD, 60 minutes, colour
IMG Sports Media/Good Guys
Media*

**WIMBLEDON 2011
Official Film**
*Narrator: Sam Hazeldine
PAL DVD, 60 minutes, colour
IMG Sports Media/Good Guys
Media*

**WIMBLEDON 2012
Official Film**
*Narrator: Tim Rice
PAL DVD, 60 minutes, colour
IMG Sports Media/Good Guys
Media*

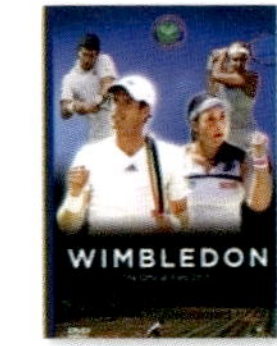

**WIMBLEDON
The Official Film 2013**
*Narrator: Tim Rice
PAL DVD, 60 minutes, colour
IMG Sports Media/Good Guys
Media*

**WIMBLEDON
The Official Film 2014**
*Narrator: John Hurt
PAL DVD, 60 minutes, colour
IMG Sports Media/Good Guys
Media*

**WIMBLEDON
The Official Film 2015**
*Narrator: Stephen Fry
PAL DVD, 60 minutes, colour
IMG Sports Media/Good Guys
Media*

**WIMBLEDON
The Official Film 2016**
*Narrator: Sophie Okonedo
PAL DVD, 60 minutes, colour
IMG Sports Media/Good Guys
Media*

**WIMBLEDON
The Official Film 2017**
*Narrator: Charles Dance
PAL DVD, 60 minutes, colour
IMG Sports Media/Good Guys
Media*

**WIMBLEDON
The Official Film 2018**
*Narrator: Michelle Dockery
PAL DVD, 54 minutes, colour
IMG Sports Media/Good Guys
Media*

Wimbledon Classic Matches

In addition to Wimbledon Official Films, complete matches from The Championships were sometimes released on video and DVD as Wimbledon Classic Matches. Early releases in this series included the 1977 Gentlemen's Singles semi-final between Bjorn Borg and Vitas Gerulaitis, and the 1978 Ladies' Singles Final between Chris Evert and Martina Navratilova. Between 2008 and 2017 a number of complete Wimbledon men's finals were released on DVD, but these were not labelled as Wimbledon Classic Matches.

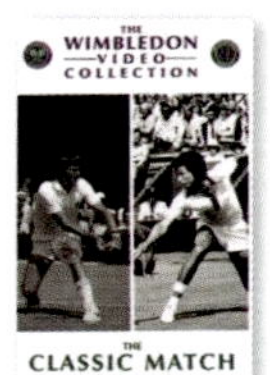

**ASHE v CONNORS
1975 FINAL**
*VHS video cassette,
140 minutes, colour
Trans World International/
Wimbledon Video Collection*

**BORG v GERULAITIS
1977 SEMI-FINAL**
*PAL DVD, 180 minutes,
colour
Trans World International/
Wimbledon Video Collection*

**NAVRATILOVA v EVERT
1978 FINAL**
*VHS video cassette & PAL
DVD, 180 minutes, colour
Trans World International/
Wimbledon Video Collection*

**BORG v McENROE
1980 FINAL**
*2 VHS video cassettes, 240
minutes, colour
Trans World International/
Wimbledon Video Collection
PAL DVD, 240 minutes, colour
IMG Sports Media/Good Guys
Media*

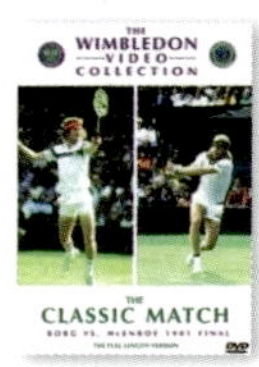

**BORG v McENROE
1981 FINAL**
*VHS video cassette, 206
minutes, colour
Trans World International/
Wimbledon Video Collection
PAL DVD, 206 minutes, colour
IMG Sports Media/Good Guys
Media*

**NOVOTNA v GRAF
1993 FINAL**
*VHS video cassette & PAL
DVD, 142 minutes, colour
Trans World International/
Wimbledon Video Collection*

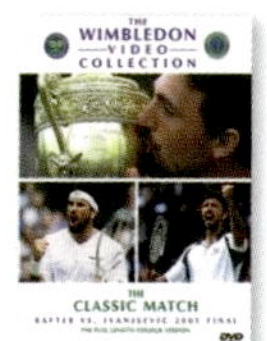

**RAFTER v IVANISEVIC
2001 FINAL**
*PAL DVD, 195 minutes,
colour
Trans World International/
Wimbledon Video Collection*

**AGASSI v RAFTER VS.
2000 SEMI-FINAL**
*VHS video cassette, 203
minutes, colour
Trans World International/
Wimbledon Video Collection*

**ANDY MURRAY v
RICHARD GASQUET**
*2008 Gentlemen's Singles 4th
Round
PAL DVD, 240 minutes, colour
IMG Sports Media/Target
Entertainment*

The thrilling fourth-round match, played on the Centre Court on Monday, 30 June 2008.

The 2008 Men's Final RAFAEL NADAL v ROGER FEDERER
*Commentators: Andrew Castle and Tim Henman
PAL DVD, 300 minutes, colour
IMG Sports Media/Target Entertainment*

Sub-titled *Rafael Nadal's Triumph at Twilight*, this film commences with Rafa and Roger reciting Rudyard Kipling's classic poem 'If', followed by interviews with the two finalists.

**The 2009 Men's Final
ROGER FEDERER v
ANDY RODDICK**
*2 PAL DVDs, 300 minutes,
colour
IMG Sports Media/Good Guys
Media*

**Men's Final 2012
ROGER FEDERER v
ANDY MURRAY**
*PAL DVD, 242 minutes, colour
IMG Sports Media/Good Guys
Media*

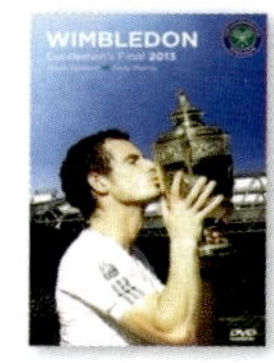

**Gentlemen's Final 2013
NOVAK DJOKOVIC v
ANDY MURRAY**
*PAL DVD, 230 minutes, colour
IMG Sports Media/Good Guys
Media*

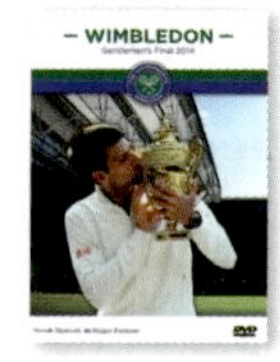

**Gentlemen's Final 2014
NOVAK DJOKOVIC v
ROGER FEDERER**
*PAL DVD, 235 minutes, colour
IMG Sports Media/Good Guys
Media*

**Gentlemen's Final 2016
ANDY MURRAY v
MILOS RAONIC**
*PAL DVD, 168 minutes, colour
IMG Sports Media/Good Guys
Media*

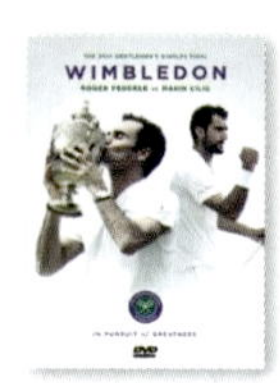

**The 2017 Gentlemen's
Singles Final
ROGER FEDERER v
MARIN CILIC**
*PAL DVD, 141 minutes, colour
IMG Sports Media/Good Guys
Media*

Legends of Wimbledon

The *Legends of Wimbledon* series profiled four of Wimbledon's greatest modern champions. The films contained match highlights and interviews with the featured players along with their doubles partners, opponents, coaches and others who knew them well.

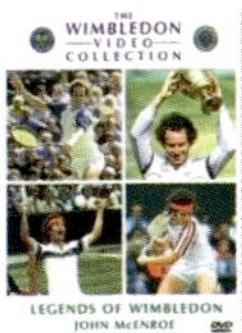

Legends Of Wimbledon
JOHN McENROE
VHS video cassette & PAL DVD, 52 minutes, colour, 1998
Trans World International/ Wimbledon Video Collection

Legends Of Wimbledon
BILLIE JEAN KING
VHS video cassette, 52 minutes, colour, 2000
Trans World International/ Wimbledon Video Collection

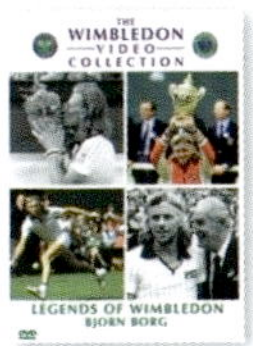

Legends Of Wimbledon
BJORN BORG
PAL DVD, 62 minutes, colour, 2004
Trans World International/ Carlton Visual Entertainment

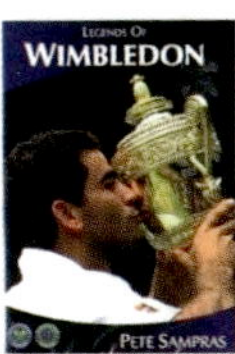

Legends Of Wimbledon
PETE SAMPRAS
PAL DVD, 52 minutes, colour, 2006
IMG Sports Media/Good Guys Media

Documentary Films

A number of interesting Wimbledon documentary films were released on video cassette and DVD between 1977 and 2013.

THE GREAT ENGLISH GARDEN PARTY
100 Years of Wimbledon
Presenter & Narrator: Peter Ustinov
VHS video cassette, 50 minutes, colour, 1977
Trans World International/IPC Video

This remarkable film recreates the garden-party scene at Worple Road during the inaugural Wimbledon Lawn Tennis Championships in 1877. Presenter Peter Ustinov mingles with the Victorian spectators and talks to William Marshall and Spencer Gore, the two finalists. The story moves through Wimbledon's first century, culminating with footage of Jimmy Connors, Ken Rosewall and other 1970s stars in action.

DECADE OF WIMBLEDON 1971–1980
VHS video cassette, 60 minutes, colour, 1981
Trans World International/EMI Video/Quadrant Video

During the first full decade of 'Open' tennis new personalities emerged and fresh rivalries were forged. Great matches were played out on Wimbledon's Centre Court, including the epic 1977 semi-final between Vitas Gerulaitis and Bjorn Borg, extensive highlights of which are included in this film.

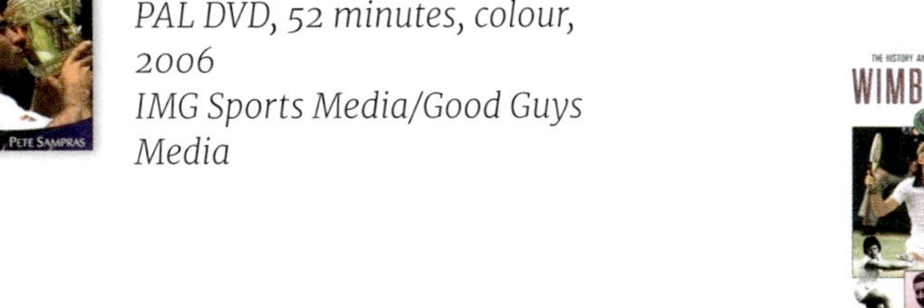

THE HISTORY AND HIGHLIGHTS OF WIMBLEDON
VHS video cassette, 55 minutes, colour, 1989
Trans World International/Castle Vision

Wimbledon's origins, history and development, featuring vintage newsreel footage.

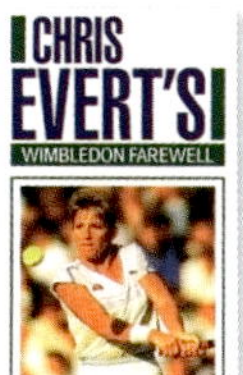

CHRIS EVERT'S WIMBLEDON FAREWELL
VHS video cassette, 52 minutes, colour, 1990
Trans World International/Parkfield Entertainment

Drawing on extensive interviews with the player herself, this film recalls the remarkable 18-year career of Chris Evert, one of Wimbledon's most popular Ladies' Singles champions of all time. There are contributions from Billie Jean King, Martina Navratilova, John Lloyd and Andy Mill.

Documentary Films

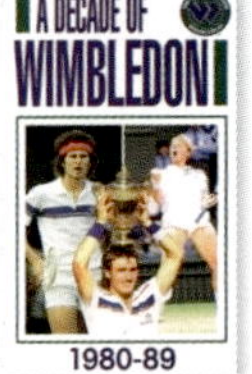

A DECADE OF WIMBLEDON 1980–1989
VHS video cassette, 52 minutes, colour, 1990
Trans World International/Parkfield Entertainment

A round-up of a remarkable decade at Wimbledon which began with Bjorn Borg's fifth and last men's singles title and ended with Boris Becker's third and last. Featured players include Evonne Cawley, John McEnroe, Martina Navratilova, Jimmy Connors, Chris Evert and Steffi Graf.

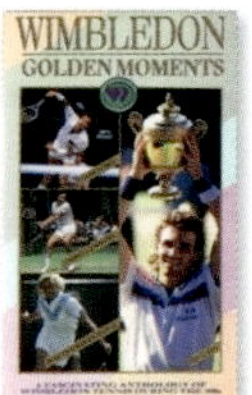

WIMBLEDON GOLDEN MOMENTS
VHS video cassette, 40 minutes, colour, 1990
Trans World International/Castle Vision

An anthology of Wimbledon tennis during the 1980s, with archive footage.

CLASSIC RALLIES
VHS video cassette, 52 minutes, colour, 1996
Trans World International/Wimbledon Video Collection

A comprehensive collection of Wimbledon's golden moments from the 1970s, 80s and 90s, introduced by John Barrett. Featured players including Ilie Nastase, Billie Jean King, Pete Sampras and Steffi Graf talk through the high points of their Wimbledon careers.

THE LIGHTER SIDE
Presenters: Cliff Richard and Andrew Castle
VHS video cassette & PAL DVD, 52 minutes,
colour, 1997
Trans World International/Wimbledon Video Collection

This entertaining film rekindles memories of humorous and controversial moments involving Tom Okker, Steffi Graf, John McEnroe, Monica Seles, Jeremy Shales, Ilie Nastase, Arantxa Sanchez Vicario and many others.

THE WORLD OF WIMBLEDON
VHS video cassette, 52 minutes, colour, 1999
Trans World International/Wimbledon Video Collection

A compendium of The Championships, with interviews, archive footage and historical material. Journalists and photographers who have covered the tournament for decades give their views on the changing Wimbledon scene, and there are interviews with Pete Sampras, Boris Becker, John McEnroe, Chris Evert and Martina Navratilova.

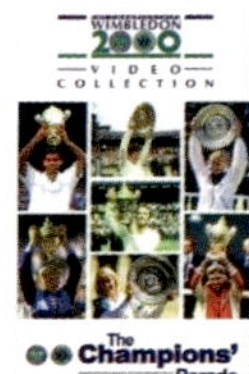

THE CHAMPIONS' PARADE
VHS video cassette, 50 minutes, colour, 2000
Trans World International/Wimbledon Video Collection

An emotional Centre Court get-together as all Wimbledon's surviving champions were invited to celebrate the new millennium on Saturday, 1 July, the middle Saturday of the 2000 Championships. John Barrett was the Master of Ceremonies for this unique occasion.

WIMBLEDON A History Of The Championships
Narrator: Robert Lindsay
2 VHS video cassettes, 208 minutes, colour, 2001
PAL DVD, 208 minutes, colour
Trans World International/Wimbledon Video Collection

The best of all the Wimbledon's documentary films is *Wimbledon – A History of The Championships*, released in 2001. The film is narrated by actor Robert Lindsay and features interviews with many past champions and a great deal of previously unreleased archive footage. The interviews were filmed during The Championships in 2000, when all the surviving past champions were invited to attend the Millennium Champions' Parade. Originally a BBC Television series, the film is in four 52-minute parts: *Dare to Dream*, *The Glory Years*, *Coming of Age* and *More Than a Game*.

DOUBLE THE FUN

VHS video cassette & PAL DVD, 52 minutes, colour, 2002
Trans World International/Wimbledon Video Collection

Over the years the doubles game has entertained and captivated audiences at Wimbledon, and this documentary features some of the greatest partnerships of all time, including Martina Navratilova and Pam Shriver, Frank Sedgman and Ken McGregor, Doris Hart and Shirley Fry, and five-times champions Todd Woodbridge and Mark Woodforde.

GREAT WIMBLEDON RIVALRIES

Narrator: Jerome Flynn
VHS video cassette, 52 minutes, colour, 2003
Trans World International/Wimbledon Video Collection

Bjorn Borg and John McEnroe, Martina Navratilova and Chris Evert, Boris Becker and Stefan Edberg, Andre Agassi and Pete Sampras: these are the enduring rivalries that made Wimbledon so compelling during the last quarter of the 20th century. This documentary puts these rivalries in the spotlight, with contributions from all eight champions.

WIMBLEDON RECORD BREAKERS

PAL DVD, 52 minutes, colour, 2005
Trans World International/Wimbledon Video Collection

Some of Wimbledon's greatest champions recall their record-breaking Wimbledon achievements. Featured players include Boris Becker, Martina Hingis, Pete Sampras, Martina Navratilova and Roger Federer.

THE CHANGING OF THE GUARD
Roger Federer v. Pete Sampras 2nd July 2001

PAL DVD, 60 minutes, colour, 2007
Trans World International/Wimbledon Video Collection

If ever a film was aptly titled, this is it. Pete Sampras had won Wimbledon seven times in the previous eight years when the burgeoning talent of Roger Federer brought an end to his reign as champion in a five-set thriller on the Centre Court. The film contains extended highlights plus interviews with both players.

ANDY MURRAY: THE MAN BEHIND THE RACQUET
plus Complete Gentlemen's Singles Final 2013

2 x PAL DVDs, 300 minutes, colour, 2013
IMG Sports Media/Good Guys Media

Released in a two-DVD 'Official Collector's Edition' along with the Complete 2013 Gentlemen's Singles Final, *Andy Murray: The Man Behind the Racquet* is a 70-minute profile which provides insights into Murray's talent, training and dedication. There are contributions from Ivan Lendl, Sir Alex Ferguson and Kevin Spacey.

WIMBLEDON The Best of 1968 and 1969

VHS video cassette, 50 minutes, colour, year not known
Trans World International/World Sports Video (Australia)

Made in Australia, this video cassette contains highlights from the Wimbledon Ladies' and Gentlemen's Singles finals of 1968 and 1969, featuring Rod Laver, Billie Jean King, Tony Roche, Ann Jones, John Newcombe and Judy Tegart.

BBC Video Releases

From 1984 to 1988 the BBC released *The Best of Wimbledon* series of documentary films covering a different aspect of The Championships each year. These were followed from 1990 to 1994 by a series of annual extended highlights films which provided an alternative view of The Championships. Produced by Martin Hopkins and edited by John Rowlinson, the BBC's films were of a very high quality with extended match footage and running times of two to three hours. The much-loved commentaries by Dan Maskell, John Barrett, Bill Threlfall, Barry Davies, Ann Jones, Paul Hutchins, Virginia Wade, David Mercer and others were a huge selling point for the BBC's films.

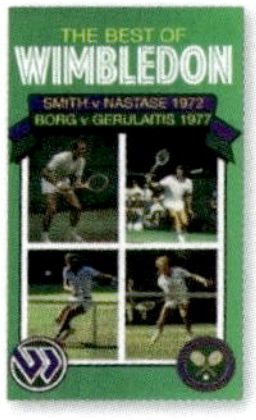

THE BEST OF WIMBLEDON
1972 and 1977
Introduced by: John Barrett
Commentary: Dan Maskell
Producer: John Vigar
VHS video cassette, 90 minutes, colour, 1984
BBC Enterprises Ltd

The final sets of two classic Wimbledon men's matches: the 1972 final between Stan Smith and Ilie Nastase, and the 1977 semi-final between Bjorn Borg and Vitas Gerulaitis.

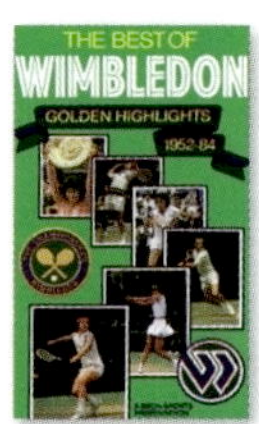

THE BEST OF WIMBLEDON
Golden Highlights 1952–1984
Written & Introduced by: John Barrett
Commentary: Dan Maskell, Peter Wilson and John Barrett
Producer: John Vigar
VHS video cassette, 82 minutes, colour, 1985
BBC Enterprises Ltd

A golden treasury of archive footage featuring Maureen Connolly, Jaroslav Drobny, Louise Brough, Ken Rosewall, Althea Gibson, Neale Fraser, Angela Mortimer, Rod Laver, Margaret Smith, Roy Emerson, Maria Bueno, Cliff Richey, Virginia Wade, Arthur Ashe, Evonne Cawley, Jimmy Connors, Andrea Jaeger, Chris Lewis and Martina Navratilova.

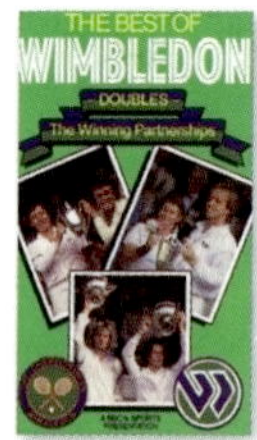

THE BEST OF WIMBLEDON
Doubles – The Winning Partnerships
Written & Narrated by: John Barrett
Commentary: Dan Maskell and others
Producer: John Vigar
VHS video cassette, 95 minutes, colour, 1986
BBC Enterprises Ltd

Featured doubles teams include Bob Hewitt and Frew McMillan, Billie Jean King and Rosie Casals, John Newcombe and Tony Roche, Patti Hogan and Peggy Michel, along with many popular mixed doubles teams from the 1960s, 70s and 80s.

THE BEST OF WIMBLEDON
The Young Champions
Presented by: John Barrett
Commentary: Dan Maskell, John Barrett, Barry Davies, Peter West and others
Producer: John Vigar
VHS video cassette, 90 minutes, colour, 1987
BBC Enterprises Ltd

A year after Boris Becker's second Wimbledon title, John Barrett remembers many outstanding young Wimbledon champions including Wilfred Baddeley, Lottie Dod, Evonne Goolagong, Chris Evert and Jimmy Connors. The film contains footage of Gabriela Sabatini in action against Martina Navratilova in 1986.

THE BEST OF WIMBLEDON 88
Presented by: Gerald Williams
Commentary: Dan Maskell, John Barrett,
Barry Davies, Ann Jones and others
Producer: John Bodnar
Editor: John Rowlinson
VHS video cassette, 105 minutes, colour, 1988
BBC Enterprises Ltd

A change of direction for the BBC's *The Best of Wimbledon* series, featuring the highlights of the 1988 Championships. Players in action include Chris Evert, Miloslav Mecir, Steffi Graf, Ivan Lendl, Martina Navratilova and 16-year-old Michael Chang.

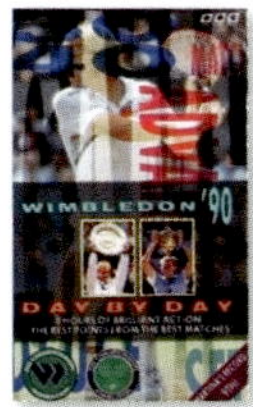
WIMBLEDON 90 Day by Day
Commentary: Dan Maskell, John Barrett, Bill Threlfall, Ann Jones, Virginia Wade, Pam Shriver, Mark Cox and others
Producers: Martin Hopkins, Penny Mills, John Vigar
Editor: John Rowlinson
VHS video cassette, 179 minutes, colour, 1990
BBC Enterprises Ltd

Extended highlights from the 1990 Championships, featuring Goran Ivanisevic, Stefan Edberg, Jennifer Capriati, Boris Becker, Martina Navratilova, Steffi Graf and Monica Seles.

Dan Maskell Selects
The Best of WIMBLEDON '91
Presented by: Dan Maskell
Commentary: Dan Maskell, John Barrett, Bill Threlfall, Ann Jones, Virginia Wade, Paul Hutchins, Mark Cox and others
Producers: Martin Hopkins & John Bodnar
Editor: John Rowlinson
VHS video cassette, 120 minutes, colour, 1991
BBC Enterprises Ltd

Extended highlights from the 1991 Championships, featuring Gabriela Sabatini, Andre Agassi, Steffi Graf, Nick Brown, Goran Ivanisevic, Stefan Edberg, Jennifer Capriati, Boris Becker, Martina Navratilova and Michael Stich.

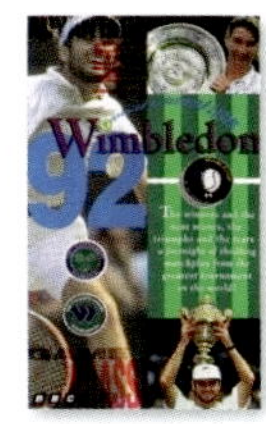
WIMBLEDON '92
Presented by: Desmond Lynam
Commentary: John Barrett, Mark Cox, Barry Davies, Ann Jones, Virginia Wade
Producers: Martin Hopkins & Nick Tilling
Editor: John Rowlinson
VHS video cassette, 120 minutes, colour, 1992
BBC Enterprises Ltd

Extended highlights from the 1992 Championships, featuring Monica Seles, Andre Agassi, Steffi Graf, John McEnroe, Gabriela Sabatini and Jeremy Bates.

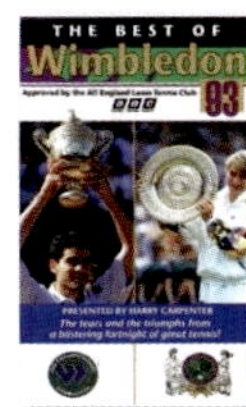
THE BEST OF WIMBLEDON '93
Presented by: Harry Carpenter
Commentary: John Barrett, David Mercer, Bill Threlfall, Mark Cox, Paul Hutchins, Virginia Wade, Ann Jones and Sue Barker
Producers: Martin Hopkins & Nick Tilling
Editor: John Rowlinson
VHS video cassette, 116 minutes, colour, 1993
BBC Enterprises Ltd

Extended highlights from the 1993 Championships, featuring Pete Sampras, Jana Novotna, Andre Agassi, Steffi Graf, John McEnroe, Gabriela Sabatini, Jim Courier, Martina Navratilova and Chris Bailey.

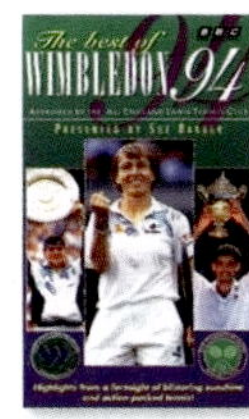
THE BEST OF WIMBLEDON '94
Presented by: Sue Barker
Commentary: John Barrett, David Mercer, Bill Threlfall, Mark Cox, John Alexander, Virginia Wade, Ann Jones and Julian Tutt
Producers: Martin Hopkins & Nick Tilling
Editor: John Rowlinson
VHS video cassette, 119 minutes, colour, 1994
BBC Enterprises Ltd

Extended highlights from the 1994 Championships, featuring Pete Sampras, Martina Navratilova, Goran Ivanisevic, Conchita Martinez, Jeremy Bates and Lori McNeil.

Other Important Video Releases

Two other tennis-related documentary films released during the 1990s are particularly worthy of the dedicated Wimblephile's attention:

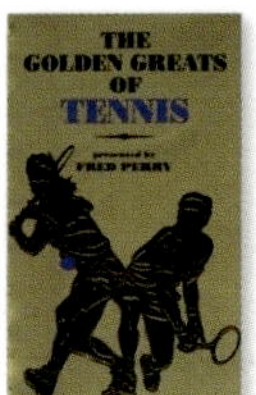

THE GOLDEN GREATS OF TENNIS
Presenter: Fred Perry
VHS video cassette, 90 minutes, colour, 1991
Tripod Films/Beckmann Home Video

This is almost certainly the finest compilation of archive tennis footage ever produced, featuring many Wimbledon champions and great personalities of the game.

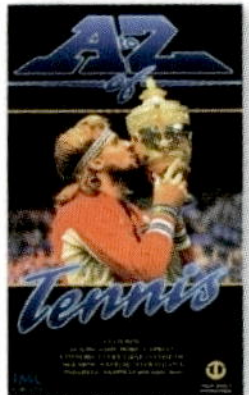

A TO Z OF TENNIS
VHS video cassette, 54 minutes, colour, 1994
Trans World International/WPE/British Pathé

This interesting compilation includes Wimbledon footage featuring Jimmy Connors, John McEnroe, Steffi Graf, Boris Becker and Martina Navratilova.

Home Recordings

During the era of video cassettes from the mid-1970s through to around 2000 many people made comprehensive home recordings of the BBC's broadcasts from Wimbledon. It was possible to record an entire day's play onto two four-hour cassettes and many people did this. A lot of these are still extant today, boxed-up in lofts and cupboards, and providing a potentially valuable resource for the tennis historians of the future. The only problem with home recordings of Wimbledon is finding the time to watch them!

Feature Films

A number of feature films have been shot on location at The All England Lawn Tennis Club over the years, most notably *Players* (1979) starring Dean Paul Martin, Ali MacGraw and Guillermo Vilas, and *Wimbledon* (2004) starring Kirsten Dunst and Paul Bettany. In the former, the only scene shot at Wimbledon showed Martin and Vilas walking onto the Centre Court ahead of their fictional Wimbledon final. This scene was filmed just before the start of the 1978 Wimbledon Ladies' Singles Final between Chris Evert and Martina Navratilova. *Players* featured cameo appearances by Pancho Gonzales, Ilie Nastase and John McEnroe. The film received poor reviews and was not a box office success.

In contrast to *Players*, large parts of *Wimbledon* were filmed at The All England Club, with a film crew, production staff and extras camped out there for several weeks during the summer of 2003. Dominic Inglot stood in for Paul Bettany in the tennis scenes, which were supervised by 1987 Wimbledon champion Pat Cash. Murphy Jensen had a cameo role, and commentators John Barrett, Mary Carillo, John McEnroe and Chris Evert brought authenticity to the film.

Wimbledon has featured in many other films over the years, notably when six-times Ladies' Singles champion Suzanne Lenglen appeared alongside Cicely Courtneidge in the 1935 British film *Things Are Looking Up*. The two stars met across the net, supposedly on Wimbledon's Centre Court, but the scene was actually filmed at Gainsborough Studios in Islington.

The All England Club has always tried to cooperate with filmmakers, and although *Wimbledon* was reasonably successful, grossing over £40m at the box office, experience shows that the magic of The Championships can never be realistically recreated in a feature film.

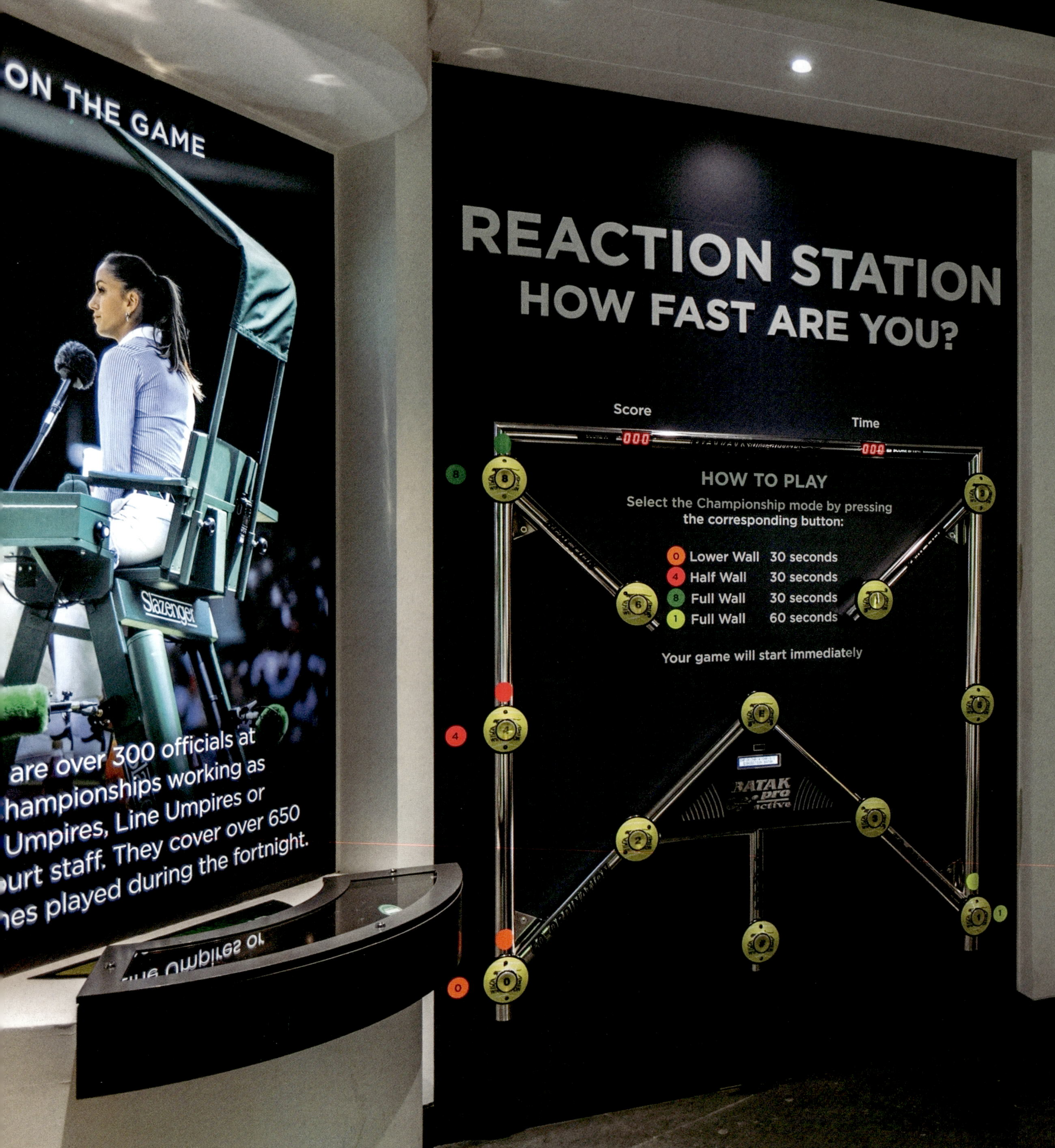
ON THE GAME
are over 300 officials at
hampionships working as
Umpires, Line Umpires or
urt staff. They cover over 650
es played during the fortnight.
Slazenger
REACTION STATION
HOW FAST ARE YOU?
Score
Time
000
000
HOW TO PLAY
Select the Championship mode by pressing
the corresponding button:
0   Lower Wall   30 seconds
4   Half Wall   30 seconds
8   Full Wall   30 seconds
1   Full Wall   60 seconds
Your game will start immediately
BATAK
pro
active

CHAPTER 13

Wimbledon Lawn Tennis Museum & Kenneth Ritchie Library

Nearly all the artworks, books, postcards, posters, programmes and other items of memorabilia featured in *Wimbledonia* are to be found in the collections of the Wimbledon Lawn Tennis Museum and the Kenneth Ritchie Wimbledon Library which are co-located within the grounds of The All England Lawn Tennis Club.

The Museum is open all year round, and for a combined entry charge offers visitors fascinating historical displays and interactive audio/visual presentations along with Blue Badge Guided Tours which take you behind the scenes of the world's most famous tennis tournament. The Library is open by prior appointment to people wishing to conduct research into the history of the game.

Whatever your area of tennis interest, Wimbledon Lawn Tennis Museum is a must-see attraction. From humble origins in a small corner of the Centre Court back in the 1970s, the Museum has expanded to become one of London's leading visitor attractions. ✒

Tennis fashion is a popular Museum theme

Wimbledon Lawn Tennis Museum

Emma Traherne, SENIOR CURATOR

Wimbledon Lawn Tennis Museum is an award-winning museum showcasing the fascinating history of The Championships and the sport of tennis. Visitors can explore the invention of the game and see a rare example of one of the first court fashions through unique clothing worn at Wimbledon by tennis superstars. Finally, visitors can come face to face with the glittering Championships trophies. As well as these authentic objects the Museum has many interactive displays and a media guide in multiple languages.

Many visitors will also choose to book a tour of the grounds with an informative guide. The tour gives visitors a chance to take a seat in the media interview room, walk through the competitors' entrance and see the iconic Centre Court.

The Museum has more than 1,000 objects on permanent display, but also holds 40,000 items in store, which explore the history of lawn tennis, The Championships and the AELTC. There is incredible variety in the collection, with objects ranging from scrapbooks created by past champions to Victorian toast racks, and from bathtubs to ball wells. Temporary exhibitions are a chance to showcase items in store which are too delicate for permanent display. They also offer wonderful opportunities to tell new stories, display recently collected objects, celebrate anniversaries and engage with different audiences.

The Collection Development Policy outlines what the Museum will collect, and staff meet monthly to discuss potential acquisitions. Factors considered include future use of the items, costs associated with acquiring, storing and researching and whether the objects may be more appropriate at another museum. Rapid contemporary collecting takes place during The Championships where the Museum aims to acquire objects which tell important stories and capture unique moments and memories both on and off the court, in the media spotlight and behind the scenes.

The collection is managed, stored and exhibited in line with national standards, codes of ethics and sector-wide best practice. Museum staff are all professionals in their areas of expertise. They care for the collection with integrity and curate exciting exhibitions with sensitivity and respect.

In the Beginning

The idea for the Museum and Library first came from the late Alan Little, as Wimbledon's official historian John Barrett recalls:

"Alan Little had the original idea for a Lawn Tennis Museum which he had suggested in an article in **Lawn Tennis and Badminton.** *Tom Todd, who lived in Guernsey, had long been a collector of tennis equipment and tennis memorabilia and his great interest in the game had led to friendships with many members at the All England Club. A keen follower of the tennis scene and a writer himself, he also was on first name terms with all the tennis journalists of the day.*

"When Tom heard that the Club was intending to launch a Museum as part of the Centenary Celebrations in 1977 he contacted the Club Secretary, David Mills, and offered to make his large collection available on permanent loan. This became the nucleus of the Wimbledon Lawn Tennis Museum which was opened in 1977 by the Club's President, the Duke of Kent, accompanied by the Club's Chairman Sir Brian Burnett.

"Tony Cooper, who had been the Club's Assistant Secretary from 1963 to 1974, became the Museum's first Curator. He was a delightfully vague fellow with a wonderful sense of humour and Museum Committee meetings which were held in the mornings and followed by lunch were always a pleasure to attend.

"'Buzzer' Hadingham, the former Chairman of Slazenger, who succeeded Sir Brian as Club Chairman in 1983, brought his commercial knowledge to bear in improving the range of articles being sold in the Museum shop. He also founded the Last 8 Club in 1986 which became a very popular meeting place for past champions who returned to Wimbledon in later years.

"Over time the Museum has become a world-class visitor attraction, winning many awards including the Visit England Gold Accolade."

Alan Little's prophetic article had appeared in the March 1967 issue of *Lawn Tennis and Badminton*, proposing the establishment of a National Museum and Library of Lawn Tennis on an adjacent plot of land recently acquired by The All England Club. Alan was passionate in promoting his idea:

"Lawn tennis was given to the world by Great Britain and therefore we should be proud of it and take an opportunity of displaying exhibits covering all facets of the game from its birth.

"There are so many things that could go on show. Take for instance the Wimbledon Trophies. Instead of being tucked away in the All England Club for 364 days a year they could be a centrepiece attraction and available for viewing six days a week."

Today the Ladies' Venus Rosewater Dish and the Gentlemen's Challenge Cup do indeed occupy a central position and are amongst the most popular of the Museum's displays.

Little was quick to trumpet the potential benefits of establishing a tennis library:

"The Library section would probably be of more material value to the tennis lover. Believe me, information on the game's history is hard to come by. It is a waste of time going to the local library for these institutions just do not cater for this sort of thing. You will be lucky to find a dozen books

Alan Little, Wimbledon's Honorary Librarian 1977–2016, by Beka Smith

on the subject and when you do they are generally biographies and autobiographies of current players. There is only one place which holds more or less each book published on the game in Great Britain and that is the British Museum. The only snag here is that entry is restricted and viewing deadly slow. So why not set up a library at Wimbledon, devoted solely to Lawn Tennis?"

Alan went on to suggest that the target date to open the new Museum and Library should be 1973 *"when our great game of lawn tennis celebrates its centenary"*. In the event, things took a little longer, but the Wimbledon Lawn Tennis Museum and the Kenneth Ritchie Library – the latter named after the late Lord Ritchie of Dundee, for many years a Member of the Committee of Management of The Championships and a former Chairman of the Stock Exchange – were formally opened in May 1977, a few weeks before the start of the Centenary Championships. ◐

The Championships trophies, always popular with visitors

The First Wimbledon Museum

Wimbledon Lawn Tennis Museum opened its doors for the first time on 19 May 1977 and it was a dark, eerie place. The spotlit showcases oozed atmosphere, and it sometimes seemed as if the spirits of the early Victorian and Edwardian champions were hovering in the shadows.

The Museum was located in the north-east corner of the Centre Court complex, on the first floor. It was reached by a long straight staircase from the Tea Lawn, or by a small lift. Immediately underneath the Museum, next to the staircase, was the Museum Tea Room, an attractive cafe with wall decoration by Wandsworth-based mural painter Michael Copus.

On entering the Museum there was a small gift shop, at the far end of which were life-sized models of six great Wimbledon champions: Dorothea Lambert Chambers, Suzanne Lenglen and Helen Wills; William Renshaw, Bill Tilden and Fred Perry. These provided ticket holders with a doorway into the Museum proper, where exhibits were clustered in a series of showcases. "The Victorian Hall", "The Victorian Parlour", and "A Victorian Tennis Tea Party", the latter featuring a backdrop painted by Michael Copus, collectively recreated the upper-class garden party days of the first three decades of the Wimbledon Championships. The mantelpiece in "The Victorian Parlour" came from Rhysnant Hall, Welshpool, the family home of Major Walter Wingfield, the man who first brought Lawn Tennis to mass attention in the 1870s.

"Gentlemen's Dressing Room, Worple Road" contained genuine fixtures and fittings brought from the All England Club's first ground, including porcelain wash basins and wooden seats, and the atmosphere was enhanced by faint sounds of a distant match in progress. "A Racket Maker's Workshop c.1900" and "Ping Pong equipment from 1900" featured antique rackets and equipment.

Fashion was a strong theme in the Museum, as it is today, and amongst the original exhibits was a pair of lace-trimmed panties created by Teddy Tinling in 1948 for 'Gorgeous Gussie' Moran. Royalty has long been associated with Wimbledon, and the Museum's displays included photographs from the collection of Lady Domini Crosfield, whose annual pre-Wimbledon garden parties were one of the highlights of the London social scene during the 1920s and 30s.

Roy McKelvie of the *Daily Mail* was duly impressed: "The story of the game and the players who have made it so universally popular in the last hundred years is well told throughout the museum." McKelvie was particularly taken by "an old wireless set on which people can listen to the first tennis broadcast, made by H.B.T. Wakelam in 1934 – the year that Fred Perry and Dorothy Round scored a British double". Another highlight was archive footage of legendary six-times champion Suzanne Lenglen practising, her balletic leaps drawing gasps from visitors.

The Museum was an immediate success with plenty of visitors during the Centenary Championships. It was an even more popular destination a year later when rain interrupted play on seven of the tournament's 12 days, including a complete wash-out on the first Thursday. Outside of 'The Fortnight', the Museum was open from 11am until 5pm on Tuesday to Saturday, and from 2pm to 5pm on Sunday.

The embryonic Kenneth Ritchie Wimbledon Library was located in a small room adjoining the Museum. Not surprisingly, Alan Little was named as the Club's first Honorary Librarian, a position he would hold for 40 years. ◍

The Museum Tea Room was decorated with attractive murals by Michael Copus

Changes

Change is a constant at Wimbledon, and the Museum and Library were no exceptions. In 1979 the Museum's offices and the Kenneth Ritchie Library moved to the second floor of the newly expanded building on the north side of the Centre Court, with the Library enjoying a wonderful view eastward across Wimbledon Park. In 1985 the Centre Court buildings overlooking the Tea Lawn were extended, enabling a redesign of the Museum with considerably more display space. In 1992 the Museum building was extended again to create a new gallery for special exhibitions, and in 1996 the display galleries dealing with the Open era were completely redesigned and rebuilt. In 2000 the popular Museum Tea Room was renamed Café Centre Court. A year later, in 2001, the Museum was extended southwards to accommodate a new audiovisual theatre and art gallery. In later years a glass 'viewing pod' was created which enabled visitors to actually see the Centre Court.

Despite all these improvements, one fact was inescapable: the Museum needed more space. This also applied to the Kenneth Ritchie Library, where Alan Little's relentless search for new acquisitions had led to a chronic shortage of shelf space. The answer came when the Club's Long Term Plan, originally unveiled in 1993, was expanded to include the construction of an entirely new Museum and Library, scheduled to open in 2006. ◌

The Museum presents original tennis artefacts in a modern interactive setting

Winning Shots

The original Wimbledon Lawn Tennis Museum and Kenneth Ritchie Wimbledon Library closed their doors to the public for the final time in October 2005. Their collections were placed in temporary storage ahead of the move to new larger accommodation in the spring of the following year.

From October 2005 until April 2006 there was no Museum at Wimbledon, but despite extensive publicity there was still a steady stream of visitors to the Club each day. Curator Honor Godfrey had anticipated this, and in order to avoid disappointment had set up a temporary Visitor Centre in the Renshaw Restaurant which was situated on the ground floor of the new No.1 Court, facing out towards Courts 14 to 17 and the northern end of Centre Court.

The Visitor Centre offered refreshments, a large seating area and a free exhibition by one of the world's leading tennis photographers. Michael Cole's *Winning Shots* featured many of the great players he had photographed during a career spanning five decades, and the exhibition was enhanced by the addition of the Ladies' and Gentlemen's Singles trophies, which were installed in high-security glass cabinets bolted to the floor. ◌

Kenneth Ritchie Wimbledon Library

Robert McNicol, CLUB HISTORIAN

The Kenneth Ritchie Wimbledon Library contains the world's most outstanding collection of tennis books, annuals, periodicals, programmes, newspaper cuttings and other items. The Library holds more than 15,000 items, originating from 90 countries. The strength of the Library is that it is a truly global tennis library, not just focusing on Wimbledon or British tennis.

The Library is named in memory of Lord Ritchie of Dundee (1902–1975), who was for many years Chairman of the London Stock Exchange and a long-serving member of the Club Committee. It was founded in 1976 by Alan Little MBE (1928–2017), who ran the Library, in his capacity of Honorary Librarian, until 2016.

Alan dedicated a large part of his life to researching tennis history and, thanks to him, we know so much more about the sport, and Wimbledon in particular, than we otherwise would.

An important function of the Library is to keep Alan's spirit alive by encouraging research into tennis history. As such, we have launched the Alan Little Bursary and, in recent years, we have held a biennial Tennis History Conference, bringing together tennis history enthusiasts of all backgrounds. We want the Library to be a hub for tennis history research, connecting everyone who shares a passion for the history of the game.

Although the contents of the Library connect us to the past, we are also looking to the future and embracing the digital age. We have

> **" *An important function of the Library is to keep Alan's spirit alive by encouraging research into tennis history.* "**

begun a digitisation project by digitising every volume of *Pastime* magazine (1883–1895) and we have teamed up with the British Library's UK Web Archive on a project to archive tennis websites.

We are often approached by members of the public who wish to donate their collections of books or programmes to the Library. Most items we are offered are ones we already have in the collection, in which case we would politely decline the offer. However, every now and again, it is very exciting to be offered an item that we don't have

and to be able to fill a gap in the Library collection.

Although the Library is very comprehensive, we do still have some gaps in the collection. We have a programme from every day of play from 1925 onwards but we are missing several from earlier years. And, although our collection of British periodicals is complete, we are missing early volumes from many other countries. Another rare item that we'd love to have is a first edition of Major Wingfield's *Sphairistike* booklet, which he sold with his lawn tennis sets.

The New Museum and Library

Immediately after the 2003 Championships the Church Road turnstiles, Barclays Bank, and the Museum Shop on the Tea Lawn Extension had all been demolished. In their place rose the New Museum Building containing turnstiles, ticket office and Wimbledon Museum Shop at ground level, and on the first floor a new suite of offices for the All England Club's administrative staff. At sub-ground level were the new Wimbledon Lawn Tennis Museum, Kenneth Ritchie Wimbledon Library and Barclays Bank.

A new, upgraded and much-expanded Wimbledon Lawn Tennis Museum opened on 12 April 2006. The opening ceremony, carried out by the Duke of Kent, the Club's President, was the culmination of three years of work to completely reconfigure the Championship Entrance Building on the Church Road side of the ground.

Reached via Gate 4 on Church Road, the new Museum presented history in a thoroughly modern environment, as Mark Hodgkinson of *The Daily Telegraph* observed: "The Curator, Honor Godfrey, has brilliantly blended the history and age-old traditions of tennis with modern, 21st-century technology. The Museum is filled with interactive touch screens, allowing visitors to learn about the sport's illustrious history, test their knowledge, or watch film clips of their favourite racket-swingers from yesteryear."

Several of the old showcases from the original Museum were retained, but they were now complemented by rackets, clothing and shoes from modern-day stars such as Andy Murray, Serena Williams, Roger Federer and Maria Sharapova. Another new innovation was a video presentation in which the ghostly form of John McEnroe showed visitors around a re-creation of the Gentlemen's locker room of the 1980s.

The new Museum is located below ground, and is entered through the much-expanded Wimbledon Museum Shop above. A special gallery hosts temporary exhibitions, with recent themes including tennis poster art, tennis on the French Riviera and Wimbledon and the BBC. The magnificent new Kenneth Ritchie Library is adjacent to the Museum, and has approximately four times as much shelf space as its predecessor. ◯

Mark Hodgkinson, *The Daily Telegraph*

Wimbledon Ephemera Collection

As well as the main collections of rackets, shoes, clothes, paintings, posters and miscellaneous objects, the Museum also has a large collection of lawn tennis ephemera which is used selectively in showcases and special exhibitions. The Museum's staff go out into the field during each year's Championships gathering exhibits for the collection which now includes such diverse items as advertisements, badges, cartoons, catalogues, dinner menus, dress patterns, drinks bottles, food wrappers, information booklets, invitations, lanyards, letters, newspapers, packaging, phonecards, postage stamps, sheet music, signage, tickets, trading cards and wristbands.

In addition to the Museum's ephemera collection, The Kenneth Ritchie Wimbledon Library for many years maintained volumes of newspaper cuttings. Annabelle Ng has been working as a temporary Library Assistant since 2017, and speaking during the 2019 Championships she explained the process: "We maintain two volumes concurrently. The first contains cuttings from *The Daily Telegraph*, which we gather all year round. The second is updated during The Championships only, with cuttings from other national newspapers. We look right through each newspaper, not just the sports section. We usually use two books for each year's Championships. If there's space in the previous year's book, we just carry straight on."

Annabelle understands the historical significance of her work: "I met Alan Little in my first year, and he impressed on me the importance of collecting contemporary press reports. During The Championships I see the volumes from past years being used by journalists and researchers – this gives me a sense that I'm continuing a worthwhile tradition."

Club Historian Robert McNicol added: "Our books of Championships cuttings date back to the 1920s, so it has been done for about 100 years. We don't know who started it off, but the Library has continued it. Alan started the year-round volumes in the early 1990s when he began bringing in his copies of *The Daily Telegraph* after he had finished with them. He considered it the best. Alan's assistant Audrey Snell did the cuttings."

> ❝ *Our books of Championships cuttings date back to the 1920s.* ❞

Librarian Robert McNicol

Ephemeral items often reveal fascinating stories about Wimbledon's past, and the changing behaviour of people attending The Championships from year to year. In the future ephemera will be used more and more in the production of digital content, too. ◓

Suzanne Lenglen sheet music, Editions Francis Salabert, 1926 (Wimbledon Lawn Tennis Museum Ephemera Collection)

Curators and Librarians

Tony Cooper was the Wimbledon Lawn Tennis Museum's first Curator, serving in that role from 1977 to 1985. Valerie Warren, Tony Cooper's former assistant, was Curator from 1985 to 1999. She was succeeded by Honor Godfrey (1999 to 2014), Anna Renton (2014 to 2018) and current incumbent Emma Traherne, who took up the post in May 2019. Adam Chadwick, formerly the Curator of the MCC Cricket Museum at Lord's, served in the role of Head of Wimbledon Museum and Tours from 2019 to 2023.

Alan Little served as Honorary Librarian from 1977 to 2016. Robert McNicol was appointed as Wimbledon's first full-time Librarian in March 2016, before moving to the role of Club Historian in 2023. Alan Little took on the new title of *Librarian Emeritus*, and was still serving in that role at the time of his death in October 2017. He was made an Honorary Member of The All England Lawn Tennis Club in 1985, and was given the Club's Distinguished Service Award in 2016. ◓

CHAPTER 14
Play is Resumed

Play is Resumed

We all start our love affair with Wimbledon the day we walk into the grounds for the first time, and for each of us the version of Wimbledon we first experience is our personal Wimbledon *forever*. It will always hold a special place in our heart. But Wimbledon is constantly changing, and I was interested to hear recently a teenager's excited anticipation of the 2026 Championships. "I simply can't wait to get inside the grounds of that wonderful place," she exclaimed.

For many the first visit to Wimbledon is preceded by several years of watching the tournament on TV. I began my Wimbledon journey on No.1 Court in 1969, but my first Wimbledon memory is of Chuck McKinley winning the men's singles in 1963. When the radio commentator said his name it sounded so *cool*, like Kookie from *77 Sunset Strip*. TV was a communal thing in the 50s and 60s and my family watched that American show religiously every Sunday evening. I was just 11, and us working-class folk were so heavily influenced by American TV back then. With Chuck McKinley bridging the gap it was only a short distance, metaphorically speaking, from Sunset Boulevard to Somerset Road.

The coolest nation had yet to reveal itself, though. The land of golden sands, endless summers and life lived permanently outdoors: Australia! That surprise lay in store half a dozen years down the line, when I made my way up Wimbledon Hill on the chartered special bus service to The Championships. I had no idea about the other courts; on TV they only had cameras trained on Centre Court and No.1. Once inside the scales quickly fell from my eyes: the outside courts, the ivy-clad water tower, and the fast-food counter underneath the South Stand of the old No.1 Court, favoured by many (including me!) for its delicious Wimpy burgers, given rave reviews by many fans but not the Wimbledon Committee who shut it down because of the smell of onions! The odd sight of houses inside the grounds, next to what are now Gates 11 and 13. The noisy arrival of the dustcart every afternoon to empty Wimbledon's bins. And a plethora of fair dinkum Aussies who had travelled across the world to play on these magical lawns.

These are just my memories, brought vividly back to life by the programmes, postcards, used tickets and press cuttings I kept along the way. Each year since 1969 Wimbledon lost some devotees but gained a whole lot more, each reserving a special place in the memory for Wimbledon the way they first saw it. The vastly expanded grounds, the new No.1 Court, the Millennium Building, and a whole lot more besides.

A lot has changed since the first Championships in 1877, not least during the last five years since the first edition of this book was published. The Covid pandemic meant that in 2020, sadly, but unavoidably, there was no Championship meeting, the first time outside two world wars that the tournament was cancelled. Fans gave vent to their frustration at the news via the burgeoning channel of social media: "Sucks. Wimbledon is my favourite." "Making this decision already? Things could be different in two months." "I know this news was expected but I can't help feeling really down about it." All messages accompanied by a liberal spread of glum and tearful emojis.

All England Club Chairman Ian Hewitt had the unenviable task of leading Wimbledon through the Covid period and the subsequent Russian invasion of Ukraine. The Club did much to assist the local community through the distribution of free meals to NHS workers and provision of extended free accommodation to players and coaches from Ukraine.

When play – and life – resumed, technology held sway and the pace of change increased. During the years that followed, public health and security could be used to justify virtually any decision organisations, including Wimbledon, wished to make. Tickets are now digital, Wimbledon is a cashless site, and computers rather than

Ian Hewitt

people call the lines. There are limits on the size of bags, which have to be transparent. Other changes are not the result of technology, but rather of the pressing needs of management. Church Road continues to be closed to vehicles during The Championships, and once inside things are different, too. The playing surface is now a hybrid mix of grass and synthetic, and there are tie-breaks in the final set of all matches.

There are on-court player interviews after matches, and since 2022 there has been scheduled play on the middle Sunday. All doubles matches are now limited to the best of three sets.

There is more downtime between matches, yet play still finishes considerably earlier. An under-14 Championship has been introduced to provide more tennis for fans to watch. The roofs on the two main show courts create a micro-climate in which the players perform before those fortunate enough to have a ticket, and, crucially, the worldwide television audience. Television viewers may be forgiven for forgetting that it ever rains at Wimbledon.

In 2024 the final of the mixed doubles event, previously scheduled for the final Sunday, was rescheduled to the second Thursday.

The result of all these changes is that Wimbledon increasingly attracts a new audience, which may be characterised as IT-literate and relatively affluent. There are not so many children to be seen around the grounds. Wimbledon is a socially desirable live event, and attendance at such events comes at a premium price. The days of ordinary folk camping out day after day just to see the tennis, as my friends and I did back in the 1970s, 80s and 90s, may be over.

I asked a couple of contributors to *The People's Wimbledon* to share their thoughts about post-pandemic Wimbledon. **Kani Bawa** of Nottingham was as enthusiastic as ever:

"Sadly, the 2020 Championships was cancelled and up to that point, I had not been successful in the ballot. 2020 ticket holders were offered priority access to purchase tickets for the same date and court in 2021, and I hadn't been successful in the 2021 ballot either. Would this be the second year since the late 1970s I would not be attending The Championships? What was I going to do? I'd have to queue instead, but the traditional Wimbledon queue was not operating in 2021 either! This meant we could not buy tickets at the turnstile or enter the grounds to purchase a resale ticket. My heart sank.

"Then, I heard tickets were being sold online on a first-come, first-served basis and capacity to the grounds was operating at 50% for the first week and full capacity in the second week. Whilst glued to my phone trying to obtain tickets via the app for The Championships, I entertained myself by going through old photos I had taken at Wimbledon over the years and decided to post one a day on my Facebook page. My friends enjoyed seeing them and I enjoyed reading their comments. They are wonderful memories.

"Around 10.30pm on 1 July 2021, I managed to secure a pair of Centre Court tickets for Saturday 3 July! Hurrah… I rang my sister who also loves tennis, to give her this amazing news. We were so excited and couldn't believe our luck. I quickly ordered our usual afternoon picnic, which has become tradition for us to eat late afternoon and started packing to travel to my sister in Windsor the next day, so we could visit The Championships together the day after.

"Of course, during our visit, restrictions were in place. We had to test negative for Covid, and have the relevant paperwork and ID, but it was a small price to pay. Also,

we were supposed to wear masks moving around the grounds but noticed that not many people were actually wearing masks. Digital tickets were used for the first time. I had always saved my paper tickets but this year, I wouldn't have a paper ticket to save. I felt robbed. There were some issues with the app. I couldn't download my tickets so that meant I wasn't able to transfer a ticket to my sister. I was live chatting on the way to the grounds whilst my sister was driving. We were reassured we'd be OK. We arrived at the gate and told them we were having issues. Apparently, it was a known issue, and we were allowed into the grounds. It was so quiet and so easy to roam around freely due to the lack of crowds. It was civilised and everybody was so friendly. We still felt a great atmosphere.

"Our first port of call is always the Champagne and Pimm's bar opposite Centre Court for a pitcher of Pimm's, some sandwiches and to enjoy some live music. But, they weren't serving Pimm's in pitchers or sandwiches at this bar, and what happened to the live band? 'Oh no,' we said. 'Maybe it's just this year and it'll be back to normal next year.' Sadly, this was not the case. Since 2021, our much-loved bar only serves Pimm's in reusable cups. The sandwiches and live music have not made a reappearance. I feel let down having known what it used to be like.

"We bought a cup of Pimm's each and paid with our cards. The venue was operating on a cashless basis only. This has also become the norm since Covid and a physical bank doesn't exist in the grounds anymore. When we finished our drinks, we decided to pick up our picnic early. It was weird walking by the turnstiles, looking out from inside the grounds and seeing them empty. We were so used to seeing the hustle and bustle around the turnstiles. We collected our picnic from near Court 18 and consumed it on The Hill (Aorangi Park), as we were there anyway. There was ample room to sit and eat. The food in the picnic bag was packed in more recycling material compared to previous years, and a £1 refund for returning reusable cups was in force, all of which remain to this day.

"When we went to sit in our seats on court, we were surprised we were all seated close together. I assumed because The Championships were working at half capacity, we would be seated apart, spread across the stadium but, we were all literally sat together filling seats at the bottom of the stadium, whilst the ones behind us, further back remained empty. It was as if a 'keep out' tape had been wrapped behind the seats, halfway up the stadium, marking a boundary nobody was allowed to cross over, as if it had been cordoned off.

"The Championships are now back to receiving large crowds and long traditional queues for entry into the grounds have returned. Being squashed like sardines in the Wimbledon shops and when spectators leave the large show courts after a match will never change. It's all part of the excitement and atmosphere. But it was lovely being able to roam around freely when the grounds were operating at half capacity during Covid. Gone are the days of applying for a Wimbledon ticket in the ballot using pen, paper and sending a stamped address envelope.

"I miss drinking Pimm's served in pitchers and eating sandwiches in the bar opposite Centre Court, listening to live music. A bank card is all you need to pay for anything within the grounds, as the venue remains cashless and makes it so easy for us to overspend. I do welcome the additional recycling material used and extra water refilling stations. It's a shame The Championships no longer sell mugs stamped with the year or sell strawberries and cream cookies in tennis ball canisters. Pencils stamped with 'Wimbledon Championships' are no longer available either. My sister used to buy loads of these. As times change, we have to adapt accordingly. I would, however, love the option of purchasing a souvenir paper ticket, as a memory of my visit to The Wimbledon Championships.

"Nothing will take away my memories as change continues. I will still attend The Championships for as long as I can. If I am not successful in the ballot, I will look for a resale ticket and if all else fails, even though my queuing days are supposed to be over, I'll be joining that ever-growing queue again!

"One of the saddest things for me was that Wimbledon 2021 proved to be Roger Federer's final appearance as he announced his retirement from professional tennis."

Another Wimbledon veteran,
Colin Triplow of New Ash Green,
had a rather different view:

"The final set tie-break was introduced in 2019 at 12 games all (the great Djokovic v Federer final that went to a final set tie-break that year). Only three years later, in 2022, the final set tie-break was slashed from 12-12 to 6-6. All Grand Slam singles matches now had tie-breaks at 6-6 in the final set, and Wimbledon had simply fallen in line with the others.

"In 2023 the men's doubles event was reduced to best of three sets from best of five, meaning that following the revamp of the Davis Cup format in 2019 there were now no best of five men's doubles matches anywhere. With virtually none of the top singles players involved in the men's doubles, I struggled to see the reasoning behind this move, feeling that it has devalued the event.

"In my view the mixed doubles also lost much of its prestige in 2024, when it was decided to play the final on the second Thursday after the two ladies' singles semi-finals, rather than at the culmination of the tournament, on the Saturday or Sunday of the finals weekend as it had been before. Perhaps it was divine intervention that persistent rain during the fortnight that year meant that the final of the mixed had to be delayed until its usual place on the last Sunday, but in 2025 it was played on the second Thursday, in front of largely empty stands.

"Wimbledon has always prided itself on being a trailblazer, and at the forefront of tennis development, but these changes make me wonder if Wimbledon now isn't so much a leader as a follower."

Wimbledon Tennis Ephemera

When it comes to ephemera things are remarkably similar to pre-pandemic days. When Wimbledon resumed in 2021 a single standard OFFICIAL PROGRAMME was produced and sold on every day of the tournament. Drawsheets were not updated daily as had previously been Wimbledon's custom. The Final Programme with Full Results usually printed a few weeks after The Championships was not produced. Happily, normal service was resumed in 2022, with a different, fully updated programme being produced on each day of The Championships, and the Final Programme with full printed results being reinstated.

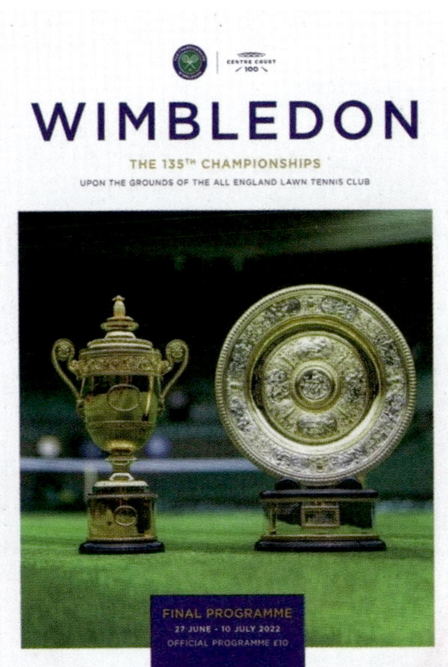

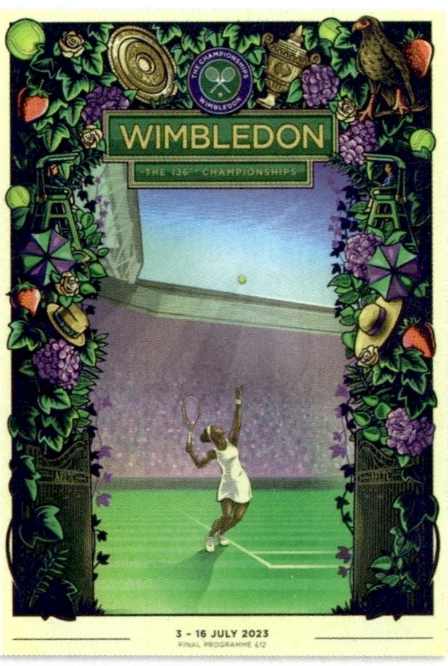

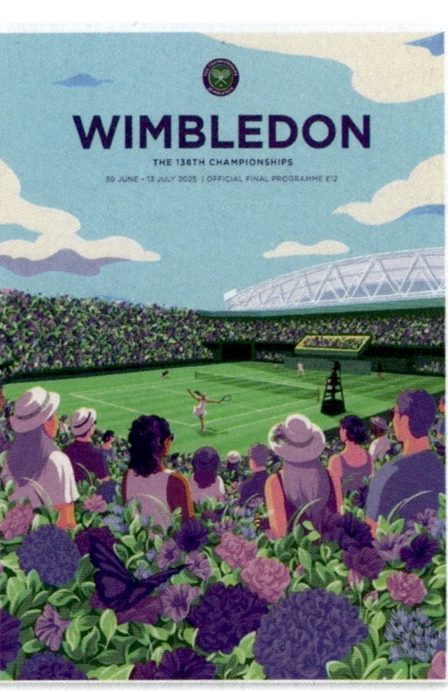

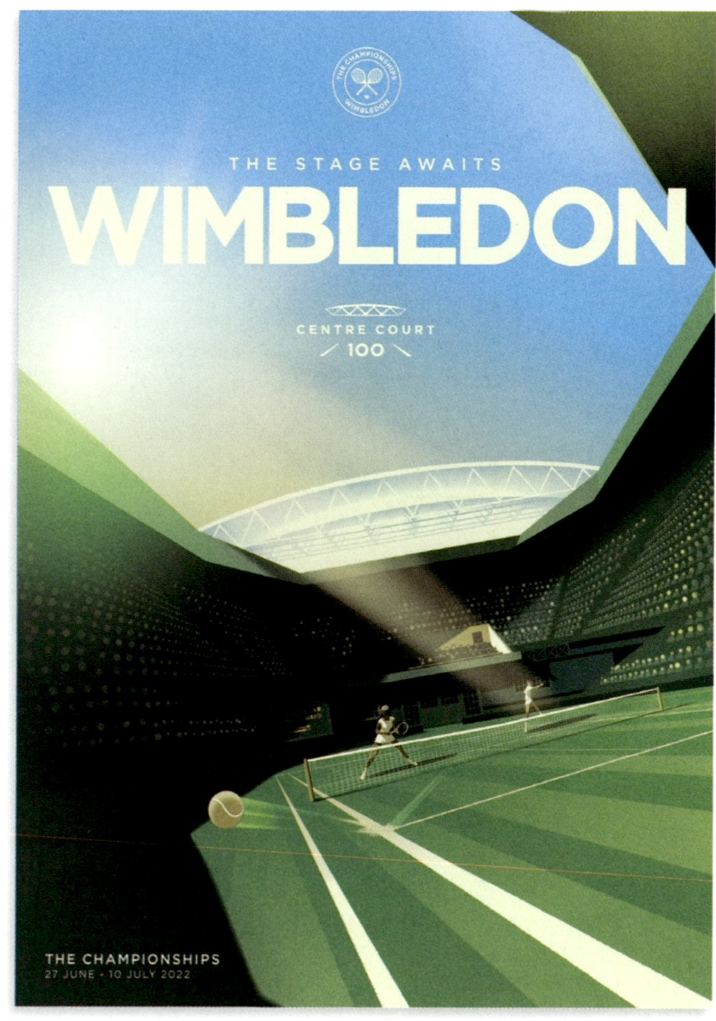

Tournament posters have been produced each year, but in smaller quantities, using inferior paper and at a higher price. They are nevertheless greatly appreciated by fans attending The Championships. In 2025 the price of the Wimbledon Official Poster was £15.

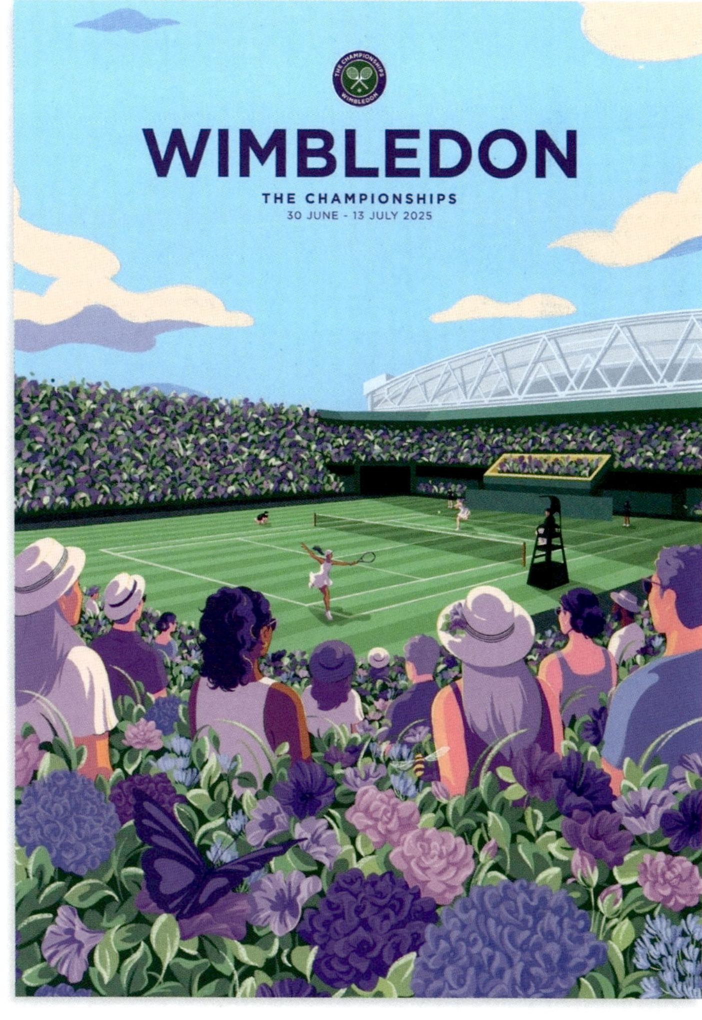

With the exception of portraits of the champions and views of the grounds, **photographs of the players** are no longer sold at Wimbledon. With everyone being required to possess a smartphone to hold their digital ticket, and with every phone containing an in-built camera, the demand for physical postcards has vastly reduced.

Sadly, and controversially, **Wimbledon tickets** are now almost entirely electronic, although it is possible to still get a physical ticket in certain circumstances. In addition, hard copy complimentary tickets are issued to All England Club members. This has created a negative reaction amongst true tennis fans who have been deprived of a physical souvenir of their day at Wimbledon. The increased price of tickets is a cause of concern, too, particularly for those wishing to attend several days of the tournament.

Physical **ephemera** still exists in the form of Wimbledon-related guides and supplements issued by the print media, but these are now a much less significant part of the Wimbledon scene.

The **Wimbledon Compendium**, now in its 36th year, is a hardback book published shortly before each Championships providing comprehensive up-to-date information about the tournament and the All England Club. The 2020 edition was published despite the fact that The Championships did not take place that year. Robert McNicol, in his new role as the All England Club's Historian, is responsible for this important work.

The **Wimbledon Official Annual** is published each autumn and provides a day-by-day illustrated report of the Fortnight just ended. Originally published in 1983 with 160 pages, by 2025 this marvellous book had grown to over 250 pages.

Vision Sports Publishing has also been responsible for a number of excellent Wimbledon-related coffee-table books. The most recent of these is *Wimbledon – The Pinnacle of Sport* by Ian Hewitt and Bob Martin (2024).

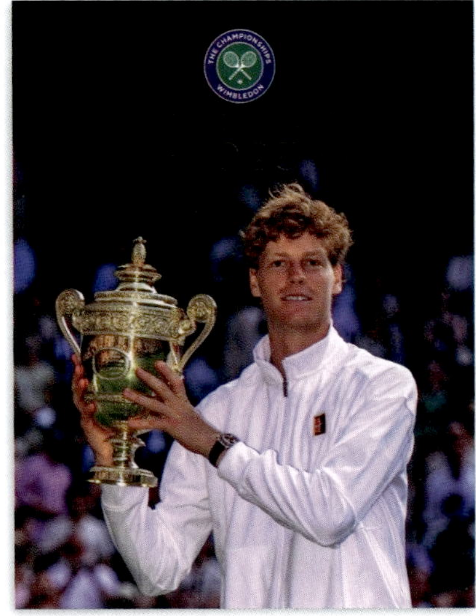

Conclusion

The end of the Federer era was almost immediately followed by the dawning of a new one: that of Carlos Alcaraz and Jannik Sinner; and of Iga Swiatek, Elena Rybakina and Aryna Sabalenka. In short, times change, both on court and off. The Wimbledon spectator of the present day has more choice of how to spend their leisure time and different priorities than his or her predecessor in times gone by, and with technological advances continuing at an ever-faster pace, who knows what the future may hold?

CONTRIBUTORS

Tim ANDREWS *BRIGHTON*
Jeff ANTHONY *WEST HARTFORD*
Patricia ARTHUR *PRENTON*

John BARRETT *WIMBLEDON*
Kani BAWA *NOTTINGHAM*
Graeme BAXTER *RANCHO MIRAGE*
Marian BOUNDY *FINCHLEY*
Jessica BOUSFIELD *NEW YORK*
Chris BOWERS *RINGMER*
Terry BRADY *HARTFORD*
Sarah BRIDGLAND *HIGH WYCOMBE*
David BROWN *FARRINGTON GURNEY*

Derek CATE *SHREWSBURY*
Sheila CHAMBERS *CROSBY*
Jeanne CHERRY *SANTA MONICA*
Kathleen CLAYDEN *PUTNEY*
Norman COHEN *STANMORE*
Michael COLE *BECKENHAM*
Suzie COLE *WIMBLEDON*
Anne COMERFORD *WEXFORD*
Carlos COSTA *PORTUGAL*

Nick DARBY *EAST GRINSTEAD*
Barry DAVIES *BARNES*
Antonio DEMASI *MERIDEN*

Tim EDSON *LEICESTER*
Paul EISENEGGER *BARNET*
Simon ETHERIDGE *BISHOP'S STORTFORD*
John EVANS *ROWLEY REGIS*
Richard EVANS *DELRAY BEACH*
Bob EVERITT *BILSTON*

John FEAVER *WIMBLEDON PARK*
Margo FITZSIMONS *BOURNEMOUTH*
Gordon FORBES *BURGERSDORP*
Chris FOULKES *COVENTRY*
Julia FREEMAN *WARGRAVE*
Andrew FULCHER *SUTTON*
Bernard FULLERTON *BRINGSTY*
Frances FUNNELL *WIMBLEDON PARK*

Geoffrey GAMMON *SURBITON*
Honor GODFREY *PUTNEY*
Chris GORRINGE *HINCHLEY WOOD*
Joan and Robert GRAHAM *BURY*

Audrey GREEN *BALDOCK*
Peter GREGORY *NORTHWICK PARK*
George GRIME *HAM*

Susan HALLIDAY *FELIXSTOWE*
Mike HANN *LONDON*
Julian HARDING *WORCESTER PARK*
Ruth HARTGILL *REIGATE*
Julie HELDMAN *SANTA MONICA*
Richard HESS *PALOS VERDES*
Ian HEWITT *LONDON*
Jenny HIGGS *REIGATE*
Richard HILLWAY *COLORADO SPRINGS*
Jeremy HUDSON *RAYNES PARK*
Myra HUNTER *RIDDRIE*

Raphael IBERG *LAUSANNE*
Keith INCH *DARTMOUTH*
John INVERDALE *KINGSTON UPON THAMES*

Aubrey JONES *MARLOW*
Christine JONES *CHESSINGTON*

Julia KILBY *HOVE*
Ian C. KING *BATTERSEA*
Billy KNIGHT *EAST HADDON*
Mark KUHN *CHARLES CITY, IOWA*

Olivia LANGINGER *LONDON*
Colin LELLIOTT *WEST WORTHING*
Alan LITTLE *BEXLEYHEATH*
John LLOYD *PALM BEACH*
Amy LUNDY *WESTPORT*
Steven LYNCH *STAINES*

Finlay MacKINNON *ISLE OF HARRIS*
Nick McCARVEL *NEW YORK*
Robert McNICOL *WIMBLEDON*
Louise MANSERGH *CAMBERLEY*
Davor MARGETIC *ZAGREB*
Geoff MASTERS *QUEENSLAND*
Roger MILNE *PULBOROUGH*
Ray MOORE *PALM DESERT*
Susan MORGAN THOMAS *TUNBRIDGE WELLS*
Luis MORRIS *BASINGSTOKE*
Angela MORTIMER *WIMBLEDON*

Annabelle NG *LONDON*
John NICHOLSON *MOTSPUR PARK*

David ORCHARD *HIGH WYCOMBE*

Denise PADDOCK *SHREWSBURY*
Will PARKER *FLEET*
Apphia and Daniel PARSONS *DULWICH*
Onny PARUN *WELLINGTON, NEW ZEALAND*
Olivier PEROTTE *LONDON*
Stuart PESKETT *FELTHAM*
Omar POPAL *LONDON*
Jane PORTNELL *INGLETON*
Doreen PRANGELL *PUTNEY*
Jim PUHL *EAU CLAIRE, WISCONSIN*

James REED *WIMBLEDON*
Ann ROBERTS *INGATESTONE*
Sandra ROBERTS *WIMBLEDON*
Elsie ROSAM *DORKING*
John ROWLINSON *LAMBOURN*
David RUTHERFORD *CROMLIX*
Bruce RYAN *SYDNEY*

Christina SAN *NEW MALDEN*
Amisha SAVANI *LONDON*
Chris SCHRUCKMAYR *ASHEVILLE*
Sarita SHARMA *SURBITON*
Keith STEPHENS *UPMINSTER*
Michael STONE *BATTERSEA*
Paul STRUDWICK *BRENTWOOD*

Jamie THOMAS *BASINGSTOKE*
Edward TIDY *WIMBLEDON PARK*
Emma TRAHERNE *WIMBLEDON*
Colin TRIPLOW *NEW ASH GREEN*
Christine TRUMAN *ALDEBURGH*

Peter WATSON *SCARBOROUGH*
Robbie WILLIAMS *MOSCOW*
Bobby WILSON *WELWYN*
Jane WILTSHIRE *CAMBERLEY*
Clare WOOD *SOUTHFIELDS*
Peter WOODMAN *HATCH END*
Jeremy WOODS *MERTON*
Peter WRIGGLESWORTH *RUISLIP*

Bendou ZHANG *SHANGHAI*

ACKNOWLEDGEMENTS

I am grateful to the late Alan Little, Wimbledon's Honorary Librarian for four decades, for lighting the blue touchpaper and getting me started on *Wimbledonia*. John Rowlinson, Wimbledon's Director of Television from 2002 to 2009, had the idea for the book's original title *The People's Wimbledon*. Alan and John, along with sports historian Ian Hewitt, who has written a wonderful Foreword, provided support and encouragement when it was needed most.

John Barrett, author of *Wimbledon – The Official History*, and formerly the "Voice of Wimbledon" on BBC Television, has been a constant source of support, encouragement and wise counsel. John has given freely of his time and expertise, and words cannot express my immense gratitude to him. John's wife Angela has been very kind and helpful, too, and we have enjoyed many light-hearted moments over the telephone whilst everyone was confined to quarters.

Tennis historian Bob Everitt believed in the project throughout, and over a four-year period designed and published a series of *Wimbledonia* articles in *The Tennis Collector* magazine. Bob's wonderful illustration of the scene at Worple Road in 1877 opens the first chapter, and many of the period images in chapters 1 and 2 are from his remarkable collection. These contributions brought the early years of Wimbledon to life. Richard Hillway, who with Bob is co-author of *The Birth of Lawn Tennis*, has been a constant source of information, advice, encouragement, and good humour. I am deeply indebted to both gentlemen.

Many of the photographs have come from the Wimbledon Lawn Tennis Museum, where I was allowed behind-the-scenes access over a three-year period to study the vast ephemera collection and conduct a photoshoot. I wish to thank everyone in the Museum team for their help, and I am particularly grateful to Anna Renton, Anna Spender, Sarah Frandsen, Malin Lundin, Annabelle Ng, Emma Traherne and Adam Chadwick. Robert McNicol, the All England Club's Historian, has been a knowledgeable and friendly ally throughout.

At the All England Club I received much-valued input from John Beddington, Chris Gorringe, Mike Hann, Ian C. King, John James, Bernard Neal and Geoff Ward. Others who spent time recalling their Wimbledon memories included Michael and Suzie Cole, Barry Davies, John Feaver, Gordon Forbes, George Grime, Julie Heldman, Jenny Higgs, Aubrey Jones, Billy Knight, Ramesh Krishnan, John Lloyd, Bir Mahajan, Geoff Masters, Ray Moore, Betty Stove, Christine Truman, Bobby Wilson and Clare Wood. I thank them all, and my good friend Bert Rowley who filmed some of those discussions.

I thank everyone listed on page 310 for their written and spoken contributions, along with Emmy Caporale, Karen Dervish, Geoffrey Dix, Charles Elstub, Paul Fendrich, Al Mawani, Dorothy Schofield, Simon Whale and many others whose excellent submissions also deserved inclusion had space allowed. Other valuable contributions came from Don Brenner, Graham Budd, Alan Chalmers, Ben Chatfield, Gianni Clerici, Martin Corrie, David Nuttall, Mary Pope, Kenneth Reed, Peter Risdon, Darren Sharwood, George Skinner, Attila Szabo, Peter Watson, and Ruth Weston.

My special thanks go to Jane Camillin and the team at Pitch Publishing for investing their resources in this book, and for allowing me to add extra pages to accommodate as many wonderful memories as possible. Andrea Dunn was an understanding and knowledgeable editor, and Duncan Olner tackled this major design challenge with skill, enthusiasm and imagination.

My heartfelt thanks go to Amisha Savani who has added a 21st century dimension to *Wimbledonia*. In the era of social media, Amisha used her "little black book" (or should that be "Contacts List"?) to commission several of the excellent reminiscences in Chapter 6. Amisha had the idea for the Wimbledon Timeline in the introduction, contributed text to Chapter 7 and brought much-needed order and structure to the book.

The final and biggest thank you goes to my wife Chris who liaised with contributors, welcomed guests, tracked down photographs, scanned documents, checked proofs and lived with *Wimbledonia* for longer than she cares to remember!

Richard Jones, March 2026

INFORMATION SOURCES

BBC Written Archives Centre, Caversham; Merton Heritage & Local Studies Centre; The Kenneth Ritchie Wimbledon Library; The Museum of Wimbledon; Wimbledon Lawn Tennis Museum; Players and Results Archive at *wimbledon.com*; Wimbledon Championships Official Programmes 1877 – 2025.

Lawn Tennis and Badminton magazine 1908 – 1967
Forty Years of First Class Lawn Tennis by G.W. Hillyard (Williams & Norgate, 1924)
Fifty Years of Wimbledon by A. Wallis Myers (AELTC, 1926)
Wimbledon Story by Norah Gordon Cleather (Sporting Handbooks, 1947)
The Twenties by Alan Jenkins (Heinemann, 1974)
Wimbledon Official Annual (various publishers, 1983 – 2019)
Historic Wimbledon by Richard Millward (Fielders, 1989)
Wimbledon – A History of The Championships (TWI video, 2001)
The 50s and 60s by Alison Pressley (Michael O'Mara Books, 2003)
From A to BIBA by Barbara Hulanicki (V&A Publishing, 2007)
Frank Pick's London by Oliver Green (V&A Publishing, 2013)
George Hillyard: The Man Who Moved Wimbledon by Bruce Tarran (Matador, 2013)
BBC Sport in Black and White by Richard Haynes (Palgrave, 2016)
You Say You Want a Revolution edited by Victoria Broackes and Geoffrey Marsh (V&A Publishing, 2016)
Wimbledon Compendium by Alan Little and Robert McNicol (AELTC, 2018)
Legacy (the story of J. Lyons & Co.) by Thomas Harding (Heinemann, 2019)
Wimbledon – The Official History by John Barrett (VSP, 2020)

A selected tennis bibliography appears on pages 268 to 273.

THE CHAMPIONSHIPS
WIMBLEDON 2017
QUEUE CARD
YOU MUST ADHERE TO
A This Queue Card is date
B It must be retained and
C This Queue Card does
D Queue jumping is not a
E The stewards are there
F Please note the alcoho
DAY 1
THE CHAMPIONSHIPS
WIMBLEDON 2017
QUEUE CARD
YOU MUST ADHERE TO
A This Queue Card is date
B It must be retained and
C This Queue Card does n
D Queue jumping is not ac
E The stewards are there t
F Please note the alcohol
DAY 1

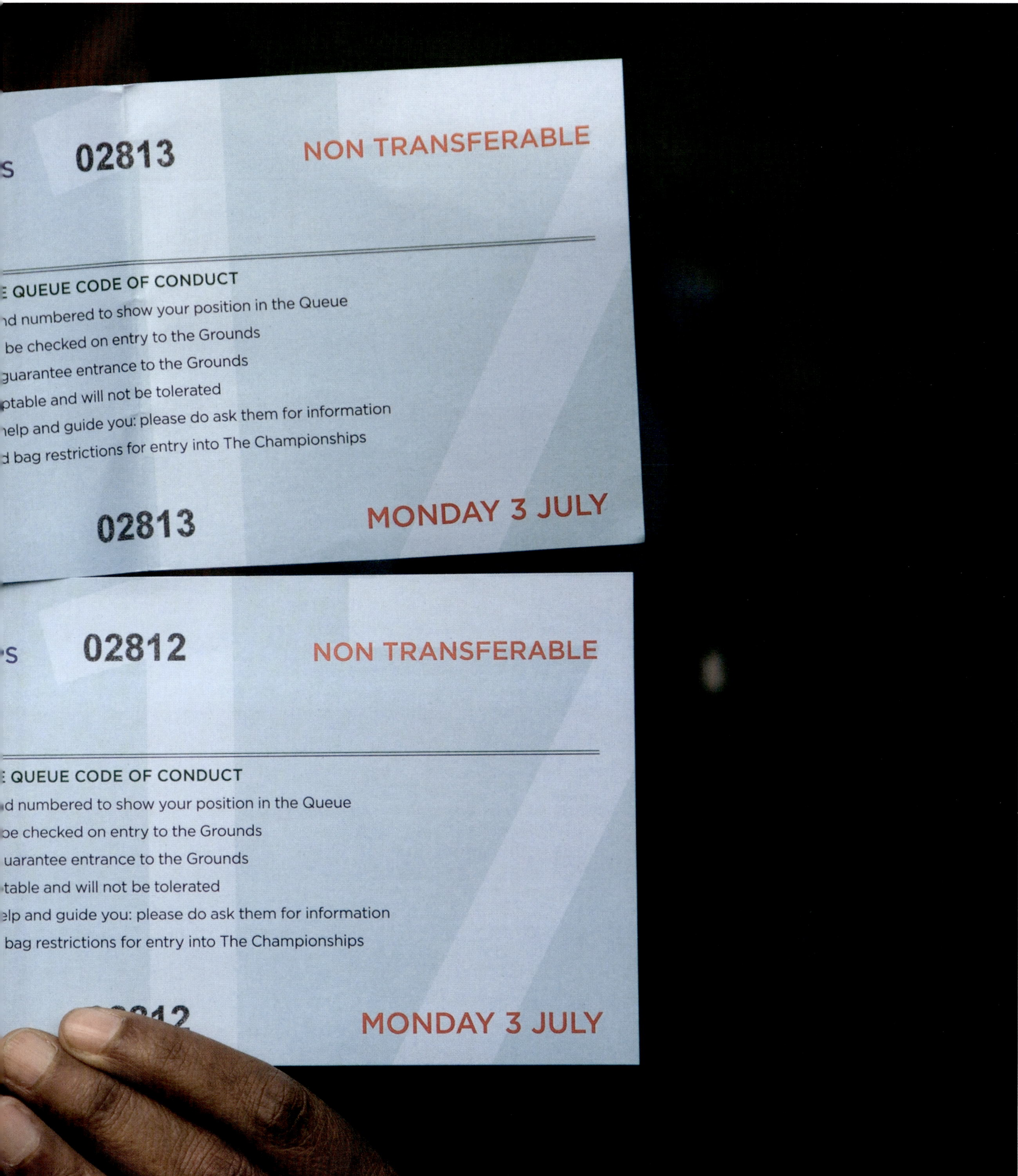
02813
NON TRANSFERABLE
E QUEUE CODE OF CONDUCT
nd numbered to show your position in the Queue
be checked on entry to the Grounds
guarantee entrance to the Grounds
ptable and will not be tolerated
help and guide you: please do ask them for information
d bag restrictions for entry into The Championships
02813
MONDAY 3 JULY
02812
NON TRANSFERABLE
E QUEUE CODE OF CONDUCT
d numbered to show your position in the Queue
be checked on entry to the Grounds
uarantee entrance to the Grounds
table and will not be tolerated
elp and guide you: please do ask them for information
bag restrictions for entry into The Championships
MONDAY 3 JULY

Tuesday, 21 June 1977

It's late, around 9.30pm, but there are still a few shafts of sunlight left. There's no play on Centre or No.1, and the outside courts are all empty. Except for one. On the Church Road side of the ground, on a court enclosed on three sides by high green surrounds, people are squashed together on tip toes, craning their necks to get a glimpse of the action as two big servers battle it out. Butch Walts and John Marks have been playing for hours, though few of these spectators have been here from the start.

Hardly anyone here knows who Walts and Marks are, save for a handful of friends, relatives and well-informed spectators, but that doesn't matter. They are tennis players, playing on the grass at Wimbledon. This is the last match of the day, and everyone still in the grounds has been drawn to it, to squeeze the final drops of nectar from their golden day at Wimbledon.

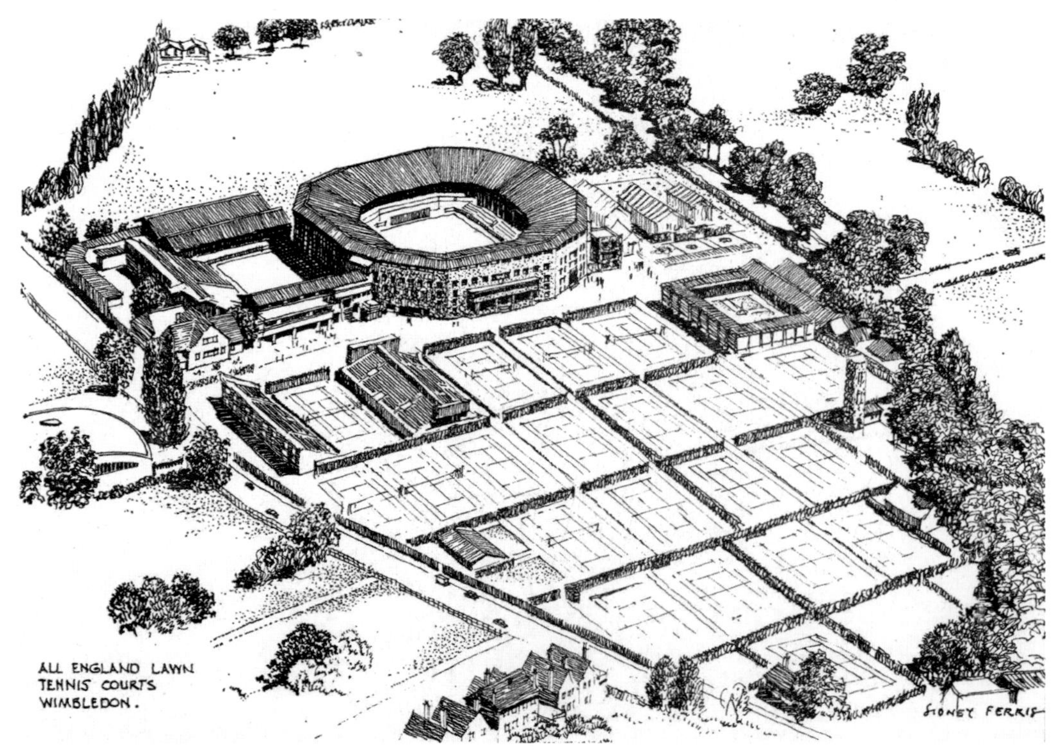

Cricket
Wimbledon Park Golf Cou
BM.74.28
L E
145
3.354
BM.75.87
F.S
All England
Lawn Tennis Ground
200
12.845
Centre Court
M B
148
1.094
BM.80.21
ROAD
97

THE STORY O